Publications
London | Paris

Neil Wilson

Edinburgh

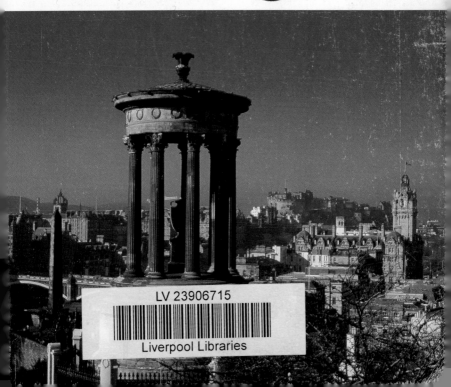

The Top Five

1 Museum of Scotland
Wander around the museum's imaginative modern interior (p63)

2 Royal Yacht Britannia
Ring the bell for royal service (p75)

3 Royal Mile
Visit St Giles Cathedral and spit on the Heart of Midlothian for good luck (p57)

4 Edinburgh Castle
Head uphill and devote an hour to the fortress on Castle Rock (p52)

5 Underground Edinburgh
Explore the haunted chambers of Real Mary King's Close (p56)

Contents

Published by Lonely Planet Publications Pty Ltd
ABN 36 005 607 983

Australia Head Office, Locked Bag 1, Footscray,
Victoria 3011, ☎ 03 8379 8000, fax 03 8379 8111,
talk2us@lonelyplanet.com.au

USA 150 Linden St, Oakland, CA 94607,
☎ 510 893 8555, toll free 800 275 8555,
fax 510 893 8572, info@lonelyplanet.com

UK 72–82 Rosebery Ave, Clerkenwell, London,
EC1R 4RW, ☎ 020 7841 9000, fax 020 7841 9001,
go@lonelyplanet.co.uk

France 1 rue du Dahomey, 75011 Paris,
☎ 01 55 25 33 00, fax 01 55 25 33 01,
bip@lonelyplanet.fr, www.lonelyplanet.fr

The Authors

NEIL WILSON

Neil was born in Glasgow, but defected to the east at the age of 18 and has now lived in Edinburgh for over 20 years. While studying geology at Edinburgh University he spent his Wednesday afternoons (while everyone else was doing sporty things) exploring the closes, wynds, courtyards and back streets of his adopted city; since then, he has continued to enjoy delving into Edinburgh's many hidden corners, and has made the study of the city's pubs and restaurants a lifetime's endeavour. Neil has been a full-time writer and photographer since 1988 and has written around 40 guidebooks for various publishers, including the Lonely Planet guides to *Scotland* and *Edinburgh*.

PHOTOGRAPHER
JONATHAN SMITH

Raised in the Scottish Highlands, Jon graduated from St Andrews University in 1994 with an MA in German. Unsure of what to do with his life, he took a flight to Vilnius and spent the next four years travelling around the former USSR. Having tried everything from teaching to translating Lithuanian cookery books into English, Jon resolved to seek his fortune as a freelance travel photographer.

Since then Jon's byline has appeared in 50 Lonely Planet titles, notably *Prague*, *Moscow* and *St Petersburg*. Currently based in Aberdeenshire, Jon has worked on several major book projects down the road in Auld Reekie. For him the main highlight of this particular assignment was being paid to explore the Edinburgh's drinking dens (hard work if you can get it). He also attended his first ever football match, though sadly his team – Leith's 'Hibbies' – lost.

Introducing Edinburgh

Edinburgh is a city that just begs to be explored. From the vaults and wynds that riddle the Old Town to the quaint urban villages of Stockbridge and Duddingston, it beckons you to go just that little bit further. It's filled with quirky, come-hither nooks that tempt you to take a look around the next bend, and every corner turned reveals sudden views and unexpected vistas – green sunlit hills, a glimpse of rust-red crags, a blue flash of distant sea.

Scotland's capital has been a top tourist destination since Sir Walter Scott invented the Scottish tourist industry in the early 19th century. Its traditional image has long been that of the 'living museum' variety, with history as the star attraction – visitors obediently trooped from the imposing castle down the Royal Mile to the Palace of Holyroodhouse; they took their photos and went back to the hotel.

But in the last two decades the city has shaken off her prim Presbyterian reserve, as if all those years of playing host to the annual bohemian excesses of the Festival and Fringe had made her see what she was missing. The booming financial services industry, a buoyant tourism sector and the return of a Scottish parliament to the city mean that Edinburgh is now awash with disposable income. Recent years have seen the city's streets produce a lush crop of designer shops, cutting-edge style bars, jazzy boutique hotels and elegant rooftop restaurants that wouldn't look out of place in London or Milan. You can still do the history thing, but there's no need to go back to your hotel afterwards – there are attractions aplenty to keep you occupied until well after bedtime.

You can always tell something about the character of a city by the nicknames it has picked up. Appropriately enough for the city that inspired the *Strange Case of Dr Jekyll and Mr Hyde*, Edinburgh has two contradictory – but complementary – ones.

Lowdown

Bus ticket 80p

Coffee £1.80

Don't say ...but it's not a real parliament, is it?

Essential accessory The latest Inspector Rebus novel, by Ian Rankin

Mid-range double room Around £80

No-no Trying to take a photo of your pal beside the Greyfriars Bobby statue during rush hour

Population 430,000

Time Zone GMT

The Athens of the North, a name inspired by the great thinkers of the Scottish Enlightenment, invokes images of high culture and lofty ideals, of art and literature, and of scientific achievement. It is here that each summer the world's biggest arts festival rises, phoenix-like, from the ashes of last year's rave reviews and broken box-office records to produce yet another string of superlatives. And it was here, in 2000, beneath the Greek temples of Calton Hill – Edinburgh's acropolis – that the Scottish parliament convened for the first time in almost 300 years.

But Edinburgh is also Auld Reekie, an altogether earthier place that thumbs its nose at the pretensions of the literati. Auld Reekie is a city of bars and clubs, of impromptu music sessions and loud singing in pubs, of overindulgence, all-night parties, and wandering home through cobbled streets at dawn. It is the city that tempted Robert Louis Stevenson from his law lectures to explore the drinking dens and lurid street life of the 19th-century Old Town. And it is the city of Beltane, the resurrected pagan May Day festival where half-naked revellers dance in the flickering firelight of bonfires beneath the stony indifference of Calton Hill's pillared monuments.

In addition to its lively cultural and social life, one of Edinburgh's greatest attractions is the way the city is intertwined with the surrounding countryside – Edinburgh is a town entangled in its landscape. The rocky peak of Arthur's Seat and the battlements of Salisbury Crags overlook one end of the Old Town – a natural counterpart to the castle walls at the other – while the leafy corridor of the Water of Leith snakes along only yards from the elegant Georgian terraces of the New Town. Fingers of greenery insinuate themselves among streets and suburbs everywhere, and you can walk or cycle across the city from the Firth of Forth to the Pentland Hills almost without touching a tarmac road.

Edinburgh is a city of many moods, rewarding you with a different experience each time you come – the castle silhouetted against a blue spring sky with a yellow haze of daffodils misting the slopes below the esplanade; a chill December morning with the haar snagging the spires of the Old Town, the dark mouths of the wynds more mysterious than ever; Festival time and a colourful crush of people on the Royal Mile, a juggler's flaming torches arcing above the sea of heads; the smell of malt wafting from the breweries on a grey Sunday afternoon, rain on the cobblestones and a warm glow beckoning from the window of a pub. Better plan for more than one visit if you want to get to know them all.

NEIL'S TOP EDINBURGH DAY

It starts with a long lie-in, of course. And it's probably May. First, a mid-morning stroll along the Meadows, then a comfortable slump over coffee and newspapers at the Elephant House Café (p104), before heading across the street to the Museum of Scotland (p63) for yet another look around – I've been visiting regularly since it opened and I still haven't seen everything. All that culture stuff makes me hungry, so I nip down to Petit Paris (p103) in the Grassmarket for a lazy lunch of *moules-frites* and Muscadet, then saunter back home through the West Port, stopping off to browse in the second-hand bookshops. The weather looks good, so to work off the lunch I get the bike out and head west along the Union Canal towpath (p97) to Ratho, enjoying the views of the Ochil Hills and the distant Highland peaks. After checking out how the new Adventure Centre (p140) is progressing – it's very impressive; my performance on the climbing wall isn't – and sneaking a quick pint at the Bridge Inn (p179), I loop south to Balerno and bike back into town along the leafy Water of Leith Walkway (p93). I've arranged to have dinner with friends, so we meet for a drink at the Caley Sample Room (p126) before walking along Dalry Rd to La Partenope (p111) where we fill our faces with the best Italian seafood in town until the juice drips off our elbows. Then home for a whisky nightcap and the prospect of another long lie-in tomorrow.

Unmissable Edinburgh

A pint of Deuchars IPA at the Bow Bar (p122)

Dinner at a rooftop restaurant (p109)

Museum of Scotland (p63)

Underground Edinburgh (pp49–50)

Winter sunset from Calton Hill (p65)

City Life

City Life

EDINBURGH TODAY

The view as you walk out of Edinburgh's Waverley train station is probably the finest first impression of any city in the world – the castle battlements rising behind the Greek temple of the National Gallery, with the lush greenery of Princes Street Gardens in the foreground. To your left, the precipitous medieval tenements of the Old Town; to your right the Gothic space rocket of the Scott Monument soaring above the commercial bustle of Princes St. And almost all of the city's top sights, best restaurants and shopping streets are within 20 minutes' walk of where you're standing.

Not only is Edinburgh one of the most beautiful cities in Europe, it also enjoys one of Europe's most beautiful settings. There are unexpected vistas from almost every street corner – a glimpse of green sunlit hills, a blue flash of sea, silhouetted spires and rust-red crags. It's a city that begs to be explored on foot – narrow alleys, flights of stairs and hidden kirkyards tempt you off the main streets at every turn.

The return of the Scottish parliament and the booming financial sector mean that Edinburgh is on the up. Unemployment is low, the population is growing, there are new building projects everywhere, and property prices are going through the roof. But the city's increasing prosperity and popularity have brought a downside in the form of severe traffic congestion, a shortage of parking spaces and, if you're a first-time buyer, property prices going through the roof.

Edinburgh consistently comes out top in travellers' polls and in surveys measuring the quality of life in UK cities. It won *Condé Nast Traveler* magazine's Best UK City Award 2001/2002, and readers of the *Guardian* newspaper voted it their favourite UK city for five years running (1999–2003). There's no denying it's a great place to live – it has all the amenities of a cosmopolitan capital city, from superb art galleries and museums to top restaurants and clubs, and, with the addition of the Christmas and New Year celebrations to the long-standing Festival and Fringe, Edinburgh has become the party capital of Europe. But the place is small enough to have a human scale; you're forever bumping into people you know. Someone once said that Edinburgh is a city the size of a town that feels like a village – spend any length of time here and you'll know what they mean.

While you're in Edinburgh, be sure to pop down to the foot of the Royal Mile to see if the Scottish Parliament Building (p60) is finished yet. Due to open by the end of 2004 – with Scottish taxpayers footing the bill for around £400 million – it was originally scheduled to be ready in 2001 at a cost of only £40 million.

Scots are never happier than when they have something to moan about, and the ever-increasing cost of the new parliament building has been a subject of vociferous complaint for the last few years. Once the parliament – acclaimed as the most important new building project in Scotland for more than a hundred years – has finally opened, it will be interesting to see

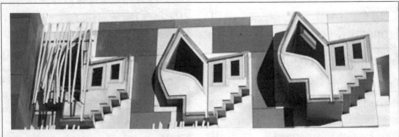

Completed section of the Scottish Parliament Building (p61) at Holyrood

whether the people embrace it or continue to condemn it.

The MSPs' offices at the western end are adorned with unusually shaped windows, said to be based on the outline of the portrait of the *Reverend Robert Walker Skating on Duddingston Loch* (see p67). These enclose a so-called 'contemplative space' in which the resident member can think over new policies. Having read the results of a forthcoming public inquiry into the spiralling costs of the project, no doubt many of them will be sitting there thinking: 'Jings, these bloody windows cost £17,000 each!'

CITY CALENDAR

Edinburgh's calendar is packed full of events and festivities; for more information check out the Festival City chapter (p19) and Holidays (p196).

CULTURE

IDENTITY

Edinburgh was once portrayed as a prim, Presbyterian city full of repressed Calvinists who would no sooner speak to a stranger in the street than they would punch a church minister. Today, however, Edinburgh is the most cosmopolitan city in Scotland – it's often described as the 'least Scottish' of Scottish cities; anyone who lives here for any length of time soon finds out that many of the people you meet are not native Edinburghers, but are incomers from somewhere else.

This cosmopolitan blend means that there's no longer any such thing as a 'typical' Edinburgher... except, perhaps, in the mind of Glaswegians, who will be happy to tell you – often at great length – that their east-coast neighbours are smug, superior, stuck-up and standoffish.

As with any stereotype, there are elements of truth in the Glasgow jibes. Writing in the late-19th century, novelist Robert Louis Stevenson described the inhabitants of his home town as 'citizens of the familiar type who keep ledgers, and attend church, and have sold their immortal portion to a daily paper...To see them thronging by, in their neat clothes and conscious moral rectitude, and with a little air of possession that verges on the absurd, is not the least striking feature of the place'.

More than a hundred years later church attendance is much reduced, but 'keeping ledgers' is still one of the city's economic mainstays, and the *Scotsman* newspaper is still the breakfast read of choice for the middle classes. You can still observe the neat clothes of the brokers and accountants as they tote their cardboard cups of Starbuck's latte back to the office, and that 'air of possession' is reflected in an instinctive (and protective) awareness of the beauty of their city; God help any neighbour who installs plastic-framed windows in a Georgian town house. As for 'conscious moral rectitude' – just read the letters page of the *Scotsman*.

Bar-room sociologists theorise that it was Edinburgh citizens' long history of living cheek-by-jowl in close-packed tenements that led to both their polite reticence (we all have to retain some privacy, after all, and respect that of others) and their feverish obsession with the doings of their neighbours. Here's Stevenson again, with another observation that still rings true today: 'Edinburgh is not so much a small city as the largest of small towns. It is scarce possible to avoid observing your neighbours; and I never yet heard of any one who tried.'

Although they're a gregarious lot, Edinburgh folk can still display a certain reticence with strangers. In pubs you'll find that the locals are rarely the ones to break the ice, but if you make the effort to get talking you'll find them to be warm and witty company, proud of their city and happy to expound on its finer points (as well as the multifarious failings of its politicians). But whatever you do, don't refer to people from Leith as Edinburghers. Although Edinburgh's port was incorporated as part of the city in 1920, its inhabitants remain fiercely independent. They're Leithers, and don't you forget it.

Edinburgh's population of 430,000 is made up of white-collar and blue-collar workers in roughly equal proportions. In fact, with so many people employed in finance, government, education, law and medicine, the city has Scotland's largest middle-class population. This class divide is mirrored in the sporting world, where rugby is traditionally seen as the preserve of former public schoolboys, while football (soccer) is for the great unwashed. Whenever two or more Edinburgh football fans get together, the first question is what team do you support? With rugby fans, it's what school did you go to?

Immigration has added a bit of spice to the city's ethnic mixture but on a smaller scale than other European capitals. Following the 19th-century famines in Ireland, many Irish settled here, as have a considerable proportion of English people. There are also many smaller ethnic communities including Italians, Poles, Indians, Pakistanis, Bangladeshis and Chinese, and there is a growing Spanish community. For much of the year the large student population adds to Edinburgh's cosmopolitanism, and during the Edinburgh Festival the city's population almost doubles with the influx of visitors.

LIFESTYLE

The old Edinburgh stereotype was the blue-rinsed and handbagged Morningside lady who spent her days drinking tea with her friends, shopping at Jenners for tweeds and twinsets, and

A Double Life

Ever since the 18th century writers have found in Edinburgh a metaphor for the duality of human nature. The image of the orderly and elegant New Town alongside the jumble and chaos of the Old has suggested the juxtaposition of respectable and bawdy, public and private, good and evil. And the city's vertical dimension – with its soaring monuments and sculpted façades rising above dark alleys, dripping vaults and chilly cellars – neatly symbolises an equivalent moral dimension with lofty ideals and ambitions raised high above festering sumps of filth and depravity.

Robert Louis Stevenson (p28) became aware of the two sides of his own nature during his student days, when he would escape the rectitude of Presbyterian family life and the monotony of his law lectures by slinking off to the pubs and brothels of the Old Town and Leith. He explored this theme more fully in his classic story of dual identity, *Strange Case of Dr Jekyll and Mr Hyde*, which, though ostensibly set in London, is undeniably an Edinburgh novel.

Along with his own adventures, Stevenson's inspiration for Jekyll and Hyde was the story of Deacon Brodie. William Brodie (1741–88) was born to a wealthy New Town family. He grew up to be a skilled cabinet-maker and a member of the city council, mingling with high society and meeting poet Robert Burns and painter Sir Henry Raeburn. But this veneer of respectability concealed a taste for Edinburgh's darker side – by night he haunted the Old Town's drinking dens, whorehouses and cockpits, maintained two mistresses and fathered half a dozen illegitimate children. He gambled away his inherited fortune and ran up huge debts.

Brodie's status as a trusted deacon (city councillor) and cabinet-maker gave him legitimate access to city shops and grand houses during the day. Using a piece of putty, he secretly took impressions of any keys he found, and paid a criminal locksmith to make copies. Thus equipped, he was able to enter his victims' properties during the night and steal at will to support his nocturnal activities.

Deacon Brodie's double life continued undetected and unsuspected for several years, until a bungled attempt to rob the Excise Office forced him to flee to Holland. But his accomplices turned King's evidence, and he was caught in the act of boarding a ship to the Americas. Tried and sentenced to death, he was hanged – in a wonderfully ironic twist – on an improved city gallows that he had himself designed.

Muriel Spark's classic novel *The Prime of Miss Jean Brodie* (p28) deals with duality in the contrast between Miss Brodie's two suitors – the respectable music teacher, Mr Lowther, and the libidinous art teacher, Teddy Lloyd – and her own inner conflict between wild romance and repressed sexuality; the choice of the heroine's surname was not accidental. More recently, Edinburgh novelist Ian Rankin (p26) has admitted that the inspiration for his first John Rebus novel *Knots and Crosses* came from Stevenson's Jekyll and Hyde; his subsequent Rebus books display a continuing fascination with the darker side of human nature and the seamier side of Scotland's capital.

Tenement Living

The tenement is a distinctive feature of Edinburgh's streetscape, from the cramped, 17th-century 'lands' that line much of the Royal Mile to the regular façades and pointy turrets of the smart Victorian tenements that spread to the south of the city centre.

A tenement is a communal building, generally four to six storeys high, that is divided into flats (apartments) opening from a common stair. Tenement flats range in size and grandeur from cramped one-bedroom places in formerly working-class areas, such as Gorgie and Abbeyhill, to the spacious, high-ceilinged, three- and four-bedroom apartments of genteel Marchmont and Newington.

The original tenements of the Old Town were a response to lack of building space within the city walls – unable to expand outwards, the city built upwards. The Victorian tenements of southern Edinburgh were built in order to squeeze as many rent-paying tenants as possible onto a landowner's property. Both meant living in close proximity to your neighbours, and the 'vertical street' of the common stair often engendered a strong feeling of community. Even now, things such as upkeep of the roof, cleaning of the stair, and payment of the electricity bill for the main-door buzzer/intercom are shared among the occupants.

Today, a spacious tenement flat in Edinburgh is a highly desirable property, especially if it retains period features such as ornate plaster cornicing and cast-iron fireplaces. At the time of writing, a three-bedroomed flat in Marchmont (just south of the Meadows) would set you back around £250,000 to £300,000.

twitching the lace curtains in the front room to keep an eye on the neighbours. The annual Festival Fringe was an occasion for writing letters of complaint to the *Scotsman* ('an affront to decent citizens' etc etc); and 'sex' was what the coalman delivered your coal in.

The Morningside ladies still exist – keep your eyes open in Jenners – but today the typical thirty-something professional Edinburgher probably lives in a tenement flat in the Southside (paid for with a hefty mortgage), works in financial services, and spends far too much time each evening circling the block in the eternal quest for a parking space. They drink wine rather than beer, latte rather than tea, and eat out at least once a week. They're obsessed with property prices, take a week or two's ski holiday each winter, and dream about owning a villa in Tuscany.

The high proportion of young professionals in Edinburgh's population means that there's a lot of disposable income floating around, much of which is channelled into restaurants, clubs, designer shops and fitness centres.

FOOD

Eating out in Edinburgh has changed beyond all recognition in the last 20 years. Back then, sophisticated dining meant a visit to the Aberdeen Angus Steak House for prawn cocktail, sirloin steak (well done) and chips, and Black Forest gateau, all washed down with Mateus Rosé. Today, the city has more restaurants per head of population than any other city in the UK, with settings ranging from cosy traditional candlelit cellars to modern glass-fronted roof-top lounges.

Traditionally, Scottish cookery was all about basic comfort food – solid, nourishing fare, often high in fat, that would keep you warm on a winter's day spent in the fields or at the fishing, and sweet treats to come home to in the evening. However, the label Modern Scottish (see p100) has been invented to describe the cuisine in many of Edinburgh's newer restaurants. This is lighter and more sophisticated, taking top-quality Scottish produce – from Aberdeen Angus beef matured in the traditional manner (hung for three weeks) to sea-scented scallops and langoustines – and preparing it using French, Italian or Asian techniques, sauces, spices or flavourings. The classic example of this approach, which appeared on the menu at Stac Polly (p108) may years ago, is haggis wrapped in a filo pastry parcel, and served with a hoisin dipping sauce.

Haggis may be the national dish that Scotland is most famous for, but when it comes to what Scottish people actually cook and eat most often, the hands-down winner has to be mince and tatties. Minced beef, browned in the pan and then stewed slowly with onion, carrot and gravy, served with mashed potatoes (with a splash of milk and a knob of butter added during the mashing) – tasty, warming, and you don't even have to chew. You'll rarely see it on an Edinburgh restaurant menu though – it's strictly a home-cooked dish.

Surprisingly few Scots eat porridge for breakfast – these days a café latte and a croissant is just as likely – and even fewer eat it in the traditional way; that is with salt to taste, but no sugar. The breakfast offered in an Edinburgh B&B or hotel usually consists of fruit juice and cereal or muesli, followed by a choice of bacon, sausage, black pudding, grilled tomato, mushrooms, and a fried egg or two. Fish for breakfast may sound strange, but many hotels still offer the traditional Scots delicacy of grilled kippers (smoked herrings) or smoked haddock (poached in

Pop Rokit pub (p125)

milk and served with a poached egg) for breakfast – delicious with lots of buttered toast.

Meat eaters will enjoy a thick fillet of world-famous Aberdeen Angus beef; venison, from Highland red deer, is leaner and also appears on many menus. Both may be served with a wine-based or creamy whisky sauce. And then there's haggis, Scotland's much-maligned national dish…

Scottish salmon is famous worldwide, but there's a big difference between farmed salmon and the leaner, more expensive, wild fish. Smoked salmon is traditionally dressed with a squeeze of lemon juice and eaten with fresh brown bread and butter. Trout, the salmon's smaller cousin – whether wild, rod-caught brown trout or farmed rainbow trout – is delicious fried in oatmeal.

As an alternative to kippers (smoked herrings) you may be offered Arbroath smokies (lightly smoked fresh haddock), traditionally eaten cold. Herring fillets fried in oatmeal are good, if you don't mind picking out a few bones. Mackerel pâté and smoked or peppered mackerel (both served cold) are also popular.

Juicy Scottish langoustines (also called Dublin Bay prawns), crabs, lobsters, oysters, mussels and scallops are also widely available in Edinburgh restaurants. Seafood soups include the delicious Cullen skink, made with smoked haddock, potato, onion and milk, and partan bree (crab soup).

Traditional Scottish puddings are irresistibly creamy, high-calorie concoctions. Cranachan is whipped cream flavoured with whisky, and mixed with toasted oatmeal and raspberries. Atholl brose is a mixture of cream, whisky and honey flavoured with oatmeal, and clootie dumpling is a rich steamed pudding filled with currants and raisins.

Haggis – Scotland's National Dish

Scotland's national dish is often ridiculed because of its ingredients, which admittedly don't sound promising – the finely chopped lungs, heart and liver of a sheep, mixed with oatmeal and onion and stuffed into a sheep's stomach bag. However, it actually tastes surprisingly good.

Haggis should be served with champit tatties and bashed neeps (mashed potatoes and turnips), with a generous dollop of butter and a good sprinkling of black pepper.

Although it's eaten year round, haggis is central to the celebrations of 25 January, in honour of Scotland's national poet, Robert Burns. Scots worldwide unite on Burns Night to revel in their Scottishness. A piper announces the arrival of the haggis and Burns' poem *Address to a Haggis* is recited to this 'Great chieftain o' the puddin-race'. The bulging haggis is then lanced with a dirk (dagger) to reveal the steaming offal within, 'warm, reekin, rich'.

Vegetarians (and quite a few carnivores, no doubt) will be relieved to know that veggie haggis is available in some restaurants.

Oat Cuisine

OATS: A GRAIN, WHICH IN ENGLAND IS GENERALLY GIVEN TO HORSES, BUT IN SCOTLAND APPEARS TO SUPPORT THE PEOPLE.

A Dictionary of the English Language, by Samuel Johnson (1709–84)

The most distinctive feature of traditional Scottish cookery is the abundant use of oatmeal. Oats *(Avena sativa)* grow well in the cool, wet climate of Scotland and have been cultivated here for at least two thousand years. Up to the 19th century, oatmeal was the main source of calories for the rural Scottish population. The farmer in his field, the cattle drover on the road to market, the soldier on the march, all would carry with them a bag of meal that could be mixed with water and baked on a girdle (a flat metal plate) or on hot stones beside a fire.

Long-despised as an inferior foodstuff (see Johnson's sneering description below), oatmeal is enjoying a return to popularity as recent research has proved it to be highly nutritious (high in iron, calcium and B vitamins) and healthy (rich in soluble fibre, which helps to reduce cholesterol).

The best-known Scottish oatmeal dish is, of course, porridge, which is simply rolled oatmeal boiled with water. A lot of nonsense has been written about porridge and whether it should be eaten with salt or with sugar. It should be eaten however you like it – as a child in the 1850s, Robert Louis Stevenson had golden syrup with his.

Oatcakes are another traditional dish that you will certainly come across during a visit to Edinburgh, usually as an accompaniment to cheese at the end of a meal. A *mealie pudding* is a sausage-skin stuffed with oatmeal and onion and boiled for an hour or so. Add blood to the mixture and you have a black pudding. *Skirlie* is simply chopped onions and oatmeal fried in beef dripping and seasoned with salt and pepper; it's usually served as a side dish. Trout and herring can be dipped in oatmeal before frying, and it can be added to soups and stews as a thickening agent. It's even used in desserts – toasted oatmeal is a vital flavouring in Cranachan, a delicious mixture of whipped cream, whisky and raspberries.

FASHION

Edinburgh has often been dismissed as a style vacuum, especially by Glasgow fashionistas who consider their city to be Scotland's capital of chic. But when Knightsbridge-based designer store Harvey Nichols (p150) opened in Edinburgh in 2003, they found their cutting-edge fashion lines – men's as well as women's – selling out faster than they did in London. The growing fashion scene was given a further boost when Kylie Minogue, Christina Aguilera, Britney Spears, Beyoncé Knowles and a host of Hollywood glamour descended on the city for the MTV Awards in October 2003.

Once a city of pinstripe suits, twinsets and tweeds, Edinburgh has become increasingly fashion-conscious in recent years, and the local Sunday newspaper supplements are filled with soft-focus spreads of the latest designer offerings. A developing taste for sharp styling and look-at-me chic is reflected in a wave of new designer boutiques, though Princes St is still a long way short of a Parisian boulevard when it comes to citizens decked out with effortless elegance.

Many of Edinburgh's clothes shops stock knitwear from the famous Pringle factory. The 200-year-old Pringle brand was a world-famous fashion name from the 1930s to the '60s (think twinsets – Pringle invented them – and diamond-pattern sweaters), but from the '70s to the '90s it fell out of the mainstream and the name came to be associated with golfers and, in the '80s, a violent faction of football fans known as 'casuals'. But Pringle was re-launched in 2000 as a designer brand, and has achieved huge success – Pringle sweaters have been seen clinging to the torsos of Sharon Stone, Tom Hanks and David Beckham.

Another traditionally Scottish fashion success story is 21st Century Kilts (see p156). Designer Howie Nicholsby created the company in 1996 in order to re-invent Scotland's national costume for the 21st century. He believes that the kilt should be a garment that can be worn in all situations, not just at weddings and Burns' Nights. His designs range from plain black barathea and formal pinstripe to more exotic variations like camouflage material and black leather; he himself has worn a kilt almost every day since 1999. Howie's kilts have been worn by celebrities such as singer Robbie Williams and Hollywood stars Mel Gibson, Samuel L Jackson and Vin Diesel, and even graced the catwalk at the 2003 Los Angeles Fashion Show.

SPORT

Football (soccer) in Scotland is not so much a sport as a religion, with thousands turning out to worship their local teams on Wednesdays and weekends throughout the season (August to May). Sacred rites include standing in the freezing cold of a February day, drinking hot Bovril and eating a Scotch pie as you watch your team getting gubbed.

Edinburgh's two main football teams are Heart of Midlothian (a.k.a. Hearts, nicknamed the Jam Tarts or Jambos), founded in 1874, and Hibernian (a.k.a. Hibs, Hibbies or Hi-bees), founded in 1875 (see also p141). On match days you'll see thousands of supporters streaming along Dalry and Gorgie Rds (Hearts) or Easter Rd (Hibs) on their way to the game.

There's intense rialry between the two clubs – both play in the Scottish Premier League – which reaches a peak when they play each other (the teams meet four times a year in a match known as the 'local Derby'). The big event in Edinburgh's football calendar was once the New Year Derby, when Hibs and Hearts faced each other on New Year's Day. However, this 100-year-old tradition was scrapped in 1999; match timing is now dictated by TV schedules.

The subject currently being debated by Edinburgh football fans in pubs throughout the city is Hearts' plan to abandon their Tynecastle stadium, which no longer complies with European rules. Various plans have been put forward for a new stadium on the edge of the city, and it has even been suggested – devout fans shudder at the thought – that Hearts and Hibs share the new stadium. But no site has yet been approved, and for the time being it looks like Hearts will move to the rugby union stadium at Murrayfield (p142) for the 2004–05 season.

Traditionally, football was the sport of Scotland's urban working classes, while rugby union was the preserve of public schoolboys, middle-class university graduates, and farmers and agricultural workers from the Borders. Although this distinction is breaking down – rugby's popularity soared after the 1999 World Cup was staged in the UK, and the middle classes have invaded the football terraces – it still persists to some extent, especially in Edinburgh.

Each year, starting in January, Scotland takes part in the Six Nations Rugby Union Championship. The most important fixture is the clash against England for the Calcutta Cup – it's always an emotive event, though Scotland has only won once in the last 10 years. The match is played at Edinburgh's Murrayfield Stadium every second year – the next one is in 2006.

MEDIA

Edinburgh has been a major publishing centre since the 18th century, and many famous names had their origins here – the *Encyclopaedia Britannica* (1768–71) and *Chambers Encyclopaedia* (1859–68) were first published in Edinburgh, and the publishing houses A&C Black and Constable were founded here. Edinburgh publishers are fewer in number these days, but include the innovative Canongate Books, led by charismatic young publisher Jamie Byng and home to bestselling authors Michel Faber *(The Crimson Petal and the White)*, Yann Martel *(The Life of Pi)* and Man-Booker Prize-winner DBC Pierre *(Vernon God Little)*.

Edinburgh's first newspaper – *Diurnal Occurrances touching the Dailie Proceedings in Parliament* – was printed in 1641. Today, the city is home to The Scotsman Publications, founded in 1817 and owned by the secretive Barclay Brothers. The group – which recently moved from its Victorian offices on North Bridge (now the Scotsman Hotel, see p161) to a modern building on Holyrood Rd – publishes the *Scotsman, Scotland On Sunday* and *Edinburgh Evening News*.

Edinburgh pretty much invented the literary magazine in the late-18th century, and the *Edinburgh Review* – founded in 1802 – is still published twice a year. Current Edinburgh-based literary magazines also include the thrice-yearly *Cencrastus* and the quarterly *Chapman*.

LANGUAGE

The language of modern Edinburgh is, of course, English. The educated Edinburgh accent at its Sunday best has a Scottish burr, but is much more clear and understandable to visitors than the broader accents of Glasgow and Aberdeen. There is, of course, a less formal Edinburgh argot, famously recorded in the expletive-strewn pages of Irvine Welsh's novel *Trainspotting*, which you'll overhear in pubs, on buses and on the football terraces. At the other end of the social spectrum, the ultimate expression of Edinburgh gentility is the Morningside accent, an over-compensated attempt to mimic the posh vowels of Southern England's Received Pronunciation, in which 'girl' becomes 'gerl' and 'friend' becomes 'fraynd'. Wonderfully rendered by Maggie Smith in *The Prime of Miss Jean Brodie*, the Morningside accent is becoming rarer but can still occasionally be heard in any tearoom with more than a hint of chintz.

However, from the 8th to the 19th centuries the common language of the city's inhabitants was Lowland Scots. Lowland Scots (sometimes called Lallans), like modern English, evolved from Old English and has Dutch, French, Gaelic, German and Scandinavian influences. As distinct from English as Norwegian is from Danish, it was the official language of the state in Scotland until the Act of Union in 1707, and was the language used by Robert Burns in much of his poetry. Following the Union, English rose to predominance as the language of government and of polite society. The spread of education and literacy in the 19th century eventually led to the Scots language being perceived as backward and unsophisticated – school children were often beaten for using Scots instead of English.

The Scots tongue persisted, however, and today it is undergoing a revival – Scots language dictionaries have been published, there are university degree courses in Scots language and literature, and Scots is studied as part of the school curriculum. A few die-hard enthusiasts even write letters to the newspapers in broad Scots.

Ken Whit Ah Mean?

Many old Scots words, and a few Gaelic ones, survive in common usage in Scotland, and you'll come across them in books, newspapers and even TV news reports as well as everyday speech. If you're intrigued by such Scotticisms, any Edinburgh bookshop will be able to sell you a Scots dictionary, where you can discover the delights of colourful words such as cantrip, dreich, and clishmaclaiver.

Auld Reekie – Edinburgh (Old Smoky)

aye – yes/always

bairn – baby or child

ben – mountain

blether – chat

brae – hill

bridie – pie filled with meat, potatoes and onion

brig – bridge

burgh – town

cairn – pile of stones to mark path or junction, also peak

ceilidh – pronounced 'kay-ley', dance

close – entrance

cratur – whisky

daur – dare

dene – valley

dinnae – don't

dram – glass of whisky

drap – drop

dun – fort

firth – estuary

glen – valley

gubbed – beaten soundly (as in a football match)

haar – fog off the North Sea

Hogmanay – New Year's Eve

howff – pub

ken – know

kipper – smoked herring

kirk – church

law – round hill

links – grass-covered, coastal sand dunes; golf course on same

neeps – turnips

Pict – early Celtic inhabitants (from the Latin *pictus*, meaning 'painted')

provost – mayor

quaich – small drinking cup

quid – pound sterling

rood – cross

sporran – purse worn on a chain round the waist, with a kilt

tatties – potatoes

tolbooth – courthouse or jail

tron – public weighbridge

vennel – narrow street

wynd – lane, alley

ECONOMY & COSTS

Edinburgh has one of the richest urban economies in the UK. Of Edinburgh's traditional industries – brewing, biscuit-making, publishing and printing – only brewing continues on a major scale, although closures, takeovers and 'rationalisations' have reduced the size of the workforce. Publishing and printing also continue on a smaller scale. Electronics and engineering are now the main industrial employers.

Edinburgh's economy today is largely based on services (which account for 85% of employment), mainly finance and tourism; in both sectors Edinburgh is second only to London. The Royal Bank of Scotland, HBOS (created in 2001 from the merger of the Bank of Scotland with the Halifax building society) and several other financial institutions have their headquarters in the city, with many financial offices clustered in the new Exchange district on the west side of Lothian Rd. Other important service sectors include retail, education, law, local government and medicine. The city's growth areas are in research, information technology, computer software and biotechnology, with many businesses located in new industrial parks in the west of the city.

Edinburgh's economy received a major boost with the creation of the Scottish parliament in 1999. New building and redevelopment projects are taking shape all over the city and the unemployment rate (around 3.3%) is below the UK average.

Edinburgh is not a cheap destination – expect to pay around £60 to £100 a night for a double room in an attractive, central hotel, and budget around £15 a head for lunch and £25 for dinner if you plan to sample the best of Edinburgh's restaurants. On the plus side, however, most of the city's art galleries and museums have free admission, and you can save on restaurant bills by looking for business lunch deals, and bargain pre- and post-theatre menus.

How Much?

1.5L bottled water 65p

1L petrol 78p

bottle of malt whisky £25

cappuccino £1.80

dinner at the Tower £25 a head

fashion kilt from £300

fish supper £3 to £4

glass of wine £2.50

pint of beer £2.20

souvenir t-shirt £10

GOVERNMENT & POLITICS

The Scottish parliament is a single-chamber system with 129 members (known as MSPs), elected through proportional representation and led by a first minister, currently Jack McConnell. It sits for four-year terms (the next elections are in 2007) and is responsible for so-called 'devolved matters' – education, health, housing, transport, economic development and other domestic affairs. It also has the power (as yet unused) to increase or decrease the rate of income tax in Scotland by up to 3%. The Scottish Executive – composed of the first minister, Scottish ministers, junior ministers and Scottish law officers – is the Scottish government, which proposes new laws and deals with the areas of responsibility outlined above, while the body of MSPs constitutes the Scottish legislature, which debates, amends and votes on new legislation.

Westminster still has power over so-called 'reserved matters' such as defence, foreign affairs and social security. Scotland is represented in Westminster by 72 Scottish members of parliament (MPs) in the House of Commons, out of a total of 659. The Scotland Office, headed by the Secretary of State for Scotland, is the Westminster department charged with ensuring Scotland's interests are represented in the UK government.

In contrast to Westminster, where the main political contest is between the Labour and Conservative parties with the Liberal Democrats coming a poor third, Scotland has four main parties – the Labour Party, the Scottish National Party (SNP), the Scottish Conservative and Unionist Party (also known as the Tory Party or just the Tories) and the Liberal Democrats (Lib Dems) – and the main struggle for power is between Labour and the SNP.

The Conservative Party was opposed to devolution (the transfer of government powers from Westminster to Scotland), a policy proposed by the Labour Party in the hope of appeasing demands for independence. The long-term goal of Scottish Nationalists is complete independence for Scotland.

In the 1997 general elections, Scotland returned no Conservative MPs at all and in the 2001 UK elections the Tories managed to claw back just one seat in Scotland, with a majority of only 48 votes. In the 2003 Scottish parliament elections, Labour won 50 seats, the SNP 27, Conservatives 18, and the Lib Dems 17; the Scottish Socialist Party took six seats and the Green Party seven seats.

Edinburgh's local government is in the hands of the City of Edinburgh Council, based in the City Chambers in the High St. The council is popularly elected and serves four-year terms.

Royal Bank of Scotland building on the east side of St Andrew Square (p68)

ENVIRONMENT

Edinburgh earned its sobriquet of Auld Reekie (Old Smoky) in the 17th century from the characteristic pall of smoke that hung over the city, caused by the huge concentration of domestic fires. With the coming of the Industrial Revolution, pollution from factories and steam trains added to the grime. Beginning in the 1950s, a series of smokeless zones were set up that now encompass the whole city.

The last decade has seen the cleaning of soot-blackened stonework on many of Edinburgh's older buildings, in the hope of restoring them to their original colour – the Royal Scottish Academy (p68) is one of the most recent structures to shed its veil. Others have not been cleaned because of the danger of damage to delicate stonework – it may be hard to believe, but the Scott Monument (p68) on Princes St was originally pale grey in colour.

THE LAND

Edinburgh is draped over and around a series of hills – the deeply eroded stumps of ancient volcanoes – between the Pentland Hills in the south and the broad Firth of Forth estuary to the north. During the last Ice Age (around 12,000 years ago) a vast ice sheet flowed from west to east around Castle Rock, creating a 'crag and tail' feature on which the Old Town was built.

Holyrood Park provides a broad swath of wild countryside in the city centre, with a varied landscape of hills, lochs and moorland. Edinburgh's only river, the Water of Leith, runs from the Pentlands northwards to the Firth of Forth at Leith, along the northwestern border of New Town.

GREEN EDINBURGH

The City of Edinburgh Council is one of the UK's more daring and forward-thinking when it comes to the subject of traffic control. In the last decade it has set up a system of dedicated bus lanes with the aim of reducing traffic congestion and vehicle pollution, and developed a growing network of cycling routes (see p191). Private cars have been banned from the east-going lane of Princes St, a congestion-charging scheme for traffic entering the city centre will be introduced in 2006, and a modern tram network is to be installed by 2009.

...nburgh was the first city in the UK to introduce a car-free housing development, 2 miles from the city centre on Gorgie Rd. Space usually allocated to car parking was given over to children's playgrounds, sports facilities and cycle paths, solar power is used to augment the electricity supply, and 'grey water' (waste water from baths and kitchen sinks) is recycled through a reed bed and reused for domestic washing.

The Water of Leith (p80) and the River Almond (at Cramond; see p76) were once industrialised and severely polluted, but both have been cleaned up in the last two decades; the Almond is now so clean that otters and salmon have been sighted in recent years.

URBAN PLANNING & DEVELOPMENT

Edinburgh is growing faster than any other city in Scotland, creating problems for the planners; the main issues are traffic congestion and a lack of building space, which is putting pressure on green-belt areas.

Plans to tackle traffic include congestion-charging (to be introduced in 2006) for vehicles entering Edinburgh. There will be two cordons – an outer one on the city boundary, and an inner one enclosing the city centre (see p192).

More ambitious plans envisage the reintroduction of trams to Edinburgh's streets, with lines running from the city centre to Leith in the north, Edinburgh Airport in the west, and Dalkeith in the south; it is hoped that the first line will open by 2009.

The most obvious building development in the city centre is the new parliament building (p61), which will completely change the face of the Holyrood district at the foot of the Royal Mile. The revamp of the Exchange financial district to the west of Lothian Rd is nearly complete, with a complex of new office buildings complementing the Edinburgh International Conference Centre and the Sheraton Grand Hotel. The next stage, under way at the time of writing, is the building of luxury residential apartments at Port Hamilton, the easterly terminus of the Union Canal, which was reopened to navigation in 2002.

The removal of the Edinburgh Royal Infirmary to a site on the southern edge of the city in 2003 has left its old home between Lauriston Pl and the Meadows ripe for redevelopment. This prime city centre location has been re-named Quartermile, and by 2010 it should have been transformed into a complex of offices, flats, shops, restaurants and a hotel (housed in the grand, Scottish Baronial shell of the old infirmary).

Probably the biggest development in the city, however, is the plan to transform the whole of Edinburgh's waterfront, from Granton to Leith. This previously industrial area, once characterised by derelict gasometers, wasteland and the smell of chemical factories, is slated to become a dazzling Riviera of luxury apartments, hotels, shopping centres and yacht marinas by 2017.

Festival City

Festival City

Since the inaugural Edinburgh International Festival of Music and Drama in 1947, the city has grown into one of the biggest party venues in the world, with a crowded calendar of contrasting festivals, ranging from science and storytelling to music, movies and marching military bands.

Although this is great news for visitors, it has led to an occasional 'Bah! Humbug!' reaction from the city's residents, who, let's face it, have to put up with major disruption to their daily lives for large chunks of the year. Fortunately, few go as far as the lady living in Ramsay Gdn, next to the Castle Esplanade, who once tried to have the Military Tattoo cancelled because of the noise.

Festival high season is August, when half a dozen festivals – including the huge Edinburgh International Festival, and the even bigger Festival Fringe – run concurrently, and late December, when the Capital Christmas and Hogmanay celebrations pull in the crowds. These and more are listed below in chronological order.

The city is at its prettiest in spring, when daffodils and cherry blossom brighten the parks, and the weather is often at its best – May and June (and September) are generally the driest and sunniest months. July and August can bring heatwaves, but also a fair bit of rain, so consider an umbrella or waterproof. Midwinter means short, dark days (the sun rises after 9am and sets before 4pm) and often cold weather – wrap up well for the Hogmanay festivities.

Only in Edinburgh

- Beltane (below)
- Caledonian Brewery Traditional Beer Festival (p21)
- Edinburgh Military Tattoo (p22)
- Edinburgh Festival Fringe (p22)
- Edinburgh's Hogmanay (p23)

Festival Tickets and Programmes

The programme for the Edinburgh International Festival is usually published at the beginning of April; the Fringe programme comes out in early June. If you want to get hold of one as soon as possible, you can register online at the relevant website, and a programme will be sent to you as soon as it's available (free for the International Festival, £2 for the Fringe).

You can start booking tickets as soon as you have a programme in your hands – by post, fax, phone or Internet, or over the counter at the box office (The Hub for the International Festival, the Fringe Office for the Fringe; see entries for details). Book as far in advance as possible for popular shows, or for anything you really, really want to see – there are few words more disappointing than 'sorry, it's sold out'.

You can find listings for all of Edinburgh's festivals on the umbrella website www.edinburgh-festivals.com.

EDINBURGH INTERNATIONAL SCIENCE FESTIVAL

☎ 530 2001; www.sciencefestival.co.uk; Roxburgh's Court, 323 High St

First held in 1987, the Science Festival hosts a wide range of events, including talks, lectures, exhibitions, demonstrations, guided tours and interactive experiments designed to stimulate, inspire and challenge. From dinosaurs and ghosts to alien life forms, there's something to interest everyone. The Science Festival runs over 10 days in the first two weeks of April.

BELTANE

☎ 228 5353; www.beltane.org; The Beltane Fire Society, 19 Leven St

Beltane is a pagan fire festival that marks the end of winter and the rebirth of spring. It was resurrected in modern form in 1988 and is now celebrated annually on the summit of Calton Hill. The spectacular rituals involve lots of fire, drumming, body paint and sexual innuendo (well, it's a fertility rite, after all). Bring your sparklers. Held annually on the night of 30 April into the early hours (around 1am) of 1 May.

SCOTTISH INTERNATIONAL CHILDREN'S FESTIVAL

☎ 225 8050; www.imaginate.org.uk; 45a George St
This is Britain's biggest festival of performing arts for children, with events suitable for kids aged from three up to 12. Groups from around the world perform classic tales such as *Hansel and Gretel*, as well as new material written especially for youngsters. The Children's Festival takes place annually in the last week of May.

CALEDONIAN BREWERY TRADITIONAL BEER FESTIVAL

☎ 228 5688; www.caledonian-events.co.uk; Caledonian Brewery, 42 Slateford Rd
A celebration of all things fermented and yeasty, Scotland's biggest beerfest is hosted by Edinburgh's leading brewer of cask-conditioned ales. You can also sample a wide range of traditionally brewed beers from around the world, while enjoying live jazz and blues music and snacking on pies and a variety of barbecued fare. Froth-topped bliss. The Beer Festival is held on the first weekend in June.

PRIDE SCOTIA

☎ 550 0898; www.pride-scotia.org; 78 Montgomery St
This annual celebration of Scotland's gay, lesbian and transgender community begins with a colourful parade along The Mound, Princes St, Leith St and Broughton St, followed by lots of eating, drinking and dancing at various venues in the Pink Triangle, Edinburgh's 'gay village'. The Pride Scotland parade and festival takes place in even years in Glasgow, odd years in Edinburgh, on the last Saturday in June.

EDINBURGH INTERNATIONAL JAZZ & BLUES FESTIVAL

☎ 553 5000; www.jazzmusic.co.uk; 29 St Stephens St
Held annually since 1978, the Edinburgh International Jazz and Blues Festival pulls in the top talent from all over the world. The first weekend sees a Mardi Gras street parade on Saturday from the City Chambers, up the Royal Mile and down into Grassmarket, for an afternoon of free, open-air music. On the Sunday there's a series of free concerts at the Ross Bandstand in Princes St Gardens. The Jazz Festival runs for nine days, beginning on the last Friday in July (ie the week before the Fringe and Tattoo begin).

EDINBURGH INTERNATIONAL GAMES

☎ 661 5351; Meadowbank Sports Centre; ticket booking ☎ 228 8616; Usher Hall, Lothian Rd
This is a one-day international athletics event featuring teams from Scotland, England,

Local brews at the Royal Oak (p138)

Festival City

21

Wales, Ireland and the United States plus individual athletes from around Europe, complemented by a programme of traditional Scottish Highland Games (tossing the caber, throwing the hammer, putting the shot), demonstrations of Highland dancing, and performances by pipe bands appearing at the Military Tattoo. It is held on the last Saturday in August.

EDINBURGH MILITARY TATTOO

☎ 225 1188; www.edintattoo.co.uk; The Tattoo Office, 32 Market St

The Military Tattoo is a spectacular display of military marching bands, massed pipes and drums, acrobats, cheerleaders and motorcycle display teams, all played out in front of the magnificent backdrop of the floodlit castle. Each show traditionally finishes with a lone piper, dramatically lit, playing a lament on the battlements. The Tattoo takes place over the first three weeks of August (from a Friday to a Saturday); there's one show at 9pm Monday to Friday, and two (at 7.30pm and 10.30pm) on Saturday, but no performance on Sunday.

EDINBURGH FESTIVAL FRINGE

☎ 226 5257; www.edfringe.com; The Fringe Office, 180 High St

When the first Edinburgh Festival was held in 1947, there were eight theatre companies who didn't make it onto the main programme. Undeterred, they grouped together and held their own mini-festival, on the fringe... and an Edinburgh institution was born. Today the Edinburgh Festival Fringe is the biggest festival of the performing arts anywhere in the world.

Since 1990 the Fringe has been dominated by stand-up comedy, but the sheer variety of shows on offer is just staggering – everything from chain-saw juggling to performance poetry to Tibetan yak-milk gargling. So how do you decide what to see? There are daily reviews in the *Scotsman* newspaper (one good *Scotsman* review, and a show sells out in hours), but the best recommendation is word of mouth. If you have the time, go to at least one unknown show – it may be crap but at least you'll have your obligatory 'worst show I ever saw' story to bandy about in the pub.

The big names play at the mega-venues such as the Assembly Rooms, the Gilded Balloon and the Pleasance, and will charge you mega-prices (from £8 per ticket and more). However, there are plenty of good shows that will only cost you a fiver and, best of all, lots of free stuff. Fringe Sunday – usually the second Sunday – is a smorgasbord of free performances. It was traditionally held in Holyrood Park, but in 2004 was moved to the Meadows.

The Fringe takes place over three-and-a-half weeks in August, the last two weeks overlapping with the first two of the Edinburgh International Festival.

EDINBURGH INTERNATIONAL FESTIVAL

☎ 473 2000; www.eif.co.uk; The Hub, Castlehill

First held in 1947 to mark a return to peace after the ordeal of WWII, the Edinburgh International Festival is festooned with superlatives – the oldest, the biggest, the most famous, the best in the world. The original was a modest affair but today hundreds of the world's top musicians and performers congregate in Edinburgh for three weeks of diverse and inspirational music, opera, theatre and dance.

The famous Fireworks Concert, held on the final Saturday of the Festival, is one of the most spectacular events of the year. A concert performed at the Ross Bandstand in Princes St Gardens (and broadcast live on radio) is accompanied by the carefully choreographed detonation of around 40 tons of artistically arranged gunpowder.

Tickets for the bandstand and gardens tend to sell out early but some are held back for personal callers at The Hub – these go on sale from the previous Sunday. If you don't manage to get a ticket, bring along a radio and join the crowds of locals on Princes St, the Mound, North Bridge, Calton Hill and Inverleith Park.

Tickets for popular events – especially music and opera – sell out quickly, so it's best to book as far in advance as possible. You can buy tickets in person at The Hub, by phone or Internet.

Edinburgh's annual culture-fest takes place over the three weeks ending on the first Saturday in September; the programme is usually available from April.

EDINBURGH INTERNATIONAL BOOK FESTIVAL

☎ 228 5444; www.edbookfest.co.uk; Scottish Book Centre, 137 Dundee St

Held in a little village of marquees right in the middle of Charlotte Square, the Book Festival is a fun fortnight of talks, readings, debates, lectures, book signings as well as meet-the-author events, with a café and tented bookshop thrown in. The Book Festival lasts for two weeks in August (usually during the first two weeks of the Edinburgh International Festival).

EDINBURGH INTERNATIONAL FILM FESTIVAL
☎ 229 2550; www.edfilmfest.org.uk; Filmhouse, 88 Lothian Rd

The Edinburgh International Film Festival is one of the original Edinburgh Festival trinity, having first been staged in 1947 along with the International Festival and the Fringe. It is a major international event, serving as a showcase for new British and European films, and staging the European premieres of one or two Hollywood blockbusters. The Film Festival last for two weeks in August (usually the first two weeks of the Edinburgh International Festival).

EDINBURGH MELA
☎ 557 1400; www.edinburgh-mela.co.uk; Arts Quarter, Gateway Theatre, Elm Row, Leith Walk

Swirling saris and skirling bagpipes, the swing of the kilt and the twang of sitars, curry washed down with Irn-Bru – the Edinburgh Mela is a colourful festival that celebrates Scotland's cultural diversity. Founded by the city's Bangladeshi, Indian and Pakistani communities back in 1995, the Mela is a weekend of multicultural music, dance, food and fashion, with plenty of children's activities, held over a weekend at the end of August or the beginning of September. The venue is Pilrig Park (Map p216).

SCOTTISH INTERNATIONAL STORYTELLING FESTIVAL
☎ 557 5724; www.scottishstorytellingcentre.co.uk; Scottish Storytelling Centre, The Netherbow, 43-5 High St

The Storytelling Centre was established in 1996 and now organises this annual celebration of the great art of spinning a yarn. Events for all ages are staged at a variety of indoor and outdoor venues, leavened with both traditional music and crafts workshops. The Storytelling Festival runs over 10 days, ending on the first Sunday in November.

EDINBURGH'S CAPITAL CHRISTMAS
☎ 529 4310; www.edinburghscapitalchristmas.org; City of Edinburgh Council, City Chambers, High St

The newest of the Scottish capital's festivals, first held in 2000, the Edinburgh Capital Christmas bash includes a big street parade, a fairground and a Ferris wheel, plus an open-air ice rink in Princes St Gdns. The celebrations are held over the three weeks prior to Christmas.

EDINBURGH'S HOGMANAY
☎ 529 4461; www.edinburghshogmanay.org; Hogmanay Box Office, The Hub, Castlehill

Traditionally, the New Year (Hogmanay) has always been a more important celebration for Scots than Christmas. In towns, cities and villages all over the country, people fill the streets at midnight on 31 December to wish each other a Guid New Year and, yes, to knock back a dram or six to keep the bitter cold at bay.

In 1993, Edinburgh's city council had the excellent idea of spicing up Hogmanay by organising some events, laying on some live

Torch-light procession to Calton Hill (p70) during Hogmanay

music in Princes St and issuing an open invitation to the rest of the world. Most of them turned up, or so it seemed, and had such a good time that they told all their pals and came back again the following year. Now Edinburgh's Hogmanay is the biggest winter festival in Europe, regularly pulling in over 250,000 partying punters.

New Year events run from 29 December to 1 January. To get into the main party area in the city centre after 8pm on 31 December you'll need a ticket – book well in advance.

Arts

Arts

Edinburgh has long dominated the Scottish arts scene, with its many galleries and theatres, and an annual feast of world-class festivals (see p19). Although it plays host to a wide cross-section of the arts, it has always been a writer's city – the main train station is named after a novel (Waverley), and its main shopping street is dominated by a towering Gothic monument to that novel's author (Sir Walter Scott). Publishing is still a major business here, and in the last decade the city has produced a flourishing new crop of best-selling authors, including Irvine Welsh, Ian Rankin and JK Rowling.

LITERATURE

Edinburgh has always been at the heart of the Scottish literary scene, from the days of the medieval makars (makers of verses; poets) William Dunbar and Gavin Douglas to the modern 'brat pack' of Iain Banks, Irvine Welsh, Ian Rankin and Christopher Brookmyre. To experience the Scottish literature scene at a reading, see p140.

POPULAR LITERATURE TODAY

Walk into any major bookshop in Edinburgh and you'll find a healthy 'Scottish Fiction' section, its shelves bulging with recently published works by best-selling Edinburgh authors like Iain Banks, Christopher Brookmyre, Quintin Jardine, Ian Rankin, Alexander McCall Smith and Irvine Welsh.

Hailed as one of the most imaginative writers of his generation, Iain Banks burst upon the Scottish literary scene in 1990 with his dazzling debut novel *The Wasp Factory*, a macabre but utterly compelling exploration of the inner world of Frank, a strange and deeply disturbed teenager. His most enjoyable books are *Complicity* (1993) a gruesome and often hilarious thriller-cum-satire on the greed and corruption of the Thatcher years, and the immensely likeable *The Crow Road* (1992), a witty and moving family saga that provides one of Scottish fiction's most memorable opening sentences: 'It was the day my grandmother exploded.' He also writes science fiction under 'the world's most penetrable pseudonym', Iain M Banks.

Christopher Brookmyre's thrillers specialise in outrageous characters (an investigative journalist-cum-cat burglar), preposterous plots (an assassin plans to murder a politician by blowing up a dam and flooding an entire valley), biting wit, and lots of violence and bad language. His more recent offerings seem to have lost the plot a little, but his early titles such as *Quite Ugly One Morning* (1997) provide laugh-out-loud entertainment. Not a suitable Christmas present for your granny, though.

Ian Rankin and Quintin Jardine have both made their names with fictional, Edinburgh-based detectives – the hard-drinking, introspective John Rebus, and the glamorous, golf-playing Bob Skinner, respectively. Rankin's Rebus novels are dark, engrossing mysteries that explore the darker side of Scotland's capital city, filled with sharp dialogue, telling detail and three-dimensional characters, while Jardine's books are fast-paced, tightly plotted thrillers. Both outsell John Grisham in Scotland.

The novels of Irvine Welsh (b 1961), who grew up in Edinburgh's working-class district of Muirhouse, describe a very different world from that inhabited by Miss Jean Brodie – the modern city's underworld of drugs, drink, despair and violence. Famous for his debut novel *Trainspotting*, Welsh's best work is probably *Marabou Stork Nightmares*, in which a soccer hooligan – paralysed and in a coma – reviews his violent and brutal life.

The latest Edinburgh author to hit the headlines is Alexander McCall Smith, a professor of medical ethics at Edinburgh University. He has written more than 50 books, but is best known for his whimsical detective stories set in Botswana, and starring the female private investigator Precious Ramotswe; the first in the series is titled *The No 1 Ladies' Detective Agency*.

Although she was born in Bristol and her books are not set in the city, the publishing phenomenon that is JK Rowling famously began her career by penning the first Harry Potter adventure while nursing a coffee in various Edinburgh cafés, because she couldn't afford to keep the heating on at home.

FROM THE BEGINNING

Gavin Douglas (1476–1522) was the son of the Earl of Angus and served as Provost of St Giles between 1502 and 1514. His poetic style ranged from colloquial to courtly and his major works include the *Tretis of the Tua Mariit Wemen and the Wedoe* (Treatise of the Two Married Women and the Widow) and a masterful translation of Virgil's *Aeneid*.

Though born in the Southern Uplands village of Leadhills, the poet Allan Ramsay (1686–1758) spent most of his life in Edinburgh. His best-known work is *The Gentle Shepherd*, a pastoral comedy that was much admired by Robert Burns. The house he built for himself on Castle Hill survives in Ramsay Garden.

Another poet who earned Burns' admiration was Robert Fergusson (1750–74), who was born in Edinburgh and wrote wittily in broad Scots about everyday city life, notably in the poem *Auld Reekie*. Tragically, he suffered a head injury after falling down stairs and died soon afterwards in a mental institution at the age of only 24.

Robert Burns (1759–96) himself spent only a few short spells in the capital between 1786 and 1788 and again in 1791, but was enthusiastically received by Edinburgh society, who hailed him 'the ploughman poet'. His love affair with the Edinburgh lady Mrs Agnes MacLehose inspired one of Burns' finest love poems, *Ae Fond Kiss*.

From the sublime to the ridiculous – if Burns was famous for the excellence of his poetry, William Topaz McGonagall (c 1825–1902) was renowned for the excruciating awfulness of his. Born in Edinburgh, he grew up in Orkney and Dundee, and lived most of his life in the latter. His *Poetic Gems* – including the appalling *Railway Bridge of the Silvery Tay* – are so bad they have become internationally famous.

James Boswell (1740–95), an Edinburgh advocate, is best known for his *Life of Johnson*, a biography of Dr Samuel Johnson, the English lexicographer who compiled the first dictionary of the English language. His *Journal of a Tour to the Hebrides* is a lively and engaging account of his expedition with Johnson to the western isles of Scotland.

1930s-style St Andrew's House and monuments on Calton Hill (p70)

Sir Walter Scott (1771–1832) is Scotland's greatest and most prolific novelist. The son of an Edinburgh lawyer, Scott was born in Guthrie St (off Chambers St; the house no longer exists) and lived at various New Town addresses before moving to his country house at Abbotsford. Scott's early works were rhyming ballads, such as *The Lady of the Lake*, and his first historical novels (Scott effectively invented the genre) were published anonymously. He almost single-handedly revived interest in Scottish history and legend in the early 19th century, and was largely responsible for organising King George IV's visit to Scotland in 1822. Plagued by debt in later life, he wrote obsessively – to the detriment of his health – in order to make money, but will always be best remembered for classic tales such as *The Antiquary*, *The Heart of Midlothian*, *Ivanhoe*, *Redgauntlet* and *Castle Dangerous*.

Along with Scott, Robert Louis Stevenson (1850–94) ranks as Scotland's best-known novelist. Born at 8 Howard Place in the Inverleith district of Edinburgh, into a family of famous lighthouse engineers, Stevenson studied law at Edinburgh University but was always intent on pursuing the life of writer. An inveterate traveller, though dogged by ill-health, he settled in Samoa in 1889, where he was revered by the natives as 'Tusitala' – the teller of tales. Stevenson is known and loved around the world for those tales – *Kidnapped*, *Catriona*, *Treasure Island*, *The Master of Ballantrae* and *Strange Case of Dr Jekyll and Mr Hyde*.

Sir Arthur Conan Doyle (1859–1930), the creator of Sherlock Holmes, was born in Edinburgh and studied medicine at Edinburgh University. He based the character of Holmes on one of his lecturers, the surgeon Dr Joseph Bell, who had employed his forensic skills and powers of deduction on several murder cases in Edinburgh.

Scotland's finest modern poet was Hugh MacDiarmid (1892–1978). Born Christopher Murray Grieve, and originally from the Dumfriesshire town of Langholm, he moved to Edinburgh in 1908 where he trained as a teacher and later a journalist, but spent most of his life in Montrose, Shetland, Glasgow and Biggar. His masterpiece is *A Drunk Man Looks at the Thistle*, a 2685-line Joycean monologue.

Born in Edinburgh and educated at the university, Norman MacCaig (1910–96) is widely regarded as the greatest Scottish poet of his generation. A primary-school teacher for almost 40 years, MacCaig wrote poetry that is witty, adventurous, moving, evocative and filled with sharp observation; poems such as *November Night, Edinburgh* vividly capture

Reading Edinburgh

- *Born Free* by Laura Hird (1999) is a gritty and tragic but heart-warming tale of modern family life in one of Edinburgh's poorer neighbourhoods, which brings vividly to life an aspect of the city that tourists never see.
- *Complicity* by Iain Banks (1993) is a gruesome and often hilarious thriller-cum-satire on the greed and corruption of the Thatcher years as it follows a strung-out journalist on the trail of a serial killer through the backdrop of Edinburgh.
- *The Falls* by Ian Rankin (2001) is a gripping noir-style crime novel that stars hard-drinking detective John Rebus, Edinburgh's answer to Sam Spade, as he struggles to solve the disappearance of a student while grappling with shades of the city's dark history.
- *The Heart of Midlothian* by Sir Walter Scott (1818) is perhaps Scott's finest and most complex work. Set in Edinburgh in the first half of the 18th century, this novel deals with justice, and the lack of it, seen through the eyes of Jeanie Deans, a heroine far ahead of her time.
- *The Prime of Miss Jean Brodie* by Muriel Spark (1962) is the story of a charismatic teacher in a 1930s Edinburgh girls school who leads her chosen girls – her 'creme de la creme' – in the pursuit of truth and beauty, with devastating consequences.
- *The Private Memoirs and Confessions of a Justified Sinner* by James Hogg (1824) is a postmodern novel some 150 years ahead of its time. This is both a murder story told from two points of view, and an ingenious deconstruction of the religious certainties of 18th-century Scotland.
- *Skinner's Rules* by Quintin Jardine (1993) is the first in a series of well-plotted detective stories centred on Edinburgh CID chief Bob Skinner; not as dark or as satisfying as Ian Rankin's Rebus novels, but gripping nonetheless.
- *Trainspotting* by Irvine Welsh (1993) is a disturbing and darkly humorous journey through the junkie underworld of 1990s Edinburgh, pulling no punches as it charts hero Renton's descent into heroin addiction.

the atmosphere of his home city. MacCaig could often be found enjoying a pint of beer with his contemporaries Robert Garioch (1909–81) and Sydney Goodsir Smith (1915–75) in Milne's Bar on the corner of Rose and Hanover Sts.

Dame Muriel Spark (b 1918) was born in Edinburgh and educated at James Gillespie's High School for Girls, an experience that provided material for her best-known novel *The Prime of Miss Jean Brodie*, a shrewd portrait of 1930s Edinburgh. A prolific writer, Dame Muriel's 22nd novel, *The Finishing School*, was published in 2004 when she was 86.

Dorothy Dunnett (b 1923) was born in Fife but went to school in Edinburgh, overlapping with Muriel Spark at Gillespie's High School. She is best known for her two series of historical novels, *The Lymond Chronicles* and *The House of Niccolo*.

ARCHITECTURE

Edinburgh and its surroundings have a remarkable heritage of superb architecture from the 12th century to the present day.

ROMANESQUE (12TH CENTURY)

The Normans were great builders and their Romanesque style – with its characteristic round arches – can be seen in the old western door of Duddingston Parish Church (p79) and in St Margaret's Chapel (p53), the oldest surviving building in Edinburgh.

GOTHIC (12TH TO 16TH CENTURY)

As the Gothic style developed in England and Europe, it was brought to Scotland and adapted by the religious orders as they built the great Border abbeys (p184) of Melrose, Dryburgh and Jedburgh. The nave of Holyrood Abbey (p59; 13th century) is all that remains in Edinburgh from the early Gothic period, while the interior of St Giles Cathedral (p57) is the only survivor from the 14th century. The more flamboyant late-Gothic style of the 15th and early 16th centuries, with its pointed arches, pinnacles and elaborate tracery, can be seen in the Trinity Apse (all that remains of the Trinity College Church; p55), just off the Royal Mile, and in the parish churches of Restalrig and Corstorphine.

POST-REFORMATION (17TH CENTURY)

After 1560 most churches were modified to suit the new Protestant religion, which frowned on ceremony and ornament. Greyfriars Kirk (p63; built in 1620 and renovated in 1722) was the first new church to be built in Edinburgh after the Reformation. The unusual Canongate Kirk (p55; 1691) also dates from this period.

GEORGIAN (18TH TO EARLY 19TH CENTURY)

Edinburgh has a rich legacy of Georgian architecture. The greatest exponents of the austere, symmetrical style in Scotland were the Adam family, in particular Robert Adam (1728–92). Among many of the neoclassical buildings he designed are the Old College (p63) of the University of Edinburgh, Register House (p67) on Princes St, Charlotte Square (p68; possibly the finest example of Georgian architecture anywhere) and also Hopetoun House (p80) near Queensferry.

VICTORIAN (19TH CENTURY)

As the Scottish identity was reaffirmed by writers such as Burns and Scott, architects turned to the towers and turrets of the past for inspiration, and produced the so-called Scottish Baronial style. Fanciful buildings such as Fettes College (built between 1864 and 1870) were created and the fashion was also displayed in many of Edinburgh's civic buildings, such as the old Royal Infirmary (built between 1872 and 1879) on Lauriston Place.

Victorian architects also looked to Europe for inspiration, but whereas the Georgians looked towards Greece, the Victorians tended to look towards Italy. The Royal Museum (p63) in Chambers St (built between 1861 and 1889) has a Venetian Renaissance façade, for example, while the Scottish National Portrait Gallery (p69; built between 1885 and 1890) is modelled on Venice's Doge's Palace.

THE 20TH CENTURY & BEYOND

The massive, modernist pile of St Andrews House (built between 1936 and 1939), sitting imperiously on Calton Hill, is one of the most impressive pieces of pre-WWII architecture in Edinburgh. Contemporary architecture has appeared all over Edinburgh during the last decade, as the city's building boom continues. The Edinburgh International Conference Centre (EICC) on Morrison St, with its huge circular auditorium, is a modern showpiece, but the building that everyone is waiting to see is the new Scottish Parliament Building at Holyrood (p60) that was designed by the Catalan architect, the late Enric Miralles.

Nearby on Holyrood Rd is the overhanging glass façade of the Tun (p121), an energetically modern complex taking in a café-bar, offices and BBC studios, plus the award-winning Scottish Poetry Library (p140), cleverly insinuated into a cramped location, and making superb use of the available light.

Edinburgh, like many other cities in the United Kingdom, suffered badly from the onslaught of the motor car, shoddy council housing and bad planning during the late 20th century. Many Edinburgh citizens still have not forgiven the university for replacing much of George Square with featureless tower blocks. Much of Princes St's northern side has given way to bland shopfronts and the St James Shopping Centre round the corner on Leith St is just plain ugly. A few fine 19th-century buildings have survived on Princes St, notably the glorious Renaissance palace of Jenners (1895), the world's oldest department store.

Top Five Beautiful Buildings

- **Nos 1–11 Charlotte Square** (p68) The elegantly proportioned Adam façade on the square's north side is the jewel in the New Town's architectural crown.
- **Dundas House** (p69) A gorgeous Palladian mansion that now houses a bank; pop into the main banking hall for a look at the dome, painted cerulean blue and studded with glazed stars.
- **Museum of Scotland** (p63) One of the best of the city's modern buildings, the museum's golden sandstone forms create echoes of castles, churches, gardens and cliffs.
- **Royal Scottish Academy** (p68) Recently stone-cleaned, this imposing William Playfair–designed Doric temple dominates the centre of Princes St.
- **Scottish Parliament Building** (p60) OK, so it wasn't quite finished at the time of writing, but the new parliament building promises to reveal the most exciting modern architecture in Scotland.

CINEMA

Scotland has never really had its own film industry, but in recent years the government-funded agency **Scottish Screen** (☎ 0141-302 1730; www.scottishscreen.com) has been created to nurture native talent and promote and develop all aspects of film and TV throughout Scotland.

Edinburgh has not played a major role in the development of British cinema, but its photogenic cityscape has drawn many film-makers. In addition to appearing as itself, it has doubled for various other places including 19th-century Oxford in *Jude* (1996), an adaptation of Thomas Hardy's novel *Jude the Obscure;* and Victorian London in *Mary Reilly* (1996), a re-telling of Edinburgh novelist Robert Louis Stevenson's *Strange Tale of Dr Jekyll and Mr Hyde.*

Tomb of Mary Queen of Scots in the Museum of Scotland (p63)

Probably the classic Edinburgh film is Ronald Neame's 1969 screen version of Muriel Spark's classic Edinburgh novel *The Prime of Miss Jean Brodie*. Set in the 1930s, it presents the two contrasting aspects of the city in the juxtaposition of the upper-middle-class Marcia Blane School for Girls (Donaldson's School for the Deaf on West Coates, just west of Haymarket) with the grim, grey tenements of the Old Town (The Vennel, Grassmarket).

Screen-writer John Hodge, who wrote the scripts for *Shallow Grave* (1994), *Trainspotting* (1996) and *A Life Less Ordinary* (1997), in collaboration with director Danny Boyle and producer Andrew Macdonald, is actually a qualified doctor who studied medicine at Edinburgh University from 1982 to 1987. The gorgeous apartment in *Shallow Grave* was actually a studio set, but its exterior was played by a Georgian terrace located in the New Town. The unforgettable opening scenes of *Trainspotting* follow Renton as he sprints along Princes St before being spreadeagled across the bonnet of a car in Calton Rd.

Michael Caton-Jones, director of *Memphis Belle* and *Rob Roy* (and another graduate of Edinburgh University), was born in West Lothian. An Edinburgh film-maker of an earlier generation was Bill Douglas (1934–91), the director of an award-winning trilogy of films documenting his childhood and early adult life; he was born in the former mining village of Newcraighall, just south of Edinburgh.

Edinburgh's most famous son – in or out of the cinema – is of course the actor Sir Sean Connery, the original and best James Bond, and star of countless hit movies since, including *Highlander* (1986), *The Name of the Rose* (1986), *Indiana Jones and the Last Crusade* (1989), *The Hunt for Red October* (1990), *Just Cause* (1995) and *The League of Extraordinary Gentlemen* (2003). Connery started his working life as 'Big Tam' Connery, sometime milkman and brickie, born in a tenement in Fountainbridge.

Edinburgh hosts a highly regarded international film festival, based at the Filmhouse in Lothian Rd (see p23). The Edinburgh International TV Festival (www.mgeitf.co.uk), held during the August bank holiday weekend, is more of an industry event, with 1700 delegates attending various discussions, lectures, previews and masterclasses.

Top Five Edinburgh Films

- *Complicity* (2000) Though not as satisfying as the novel (see p26), this fast-paced thriller keeps you watching as it follows cocaine-fuelled Edinburgh journalist Cameron Colley on the trail of a serial killer.
- *Greyfriars Bobby* (1961) Walt Disney's film version of the life of Edinburgh's most famous pooch is still a watchable, if somewhat saccharine, children's movie.
- *The Prime of Miss Jean Brodie* (1969) Classic evocation of 1930s Edinburgh, with a charismatic school teacher attempting to mould her young 'gerls' in her own image, with tragic results.
- *Restless Natives* (1985) A whimsical comedy that follows two disillusioned Edinburgh lads as they embark on a highwayman's spree of nonviolent robberies of tourist coaches, becoming folk heroes in the process.
- *Trainspotting* (1996) A gritty and groundbreaking look at life among Edinburgh's heroin addicts, filled with memorable scenes, sharp dialogue and a pounding soundtrack.

MUSIC HALL & THEATRE

These days not everyone will have heard of the Scottish music-hall entertainer Sir Harry Lauder (1870–1950), but they will almost certainly have heard one or more of his songs. Born in Portobello, he worked as a flax spinner in Arbroath while still at school, then as a pitboy in a Lanarkshire coal mine in his teens. He won several talent competitions before achieving professional success in Glasgow. When he moved to London he was an immediate hit and then went on to wow audiences in the USA and around the world.

Two of his most famous songs, *Roamin' in the Gloamin* and *I Love a Lassie*, were written for his wife. Another, *Keep Right on to the End of the Road*, was written after their only son was killed in battle in WWI. Although he continued to perform he never fully recovered from this tragedy. Sometimes derided for his stage persona of a stereotypical Scot in kilt and bonnet, he was enormously talented and his musical legacy lives on.

Edinburgh's world-famous Traverse Theatre (p144) has a well-deserved reputation for producing contemporary drama of the highest quality. It was founded during the 1962 Edinburgh Festival in a former brothel in James Court, off the Royal Mile, and from 1969 to 1992 was based in West Bow in Grassmarket. It is now housed in a purpose-built theatre next to the Usher Hall in Lothian Rd.

The first Edinburgh International Festival (p22) in 1947 was launched as a temporary alternative to the great music and drama festivals of Salzburg and Munich while those cities recovered after WWII. Eight theatre groups turned up uninvited and staged their own 'fringe' events; since then, the Fringe (see p22) has overtaken the official Festival to become the world's largest arts festival.

Despite its size, the Fringe is still true to its origins in three fundamental respects – performers are not invited to the event (they must make their own arrangements); they make use of unusual and unconventional theatre spaces; and they take all their own financial risks – and it continues to be one of the world's most exciting and innovative drama events.

MUSIC

When it comes to new bands, Edinburgh tends to be eclipsed by the hipper metropolis of Glasgow and the temptations of London. The city's contribution to the contemporary music scene includes the rock band Idlewild as well as the Proclaimers, Beta Band, Bay City Rollers, The Rezillos, Ballboy, Bert Jansch, Pilot and EMF; reggae-soul-pop singer Finlay Quaye; Shirley Manson, lead singer of Garbage; and the red-hot jazz saxophonist Tommy Smith.

Edinburgh rock musicians who made their names in the 1970s and '80s include Iain Anderson, front man for Jethro Tull, and Mike Scott of the Waterboys. Fish, the lead singer in Marillion, now produces solo albums and runs a successful recording studio in East Lothian. Barbara Dickson and Nazareth hail from Dunfermline, just across the Firth of Forth.

Scotland has always had a strong folk tradition, which underwent an Edinburgh-based revival in the 1960s and '70s. Robin Hall and Jimmy MacGregor, the Corries and the hugely talented Ewan McColl worked the pubs and clubs in the capital and up and down the country. During this time the Incredible String Band and the Boys of the Lough successfully combined folk and rock and have been followed by Runrig (who write songs in Gaelic), the Battlefield Band, Alba, Capercaillie and others. Though folk music rarely hits the headlines these days, the Edinburgh folk scene is alive and kicking (see p137); performers to look out for include the Mick West Band, Jock Tamson's Bairns and Tony McManus.

As for classical music, Sir John Clerk of Penicuik (1676–1755), a leading Scottish patron of the arts, was a notable composer, violinist and harpsichordist, who studied in Europe under the master Arcangelo Corelli. He paved the way for a flowering of Scottish music during the Enlightenment, when Edinburgh composers William McGibbon (c 1690–1756) and James Oswald (1710–69) adapted traditional Scots tunes to the classical Italian style. Thomas Erskine (1732–81), sixth earl of Kelly (known as 'Fiddler Tam'), was one of the most important British composers of the 18th century and a noted Edinburgh *bon viveur*. He was the first Scottish musician to produce a symphony.

Sir Alexander Campbell MacKenzie (1847–1935), the son of a noted Edinburgh violinist, and himself a professional violinist by the age of 11, was one of the finest British musicians and composers of his time; his best works include his *Piano Quartet* and the choral oratorio *Rose of Sharon*.

Scotland did not have a full-time symphony orchestra until the mid-1930s, and institutions such as the Scottish Opera and Scottish Ballet (based in Glasgow but performing regularly in Edinburgh) were not founded until the 1960s.

See p137 for details on the live-music scene in Edinburgh.

Top Five CDs

- *100 Broken Windows* Idlewild
- *Maverick A Strike* Finlay Quaye
- *Rollin'* Bay City Rollers
- *Sunshine on Leith* Proclaimers
- *The Three E.P.'s* Beta Band

VISUAL ARTS

Scottish painting only really emerged in the mid-17th century with portraits by George Jameson (c 1589–1644), an Aberdonian who moved to Edinburgh in 1633 to paint decorations for Charles II's visit, and his pupil John Wright (1617–1700).

Scottish portraiture reached its peak during the Scottish Enlightenment in the second half of the 18th century with the Edinburgh-born figures of Allan Ramsay the Younger (1713–84), son of the poet Allan Ramsay, and Sir Henry Raeburn (1756–1823).

Alexander Nasmyth (1758–1840), a pupil of Allan Ramsay, set up as a portraitist in 1778, but emerged as an important landscape painter whose work had a great impact on 19th-century Scottish art.

A Fife lad who learned his craft at the Trustees' Academy in Edinburgh between 1799 and 1805, Sir David Wilkie (1785–1841) spent most of his life in London. One of the top Scottish artists of the 19th century, his paintings depict simple scenes of Scottish rural life.

The Trustees' Academy, particularly under the direction of Robert Scott Lauder (1803–69), was very influential and produced many of the great 19th-century painters, most notably William McTaggart (1835–1910). Exhibitions at the Royal Scottish Academy (RSA) in Edinburgh also helped to promote Scottish painters. Many works by the painters mentioned above can be seen at the National Gallery of Scotland (p67).

David Octavius Hill (1801–70), a portrait painter and secretary of the RSA, was an important early pioneer of portrait photography. He and his partner Robert Adamson (1821–48) produced around 1800 magnificent photographs of Edinburgh people, from Newhaven fishwives to Church of Scotland ministers. Examples of these early works are occasionally displayed in temporary exhibitions at the Scottish National Portrait Gallery (see p69), and can also be seen in books such as *Facing the Light: The Photography of Hill and Adamson* (2002) by Sara Stevenson.

Three out of the four artists known as the Scottish Colourists – Samuel J Peploe (1871–1935), Francis CD Cadell (1883–1937) and John D Fergusson (1874–1961) from Leith – were

Top Five Art Galleries

- **City Art Centre** (p62) Populist and popular, mixing permanent collection of 17th- to 20th-century Scottish art with blockbusting temporary exhibitions.
- **Fruitmarket Gallery** (p61) Minimalist, modern, art-student hang-out.
- **National Gallery of Scotland** (p67) The country's main collection of both Scottish and international pre-20th-century art.
- **Royal Scottish Academy** (p68) Greek temple on Princes St hosting crowd-pulling travelling exhibitions from around the world.
- **Scottish National Gallery of Modern Art** (p72) Grand mansion in beautiful grounds makes a great setting for 20th-century art.

born in Edinburgh. Their striking paintings drew upon both French post-impressionism and Fauvism.

The Edinburgh School of the 1930s was a group of modernist painters who depicted the Scottish landscape. Chief among them were William Gillies (1898–1973), Sir William MacTaggart (1903–81; grandson of his earlier namesake) and Anne Redpath (1895–1965). Following WWII, artists such as Alan Davie and Sir Eduardo Paolozzi gained international reputations in abstract expressionism and pop art. Today, the focus of Scottish painting has swung back to the west, where the 'New Glasgow Boys' (Peter Howson, Steven Campbell, Ken Currie) are producing work characterised by a concern for social issues. Works by the Scottish Colourists, the Edinburgh School and the New Glasgow Boys can be seen at the Scottish National Gallery of Modern Art (p72), while the neighbouring Dean Gallery (p72) has an extensive collection of Paolozzi's sculpture.

History

History

THE RECENT PAST

Since devolution and the re-instatement of the Scottish Parliament in 1999 Edinburgh has experienced a surge in its fortunes, with near-full employment, a growing population and sky-rocketing property prices. The skyline bristles with tower cranes as new building projects sprout up on every other street corner, and city councillors tear their hair out trying to find ways to manage the problem of Edinburgh's increasingly congested traffic. A brand new car ferry service now links nearby Rosyth to Zeebrugge in Belgium, and there are plans to build a second runway at Edinburgh's fast-growing international airport.

The city's once-stern image of Presbyterian rectitude has been replaced by a reputation as one of Europe's biggest party venues, with the Festival (p22) and the Christmas/Hogmanay celebrations pulling in hundreds of thousands of revellers. Meanwhile, the Scottish public wait with bated breath for the scaffolding to come off their shiny new parliament building at Holyrood – and for the final bill.

Top Five Books on Edinburgh's History

- *Capital of the Mind: How Edinburgh Changed the World* by James Buchan (2003) is a vivid and engrossing account of the Scottish Enlightenment (1745–1820) in Edinburgh, which saw the capital's transformation from a squalid slum into the Athens of the North.
- *Edinburgh: Picturesque Notes* by Robert Louis Stevenson (1879, re-published in 2001) is a fascinating picture of the city in Victorian times by one of Edinburgh's most famous sons.
- *The Making of Classical Edinburgh* by AJ Youngson (1993) is a detailed, scholarly and well-illustrated history of the building and architecture of Edinburgh's Georgian New Town.
- *She Was Aye Workin': Memories of Tenement Women in Edinburgh and Glasgow* by Helen Clark & Elizabeth Carnegie (2003) is a lively and colourful oral history that brings alive the everyday lives of families living in Edinburgh (and Glasgow) tenements in the early 20th century.
- *The Town Below the Ground* by Jan-Andrew Henderson (1999) is a humorous trawl through the myths and legends surrounding Edinburgh's hidden vaults and buried closes.

FROM THE BEGINNING

FIRST IMMIGRANTS

Scotland's earliest inhabitants were hunter-gatherers, who began pushing northwards from England, Ireland and northern Europe as the glaciers retreated in the wake of the last Ice Age around 10,000 BC. Over the next few thousand years these colonisers came in waves to different parts of the country. There are indications of Baltic cultures in eastern Scotland and Irish cultures on the western islands. Mesolithic flints from northern France have been found at many sites.

Recent archaeological investigations at Cramond (p76), on the northwestern edge of Edinburgh, have uncovered evidence of habitation there dating to 8500 BC – the earliest

TIMELINE	10,000 BC	8500 BC	900 BC
	Hunter-gatherers push northwards from Northern Europe	Evidence of habitation at Cramond is the earliest known sign of human activity in Scotland	Earliest signs of human habitation at Edinburgh's Castle Rock and Arthur's Seat

known traces of human activity in Scotland. These early inhabitants made good use of the oyster and mussel beds of the Firth of Forth (they left behind huge piles of discarded shells), a natural resource that Edinburgh folk continued to exploit until the early 20th century.

The Neolithic era, beginning in the 4th millennium BC, brought a new way of life, with agriculture, stock breeding and trading. These changes caused an increase in population, and more complex patterns of social organisation evolved to control them. With organised groups of workers, more ambitious construction projects became possible.

Edinburgh's Castle Rock, a volcanic crag with three vertical sides, dominates the city centre. This natural defensive position attracted the first settlers; the earliest signs of habitation on the rock date back to around 900 BC. There is also evidence of ancient habitation on Arthur's Seat (p58), where traces of cultivation terraces have been found.

Entrance Gateway, Edinburgh Castle (p52)

ROMAN INVASION

The Roman invasion of Britain began in 55 BC, when Julius Caesar's legions first crossed the English Channel. However, the Roman onslaught ground to a halt in the north. Between AD 78 and 84, the Roman governor Agricola (whose son-in-law, Tacitus, named the northern part of Scotland Caledonia after the Caledones – the first tribe he came across) marched northwards and spent several years trying to subdue the wild tribes the Romans called the Picts.

By the 2nd century, Emperor Hadrian had decided that this inhospitable land of mist, bogs, midges and warring tribes had little to offer the Roman Empire and built the wall (AD 122–28) that took his name (close to the modern border between Scotland and England). Two decades later Hadrian's successor, Antoninus Pius, invaded Scotland again and built a turf rampart, the Antonine Wall, between the Firth of Forth and the River Clyde. An important Roman fort and supply station was built at Cramond (p76), with other garrisons at Inveresk and Dalkeith, but they were only manned for about 40 years before the Romans again withdrew. Cramond's Roman remains are uninspiring, but the village has provided one of Britain's most impressive Roman sculptures (see The Cramond Lioness, p77).

CELTS & NORTHUMBRIANS

When the Romans first arrived in the Lothian region, the chief tribe they encountered was the Votadini, who had settlements on Castle Rock, Arthur's Seat and Blackford Hill. Little is known about them but it seems likely that these ancient Britons were the ancestors of the Gododdin, who are mentioned by the Welsh bard Aneirin in a 7th-century manuscript. Aneirin relates how Mynyddog Mwynfawr, king of the Gododdin, feasted with his warriors

55 BC	AD 78–84	AD 122–28	AD 142
Roman invasion of Britain	Roman governor Agricola marches northwards to Scotland to subdue the Picts	Emperor Hadrian builds a wall close to the modern border between Scotland and England	Building of Antonine Wall marks northern limit of Roman Empire

in the 'halls of Eidyn' before going into battle with the Angles (the tribe who gave their name to Angle-land, or England) at Catraeth (Catterick, in Yorkshire).

The 'capital' of the Gododdin was called Dun Eiden, which meant 'Fort on the Hill Slope', and almost certainly referred to Castle Rock. The Angles, from the kingdom of Northumbria in northeastern England, defeated the Gododdin and captured Dun Eiden in 638. It is thought that the Angles took the existing Celtic name 'Eiden' and tacked it onto their own Old English word for fort, 'burh', to create the forerunner of the name Edinburgh.

History – From the Beginning

Exploring Your Scottish Roots

Genealogy is a hugely popular pastime, and many visitors to Edinburgh take the opportunity to do some detective work on their Scottish ancestry.

The main records used in Scottish genealogical research – the Statutory Registers of births, marriages and deaths (1855–the present), the Old Parish Registers (1533–1854), and the 10-yearly census returns from 1841 to 1901 – are held at the **General Register Office** (Map pp218–20; GRO; ☎ 314 4433; www.gro-scotland.gov.uk; New Register House, 3 West Register St; admission per full/half day £17/10; ☺ 9am-4.30pm Mon-Fri), where you can do your own research. The registration of births, marriages and deaths became compulsory in Scotland on 1 January 1855 – before that date, the ministers of the Church of Scotland kept registers of baptisms and marriages. The oldest surviving parish registers date back to 1553, but these records are far from complete, and many births and marriages before 1855 went unrecorded. Next door to the GRO is the **National Archives of Scotland** (Map pp218–20; NAS; ☎ 535 1334; www .nas.gov.uk; 2 Princes St; admission free; ☺ 9am-4.45pm Mon-Fri), which holds records of wills, property transactions and many other items of interest to genealogists. On your first visit to the NAS you will need to ask for a reader's ticket (free) – bring some form of ID bearing your name and signature (eg passport, driving licence, bank card). Use of the Historical Search Room is free, and is first-come, first-served – you can't book a seat here.

You can consult all these records yourself, but make sure you do some research before leaving home – gather as much information as possible from birth, marriage and death certificates and other family papers in your possession, and interview elderly relatives. You will need full names, dates and places of birth, marriage or death in Scotland. One of the best guides is the book *Tracing Your Scottish Ancestry* by Kathleen B Cory, and there are many useful websites too – GenUKI (www.genuki.org.uk) is a good starting point.

At the Scotlands People website (www.scotlandspeople.gov.uk) you can search the indexes to the Old Parish Registers and Statutory Registers up to 100 years ago (75 years ago for deaths), and the indexes to the 1881, 1891 and 1901 census returns, on a pay-per-view basis. The International Genealogical Index (www.familysearch.com), compiled by the Mormon Church, includes freely searchable records of Scottish baptisms and marriages from 1553 to 1875.

Another useful resource is the **Scottish Genealogy Society Library & Family History Centre** (Map pp224–5; ☎ 220 3677; www.scotsgenealogy.com; 15 Victoria Tce; ☺ 10.30am-5.30pm Tue & Thu, 10.30am-8.30pm Wed, 10am-5pm Sat), which maintains the world's largest library of Scottish gravestone inscriptions. Entry is free to society members and £5 for nonmembers.

THE MacALPIN KINGS

The name Scotland is thought to be derived from the Scotti, or Scots, a Gaelic-speaking Irish tribe that colonised the west of Scotland in the 6th century. The Scots and Picts were drawn together by the threat of invasion by the Norsemen (Vikings) and by their common Christianity.

In 843 Kenneth MacAlpin, the king of Dalriada (modern-day Kintyre and Argyll) and son of a Pictish princess, took advantage of the custom of matrilineal succession to take over the Pictish throne, uniting Scotland north of the Firth of Forth into a single kingdom. He made Scone (near Perth) his capital and brought to it the sacred Stone of Destiny (see p53) used in the coronation of Scottish kings. Thereafter the Scots gained cultural and political ascendancy.

4th century	638	843	1018
Romans leave Britain	Angles defeat Gododdin and capture Dun Eiden	Kenneth MacAlpin unites Scotland north of the Firth of Forth	Battle of Carham: Edinburgh and the Lothian region brought under Scottish control

Nearly 200 years later, Kenneth MacAlpin's great-great-great-grandson, Malcolm II (r 1005–18), defeated the Northumbrian Angles led by King Canute at the Battle of Carham (1018) near Roxburgh on the River Tweed. This victory brought Edinburgh and the Lothian region under Scottish control and extended Scottish territory as far south as the Tweed.

THE CANMORE DYNASTY

Malcolm II's grandson was Malcolm III Canmore (r 1057–93). Malcolm III's father Duncan was murdered by Macbeth (as described in Shakespeare's eponymous play), and Macbeth himself was killed by Malcolm at Lumphanan in 1057. With his Saxon queen, Margaret, Malcolm Canmore founded a solid dynasty of able Scottish rulers. They introduced new Anglo-Norman systems of government and religious foundations. Malcolm and Margaret had their main home in Dunfermline but regularly visited the castle at Edinburgh.

Until this period there was no record of a town at Edinburgh – just the castle – but from the 11th century a settlement grew along the ridge to the east of Castle Rock. It was made into a royal burgh (a self-governing town with commercial privileges) no later than 1124, when Malcolm's son, David I (r 1124–53), held court at the castle and founded the abbey at Holyrood (p59).

David's mother Margaret had been a deeply religious woman and either he or his brother, Alexander I (r 1107–24), built a church in her honour on Castle Rock. It survives today as St Margaret's Chapel (p53), the city's oldest building. David I increased his power by adopting the Norman feudal system, granting land to noble Norman families in return for their acting as what amounted to a royal police force.

The royal burghs – which included Edinburgh and its suburb, Canongate – were permitted to conduct foreign trade, for which purpose Edinburgh created a port at nearby Leith. Edinburgh at the beginning of the 12th century was still something of a backwater, playing second fiddle to the wealthy burghs of Stirling, Perth and Berwick. That all changed when David I's successor Malcolm IV (r 1153–65) made the castle in Edinburgh his chief residence and royal treasury.

WARS OF INDEPENDENCE

Two centuries of the Canmore dynasty came to an end in 1286 when Alexander III fell to his death over a sea-cliff at Kinghorn in Fife. He was succeeded by his four-year-old grand-daughter, Margaret (the Maid of Norway), who was engaged to the son of King Edward I of England.

Sadly, Margaret died in 1290 during the sea voyage to Scotland from her home in Norway, and there followed a dispute over the succession to the throne. There were no less than 13 claimants, but in the end it came down to two: Robert de Brus, lord of Annandale, and John Balliol, lord of Galloway. As the greatest feudal lord in Britain, Edward I of England was asked to arbitrate – he chose Balliol, whom he thought he could manipulate more easily. Instead of withdrawing, as the Scots nobles expected, Edward tightened his feudal grip on Scotland, treating the Scots king as his vassal rather than his equal. The humiliated Balliol finally turned against Edward and made a treaty with France in 1295, thus beginning the enduring 'Auld Alliance'.

The English king responded with a bloody attack. In 1296 he marched on Scotland with an army of 30,000 men, razed the ports of Berwick and Dunbar and butchered the citizens, and captured the castles of Berwick, Edinburgh, Roxburgh and Stirling. Balliol was incarcerated in the Tower of London, oaths of allegiance were demanded from Scottish nobles and, in a final blow to Scottish pride, Edward I removed the Stone of Destiny, the coronation stone of the kings of Scotland, from Scone and took it back to London (see p53).

1124	1295	1296	1297
Edinburgh made into a royal burgh during rule of the Canmore Dynasty	Scots form the Auld Alliance with France	King Edward I invades Scotland and moves the Stone of Destiny from Perth to London	William Wallace defeats the English at the Battle of Stirling Bridge

BRAVEHEART

Bands of rebels led by local warlords attacked and harried the English occupiers. One such band, led by William Wallace (whose life was romanticised in the popular 1995 film *Braveheart*), defeated the English army at the Battle of Stirling Bridge in 1297, but Wallace was captured and executed in London in 1305. The Scots nobles, inspired by Wallace's example, looked around for a new leader and turned to Robert the Bruce, grandson of the lord of Annandale who had been rejected by Edward in 1292. Bruce murdered his rival, John Comyn, in February 1306 and had himself crowned king of Scotland at Scone the following month.

Bruce mounted a campaign to drive the English out of Scotland but suffered repeated defeats. According to legend, while Bruce was on the run he was inspired by a spider's persistence in spinning its web to renew his own efforts. He went on to win a famous victory over the English, led by Edward II, at the Battle of Bannockburn in 1314. Continued raids on the north of England forced Edward II to sue for peace and, in 1328, the Treaty of Northampton (also known as the Treaty of Edinburgh) gave Scotland its independence, with Robert I, the Bruce, as its king.

One of Robert's last acts before his death in 1329 was to grant Edinburgh a charter giving it control over the port of Leith, the mills on the Water of Leith and much of the surrounding countryside, effectively making it Scotland's most important royal burgh.

STEWART DYNASTY

Bannockburn and the Treaty of Northampton had no lasting effect. After the death of Robert I, the country was ravaged by civil disputes and continuing wars with England. Edinburgh was occupied several times by English armies, and in 1385 the Kirk of St Giles was burnt to the ground. Robert was succeeded by his five-year-old son, David II (r 1329–71), who returned from exile in France in 1341 and made Edinburgh his main residence, building a tower house on the site of what is now the Half Moon Battery in Edinburgh Castle. When David II died without a son, the crown passed to his nephew, Robert II (r 1371–90), the child of his sister Marjory and her husband Walter, the third high steward of Scotland. Thus was born the Stewart dynasty, which would rule Scotland and Britain for the next 300 years.

By the mid-15th century, Edinburgh was the de facto royal capital and political centre of Scotland. The coronation of James II (r 1437–60) was held in the abbey at Holyrood and the Scottish parliament met in the Tolbooth on High St or in the castle. The city's first effective town wall was constructed at about this time, enclosing the Old Town as far east as the Netherbow, and the Grassmarket. This overcrowded area – now the most populous town in Scotland – became a medieval Manhattan, forcing its densely packed inhabitants to build upwards instead of outwards, creating tenements that towered up to 12 storeys high.

RENAISSANCE

James IV (r 1488–1513) married the daughter of Henry VII of England, the first of the Tudor monarchs, thereby linking the two royal families through 'the Marriage of the Thistle and the Rose'. This didn't prevent the French from persuading James to go to war against his in-laws, and he was killed at the Battle of Flodden in 1513, along with 10,000 of his subjects. To protect Edinburgh from a feared English invasion its citizens hurriedly built another wall – the Flodden Wall (see p62) – around the city. The wall, which took over 40 years to build, was over 1.25 miles long, 25ft (7.5m) high and 5ft (1.5m) thick.

1314	1328	1371	1488–1513
Battle of Bannockburn: Robert the Bruce defeats Edward II	Treaty of Northampton (Treaty of Edinburgh) makes Robert I, the Bruce, king of Scotland	Stewart dynasty established	Renaissance; the rise of Protestantism

Coat of arms above the entrance to the Palace of Holyroodhouse (p59)

James IV's death ended a golden era that had seen the foundation of Edinburgh's Royal College of Surgeons in 1505, the establishment of a supreme law court and the introduction of printing to Edinburgh. Much graceful Scottish architecture dates from this time, and the Renaissance style can be seen in the alterations and additions made to the royal palaces at Holyroodhouse (see p59), Stirling, Linlithgow and Falkland.

Renaissance ideas flourished throughout James IV's reign. Scottish poetry thrived, created by 'makars' (makers of verses) such as William Dunbar, the court poet of James IV, and Gavin Douglas. The intellectual climate provided fertile ground for the rise of Protestantism, a reaction against the perceived wealth and corruption of the medieval Roman Catholic Church that would eventually lead to the Reformation.

MARY QUEEN OF SCOTS

In 1542, King James V lay on his deathbed in Falkland Palace in Fife – broken-hearted, it is said, after his defeat by the English at Solway Moss. His French wife, Mary of Guise, had borne him two sons but both had died in infancy. On 8 December a messenger brought word that his wife had given birth to a baby girl at the Palace of Linlithgow. Fearing the end of the Stewart dynasty and recalling its origin through Robert the Bruce's daughter, James sighed, 'It cam' wi' a lass, and it will gang wi' a lass'. He died a few days later, leaving his week-old daughter Mary to inherit the throne as queen of Scots.

In 1548 Mary (r 1542–67) was sent to France, leaving the country to be ruled by regents who rejected overtures from Henry VIII of England urging them to wed the infant queen to his son. Henry was furious and sent his armies to take vengeance on the Scots. Parts of Edinburgh were razed, Holyrood Abbey was sacked and the Border abbeys of Melrose, Dryburgh and Jedburgh were burnt down. The Rough Wooing, as it was called, failed to persuade the Scots of the error of their ways; in 1558 Mary was married to the French dauphin and became queen of France as well as Scotland.

1513	1560s	1603	1638
James IV killed at the Battle of Flodden	Reformation; Mary, Queen of Scots, abdicates	Union of the Crowns; Scotland and England joined under a single monarch·	National Covenant signed in Edinburgh to protect the Protestant religion in Scotland

THE REFORMATION

While Mary was in France being raised as a Roman Catholic, the Reformation tore through Scotland where the preachings of John Knox, a pupil of the Swiss reformer Calvin, found sympathetic ears. In 1560 the Scottish parliament created a Protestant church that was independent of Rome and of the monarchy. Latin Mass was abolished and the pope's authority denied.

Following the death of her sickly husband, the 18-year-old Queen Mary returned to Scotland, arriving at Leith on 19 August 1561. A week later she was formally welcomed to her capital city, dining in Edinburgh Castle before proceeding down the Royal Mile to the Palace of Holyroodhouse, where she held a famous audience with John Knox. The great reformer harangued the young queen and challenged her Catholic faith; she later agreed to protect the Protestant Church in Scotland while continuing to hear Mass in private.

She married Henry Stewart, Lord Darnley, in the Chapel Royal at Holyrood and gave birth to a son (later James VI) in Edinburgh Castle in 1565. Any domestic bliss was short-lived and, in a dramatic train of events, Darnley was involved in the murder of Mary's Italian secretary Rizzio (rumoured to be her lover), shortly before he himself was murdered at his Edinburgh home, probably by Mary's new lover and second-husband-to-be, the earl of Bothwell.

Mary's enemies – led by her bastard half-brother Lord James Stewart, the earl of Moray – finally confronted her at Carberry Hill, just east of Edinburgh, and Mary was forced to abdicate in 1567. Her son, the infant James VI (r 1567–1625), was crowned at Stirling and a series of regents ruled in his place. When Queen Elizabeth I of England died childless in 1603, James VI of Scotland inherited the English throne in the so-called Union of the Crowns, thus becoming James I of Great Britain (usually written as (VI/I). James moved his court to London and, for the most part, the Stewarts ignored Edinburgh from then on. Indeed, when Charles I (r 1625–49) succeeded James in 1625, he couldn't be bothered to come north to Edinburgh to be formally crowned as king of Scotland until 1633.

COVENANTERS & CIVIL WAR

The 17th century was a time of civil war in Scotland and England. The arrogant attempts by Charles I to impose episcopacy (the rule of bishops) and an English liturgy on the Scottish Church set off public riots in Edinburgh (see p57). The Presbyterian Scottish Church believed in a personal bond with God that had no need of mediation through priests, popes and kings, and on 28 February 1638 hundreds gathered in Greyfriars Kirkyard (p62) to sign a National Covenant, affirming their rights and beliefs. Scotland became divided between the Covenanters and those who supported the king.

Edinburgh remained mostly unaffected by the civil wars of the 1640s but was laid low by the plague that raged between 1644 and 1645, when a fifth of the population died. Although the Scots opposed Charles I's religious beliefs and autocratic rule, they were appalled when Oliver Cromwell's parliamentarians executed the king in 1649. They offered his son the Scottish crown as long as he signed the Covenant, which he did. Charles II (r 1649–85) was crowned at Scone on 1 January 1651 but was soon forced into exile by Cromwell, who invaded Scotland and captured Edinburgh.

Following Charles II's restoration in 1660, he reneged on the Covenant; episcopacy was reinstated and hard-line Presbyterian ministers were deprived of their churches. Even so, many clergymen rejected the bishops' authority and started holding outdoor services, or conventicles. Charles' brother and successor, James VII/II (r 1685–89) was a Catholic who made worshipping as a Covenanter a capital offence. It was during this period that Greyfriars Kirkyard was used as a Covenanters' prison (see p64).

1640s–90s	1695	1707	1746
Civil War ends with the death of Bonnie Dundee at the Battle of Killiecrankie	Bank of Scotland founded	Act of Union passed; Scottish parliament dissolved	Jacobites defeated at the Battle of Culloden

With the arrival in England of the Protestant William of Orange in 1688, the Catholic Stuart monarchy was doomed (the spelling 'Stuart' was preferred to 'Stewart' after 1603, in deference to their French allies, whose alphabet has no 'w'). Scottish royalists held on to Edinburgh Castle in the name of King James during the Long Siege of 1689. Their leader, the duke of Gordon, held a famous conference with John Graham of Claverhouse (known as 'Bonnie Dundee') at the western postern of the castle. Dundee then rode off to raise a Jacobite army and began five more months of civil war that ended with his death at the Battle of Killiecrankie.

UNION WITH ENGLAND

By the end of the 17th century, Edinburgh was indisputably Scotland's most important city. It had been made a cathedral city by Charles I in 1633; the Parliament Hall (p56) was built next to St Giles in 1639; and the Bank of Scotland (p55) was founded there in 1695. But civil war had left the country and its economy ruined. In the 1690s, famine killed up to a third of the population in some areas. The situation was exacerbated by the failure of an investment venture in Panama (the so-called Darien Scheme, set up by the Bank of England to boost the economy), which resulted in widespread bankruptcy.

The failure of the Darien Scheme made it clear to wealthy Scottish merchants and stockholders that the only way to gain access to the lucrative markets of developing colonies was through union with England. The English parliament favoured union through fear of their French enemies exploiting Jacobite sympathies in Scotland; it threatened to end the Scots' right to English citizenship and ban the duty-free export of their goods to England. They also offered a financial incentive to those who lost money in the Darien Scheme. Despite opposition, the Act of Union – which brought the two countries under one parliament, one sovereign and one flag, but preserved the independence of the Scottish Church and legal system – took effect on 1 May 1707.

On receiving the Act in Edinburgh, the chancellor of Scotland, Lord Seafield – the leader of the parliament that the Act abolished – is said to have murmured: 'Now there's an end to an auld sang.' Robert Burns later castigated the wealthy politicians who engineered the Union in characteristically stronger language: 'We're bought and sold for English gold – such a parcel of rogues in a nation!'

THE JACOBITES

The Jacobite rebellions of the 18th century sought to displace the Hanoverian monarchy (chosen by the English parliament in 1701 to succeed the house of Orange) and restore a Stuart king to Britain's throne. (The name Jacobite comes from Jacob, the Latin form of James; the Jacobites were originally supporters of the exiled James VII/II.)

James Edward Stuart, known as the Old Pretender, was the son of James VII/II. With French support he arrived in the Firth of Forth with a fleet of ships in 1708, causing panic in Edinburgh, but was seen off by English men o' war. Another attempt in 1715 fizzled out after the inconclusive Battle of Sheriffmuir, but prompted the building of stronger defences at Edinburgh Castle.

In 1745 the Old Pretender's son, Charles Edward Stuart (Bonnie Prince Charlie), landed in Scotland to claim the crown for his father. Supported by an army of Highlanders, he captured Edinburgh (except for the castle) in September 1745, holding court at the Palace of Holyroodhouse before defeating the Hanoverian forces of Sir John Cope at Prestonpans (near Musselburgh, just east of the capital). He got as far south as Derby in England but success was short-lived; a Hanoverian army led by the duke of Cumberland harried him all the way back to the Highlands, where Jacobite dreams were finally extinguished at Culloden in 1746. Jacobite prisoners were held in Edinburgh Castle, which became an important military garrison.

1740s–1830s	1843	19th century	1902
Scottish Enlightenment	The Disruption marks the founding of the Free Church of Scotland	Industrial Revolution	Hibs win the Scottish Cup

THE SCOTTISH ENLIGHTENMENT

Increasing stability in the second half of the 18th century allowed Edinburgh to expand. Desperate to relieve the pressure on the overcrowded and insanitary Old Town, the city council proposed to 'boldly enlarge Edinburgh to the utmost'. The council sponsored an architectural competition to design a 'New Town'; the winner was the unknown, 23-year-old James Craig. Over the next 50 years, elegant Georgian terraces spread across the low ridge to the north of the castle. Many of the finest houses were designed by architect Robert Adam, whose neoclassical style – a revival of Greek and Roman forms – swept through Europe in the late-18th and early 19th centuries.

Following the removal of the Scottish parliament in 1707, Edinburgh declined in political importance but its cultural and intellectual life flourished. During the period known as the Scottish Enlightenment (roughly 1740–1830), Edinburgh became known as 'a hotbed

The Resurrection Men

In 1505, Edinburgh's newly-founded Royal College of Surgeons was officially allocated the corpse of one executed criminal per year for the purposes of dissection. But this was not nearly enough to satisfy the curiosity of the city's anatomists, and in the following centuries an illegal trade in dead bodies emerged, which reached its culmination in the early 19th century, when the anatomy classes of famous surgeons such as Professor Robert Knox drew audiences of up to 500 people.

The readiest supply of corpses was to be found in the city's graveyards, especially Greyfriars. Grave robbers – who came to be known as 'resurrection men' – plundered newly interred coffins and sold the cadavers to the anatomists, who turned a blind eye to the source of their research material.

This gruesome trade led to a series of countermeasures, including the mort-safe – a metal cage that was placed over a coffin until the corpse had begun to decompose; you can see examples in Greyfriars Kirkyard (p62) and on Level 5 of the Museum of Scotland (p63) – and watch towers, where a sexton, or relatives of the deceased, would keep watch over new graves. There are still watch towers in St Cuthbert's (p66) and Duddingston (p79) kirkyards.

The notorious William Burke and William Hare, who kept a lodging house in Tanner's Close at the west end of the Grassmarket, took the body-snatching business a step further. When an elderly lodger died without paying his rent, Burke and Hare stole his body from the coffin and sold it to the famous Professor Knox. Seeing a lucrative business opportunity, they figured that rather than waiting for someone else to die, they could create their own supply of fresh cadavers by resorting to murder.

Burke and Hare preyed on the poor and weak of Edinburgh's Grassmarket, luring them back to Hare's lodging house, plying them with drink, and then suffocating their victims. Between December 1827 and October 1828, they murdered at least 16 people, selling their bodies to Professor Knox. When the law finally caught up with them, Hare turned King's evidence and testified against Burke.

Burke was hanged outside St Giles Kirk in the High St in January 1829 and, in an ironic twist, his body was given to the anatomy school for public dissection. His skeleton, and a wallet made from his skin, are still on display in the pathology museum in Surgeons' Hall (p65). Although he was never charged with any crime, Knox's reputation was blackened, and he took to carrying a loaded pistol and a dagger for protection from the public. A rhyme that became popular in the city at the time ran:

Doon the close and up the stair,
But and ben with Burke and Hare;
Burke's the butcher, Hare's the thief,
And Knox the boy that buys the beef!

It was as a result of the Burke and Hare case that the Anatomy Act of 1832 – regulating the supply of cadavers for dissection, and still in force today – was passed.

1914–18	1939–45	1940s	1947
WWI: Scottish soldiers account for 20% of British casualties (Scots only 10% of GB population)	WWII: The shipyards of Clydebank are bombed by the Luftwaffe; Edinburgh escapes	Edinburgh University established as a teaching and research centre of international importance	Edinburgh International Festival and the Fringe both held for the first time

of genius'. The philosophers David Hume and Adam Smith and the sociologist Adam Ferguson emerged as influential thinkers, nourished on generations of theological debate. Medic William Cullen produced the first modern pharmacopoeia, chemist Joseph Black advanced the science of thermodynamics, and geologist James Hutton challenged long-held beliefs about the age of the Earth.

After centuries of bloodshed and religious fanaticism, people applied themselves with the same energy to the making of money and the enjoyment of leisure. There was a revival of interest in Scottish history and vernacular literature, reflected in Robert Fergusson's satires and Alexander MacDonald's Gaelic poetry. The poetry of Robert Burns, a man of the people, achieved lasting popularity. Sir Walter Scott, the prolific novelist and ardent patriot, unearthed the Scottish crown jewels and had them put on public display in the castle.

The infamous bodysnatcher William Burke at the White Hart Inn (p122)

THE 19TH CENTURY

The renaissance of Scottish culture brought about by the Enlightenment awakened interest in Scotland elsewhere. In 1822, King George IV (r 1820–30) made the first state visit to Scotland by a reigning monarch since Charles II's coronation visit during December 1650 and January 1651. His procession through Edinburgh, clad in Highland dress, was stage-managed by Sir Walter Scott and marked the beginnings of Edinburgh's tourist industry. The royal association was cemented by Queen Victoria (r 1837–1901), who was famously besotted with all things Scottish, and wrote, 'The impression Edinburgh has made on me is very great; it is quite beautiful, totally unlike anything else I have ever seen.'

Religious tensions, never far from the surface, broke out again over who had the right to appoint Church of Scotland ministers. Since 1712, the civil authorities had held that power; the dissenters supported the right of the congregation to appoint their own minister. It all came to a head in Edinburgh in 1843, when 190 clergymen walked out of the General Assembly, then being held in the Church of St Andrew and St George on George St (p69). The Disruption, as it came to be known, marked the founding of the Free Church of Scotland.

Although the Industrial Revolution affected Edinburgh on a much smaller scale than Glasgow, it brought many changes. Ironworks, potteries, glass factories and light engineering were added to the traditional industries of baking, brewing, distilling and publishing. Edinburgh's population increased rapidly, quadrupling in size to 400,000 – not much less than it is today. The Union Canal was completed in 1822, allowing coal from the Midlothian mines to be transported by barge to the Forth and Clyde canal and on to Glasgow. No sooner had the canal gone into operation than it was rendered largely obsolete by the arrival of the railways. New suburbs of Victorian tenement blocks spread over the country estates south of the Old Town as the city expanded, swallowing up nearby villages such as Stockbridge and Dean (p71).

1975	1979	1995	1996
Reorganisation of Scottish local government allows Edinburgh to expand westwards	Referendum held on whether to elect a Scottish Assembly: rejected	Edinburgh's Old and New Towns declared Unesco World Heritage Sites	Stone of Destiny returned to Edinburgh

THE 20TH CENTURY

In the 1920s the city's borders expanded again to encompass Leith in the north, Cramond in the west and the Pentland Hills in the south. Following the reorganisation of Scottish local government in 1975, the city expanded westwards to absorb Queensferry, Ratho and Kirkliston.

Following WWII, the city's cultural life blossomed, initiated by the Edinburgh International Festival and its fellow traveller the Fringe, both held for the first time in 1947 and now recognised as world-class arts festivals. The University of Edinburgh established itself as a teaching and research centre of international importance in areas such as medicine, electronics and artificial intelligence.

Ill-conceived development plans in the 1960s and '70s resulted in the demolition of large parts of Greenside (at the top of Leith Walk), St Leonards, Dalry and Tollcross, and the construction of various concrete monstrosities in and around the city centre, notably the St James Centre at the eastern end of Princes St. Fortunately, not all of the plans were realised, and Edinburgh was spared the horror of a motorway running the length of Princes St Gdns. In reaction, a strong conservation movement emerged to preserve and restore the city's old buildings and to control the impact of any new developments on the city's character. In 1995 both the Old and New Towns were declared Unesco World Heritage Sites.

SCOTTISH DEVOLUTION

Both Labour and Conservative governments had toyed with the idea of offering Scotland devolution, or a degree of self-government, and in 1979 a referendum was held on whether to set up a directly elected Scottish Assembly. Fifty-two percent of those who voted said 'yes' to devolution but the Labour Prime Minister, James Callaghan, decided that everyone who didn't vote should be counted as a 'no'. By this devious reasoning, only 33% of the electorate had voted 'yes', so the Scottish Assembly was rejected.

From 1979 to 1997, Scotland was ruled by a Conservative government in London for which the majority of Scots hadn't voted. Separatist feelings, always present, grew stronger. Following the landslide victory of the Labour Party in May 1997, another referendum was held over the creation of a Scottish parliament. This time the result was overwhelmingly and unambiguously in favour.

Elections to the new parliament took place on 6 May 1999 and the Scottish parliament convened for the first time on 12 May in the Assembly Rooms of the Church of Scotland at the top of the Royal Mile. The parliament was officially opened by Queen Elizabeth II on 1 July 1999. Donald Dewar (1937–2000), formerly the Secretary of State for Scotland, was nominated as first minister (the Scottish parliament's equivalent of prime minister). A new parliament building at Holyrood is nearing completion (see p60).

1997	1998	1999	2004
Referendum held over the creation of a Scottish Parliament: accepted	Hearts win the Scottish Cup	Scottish Parliament convenes on May 12; officially opened on 1 July by Queen Elizabeth	Scottish Parliament building completed...

Neighbourhoods

Neighbourhoods

Modern Edinburgh sprawls over an area of 100 sq miles, from the shores of the Firth of Forth in the north to the foothills of the Pentlands in the south, and from the riverside cottages of Cramond in the west to the seaside suburb of Portobello in the east. Even the separate village of Queensferry, 8 miles to the west of the city centre, now falls within the city's jurisdiction.

Fortunately, most places of interest are concentrated within the city centre – in the medieval core of the Old Town, clustered around Edinburgh Castle and the Royal Mile, and in the orderly grid of the 18th-century New Town immediately to its north. We have grouped the rest of the city's attractions under the convenient headings of four further neighbourhoods – Edinburgh West and Edinburgh South, to the west and south of the city centre; Waterfront Edinburgh, stretching along the Forth from Cramond to Portobello; and Greater Edinburgh, which takes in the outlying areas of Queensferry, Corstorphine, Swanston, Blackford Hill and Duddingston. See the transport boxed texts in this chapter and p190 for advice about transport to and around Edinburgh.

ITINERARIES

One Day

It would be deeply wrong to visit Edinburgh without seeing Edinburgh Castle (p52), so if you only have a day to spare, devote an hour or so to the fortress first thing in the morning and then take a leisurely stroll down the Royal Mile (p55), stopping off at any of the museums or attractions that take your fancy – but be sure to take a quick peek inside St Giles Cathedral (p57). In the afternoon, spend an hour or two in the Museum of Scotland (p63) and then, if the weather's fine, take an evening walk up Calton Hill (p70). Round off the day with dinner at a restaurant with a view such as the Tower (p103).

Two Days

Kick off with morning coffee and people-watching in the Grassmarket – an outside table at Made in Italy (p105) will do – then head uphill to Edinburgh Castle (p52) to do the touristy bit. Afterwards, begin strolling down the Royal Mile (p55) – Walk 1 (p92) would make an interesting start – and think about where to have lunch; the Doric Wine Bar & Bistro (p102) and David Bann (p102) are temptingly close by. Once you've eaten, continue to the foot of the Royal Mile to see if the new Scottish Parliament Building (p60) is finished yet, then work up an appetite by climbing Arthur's Seat (p58) – or, for the less outdoorsy, ogling the designer shoes in Harvey Nichols (p150). Satisfy your hunger with dinner at Oloroso (p108), while you watch the sun set over the Firth of Forth.

On day two, spend the morning soaking up some history in the Museum of Scotland (p63), and in the afternoon catch the bus to Leith for a visit to the Royal Yacht Britannia (p75). In the evening, have an early dinner at Daniel's Bistro (p116) or Witchery by the Castle (p104), then scare yourself silly on a guided ghost tour with Black Hart Storytellers (p50).

One Week

If you're lucky enough to have a week in Edinburgh, follow the 'Two Days' itinerary, then spend your third morning exploring the New Town (p65) – Walk 2 (p93) would be ideal – and have a lazy lunch at Circus Café (p106) in Stockbridge before strolling north to the Royal Botanic Gardens (p72) or south to the Scottish National Gallery of Modern Art (p72). On day four, take it easy with a pampering treatment at One Spa (p143), a spot of self-indulgent shopping in Stockbridge (p152) and a romantic dinner at Stac Polly (p108).

Day five can be a day at the seaside – take the bus to **Cramond** (p76) for a riverside stroll and have lunch at the **Cramond Inn** (p117), then in the afternoon cross the river to visit **Dalmeny House** (p77) or (tides allowing) take a walk out to **Cramond Island** (p77). In the evening, head for Leith to sample some of the city's finest seafood at **Fishers** (p106). On day six, take an excursion out of the city to the mysterious **Rosslyn Chapel** (p186). Day seven should be saved for a shopping spree from the **West End** (p126) along George St to the consumerist shrine of **Harvey Nichols** (p150), and cap the week with an unforgettable dinner at the sumptuous **Rhubarb** (p113) in the Prestonfield House Hotel.

Underground Edinburgh

As Edinburgh expanded in the late 18th and early 19th centuries, many old tenements were demolished and new bridges were built to link the Old Town to the newly built areas to its north and south. South Bridge (built between 1785 and 1788) and George IV Bridge (built between 1829 and 1834) lead southwards from the Royal Mile over the deep valley of Cowgate, but since their construction so many buildings have been built closely around them that you can hardly tell they are bridges – George IV Bridge has a total of nine arches but only two are visible; South Bridge has no less than 18 hidden arches.

These subterranean vaults were originally used as storerooms, workshops and drinking dens. But as early-19th-century Edinburgh's population was swelled by an influx of penniless Highlanders cleared from their lands and Irish refugees from the potato famine, the dark, dripping chambers were given over to slum accommodation and abandoned to poverty, filth and crime.

The vaults were eventually cleared in the late 19th century, then lay forgotten until 1994 when the South Bridge vaults were opened to guided tours (see p4). Certain chambers are said to be haunted and one particular vault was investigated by paranormal researchers in 2001 (see p64).

However, the most notorious legend of underground Edinburgh dates from much earlier – from the plague that struck the city in 1645. Legend has it that the disease-ridden inhabitants of Mary King's Close (a lane on the northern side of the Royal Mile on the site of the City Chambers) were walled up in their houses and left to perish. When the lifeless bodies were eventually cleared from the houses, they were so stiff that workmen had to hack off limbs to get them through the small doorways and narrow, twisting stairs.

Satisfyingly gruesome though it is, the story isn't true – plague did strike, but no one was walled in – but from that day on, the close was said to be haunted by the spirits of the plague victims. The few people who were prepared to live there reported seeing apparitions of severed heads and limbs, and the largely abandoned close fell into ruin. When the Royal Exchange (now the City Chambers) was constructed between 1753 and 1761, it was built over the lower levels of Mary King's Close, which were left intact beneath the building.

Interest in the close revived in the 20th century when Edinburgh's city council began to allow occasional guided tours to enter. Since then, visitors have reported many supernatural experiences – the most famous ghost is 'Sarah', a little girl whose sad tale has prompted people to leave gifts of dolls in a corner of one of the rooms. In 2003 the close was opened to the public as the **Real Mary King's Close** (p56–7).

Neighbourhoods

ORGANISED TOURS

Bus Tours

Open-topped buses leave from Waverley Bridge outside the main train station and offer hop-on/hop-off tours of the main sights, taking in New Town, Grassmarket and the Royal Mile. They're a good way of getting your bearings, although with a bus map and a Day Saver bus ticket (£2.50) you could do much the same thing without the commentary. Tours run daily, year-round (except for 24 and 25 December), every 20 or 30 minutes, from 9.45am to 4.45pm; tickets remain valid for 24 hours.

BRITANNIA TOUR

☎ 220 0770; adult/child £8.50/2.50

The Britannia tour bus runs every 30 minutes (every 15 minutes in July and August) from Waverley Bridge to the Royal Yacht *Britannia* (p75) at Ocean Terminal via the Royal Botanic Garden (p72).

EDINBURGH TOUR

☎ 555 6363; adult/child £7.50/2.50

Lothian Buses' bright red open-top buses depart every 10 minutes from Waverley Bridge; the one-hour tour covers Old Town, New Town, Calton Hill, Grassmarket, Greyfriars and Holyrood.

MAC TOURS
☎ 220 0770; adult/child £8.50/2.50
Offers similar tours every 20 minutes, but in a vintage open-top bus.

Cycling Tours
ADRIAN'S EDINBURGH CITY CYCLE TOUR
☎ 07966447206; www.pedalculture.com; adult/child £15/10; ☺ 10am & 2.30pm
This 5-mile guided cycle tour makes use of back streets and short cuts to avoid steep hills and the worst of the traffic. Tours, which last three hours, begin at the gates of the Palace of Holyroodhouse (p59). Bikes are provided, though you can bring your own if you prefer.

Helicopter Tours
LOTHIAN HELICOPTERS
☎ 01875320032; www.lothianhelicopters.co.uk; Ste 1, Vineyard Business Centre, Tynehead, Pathhead; tours £40-160; ☺ by arrangement
This company offers sightseeing flights over Edinburgh and the Forth Bridges in a seven-seat Bell 206L-4. Prices range from £40 per person for a 10-minute flight, to £160 for 45 minutes.

Walking Tours
There are lots of organised walks around Edinburgh, many of them related to ghosts, murders and witches. For starting times, phone or check the websites listed below.

AULD REEKIE TOURS
☎ 557 4700; www.auldreekietours.co.uk; 45-7 Niddry St; adult/child £6/4; ☺ hourly 7-10pm
More interested in the blood-and-guts aspects of medieval torture than in real history, Auld Reekie can boast a 'working pagan temple' complete with witches' coven. Tours start from the Tron Kirk (p58).

BLACK HART STORYTELLERS
☎ 221 1249; www.blackhart.uk.com; adult/child £6/5; ☺ 7.30pm & 8.30pm
Not suitable for children. The 'City of the Dead' tour of Greyfriars Kirkyard is probably the best of Edinburgh's 'ghost' tours. Many people have reported encounters with the 'MacKenzie Poltergeist'. Tours depart from the Mercat Cross (p57).

CADIES & WITCHERY TOURS
☎ 225 6745; www.witcherytours.com; 84 West Bow; adult/child £7/4; ☺ hourly 7-10pm
The becloaked and pasty-faced Adam Lyal (deceased) leads a 'Murder & Mystery' tour of the Old Town's darker corners. These tours are very famous for their 'jumper-ooters' – costumed actors who 'jump oot' when you least expect it. Ooooh, scary. Tours begin outside the Witchery by the Castle restaurant (p104).

CELTIC TRAILS
☎ 477 5419; www.celtictrails.co.uk; tours £22-27; ☺ times by arrangement
A refreshing alternative to mainstream walking tours is offered by Jackie Queally, who leads guided tours of Edinburgh's ancient and sacred sites, covering subjects such as Celtic mythology, geomancy, sacred geometry and the Knights Templar. Tours must be arranged in advance.

EDINBURGH LITERARY PUB TOUR
☎ 226 6665; www.scot-lit-tour.co.uk; adult/student £7/5; ☺ 7.30pm daily Jun-Sep, 7.30pm Thu-Sun Apr, May & Oct, 7.30pm Fri Nov-Mar
An enlightening two-hour trawl through Edinburgh's literary history – and its associated howffs – in the entertaining company of Messrs Clart and McBrain. One of the best of Edinburgh's walking tours. Tours begin at the Beehive Inn (p121).

GEOWALKS
☎ 555 5488; www.geowalks.demon.co.uk; tours £7-10; ☺ see website for details
For those of you that are interested in history that goes back for millions, rather than just hundreds of years, geologist Dr Angus Miller leads walks that explore the geological history of Edinburgh's very own extinct volcano, Arthur's Seat, and the surrounding countryside.

MERCAT TOURS
☎ 557 6464; www.mercat-tours.co.uk; Mercat house, Niddry St South; adult £6-7.50, child £4-5.50; ☺ 11am-8pm
Mercat Tours offer a wide range of fascinating tours including informative history walks in the Old Town and Leith, 'Ghosts & Ghouls' tours, and visits to haunted underground vaults. Tours begin from the Mercat Cross (p57).

OLD TOWN

Eating p101; Drinking p120; Shopping p147; Sleeping p159

Edinburgh's Old Town stretches along a ridge between the castle and Holyrood, and tumbles southward down Victoria St and West Bow to the broad expanse of the Grassmarket and the mossy stones of Greyfriars Kirkyard. It's a jagged, jumbled maze of masonry riddled with closes, wynds (narrow alleys), stairs and vaults, and is cleft along its spine by the cobbled ravine of the Royal Mile.

Until the founding of the New Town in the 18th century, old Edinburgh was an overcrowded and insanitary hive of humanity. Constrained between the boggy ground of the Nor' Loch (now drained and occupied by Princes St Gardens) to the north and the city walls to the south and east, the only way for the town to expand was upwards. The five- to eight-storey tenements that were raised along the Royal Mile in the 16th and 17th centuries were the skyscrapers of their day, remarked upon with wonder by visiting writers such as Daniel Defoe. All classes of society, from beggars to magistrates, lived cheek by jowl in these urban ants' nests, the wealthy occupying the middle floors – high enough to be above the noise and stink of the streets, but not so high that climbing the stairs would be too tiring (middle-class folk had to make that climb!) – while the poor squeezed into attics, basements, cellars and vaults amid the rats, rubbish and raw sewage.

Edinburgh Castle (p52) viewed from Arthur's Seat (p58)

The renovated Old Town tenements still support a thriving city-centre community, but today the street level is crammed with cafés, restaurants, bars, backpacker hostels and tacky souvenir shops. Few visitors wander beyond the main drag of the Royal Mile, but it's worth taking time to explore the countless closes and wynds that lead off the street into quiet courtyards, often with unexpected views of cityscape, sea and hills.

Transport

Bus Lothian bus 28 runs from St Andrew Sq to the Lawnmarket at the top of the Royal Mile, close to the castle; bus 35 runs along the lower part of the Royal Mile from George IV Bridge to the Palace of Holyroodhouse. Buses 23, 27, 41 and 42 run along the Mound and George IV Bridge, giving access to the Royal Mile and Grassmarket (via Victoria St or Candlemaker Row).

Parking Cars are not allowed on the central part of the Royal Mile between George IV Bridge and North Bridge. There are large car parks at Castle Tce and on New St; outside the Festival period, there is also parking on the Castle Esplanade.

CASTLEHILL

Lined with tall buildings, this narrow street at the top of the Royal Mile is a bustling bottle-neck through which tides of tourists ebb and flow on their way to and from the castle.

EDINBURGH CASTLE Map p226

☎ 225 9846; Castlehill; adult/concession/child including audioguide £8.50/6.25/2; ☯ 9.30am-6pm Apr-Sep, 9.30am-5pm Oct-Mar; last ticket sold 45 mins before closing; bus 28

The brooding, black crags of the Castle Rock, shouldering above Princes St Gardens, are the very reason for Edinburgh's existence. This rocky hill – the glacier-worn stump of an ancient volcano – was the most easily defended hilltop on the invasion route between England and central Scotland, a route followed by countless armies from the Roman legions of the 1st and 2nd centuries AD to the Jacobite troops of Bonnie Prince Charlie in 1745. No-one knows when the rock was first fortified but archaeological excavations have uncovered evidence of habitation from as early as 900 BC.

The castle has played a pivotal role in Scottish history, both as a royal residence – King Malcolm Canmore (r 1057–93) and Queen Margaret made their home here in the 11th century – and as a military stronghold. From the 16th century the royal family favoured comfortable domestic accommodation at Holyrood and Linlithgow, and the castle became a seat of government and military power. However, in 1566 Mary Queen of Scots underlined its continuing symbolic importance when she chose to give birth to her son, King James VI, in the castle.

The castle suffered extensive damage during the Lang Siege, between 1571 and 1573,

when supporters of Mary Queen of Scots held out against the forces of James Douglas, Earl of Morton. It was occupied by English soldiers from 1650 to 1660 during Oliver Cromwell's invasion of Scotland and by Jacobites during the siege of 1689, when the Duke of Gordon faced off against William of Orange.

But when the army of Bonnie Prince Charlie passed through Edinburgh in 1745, they made only a cursory attempt to take the castle before moving quickly on. That was the last time the castle saw military action, and from then until the 1920s it served as the British army's main base in Scotland.

Edinburgh Castle is now Scotland's most popular pay-to-enter tourist attraction, pulling in over 1.7 million visitors in 2003. The **Esplanade**, a parade ground dating from 1820, is now a car park with superb views south over the city towards the Pentland Hills. On the northern side is an equestrian **statue of Field Marshall Earl Haig** (1861–1928). Haig was commander-in-chief of British forces during WWI and was responsible for the policy of attrition and trench warfare that killed thousands of troops.

The **Entrance Gateway** dates from between 1886 and 1888, and is flanked by statues of Robert the Bruce and William Wallace. Above the gate is the Royal Standard of Scotland – a red lion rampant on a gold field – and the Scottish Royal motto in Latin, 'NEMO ME IMPUNE LACESSIT'. This is translated into Scots as 'wha daur meddle wi' me', and into English as 'watch it, pal' (OK, it literally means 'no one provokes me with impunity'). Inside, a lane leads up beneath the 16th-century **Portcullis Gate**, topped by the 19th-century **Argyle Tower**, and past the cannon of the **Argyle** and **Mills Mount batteries**. The battlements here have great views over New Town to the Firth of Forth.

At the far end of Mills Mount Battery, to the right of the **Cart Shed** (which houses a café and restaurant), is the **One O'Clock Gun** (p67), a gleaming WWII 25-pounder that fires an ear-splitting time signal at 1pm every day (except Sunday, Christmas Day and Good Friday). Beyond lie the **Western Ramparts**, a battlement walk with views over Edinburgh's West End. To the left of the Cart Shed, a road leads down to the **National War Museum of Scotland** (p54).

South of Mills Mount, the road curls up leftwards through **Foog's Gate** to the highest part of the Castle Rock, crowned by the tiny **St Margaret's Chapel**, the oldest surviving building in Edinburgh. It's a simple Romanesque structure that was probably built by David I or Alexander I in memory of their mother Queen Margaret sometime around 1130 (she was canonised in 1250). Following Cromwell's capture of the castle in 1650 it was used to store ammunition until it was restored at the order of Queen Victoria; it was rededicated in 1934. The tiny stained-glass windows – depicting Margaret, St Andrew, St Columba, St Ninian and William Wallace – date from the 1920s. Immediately north of the chapel is **Mons Meg**, a giant 15th-century siege gun built at Mons in Belgium in 1449. The gun was last fired in 1681, as a birthday salute for the future King James VII/II, when its barrel burst. Take a peek over the wall to the north of the chapel and you'll see a charming little garden that was used as a **pet cemetery** for officer's dogs.

Beyond is the **Half Moon Battery**, which was built around and over the ruins of **David's Tower** –

the royal residence of David II (1329–71) – after it was destroyed in the Lang Siege of 1571–73; you can visit the ruined vaults of the tower via a stairway beneath the battery.

The main group of buildings on the summit of the castle rock are arranged around **Crown Square**, dominated by the hushed shrine of the **Scottish National War Memorial**. Opposite is the **Great Hall**, built for James IV (r 1488–1513) as a ceremonial hall and used as a meeting place for the Scottish Parliament until 1639. Its most remarkable feature is the original, 16th-century hammer-beam roof.

On the eastern end of the square is the **Royal Palace**, built during the 15th and 16th centuries, where a series of historical tableaux leads to a strongroom housing the **Honours of Scotland** (the Scottish crown jewels), the oldest surviving crown jewels in Europe. Locked away in a chest following the Act of Union in 1707, the crown (made in 1540 from the gold of Robert the Bruce's 14th-century coronet), sword and sceptre lay forgotten until they were unearthed at the instigation of the novelist Walter Scott in 1818. Also on display here is the **Stone of Destiny** (see below).

Among the neighbouring **Royal Apartments** is the bedchamber where Mary Queen of Scots gave birth to her son James VI, who was to unite the crowns of Scotland and England in 1603.

The **Castle Vaults** beneath the Great Hall were used at various times as storerooms, bakeries and prisons – French prisoners in the 18th century carved the graffiti on the walls.

The Stone of Destiny

On St Andrew's Day 1996, with much pomp and ceremony, a block of sandstone – 26½ inches by 16½ inches by 11 inches in size – with rusted iron hoops at either end was installed in Edinburgh Castle. For the previous 700 years it had lain in London, beneath the Coronation Chair in Westminster Abbey. Almost every English, and later British, monarch from Edward II in 1307 to Elizabeth II in 1953 had parked their backside firmly over this stone during their coronation ceremony.

The legendary Stone of Destiny – said to have originated in the Holy Land, and on which Scottish kings placed their feet during their coronation (not their bums; the English got that bit wrong) – was stolen from Scone Abbey near Perth by King Edward I of England in 1296. It was taken to London and there it remained for seven centuries – except for a brief removal to Gloucester during WWII air raids, and a three-month sojourn in Scotland after it was stolen by Scottish students at Christmas in 1950 – an enduring symbol of Scotland's subjugation by England.

The Stone of Destiny returned to the political limelight in 1996, when the then Scottish Secretary and Conservative Party MP, Michael Forsyth, arranged for the return of the sandstone block to Scotland. A blatant attempt to boost the flagging popularity of the Conservative Party in Scotland prior to a general election, Forsyth's publicity stunt failed miserably. The Scots said thanks very much for the stone and then, in May 1997, voted every Conservative MP in Scotland into oblivion.

Many people, however, believe that Edward I was fobbed off with a shoddy imitation in 1296 and that the true Stone of Destiny remains safely hidden somewhere in Scotland. This is not impossible – some descriptions of the original state that it was made of black marble and decorated with elaborate carvings. Interested parties should read *Stone of Destiny* (1997), by Pat Gerber, which details the history of Scotland's most famous lump of rock.

HIGHLAND TOLBOOTH KIRK Map pp224–5
Castlehill; bus 28

With Edinburgh's tallest spire (71.7m), this church is a prominent feature of the Old Town skyline. It was built in the 1840s by James Graham and Augustus Pugin (architect of London's Houses of Parliament) and takes its name from the Gaelic services that were held here in the 19th century for Edinburgh's Highland congregations. The interior has been refurbished and it now houses the **Hub** (☎ 473 2000; www .eif.co.uk/thehub; admission free; ticket centre ☒ 10am-5pm Mon-Sat), the ticket office and information centre for the Edinburgh Festival. There's also a good café here (see p102).

Opposite the kirk are the Assembly Rooms of the Church of Scotland, which are the temporary home of the debating chamber of the new **Scottish Parliament** (p60; visitors entrance is in Milne's Court, beside Ensign Ewart).

NATIONAL WAR MUSEUM OF SCOTLAND Map p226
☎ 225 7534; admission included in Edinburgh Castle ticket; ☒ 9.45am-5.30pm Apr-Nov, 9.45am-4.30pm Dec-Mar; bus 28

Opened in 2000, this museum brings Scotland's military history vividly to life. The exhibits have been personalised by telling the stories of the original owners of the objects on display, making it easier to empathise with the experiences of war than any dry display of dusty weaponry ever could. You'll see more than one person brushing away a tear as they pass through.

National War Museum of Scotland

Trunk and Disorderly

One of the most unusual exhibits in the National War Museum of Scotland is a set of sawn-off elephant's toenails. They belonged to a beast that was adopted as a regimental mascot by the 78th Regiment of Foot (the Ross-shire Buffs) while they were serving in Ceylon (now Sri Lanka) in the 1830s, and travelled back to Edinburgh with them on their return to Scotland. The elephant lived in stables at Edinburgh Castle and was trained to march at the head of the regiment during parades. It was looked after by Private James McIntosh, a bibulous Highlander who regularly retired to the canteen in the evenings to partake of alcoholic refreshment.

The elephant, no doubt feeling lonely and a little disoriented, would follow him to the canteen and loiter with intent, regularly extending its trunk through the window where the amused clientele would serve it large quantities of beer. Legend has it that both McIntosh and the elephant would then retire to the stable and sleep it off together.

OUTLOOK TOWER & CAMERA OBSCURA Map pp224–5
☎ 226 3709; Castlehill; adult/child £5.95/3.70; ☒ 9.30am-7.30pm Jul & Aug, 9.30am-6pm Apr-Jun, Sep & Oct, 10am-5pm Nov-Mar; bus 28

The 'camera' itself is a curious device (originally dating from the 1850s, although improved in 1945) a bit like a periscope, which uses lenses and mirrors to throw a live image of the city onto a large horizontal screen. The accompanying commentary is entertaining and the whole exercise has a quirky charm. The Outlook Tower offers great views over the city.

SCOTCH WHISKY HERITAGE CENTRE
Map pp224–5
☎ 220 0441; 354 Castlehill; adult/child including tour & tasting £7.50/3.95; ☒ 9.30am-6.30pm May-Sep, 10am-5pm Oct-Apr; bus 28

Housed in a former school, the centre explains the making of whisky from barley to bottle, in a series of exhibits that combine sight, sound and smell. The first, and more interesting, part is led by a guide, while the second part consists of riding a 'barrel car' past several tableaux depicting the history of the 'water of life' – Johnnie Walker meets Walt Disney. As a reward, you get a wee taste of the real thing, before being channelled into a shop full of whisky (though it's cheaper at Oddbins off-licence five minutes down the road).

ROYAL MILE

The Royal Mile, Edinburgh's oldest street, connects the castle to the Palace of Holyroodhouse. Hemmed in for much of its gently snaking length with tall, 17th- to 19th-century tenement buildings, it retains a grand, baronial atmosphere, heightened in festival time when the pedestrianised central section is crowded with tourists and performers.

The Royal Mile is split into four named sections: **Castlehill** (p52), the Lawnmarket, the High Street and the Canongate. A corruption of 'Landmarket', **Lawnmarket** takes its name from the large cloth market (selling goods from the land outside the city) that flourished here until the 18th century; this was the poshest part of the Old Town, where many of its most distinguished citizens made their homes.

High St, which stretches from George IV Bridge down to St Mary's St, is the heart and soul of the Old Town, home to the city's main church, the Law Courts, the city council and – until 1707 – the Scottish Parliament. High St ends at the intersection with St Mary's and Jeffrey Sts, where the Old Town's eastern gate, the **Netherbow Port** (part of the Flodden Wall) once stood. Though it no longer exists, its former outline is marked by brass strips set in the road.

The **Canongate** – the section between the Netherbow and Holyrood – takes its name from the Augustinian canons (monks) of Holyrood Abbey. From the 16th century it was home to aristocrats attracted to the Palace of Holyroodhouse. Originally governed by the monks, the Canongate remained an independent burgh until 1856.

BANK OF SCOTLAND MUSEUM

Map pp224–5

☎ 529 1288; the Mound; admission free; ☽ 10am-4.45pm Mon-Fri mid-Jun–Aug; bus 2, 23, 27, 28, 41, 42
Housed in the Bank of Scotland's splendid Georgian HQ, this little museum is a treasure trove of gold coins, bullion chests, safes, banknotes, forgeries, cartoons and lots of fascinating old documents and photographs charting the history of Scotland's oldest bank.

BRASS RUBBING CENTRE Map pp224–5

☎ 556 4364; Trinity Apse, Chalmers Close; admission free; ☽ 10am-5pm Mon-Sat year round, noon-5pm Sun Aug; bus 35
Across the street from the Museum of Childhood, Chalmers Close leads down to

Trinity Apse, the only surviving part of the 15th-century Trinity College Church. The Gothic apse now houses a Brass Rubbing Centre where you can learn how to take rubbings from the centre's collection of medieval brasses and replicas of Pictish and Celtic stones. Though admission is free, rubbings cost from £1.20.

CANONGATE KIRK Map pp218–20

☎ 226 5138; Canongate; admission free; ☽ 9am-6pm; bus 35
A short distance downhill from the Canongate Tolbooth (following) is the attractive curved gable of **Canongate Kirk**, built in 1688. In 1745 Charles Edward Stuart (Bonnie Prince Charlie) used it to hold prisoners taken at the Battle of Prestonpans. The surrounding kirkyard contains the graves of several famous people, including the economist **Adam Smith** (1723–90), author of The Wealth of Nations, who lived nearby in Panmure Close, and **Mrs Agnes MacLehose** (the 'Clarinda' of Robert Burns' love poems). Walk down the left-hand side of the church to a tree and turn left – the grave with the low iron railing belongs to the 18th-century poet **Robert Fergusson** (1750–74). He was much admired by Robert Burns, who paid for the gravestone and penned the epitaph – take a look at the inscription on the back.

CANONGATE TOLBOOTH Map pp218–20

☎ 529 4057; 163 Canongate; admission free; ☽ 10am-5pm Mon-Sat year-round, plus 2-5pm Sun during the Edinburgh Festival; bus 35
The Tolbooth is one of the surviving symbols of Canongate's former independence. Built in 1591, it served successively as a collection point for tolls (taxes), a council house, a courtroom and a jail. With its picturesque turrets and projecting clock, it's a splendid example of 16th-century architecture. It now houses a fascinating museum, the **People's Story**, recording the life, work and pastimes of ordinary Edinburgh folk from the 18th century to the present day.

CITY CHAMBERS Map pp224–5

High St; not open to the public; bus 35
The imposing Georgian City Chambers, home to Edinburgh City Council, was originally built by John Adam (brother of Robert) between 1753 and 1761 to serve as the Royal Exchange – a covered meeting place for city merchants – replacing the traditional meeting place of the Mercat Cross (p57). However, the merchants

continued to prefer their old stamping grounds in the street and the building became the offices of the city council in 1811. Though only four storeys high on the Royal Mile side, the building plummets 12 storeys on the northern side, overlooking Cockburn St.

It was built over the sealed-off remains of three Old Town closes; the spooky remains of these can be explored on a guided tour of the famous Mary King's Close (see p56).

GLADSTONE'S LAND Map pp224-5

☎ 226 5856; 477 Lawnmarket; adult/child £3.50/2.60; ☺ 10am-5pm Mon-Sat & 2-5pm Sun Apr-Oct; bus 28

In 1617 Thomas Gledstanes, a 17th-century merchant – and ancestor of the 19th-century British prime minister William Gladstone – bought the tenement later known as Gladstone's Land. Built in the mid-16th century and extended in the 17th, it gives a fascinating glimpse of the Old Town's past. The comfortable interior contains fine painted ceilings, walls and beams and some splendid furniture from the 17th and 18th centuries. The volunteer guides provide a wealth of stories and detailed history.

JOHN KNOX HOUSE Map pp224-5

☎ 556 2647; 43-5 High St; adult/child £2.25/75p; ☺ 10am-5pm Mon-Sat Sep-Jul, 10am-7pm Mon-Sat Aug, plus noon-4pm Sun Jul & Aug; bus 35

The Royal Mile narrows at the foot of the High St beside the jutting façade of John Knox House. It is the oldest surviving tenement in Edinburgh, dating from around 1490, and the outside staircase, overhanging upper floors and crow-stepped gables are all typical of a 15th-century town house. John Knox is thought to have occupied the second floor from 1561 to 1572. The labyrinthine interior has some beautiful painted timber ceilings and an interesting display on Knox's life and work. At the time of writing the house was undergoing renovation, and was due to reopen by summer 2005.

MUSEUM OF CHILDHOOD Map pp224-5

☎ 529 4142; 42 High St; admission free; ☺ 10am-5pm Mon-Sat year-round, 2-5pm Sun Jul & Aug; bus 35

Halfway down the High St is 'the noisiest museum in the world' – the Museum of Childhood. Often overrun with screaming kids, it covers serious issues related to childhood – health, education, upbringing and so on – but also has an enormous collection of toys, games and books: everything from Victorian dolls to a video history of the 1960s Gerry Anderson TV puppet series Thunderbirds.

MUSEUM OF EDINBURGH Map pp218-20

☎ 529 4143; 142 Canongate; admission free; ☺ 10am-5pm Mon-Sat year-round, 2-5pm Sun during the Edinburgh Festival; bus 35

Across the street from the Canongate Tolbooth is Huntly House. Built in 1570, it is a good example of the accommodation that aristocrats built for themselves along the Canongate – the projecting upper floors of plastered timber are typical of the period. It now houses the Museum of Edinburgh, whose exhibits cover the history of the city from prehistory to the present.

The labyrinth of oak-panelled rooms with creaky, polished wooden floors houses a lot of less-than-riveting displays of weights and measures, shop signs and silverware. There are some gems worth seeking out, however, most notably an original copy of the National Covenant signed in Greyfriars Kirkyard in 1638, and tasselled with the seals of countless Scottish noblemen. There is also an interesting display on the history of the One O'Clock Gun (see p67), but the big crowd-pleaser is the case containing the dog collar and feeding bowl that belonged to Greyfriars Bobby (see p63), the city's most famous canine citizen.

PARLIAMENT HALL Map pp224-5

☎ 348 5355; 11 Parliament Sq; admission free; ☺ 10am-4pm Mon-Fri; bus 35

Around St Giles Cathedral (p57) is the cobbled expanse of Parliament Square, flanked to the south by Parliament House, the meeting place of the Scottish Parliament from 1639 to 1707 (the neoclassical façade was added in the early 19th century). After the Act of Union the building became the centre of the Scottish legal system, housing the Court of Session and the High Court, a function which it still serves today. The most interesting feature is the 17th-century Parliament Hall (dating from 1639), where the parliament actually met. Now used by lawyers and their clients as a meeting place, it boasts its original oak hammer-beam roof and magnificent 19th-century stained-glass windows depicting the inauguration of the Court of Session by King James V in 1532.

To find the Parliament Hall at No 11 Parliament Square (there's a sign outside saying Parliament Hall; Court of Session), go through the double doors immediately on your right.

REAL MARY KING'S CLOSE Map pp224-5

☎ 0870 243 0160; 2 Warriston's Close, Writers Court, High St; adult/child £7/5; ☺ 10am-9pm Apr-Oct, 10am-4pm Nov-Mar; bus 35

The City Chambers were built over the sealed-off remains of Mary King's Close, and the lower levels of this medieval Old Town alley have survived almost unchanged in the foundations for 250 years. Now open to the public, this spooky, subterranean labyrinth gives a fascinating insight into the everyday life of 17th-century Edinburgh. A costumed drama student in period costume will take you on a guided tour through the vaults, whilst practising his or her dramatic enunciation.

The scripted tour, with its ghostly tales and gruesome tableaux, can seem a little naff, milking the scary and scatological aspects of the close's history for all they're worth, but there are things of genuine interest to see – there's something about the crumbling 17th-century tenement room, with tufts of horsehair poking from the collapsing lath-and-plaster walls, the ghost of a pattern on the walls, and the ancient smell of stone and dust thick in your nostrils, that makes the hairs rise on the back of your neck.

Then there's wee Annie's room, where a psychic once claimed to have been approached by the ghost of a little girl. It's hard to tell what's more frightening – the story of the ghostly girl, or the bizarre heap of tiny dolls and teddies left in a corner by sympathetic visitors.

Weirdest of all is standing at the foot of Mary King's Close itself, with the old tenement walls rising on either side, and feeling the weight of those 11 storeys – and some 250 years of history – pressing down all around you.

ST GILES CATHEDRAL Map pp224–5
☎ 225 9442; High St; admission free but donations welcome; ☼ 9am-7pm Mon-Fri, 9am-5pm Sat, 1-5pm Sun May-Sep, 9am-5pm Mon-Sat & 1-5pm Sun Oct-Apr; bus 35

Dominating High St is the great grey bulk of St Giles Cathedral. Properly called the High Kirk of Edinburgh (it was only a true cathedral – ie the seat of a bishop – from 1633 to 1638 and from 1661 to 1689), St Giles was named after the patron saint of cripples and beggars. There has been a church on this site since the 9th century. A Norman-style church was built in 1126 but was destroyed by English invaders in 1385; the only substantial remains are the central piers that support the tower. The present church dates largely from the 15th century – the beautiful crown spire was completed in 1495 – but much of it was restored in the 19th century.

St Giles was at the heart of the Scottish Reformation. John Knox served as minister here from 1559 to 1572, preaching his uncompromising Calvinist message, and when Charles I attempted to re-establish episcopacy in Scotland in 1637 by imposing a new liturgy, he only hardened the Scots' attitude against him. As the service from Charles I's *Book of Common Prayer* was read out for the first time in St Giles, a local woman called Jenny Geddes hurled her stool at the Dean and called out, 'De'il colic the wame o' thee – wouldst thou say Mass at ma lug?' (The devil buckle your belly – would you say Mass in my ear?) – and ignited a riot whose aftermath led to the signing of the National Covenant at Greyfriars the following year. A plaque marks the spot where Geddes launched her protest and a copy of the National Covenant is displayed on the wall.

There are several ornate monuments in the church, including the tombs of James Graham, Marquis of Montrose, who led Charles I's forces in Scotland and was hanged in 1650 at the Mercat Cross; and his Covenanter opponent Archibald Campbell, Marquis of Argyll, who was decapitated in 1661 after the Restoration of Charles II. One of the most interesting corners of the church is the **Thistle Chapel**, built between 1909 and 1911 for the Knights of the Most Ancient & Most Noble Order of the Thistle. The elaborately carved Gothic-style stalls have canopies topped with the helms and arms of the 16 knights – look out for the bagpipe-playing angel amid the vaulting.

By the side of the street outside the western door of St Giles, a cobblestone **Heart of Midlothian** is set in the paving. Passers-by traditionally spit on it for luck (don't stand downwind!). This was the site of the Tolbooth, originally built to collect tolls, but subsequently a meeting place for parliament, the town council and the General Assembly of the Reformed Kirk, then law courts and, finally, a notorious prison and place of execution. The Tolbooth was immortalised in Sir Walter Scott's novel *The Heart of Midlothian*.

At the other end of St Giles is the **Mercat Cross**, a 19th-century copy of the 1365 original, where merchants and traders met to transact business and Royal Proclamations were read. In a revival of this ancient tradition, the dissolution of the Westminster Parliament prior to the 2001 general election was proclaimed here by costumed officials, much to the bemusement of tourists and locals alike.

SCOTTISH PARLIAMENT VISITOR CENTRE Map pp224–5

☎ 348 5000; www.scottish.parliament.uk; George IV Bridge; admission free; ⏱ 10am-5pm Mon-Fri, opens earlier when parliament is sitting; bus 2, 23, 27, 28, 41, 42

The centre explains the workings of the new parliament, which was officially opened on 1 July 1999 – the first Scottish parliament to sit for almost 300 years. You can visit the debating chamber when parliament is not sitting (usually from 10am to noon and 2pm to 4pm Monday and Friday), or you can phone ahead (☎ 348 5411, no more than a week in advance) to arrange free tickets for the public gallery while parliament is sitting.

TRON KIRK Map pp224–5

☎ 225 8408; cnr High St & South Bridge; admission free; ⏱ 10am-5.30pm Apr-Oct, noon-5pm Nov-Mar; bus 35 & all South Bridge buses

At the southwestern corner of the intersection with South Bridge is the Tron Kirk, which takes its name from the *tron*, or public weighbridge, that once stood on the site. It was built in 1637 by John Mylne, the king's master mason, but remodelled in the late 18th century during the construction of South Bridge. The original wooden spire was lost in the great fire of 1824 – you can still see scorch marks around the arch inside the doorway – and was replaced with a much taller stone spire in 1828.

The interior has been gutted, except for the magnificent oak hammer-beam roof, which rivals that in the Great Hall at Edinburgh Castle, and the floor has been excavated by archaeologists to reveal the cobbled surface of **Marlin's Wynd**, a late-16th-century alley with the remains of cellars, staircases and medieval drains on either side.

WRITERS' MUSEUM Map pp224–5

☎ 529 4901; Lady Stair's Close, Lawnmarket; admission free; ⏱ 10am-5pm Mon-Sat year-round, also 2-5pm Sun during Edinburgh Festival; bus 28

Tucked down a close to the east of Gladstone's Land is this little museum dedicated to Robert Burns, Sir Walter Scott and Robert Louis Stevenson. The building alone is worth a visit – Lady Stair's House was built in 1622, and the interior has been restored in grand Jacobean style, with a huge original fireplace, an ornate gallery and panelled ceiling, and an intriguing staircase hidden in a wall, with steps of uneven height designed to trip up intruders. The museum contains portraits, letters and a varied collection of memorabilia, including Burns' diminutive writing desk and Scott's dining room table. Head downstairs to the Stevenson display for a look at the tall mahogany cabinet that was built by none other than the notorious Deacon Brodie (see p10). It sat in Robert Louis Stevenson's bedroom when he was a child, and no doubt its history played a part in the author's inspiration for *The Strange Tale of Dr Jekyll and Mr Hyde*.

HOLYROOD

The district at the foot of the Royal Mile is undergoing a major upheaval during the construction of the new Scottish Parliament Building (due for completion by the end of 2004).

HOLYROOD PARK Map pp214–15, pp218–20 & pp222–3

In Holyrood Park, Edinburgh is blessed with a little bit of wilderness in the heart of the city. The former hunting ground of Scottish monarchs, the park covers 650 acres of varied landscape, including crags, moorland and lochs. The highest point is the summit of **Arthur's Seat** (251m), the deeply eroded remnant of a long-extinct volcano, but the most dramatic feature is the long, curving sweep of **Salisbury Crags**, a russet curtain of columnar basaltic cliffs that rises to the southeast of the Old Town.

The stony path along the foot of the crags is known as the **Radical Road** – it was built in 1820 at the suggestion of Sir Walter Scott, to give work to unemployed weavers (from whose politics it took its name). The path makes a good short walk from Holyrood, with fine views over the Old Town.

At the southern end of Salisbury Crags is the most famous rock outcrop in Edinburgh. Known as **Hutton's Section**, it was used by the pioneering Scottish geologist James Hutton in 1788 to bolster his theory that the basaltic rocks of Salisbury Crags were formed by the cooling of molten lava. An information board nearby explains what to look for.

Dug into the hillside near the northern end of the crags is **St Margaret's Well**, a beautiful, late-15th-century Gothic well-house. It was moved, stone by stone, to this location in 1860 when its original site in Meadowbank was taken over by a railway depot. You can't get into the chamber – all you can do is peek at the ornate vaulting through the metal grille at the entrance.

About 300m to the south, on a small hill overlooking St Margaret's Loch, are the ruins of **St Anthony's Chapel**. Dating from the 15th century, its origins are obscure; it may have been associated with a hospital in Leith donated by King James I (for the treatment of the skin disease erysipelas, also known as St Anthony's Fire), or it may have been a beacon for ships in the Firth of Forth. Nearby is a rough stone basin under a large boulder, known as **St Anthony's Well**, whose waters are said to have a curative effect. According to another (and probably related) legend, if you wash your face in the dew on Arthur's Seat on the morning of 1 May, you will be made beautiful.

Holyrood Park can be circumnavigated by car or bike along Queen's Drive – note that the western half of the drive is a major traffic route between the southern and eastern parts of the city, and the eastern half is closed to motorised traffic on Sunday. The parking area beside Dunsapie Loch is only a 15-minute hike away from the summit of Arthur's Seat. See p95 for details of a walk through the park via Arthur's Seat.

OUR DYNAMIC EARTH Map pp218–20
☎ 550 7800; Holyrood Rd; adult/child £7.95/5.45;
☯ 10am-6pm Apr-Oct, 10am-5pm Wed-Sun Nov-Mar, last admission 40 min before closing; bus 35, 64

A modernistic white marquee roof pitched beneath Salisbury Crags marks the site of Our Dynamic Earth. Advertised with the slogan

Gate to the Palace of Holyroodhouse

Mystery of the Miniature Coffins

In July 1836, five boys were hunting for rabbits on the slopes of Arthur's Seat when they made a gruesome discovery – in a hollow beneath a rock, arranged on a pile of slates, were 17 tiny, wooden coffins.

Each coffin was just four inches (10cm) long, and each contained a roughly carved human figure dressed in hand-made clothes. Articles in local newspapers at the time denounced the coffins as the work of witches, but from that day to this no one has ever found out who placed them there, or why.

The most convincing theory, put forward by researchers in 2000, is that the coffins were made in response to the infamous Burke and Hare murders (see p44), which were committed in 1831–32 – the number of coffins matches the number of known victims. It was a common belief that people whose bodies had been dissected by anatomists could not enter the Kingdom of Heaven, and it is thought that someone fashioned the tiny figures in order to provide the murder victims with a form of Christian burial.

Eight of the seventeen coffins survive, and can be seen in the Museum of Scotland (see p63).

'Live 4500 million years in one day!', it's billed as an interactive, multimedia 'journey of discovery' through Earth's history from the Big Bang to the present day. Hugely popular with kids of all ages, it's a slick extravaganza of whizz-bang special effects cleverly designed to fire up young minds with curiosity about all things geological and environmental. Its true purpose, of course, is to disgorge you into a gift shop where you can buy model dinosaurs and souvenir T-shirts.

The highlights include earthquake simulators, a vertigo-inducing, giant-screen video flypast over the glaciers of Norway, and a huge, artificial rainforest that gets drenched with an indoor tropical downpour every five minutes or so. There are loads of hands-on exhibits for the kids, and a soft play area for under-10s.

PALACE OF HOLYROODHOUSE & HOLYROOD ABBEY Map pp218–20
☎ 556 5100; Canongate; adult/child £7.50/4;
☯ 9.30am-6pm Apr-Oct, 9.30am-4.30pm Nov-Mar; bus 35, 64

Mary Queen of Scots spent six eventful years (1561–67) living in the Palace of Holyroodhouse, which dominates the eastern end of the Royal Mile. During this time she married

Lord Darnley (in the neighbouring abbey) and Bothwell (in what is now the Picture Gallery). It was here that she debated with John Knox and witnessed the murder of her secretary Rizzio.

The palace developed from a guesthouse attached to Holyrood Abbey, which was extended by King James IV in 1501 to create more comfortable living quarters than were possible in the exposed and windy hill-top castle. The oldest surviving section of the building, the northwestern tower, was built in 1529 as a royal apartment for James V and his wife, Mary of Guise.

Although Holyrood was never again used as a permanent royal residence after James VI departed for London in 1603, it was further extended during Charles II's reign, completing the great quadrangle you see today. It lay neglected through much of the 18th century – though Bonnie Prince Charlie briefly held court here in 1745 on his way south to Derby – but was gradually renovated as royal interest in Scotland revived following George IV's visit in 1822.

The guided tour leads you through a series of impressive royal apartments, ending in the **Great Gallery**. The 89 portraits of Scottish kings, commissioned by Charles II, supposedly record his unbroken lineage from Scota, the Egyptian pharaoh's daughter who discovered the infant Moses in a reed basket on the banks of the Nile.

The highlight of the tour is **Mary Queen of Scots' Bed Chamber** in the 16th-century tower house. This bedroom – with its low, painted ceilings and secret staircase connecting to her husband Lord Darnley's bedroom – was home to the unfortunate Mary from 1561 to 1567. It was here that her jealous husband restrained the pregnant queen while his henchmen murdered her secretary – and favourite – David Rizzio. In her own words, they '…dragged David forth with great cruelty from our cabinet and at the entrance of our chamber dealt him 56 dagger blows'. A plaque in the next room marks the spot where he bled to death. The exit from the palace leads into Holyrood Abbey.

King David I founded **Holyrood Abbey** here in the shadow of Salisbury Crags in 1128. It was probably named after a fragment of the True Cross (*rood* is an old Scots word for cross) said to have been brought to Scotland by his mother St Margaret. As it lay outside the city walls it suffered repeated attacks by English invaders, and the great abbey church was demolished in 1570, except for the nave, which remained in use as Canongate parish church until it col-

lapsed in 1768. Most of the surviving ruins date from the 12th and 13th centuries, although a doorway in the far southeastern corner has survived from the original Norman church. The bay on the right, as you look at the huge, arched, eastern window, is the royal burial vault, which holds the remains of kings David II, James II and James V, and of Mary's husband Lord Darnley.

In the gardens to the north of the palace is the tiny, turreted lodge known as **Queen Mary's Bath House**. According to legend, Mary Queen of Scots used to bathe in white wine here. It is more likely to have been a dovecote or summer house.

QUEEN'S GALLERY Map pp218–20

☎ 556 5100; Horse Wynd; adult/child £4/2; ◷ 9.30am-6pm Apr-Oct, 9.30am-4.30pm Nov-Mar; bus 35, 64

This stunning new gallery was opened in November 2002 as a showcase for exhibitions of art from the Royal Collections. The exhibitions change every six months or so; for details of the latest, check the Art and Residences/Royal Residences/Queen's Gallery link on www.royal .gov.uk. A combined ticket for admission to both the Queen's Gallery and the Palace of Holyroodhouse costs £10/5.

SCOTTISH PARLIAMENT BUILDING
Map pp218–20

☎ no phone; Holyrood Rd; not open to public; bus 35, 64
The new Scottish Parliament Building (see p60) is being built on the site of a former brewery at the foot of the Royal Mile, and is due to open in late 2004. The temporary **Parliament Building Visitor Centre** (the Tun, Holyrood Rd; admission free; ◷ 10am-4pm) records the development of the project from the initial architectural design competition to the current state of construction. The competition to design the new building was won in July 1998 by the late Catalan architect Enric Miralles, who envisaged a group of lenticular buildings with curved roofs inspired by upturned boats seen on a beach in northern Scotland.

Queensberry House, a 17th-century mansion once owned by the dukes of Queensberry, occupies the northern part of the site. It has been restored inside and out and will be incorporated as part of the parliament complex. Ironically, James, the second duke of Queensberry, was Commissioner to Parliament for King William and was instrumental in securing the passage of the Act of Union that brought about the end of the Scottish Parliament in 1707.

The Bottomless Pit?

It has been called Scotland's answer to the Sydney Opera House, and the most jinxed public building in Scottish history. Designed by Catalan architect Enric Miralles (who died of a brain tumour in July 2000, not long after the project got under way) the new parliament complex promises to be Scotland's most spectacular and controversial building – a flagship architectural project that has gone way over budget, way over schedule, and has been dogged by contention at every step.

At the time of writing, the new Scottish Parliament Building at the foot of the Royal Mile was nearing completion. It had long been thought that if Scotland was ever granted a devolved parliament it would be housed in the former Royal High School on Calton Hill, which had already been restored and fitted with a debating chamber in anticipation of such an event. The option of siting the new parliament in Leith was also discussed.

Instead, the Labour government in Westminster chose Holyrood – because, they claimed, it was the least expensive, best-value alternative. But it has been suggested that the siting of the Parliament Building was a political, not an economic, decision, and that the Labour Party – whose main opposition in Scotland is from the Scottish National Party (SNP) – decided against the Calton Hill site because it was favoured by the nationalists and had become associated in the public mind with full independence rather than devolution.

When a new home for the Scottish Parliament was first discussed in London in 1997, price estimates ranged from £10 million to £40 million, and it was expected to be ready by 2001. By the time the Scottish Parliament had convened for the first time in 1999, the cost estimate had been revised to £109 million. As the project went one, then two, then three years beyond schedule, mounting indignation was accompanied by steadily mounting costs – by February 2004 the bill had risen to £420 million and rising, with a completion date pencilled in for September 2004.

What rankles with many people and politicians is that all the main financial decisions on the Parliament Building – the site, the design, the architect, the construction contracts – were taken by Labour cabinet ministers in London before the Scottish Parliament had even been elected, and yet the ever-increasing cost of the project has to be met entirely out of Scottish Parliament funds.

In June 2003, an inquiry headed by the judge Lord Fraser of Carmyllie was set up to investigate the management of the building project. The inquiry is ongoing; for more information check out www.holyroodinquiry.org.

Hopefully the completed parliament complex will turn out to be a world-class building of which Scotland can be proud, but there is little doubt that the trials and tribulations surrounding its construction will cast a shadow over the project for years to come…

COCKBURN & MARKET STS

Cockburn St, lined with fashion, jewellery and music shops, leads down from the Royal Mile to Waverley Bridge. Cockburn St was opened in 1856, the first road to give direct access by horse-drawn carriage between the Royal Mile and the recently opened train stations on the site now occupied by Waverley station.

COLLECTIVE GALLERY Map pp224–5

☎ 220 1260; www.collectivegallery.net; 22-8 Cockburn St; admission free; 11am-5.30pm Tue-Sat

Halfway down on the left is the Collective Gallery, an artist-run gallery with exhibitions by contemporary Scottish artists and others.

STILLS GALLERY Map pp224–5

☎ 622 6200; www.stills.org; 23 Cockburn St; admission free; 11am-6pm

Across the street from the Collective Gallery you'll find Scotland's top photographic gallery, which exhibits the best of international contemporary photography.

EDINBURGH DUNGEON Map pp224–5

☎ 240 1000; 31 Market St; adult £10.45, child aged 10-15 £8.45, child aged 4-9 £6.45; 10am-7pm Jul & Aug, 10am-5pm Apr-Jun, Sep & Oct, 11am-4pm Mon-Fri, 10.30am-4.30pm Sat & Sun Nov-Mar; bus 64

Opposite the foot of Cockburn St, this manufactured attraction combines a gruesome tableaux of torture and degradation with live actors who perform scary little sketches along the way. Mildly amusing in a large group, mildly embarrassing in a small one and genuinely terrifying for small children. Seriously – not recommended for kids under eight.

FRUITMARKET GALLERY Map pp224–5

☎ 225 2383; www.fruitmarket.co.uk; 45 Market St; admission free; 11am-6pm Mon-Sat, noon-5pm Sun; bus 64

One of the city's most innovative galleries, the Fruitmarket showcases contemporary Scottish and international artists; it also has an excellent arts bookshop and café (see p104). There are around half a dozen exhibitions a year, ranging from paintings to installations to light-based artworks. Recent exhibitions have seen works as diverse as an installation consisting of 25 geraniums on a potting-shed table (part of a work exploring the theme of growth and change), and a display of spectacular glacier images by Swiss photographer Balthasar Burkhard.

CITY ART CENTRE Map pp224–5
☎ 529 3993; 2 Market St; admission free except for temporary exhibitions; 🕙 10am-5pm Mon-Sat year-round, noon-5pm Sun Aug; bus 64

Across the street from the Fruitmarket Galley is the City Art Centre, the largest and most populist of Edinburgh's smaller galleries. Owned by Edinburgh City Council, and housed in a former newsprint warehouse, its six floors are home to the city's collection of Scottish art, ranging from the 17th century to the 20th. There are also many fine paintings, engravings and photographs showing views of Edinburgh at various stages of its history. The centre regularly hosts crowd-pleasing, touring exhibitions such as the Gold of the Pharaohs and the Art of Star Wars.

GRASSMARKET

The site of a market from the 15th century until the start of the 20th, the Grassmarket has always been a focal point of the Old Town. As well as being a cattle market, this was the main place of execution in the city, and over 100 martyred Covenanters are commemorated by a monument at the eastern end, where the gallows used to stand. The notorious murderers Burke and Hare operated from a now vanished close off the west end. In 1827 they enticed at least 18 victims to their boarding house, suffocated them and sold the bodies to Edinburgh's medical schools (see p44).

Nowadays, the broad, open square, lined with tall tenements and dominated by the looming castle has many lively pubs and restaurants, including the White Hart Inn (p122) which was once patronised by Robert Burns. The Cowgate – the long, dark ravine leading eastwards from the Grassmarket – was once the road along which cattle were driven from the pastures around Arthur's Seat to the safety of the city walls. Today it is the heart of Edinburgh's nightlife, with a few dozen clubs and bars within five minutes' walk of each other (see p120 and p133).

At the western end of the Grassmarket, a narrow close called the Vennel leads steeply

Half-Hangit Maggie

The Grassmarket pub called Maggie Dickson's, just opposite the point where the gallows used to stand, is named after a Musselburgh woman who was hanged in 1724 for the crime of concealing the death of her prematurely born, illegitimate child. Her corpse was taken down from the gallows, placed in a casket and put on a cart for the journey back to Musselburgh. On the way, an argument erupted between Maggie's relatives and friends, who wanted to give her a Christian burial, and a group of surgeons' apprentices, who wanted the corpse for dissection. (At that time, executed criminals provided the only legal source of bodies for medical research.)

The argument was settled by the corpse itself, when noises were heard coming from within the coffin. The rope had not done its job properly and Maggie had revived – much to the consternation of both family and apprentices. Maggie Dickson made a full recovery and legal opinion was that someone who had already been pronounced dead could not be hanged again. She lived for another 30 years, and was ever after known in the town as 'Half-Hangit Maggie Dickson'.

up to one of the few surviving fragments of the Flodden Wall, the city wall that was built in the early 16th century as protection against a feared English invasion. Beyond it is the Telfer Wall, a later extension that continues to Lauriston Pl.

GEORGE HERIOT'S SCHOOL Map pp224–5
☎ 229 7263; Lauriston Pl; admission free; tours during summer holidays, Jun, Jul & first 2 weeks in Aug

East of the wall lies George Heriots, one of the most impressive buildings in the Old Town. Built in the 17th century with funds bequeathed by George Heriot (goldsmith and banker to King James VI, and popularly known as Jinglin' Geordie), it was originally a school and home for orphaned children, but became a fee-paying public school in 1886. Senior pupils conduct guided tours – phone ahead to book.

GREYFRIARS

Candlemaker Row leads up from the eastern end of Grassmarket alongside one of Edinburgh's most famous graveyards. Hemmed in by high walls and overlooked by the brooding presence of the castle, Greyfriars Kirkyard is one of Edinburgh's most evocative spots, a peaceful green oasis dotted with elaborate monuments. Many famous Edinburgh names are buried here, including poet Allan Ramsay (1686–1758), architect William Adam (1689–1748) and William Smellie (1740–95), editor of the first edition of *Encyclopaedia Britannica*. On the western side, to the left of the gate into George Heriot's School, a small plaque commemorates William Topaz McGonagall (c 1825–1902) – famed as the world's worst poet – who is buried nearby.

However, the memorial that draws in the biggest crowds by far is the tiny statue of **Greyfriars Bobby**, directly in front of the pub beside the kirkyard gate. Bobby was a Skye terrier who maintained a vigil over the grave of his master, an Edinburgh police officer, from 1858 to 1872. The story was immortalised (and romanticised) by Eleanor Atkinson in her 1912 novel, and in 1963 it was made into a movie by – who else? – Walt Disney.

GREYFRIARS KIRK Map pp224–5

☎ 226 5429; Candlemaker Row; admission free; ☽ 10.30am-4.30pm Mon-Fri & 10.30am-2.30pm Sat Apr-Oct, 1.30-3.30pm Thu Nov-Mar; all George IV Bridge buses

The church of Greyfriars was built on the site of a Franciscan friary and opened for worship on Christmas Day 1620. In 1638 the National Covenant was signed here, rejecting Charles I's attempts to impose episcopacy and a new English prayer book, and affirming the independence of the Scottish Church. Many who signed it were later executed in the Grassmarket and, in 1679, 1200 Covenanters were held prisoner in terrible conditions in an enclosure in the kirkyard.

Inside the church is a small exhibition on the National Covenant, and an original portrait of Greyfriars Bobby dating from 1867. In the kirk you can buy *Greyfriars Bobby – The Real Story at Last* (£4.50), Forbes MacGregor's debunking of some of the myths. Bobby's grave – marked by a small, pink granite stone – is just inside the entrance to the kirkyard. His original collar and bowl are in the Museum of Edinburgh (see p56). At 12.30pm on Sundays there are church services in Gaelic, at which visitors are welcome.

CHAMBERS ST

Broad and elegant Chambers St stretches from Greyfriars Bobby to South Bridge, bordered on its southern side by the twin façades, modern and Victorian, of the Museum of Scotland and the Royal Museum, respectively.

At the eastern end of Chambers St is Edinburgh University's **Old College** (also called the Old Quad; it now houses the Law Faculty), a neoclassical masterpiece designed by Robert Adam in 1789 but not completed till 1834. Inside the Old College, at the College Wynd end, is the Talbot Rice Gallery.

ROYAL MUSEUM & MUSEUM OF SCOTLAND Map pp224–5

☎ 247 4219; www.nms.ac.uk; Chambers St; admission free, except for special exhibitions; ☽ 10am-5pm Mon & Wed-Sat, 10am-8pm Tue, noon-5pm Sun; bus 2, 23, 27, 41, 42

The 19th-century Royal Museum and the late-20th-century Museum of Scotland sit next to each other in Chambers St, one the epitome of Victorian elegance, the other a striking modern edifice in glowing, golden stone.

The **Museum of Scotland** – opened in 1998 – is one of the city's most distinctive new landmarks, and the imaginative interior design is an attraction in itself. The five floors of the museum trace the history of Scotland from its geological beginnings to the 1990s, with many imaginative and stimulating exhibits – it would

South Bridge vaults (p49)

The MacKenzie Poltergeist

Two centuries ago, boys from George Heriot's School would climb over the wall from the school grounds into Greyfriars Kirkyard to dodge lessons. One of their schoolboy dares was to go up to the mausoleum of Sir George MacKenzie, and yell through the keyhole, *'Bluidy MacKenzie come out if ye daur, Lift the sneck and draw the bar'*, before running away giggling and screaming. The tomb was described as long ago as 1824 as 'a place of peculiar horror, as it was supposed to be haunted by the spirit of the bloody persecutor'.

Sir George MacKenzie (1636–91) was the King's Advocate (the chief law officer in Scotland) and was responsible for the persecution of the Covenanters, sending many of them to the gallows – hence his popular nickname, 'Bloody MacKenzie'. Just around the corner from his domed tomb is the Covenanters Prison, a long, narrow corner of Greyfriars Kirkyard where around 1200 Covenanters were incarcerated for five months in appalling conditions, while awaiting trial after the Battle of Bothwell Brig (1679).

In 1999 a homeless man, looking for shelter in the kirkyard on a cold and rainy night, wandered into Bloody MacKenzie's mausoleum. Perhaps fortified by some Buckfast tonic wine, he lifted the metal grating in the floor and descended into the vault. There he found a second, smaller grating in the floor and lifted it too…then accidentally tumbled into the dark hole. The story goes that he found himself sprawled in a mossy heap of human bones, grinning skulls and half-decayed flesh.

Just at that moment, the Greyfriars caretaker passed by, and noticed the door to MacKenzie's tomb was open. He edged inside with his torch, only to be faced with a deranged figure charging up from the vault, wailing and screaming like a madman. Paranormal investigators have theorised that it was the incredible bolt of fear given off by these two men that awakened what has come to be known as the MacKenzie Poltergeist.

Since 1999, the guides who lead ghost tours around Edinburgh's vaults and graveyards have logged around 200 cases of high-level poltergeist activity, including punching, bruising, scratching, hair-pulling and ankle-grabbing, both in the South Bridge vaults (near the former home of Sir George MacKenzie) and in the Covenanters Prison. There have been around 30 incidents where people have actually been rendered unconscious.

The MacKenzie Poltergeist is now the best-documented case of poltergeist activity ever studied. During the Science Festival in 2001, the well-known psychologist and paranormal investigator Dr Richard Wiseman conducted a large-scale experiment in the 'haunted vaults' beneath South Bridge, and concluded that there was a measurable phenomenon that was worthy of further scientific investigation.

Whether that phenomenon is truly paranormal, or just some sort of psychological effect, remains to be seen. Meanwhile, ghost-tour customers are queuing up to scare themselves silly by repeating that ancient schoolboy dare. Bloody MacKenzie come out if ye daur…

take several visits to do it justice. Audioguides are available in several languages.

Highlights of the **Early Peoples** galleries on Level 0, in the basement, include a Roman sculpture of a lioness clutching a human head in her jaws, the 20kg of 5th-century silver that makes up the Traprain Treasure, and heavy silver chains dating from the 5th to 9th centuries that would put a gangsta rapper to shame. Also well worth checking out are the beautiful installations by sculptor Andy Galsworthy, from the huge stacks of old roofing slates to a sphere made entirely of stacked whale bones.

The treasures in the **Kingdom of the Scots** galleries, on Levels 1 and 2, include the famous Monymusk Reliquary, a tiny silver casket dating from AD 750, which is said to have been carried into battle with Robert the Bruce at Bannockburn in 1314; a set of charming, 12th-century chess pieces made from walrus ivory; and the ornate crosier that once belonged to the 8th-century St Fillan.

Levels 3 and 4 follow Scotland's progress through the Industrial Revolution, potently symbolised by the towering Newcomen atmospheric engine that once pumped water from flooded Ayrshire coalmines. The **Ways of Death** exhibit on Level 5 – a Goth's paradise of jet jewellery and mourning bracelets made from human hair – contains several fascinating objects, including eight of the 17 tiny coffins that were discovered on the slopes of Arthur's Seat in 1836 (see p59).

Level 6 is given over to the **Twentieth Century**, with a gallery of objects that were chosen by celebrities and members of the general public as representing their lives. These range from footballer Jim Baxter's shirt, worn when Scotland beat newly crowned world champions England at Wembley in 1967 (nominated by Irvine Welsh) and mountaineer Hamish McInnes's innovative all-metal ice axes, to TV presenter Kirsty Wark's Saab convertible and Prime Minister Tony Blair's Fender Stratocaster electric guitar – make of that what you will. And if you want to feel old, there's nothing like seeing familiar objects that you grew up with confined to museum display cases – everything from a 1970s Trimphone to the original PlayStation is on show here. Don't forget to take the lift to the Roof Terrace for a fantastic view of the castle.

The Museum of Scotland connects with the original **Royal Museum**, dating from 1861, whose stolid, grey exterior gives way to a bright and airy, glass-roofed atrium. The museum houses an eclectic collection covering the natural world (evolution, natural history, minerals, fossils and so on), archaeology, scientific and industrial technology, and the decorative arts of ancient Egypt, Islam, China, Japan, Korea and the West. Volunteers give free, 45-minute guided tours of the Royal Museum (at 3pm daily except Tuesday and Thursday) and Museum of Scotland (at 2pm daily and also at 6pm on Tuesday).

TALBOT RICE GALLERY Map pp224–5

☎ 650 2210; www.trg.ed.ac.uk; Old College, South Bridge; admission free; ☾ 10am-5pm Tues-Sat year-round, 10am-5pm daily during Edinburgh Festival; all South Bridge buses

Established by Edinburgh University in 1975, this small art gallery has two exhibition spaces. The neoclassical Red Gallery was designed by William Playfair, and houses a permanent collection of works by old masters, including Dutch landscapes by Van der Velde and Van der Meulen, and a striking bronze anatomical figure of a horse, created in Florence in 1598.

The **White Gallery** is a more modern space that is used to exhibit the works of contemporary Scottish painters and sculptors.

SURGEON'S HALL MUSEUMS

Map pp224–5

☎ 527 1600; 9 Hill Sq; admission free; ☾ noon-4pm Mon-Fri; all South Bridge buses

Surgeons' Hall, a grand Ionic temple designed by William Playfair, was built in 1832 to house the Royal College of Surgeons of Edinburgh, founded in 1505, one of the oldest surgical corporations in the world. The building's massive portico dominates Nicolson St opposite the Festival Theatre, but the entrance to the museums is around the back in Hill Sq, reached via Hill Pl.

The **Sir Jules Thorn Exhibition** is a fascinating exposition on the history of surgery from the 15th century, when barbers supplemented their income by performing blood-letting, dental extractions, amputations and other surgical procedures, to the present day. The adjacent **Menzies Campbell Dental Museum**, with its collections of wince-inducing extraction tools and inventive dentures, covers the same ground for dentistry.

The more famous **Museum of Anatomy and Pathology** (in the same building), can only be visited by groups of 12 to 24, by prior arrangement; write to the Museum Office at the above address, or email to museum@rcsed.ac.uk. There is no charge for the guided tour, but a donation to cover staff costs is appreciated. Housed in the magnificent Playfair Hall, the museum displays a gruesome but compelling 19th-century teaching collection of diseased organs, tumours and deformed infants pickled in formaldehyde; its most famous exhibit is a wallet fashioned from the skin of the murderer William Burke, who was hanged in the Lawnmarket in 1829.

Neighbourhoods – New Town

NEW TOWN

Eating p105; Drinking p123; Shopping p149; Sleeping p162
Edinburgh's New Town lies north of the Old, on a ridge running parallel to the Royal Mile and separated from it by the valley of Princes St Gardens. Its regular grid of elegant, Georgian terraces is a complete contrast to the chaotic tangle of tenements and wynds that characterises the Old Town.

Between the end of the 14th century and the start of the 18th, the population of Edinburgh – still confined within the walls of the Old Town – increased from 2000 to 50,000. The tottering tenements were unsafe and occasionally collapsed, fire was an ever-present danger and the overcrowding and squalor became unbearable. There was no sewer system and household waste was disposed of by flinging it from the window into the street with a euphemistic shout of 'Gardyloo!' (from the French *'gardez l'eau'* – beware of the water). Passers-by replied with 'Haud yer haun'!' (Hold your hand) but were often too late. The stink that rose from the streets was ironically referred to as 'the floo'rs o' Edinburgh' (the flowers of Edinburgh).

So when the Act of Union in 1707 brought the prospect of long-term stability, the upper classes wanted healthier, spacious living quarters, and in 1766 the Lord Provost of Edinburgh announced a competition to design an extension to the city. It was won by an unknown 23-year-old, James Craig, a self-taught architect whose elegant plan envisaged the New Town's main axis, George St, following the crest of a ridge to the north of Old Town, with squares at each end. Building would be restricted to one side of Princes and Queen Sts, so that the houses had views over the Firth of Forth to the north, and to the castle and Old Town to the south.

During the 18th and 19th centuries, the New Town continued to sprout squares, circuses, parks and terraces, with some of its finest neoclassical architecture designed by Robert Adam. Today, the New Town remains the world's most complete and unspoilt example of Georgian architecture and town planning; along with the Old Town, it was declared a Unesco World Heritage Site in 1995.

Transport

Bus Just about every bus service in Edinburgh runs along Princes St at some point in its journey. But note that not all buses stop at every bus stop – if you're looking for a particular bus, check the route numbers listed on the bus stop sign.

Parking There are multistorey car parks on Castle Tce, just off Lothian Rd at the west end of Princes St, and in the St James Shopping Centre at the east end. There is metered on-street parking in George St, but don't bet on finding a place easily.

PRINCES ST

Princes St is one of the world's most spectacular streets. Built up on one side only – the northern side – it catches the sun in summer and allows expansive views across Princes St Gardens to the castle and the crowded skyline of the Old Town. Sadly, much of its original Georgian elegance was destroyed in the 1960s and '70s with the building of concrete façades and modern shop-fronts; today it is lined with the gaudy colours of all the big players in UK high-street shopping, from Marks & Spencer to MacDonald's. But what a view…

The western end of Princes St is dominated by the red-sandstone edifice of the Caledonian Hotel and the tower of St John's Church, worth visiting for its fine Gothic Revival interior. It overlooks St Cuthbert's Parish Church, built in the 1890s on a site of great antiquity – there has been a church here

New College, Edinburgh University

since at least the 12th century, and perhaps since the 7th century. There is a circular **watch tower** in the graveyard – a reminder of the days when graves had to be guarded against bodysnatchers (see p44).

At the eastern end is the prominent clock tower – traditionally three minutes fast so that you don't miss your train – of the Balmoral Hotel, and the beautiful Register House (1788), designed by Robert Adam, with a statue of the Duke of Wellington on horseback in front. It houses the National Archives of Scotland (see p38).

NATIONAL GALLERY OF SCOTLAND

Map pp224–5

☎ 624 6200; www.nationalgalleries.org; the Mound; admission free, special exhibitions £1-5; ☻ 10am-5pm Fri-Wed, 10am-7pm Thu; all Princes St buses

The National Gallery of Scotland is an imposing neoclassical building with Ionic porticoes, designed by William Playfair and dating from the 1850s. Its octagonal rooms, lit by skylights, have been restored to their original Victorian décor of deep-green carpets and dark-red walls, and occasionally experience a deep rumble from trains passing through the tunnel underneath the building. Annually (in January) the gallery exhibits its collection of Turner watercolours, bequested by Henry Vaughan in 1900.

Highlights of the main galleries include Titian's *Three Ages of Man* (Room I), a meditation on the nature of love with some rather suggestive flute-playing from the shepherdess on the left, and his impressive renderings of *Diana and Actaeon* and *Diana and Callisto* (Room II).

Allegory of the Sense of Smell by 17th-century Dutch artist Jan Weenix is of interest in having once been owned by US press magnate William Randolph Hearst; it also appeared briefly as a backdrop in *Monsieur Beaucaire*, a 1946 movie starring Bob Hope. Rubens' *Salome* and Gainsborough's exquisite portrait of *The Honourable Mrs Graham* are in Room X, while Room XI contains Constable's classic landscape, the *Vale of Dedham,* and a glowing picture of *Niagara Falls* – you can almost hear the thunder of the water – by Frederic Edwin Church.

Room XII is normally graced by Antonio Canova's white marble sculpture of the *Three Graces;* it is owned jointly with London's Victoria & Albert Museum, where it was on display at the time of writing; it will return to the National Gallery of Scotland in 2007.

The upstairs galleries house portraits by Sir Joshua Reynolds and Sir Henry Raeburn, and a clutch of Impressionists including Monet's luminous *Haystacks,* Van Gogh's demonic *Olive Trees,* and Gauguin's hallucinatory *Vision After the Sermon.* But the painting that really catches your eye is the gorgeous portrait of *Lady Agnew of Lochnaw* by John Singer Sargent, with its barely repressed erotic charge – that ever-so-slightly raised right eyebrow speaks volumes.

The basement galleries dedicated to Scottish art includes glowing portraits by Allan Ramsay and Sir Henry Raeburn, rural scenes by Sir David Wilkie and impressionistic landscapes by William MacTaggart. Look out for Raeburn's iconic *Revd Dr Robert Walker Skating on Duddingston Loch,* and Sir George Harvey's hugely entertaining *A Schule Skailin* (A School Emptying) – a stern dominie (teacher) looks on as the boys stampede for the classroom door, one reaching for a spinning top confiscated earlier. Kids will love the fantasy paintings of

The Daily Bang

On Princes St, you can tell locals and visitors apart by their reaction to the sudden explosion that rips through the air each day at one o'clock. Locals check their watches, while visitors shy like startled ponies. It's the One O'Clock Gun, fired from Mills Mount Battery on the castle battlements at 1pm sharp every day except Sunday.

The gun's origins date from the mid-19th century, when the accurate setting of a ship's chronometer was essential for safe navigation (finding your longitude at sea depended on knowing the exact time in your home port). The city authorities installed a time-signal on top of the Nelson Monument on Calton Hill – a ball that was hoist to the top of a flagstaff and dropped exactly on the stroke of one o'clock – that was visible to ships anchored in the Firth of Forth. The gun was added as an audible signal that could be used when rain or mist obscured the ball.

Of course, the ship-bound navigators – and the Edinburgh public – had to make an allowance for the time it took for the sound of the gun (travelling at 330m/s) to reach them. The Edinburgh Post Office Directory used to publish Maps showing the time delay for various places – two seconds for New Town, 11 seconds for Leith and up to 15 seconds for vessels anchored offshore. An interesting little exhibition in the Museum of Edinburgh (see p56) details the history and workings of the One O'Clock Gun.

Sir Joseph Noel Paton in Room B5, incredibly detailed canvases crammed with hundreds of tiny fairies, goblins and elves.

A major building project that will link the Royal Scottish Academy (p68) and the National Gallery via an underground mall was nearing completion at the time of writing. This will increase their gallery space by 4500 sq m, giving them twice the temporary exhibition space of the Prado in Madrid, and three times that of the Royal Academy in London. The project includes a café and restaurant overlooking Princes St Gardens.

PRINCES ST GARDENS Map pp218–20

Princes St; admission free; ☽ dawn to dusk; all Princes St buses

These beautiful gardens lie in a valley that was once occupied by the Nor' Loch (North Loch), a boggy depression that was drained in the early 19th century. They are split in the middle by the **Mound** – around two million cartloads of earth dug out from foundations were dumped here during the construction of the New Town, to provide a road link across the valley to the Old Town. It was completed in 1830.

In the middle of the western part of the gardens is the **Ross Bandstand**, a venue for open-air concerts in summer and during the Hogmanay celebrations, and the stage for the famous Fireworks Concert during the Edinburgh Festival. At the gate beside the Mound is the **Floral Clock**, a working clock laid out in flowers; it was first created in 1903, and the design changes every year.

ROYAL SCOTTISH ACADEMY

Map pp218–20

RSA; ☎ 225 6671; www.royalscottishacademy.org; the Mound; admission free, £3-8.50 for special exhibitions; ☽ 10am-5pm Fri-Wed, 10am-7pm Thu; all Princes St buses

The distinguished Greek Doric temple at the corner of the Mound and Princes St, its northern pediment crowned by a seated figure of Queen Victoria, is the home of the Royal Scottish Academy (RSA). Designed by William Playfair and built between 1823 and 1836, it was originally called the Royal Institution; the RSA took over the building in 1910. The galleries display a collection of paintings, sculptures and architectural drawings by academy members dating from 1831. It also hosts temporary exhibitions throughout the year – details are posted on the academy's website.

SCOTT MONUMENT Map pp218–20

☎ 529 4068; East Princes St Gardens; admission £2.50; ☽ 9am-6pm Mon-Sat & 10am-6pm Sun Apr-Sep, 9am-3pm Mon-Sat & 10am-3pm Sun Oct-Mar; all Princes St buses

The eastern half of Princes St Gardens is dominated by the massive Gothic spire of the Scott Monument. Built by public subscription in memory of the novelist Sir Walter Scott after his death in 1832, it testifies to a popularity largely inspired by his role in rebuilding pride in Scottish identity. You can climb the 287 steps to the top for a superb view of the city; the stone figures that decorate the niches on the monument represent characters from Scott's novels. The statue of Scott, with his favourite deerhound Maida, at the base of the monument was carved from a single, 30-tonne block of white Italian marble.

GEORGE ST

Until recently, George St – the major axis running through the New Town – was the centre of Edinburgh's financial industry and Scotland's equivalent of Wall St. Now many of the big financial firms have relocated to premises in the new Exchange district west of Lothian Rd, and George St's banks and office buildings have been taken over by designer boutiques, trendy bars and upmarket restaurants.

At the western end of George St is **Charlotte Square**, the architectural jewel of the New Town, designed by Robert Adam shortly before his death in 1791. The northern side of the square is Adam's masterpiece and one of the finest examples of Georgian architecture anywhere. **Bute House**, in the centre at No 6, is the official residence of Scotland's first minister. Just off the southeastern corner of the square, at 16 South Charlotte St, a plaque marks the house where **Alexander Graham Bell**, the inventor of the telephone, was born in 1847.

On the western side of Charlotte Sq, the former St George's Church (1811) is now **West Register House**, an annexe to Register House in Princes St. It houses Maps and plans owned by the National Archives of Scotland and mounts occasional exhibitions in the entrance hall.

St Andrew Square is not as distinguished architecturally as its sister at the opposite end of George St. This is where the first houses in the New Town were built – compare the rubble walls (originally covered in stucco)

of Nos 23 to 26 on the northern side of the square (built in 1772), with the smooth, ashlar masonry and unified façades of Charlotte Sq.

Dominating St Andrew Sq is the fluted column of the **Melville Monument**, commemorating Henry Dundas, first viscount Melville (1742–1811), who was the most powerful Scottish politician of his time, often referred to when alive as the 'Harry IX, the Uncrowned King of Scotland'. The impressive Palladian mansion of **Dundas House** (built between 1772 and 1774) on the eastern side of the square was built for Sir Laurence Dundas (1712–81) – no relation to Viscount Melville. It has been the head office of the Royal Bank of Scotland since 1825 and has a spectacular domed banking hall dating from 1857 (you can nip inside for a look).

A short distance along George St is the **Church of St Andrew & St George**, built in 1784, with an unusual oval nave. It was the scene of the Disruption of 1843, when 451 dissenting ministers left the Church of Scotland to form the Free Church.

GEORGIAN HOUSE Map pp218–20

☎ 226 2160; 7 Charlotte Sq; adult/child £5/3.75; ☼ 10am-5pm Apr-Oct, 11am-3pm Mar & 1 Nov-24 Dec; bus 13, 19, 36, 37, 41

Owned by the National Trust for Scotland (NTS), the Georgian House (dating from 1796) has been beautifully restored to show how Edinburgh's wealthy elite lived at the end of the 18th century. The rooms are furnished with the finest period furniture and the walls are decorated with paintings by Allan Ramsay, Henry Raeburn and Sir Joshua Reynolds. There are costumed guides on hand to add a bit of character, and a 35-minute video presentation helps to bring the place to life.

NATIONAL TRUST FOR SCOTLAND

Map pp218–20

NTS; ☎ 243 9300; www.nts.org.uk; 28 Charlotte Sq; admission free; ☼ 10am-5pm Mon-Sat; bus 13, 19, 36, 37, 41

The headquarters of the NTS is on the southern side of Charlotte Sq. As well as a shop, café and information desk the building contains a restored 1820s **drawing room** (☼ 11am-3pm Mon-Fri) with Regency furniture and a collection of 20th-century Scottish paintings.

SCOTTISH NATIONAL PORTRAIT GALLERY Map pp218–20

☎ 624 6200; 1 Queen St; admission free; ☼ 10am-5pm Mon-Sat & noon-5pm Sun, hours extended during Edinburgh Festival; all York Pl buses

Just north of St Andrew Sq, at the junction with Queen St, is the Venetian Gothic palace of the Scottish National Portrait Gallery. Its galleries depict Scottish history through portraits and sculptures of famous Scottish personalities, from Robert Burns and Bonnie Prince Charlie to Sean Connery and Billy Connolly. It also houses the National Photography Collection, which includes works by David Octavius Hill and Robert Adamson, the 19th-century Scottish pioneers of portrait photography.

Edinburgh for Children

The Edinburgh and Scotland Information Centre (p199) has lots of info on children's events, and the handy guidebook *Edinburgh for Under Fives* (£5.95) can be found in most bookshops. *The List* magazine (£2.20; www.list.co.uk) has a special Kids' section listing children's activities and events in and around Edinburgh. The week-long **Children's International Theatre Festival** (☎ 225 8050; www.edinburgh-festivals.com/childrens) takes place each year in late May/early June.

There are good, safe **playgrounds** in most Edinburgh parks, including Princes St Gardens West, Inverleith Park (opposite the Royal Botanic Garden), George V Park (New Town), the Meadows and Bruntsfield Links.

Ideas for outdoor activities include: going to see the animals at **Edinburgh Zoo** (p78); exploring the **Royal Botanic Garden** (p72); visiting **Greyfriars Bobby's statue** (p63); and feeding the swans or playing on the beach at **Cramond** (p76). During the Festival and Fringe there's lots of **street theatre** for kids, especially on the High St and at the foot of the Mound, and in December there's an **open-air ice rink** and **fairground rides** in Princes St Gardens.

If it's raining, you can visit the **Museum of Scotland** (p63), which offers the Discovery Centre, a hands-on activity zone on Level 3, and the dioramas of ancient forests on Level 0, where you can play 'spot the animals'; play on the flumes at the **Royal Commonwealth Pool** (p143); try out the earthquake simulator at **Our Dynamic Earth** (p59); or take a tour of the haunted **Real Mary King's Close** (p56-7).

CALTON HILL

Calton Hill (100m), which rises dramatically above the eastern end of Princes St, is Edinburgh's acropolis, its summit scattered with grandiose memorials, mostly dating from the first half of the 19th century. It is also one of the best viewpoints in Edinburgh, with a panorama that takes in the castle, Holyrood, Arthur's Seat, the Firth of Forth, New Town and the full length of Princes St.

Approaching from Princes St along Waterloo Pl, you pass over **Regent Bridge**, built across the chasm of Calton St between 1816 and 1819 to give access to Calton Hill and allowing the development of the exclusive Georgian terraces on its northern and southeastern sides. (Fans of the film *Trainspotting* might recognise Calton St – it's where Renton spreadeagles himself across a car bonnet in the opening sequence of the movie.)

Old Calton Burying Ground, on the southern side of Waterloo Pl, is one of Edinburgh's many atmospheric old cemeteries. It is dominated by the tall black obelisk of the Political Martyrs' Monument, which commemorates those who suffered in the fight for electoral reform in the 1790s. In the southern corner is the massive, cylindrical grey stone tomb of David Hume (1711–76), Scotland's most famous philosopher. Hume was a noted atheist, prompting rumours that he had made a Faustian pact with the devil; after his death his friends held a vigil at the tomb for eight nights, burning candles and firing pistols into the darkness lest evil spirits should come to bear away his soul. Near the tomb is a statue of Abraham Lincoln, commemorating Scots-Americans who died in the American Civil War.

Beyond Waterloo Pl, on Regent Rd, is the modernist façade of **St Andrew's House** (built between 1936 and 1939), which housed the civil servants of the Westminster government's Scottish Office until they were moved to the new Scottish Executive building in Leith in 1996. It was built on the site of Calton Gaol, the successor to the much-despised Tolbooth in the High St, and once the biggest prison in Scotland. All that remains is the distinctive turreted building just west of St Andrew's House, and well seen from North Bridge – this was the **Governor's House**, built in 1817.

Just beyond St Andrew's House, on the opposite side of the road, is the imposing Royal High School building, dating from 1829 and modelled on the Temple of Theseus in Athens. Former pupils include 18th-century architect Robert Adam, Alexander Graham Bell (inventor of the telephone) and novelist Sir Walter Scott. The building was at one time cited as a potential home for the new Scottish parliament, but it now stands empty. To its east, on the other side of Regent Rd, is the **Burns Monument** (1830), a Greek-style memorial to Robert Burns. It was designed by Thomas Hamilton, another former pupil of the school.

You can reach the summit of Calton Hill by the road that runs behind the Royal High School or via the stairs at the eastern end of Waterloo Pl. The largest structure on the summit is the **National Monument**, a rather over-ambitious attempt to replicate the Parthenon and intended to honour Scotland's dead in the Napoleonic Wars. Construction – paid for by public subscription – began in 1822 but funds ran dry when only 12 columns had been erected. It became known locally as 'Edinburgh's Disgrace'.

The design of the **City Observatory**, built in 1818, was based on the ancient Greek Temple of the Winds in Athens. Its original function was to provide a precise, astronomical time-keeping service for marine navigators. Smoke from Waverley train station forced the astronomers to move to Blackford Hill (see p78) in 1895, and since 1953 the City Observatory has been home to the Astronomical Society of Edinburgh (☎ 556 4365; www.astronomyedinburgh.org). Visitors with an interest in astronomy are welcome to attend when the telescopes are in operation (most Friday evenings when the sky is clear, between 8pm and 10pm).

Just downhill from the observatory is the small, circular **Monument to Dugald Stewart** (1753–1828), who was Professor of Mathematics and of Moral Philosophy at Edinburgh University.

NELSON MONUMENT Map pp218–20

☎ 556 2716; Calton Hill; admission £2; ☿ 1-6pm Mon & 10am-6pm Tue-Sat Apr-Sep, 10am-3pm Mon-Sat Oct-Mar; all Leith St buses

Looking a bit like an upturned telescope – the similarity is intentional – and offering superb views, the Nelson Monument was built to commemorate Admiral Lord Nelson's victory at Trafalgar in 1805. In 1852 a time-ball was added as a time signal for ships anchored in the Firth of Forth (see p67) – it still drops from the cross-bars of the mast at the top of the monument at 1pm every day.

BROUGHTON

The bohemian neighbourhood of Broughton, centred on Broughton St at the north-eastern corner of the New Town, is the focus of Edinburgh's gay nightlife (see p133) and home to many good bars (p125) and restaurants (p105).

Transport

Bus Nos 8 and 17 go to Broughton St, from Princes St and South Bridge, respectively.

Parking There is limited, metered on-street parking, but it's better to use the multistorey car parks in the St James Centre and Omni Centre.

EDINBURGH PRINTMAKERS' WORKSHOP & GALLERY Map pp218–20
☎ 557 2479; 23 Union St; ☽ 10am-6pm Tue-Sat; bus 8, 17

Founded in 1967, this was the UK's first 'open-access' print-making studio, providing studio space and equipment for professional artists and beginners alike. You can watch printmakers at work in the ground floor studio, while the first floor gallery hosts exhibitions of lithographs and screenprints by local artists. If you fancy having a go yourself, the workshop offers two-day weekend courses (£95) in screenprinting, lithography, etching and relief printing.

MANSFIELD PLACE CHURCH

Map pp218–20
☎ 474 8033; www.mansfieldtraquair.org.uk; Mansfield Pl; ☽ 1-4pm 2nd Sun of month Jul-Dec, 10-11.45am Mon-Sat during Edinburgh Festival; bus 8, 13, 17

In complete contrast to the austerity of most of Edinburgh's religious buildings, the 19th-century, neo-Romanesque Mansfield Place Church at the foot of Broughton St contains a remarkable series of Renaissance-style frescoes painted in the 1890s by Irish-born artist Phoebe Anna Traquair (1852–1936). The church has been converted for use as office space, but the murals – now undergoing restoration – are on view to the public at certain times (check the website for the latest details).

STOCKBRIDGE & DEAN VILLAGE

The New Town's Georgian architecture extends north into Stockbridge, a trendy district with its own distinct identity, some interesting shops and a good choice of pubs and restaurants. Originally a milling community, Stockbridge was developed in the early 19th century on lands owned largely by the painter, Sir Henry Raeburn. The garden villas along **Ann St**, named after Raeburn's wife and dating from 1817, are among the most beautiful and desirable houses in Edinburgh, while the giant Doric columns that line **St Bernard's Crescent** are the most grandiose decoration on any private residence in the city.

If you follow Queensferry St northwards from the western end of Princes St, you come to the **Dean Bridge**, designed by Thomas Telford and built between 1829 and 1832. Vaulting gracefully over the narrow, steep-sided valley of the Water of Leith, it was built to allow the New Town to expand to the northwest. It became notorious as a suicide spot – it soars 27m above the river – and in 1912 the parapets were raised to deter jumpers.

Down in the valley, just west of the bridge, is **Dean Village** (*dene* is a Scots word for valley); to get there, descend the steep, cobbled lane of Bell's Brae at the southern end of Dean Bridge. The village was founded as a milling community by the canons of Holyrood Abbey in the 12th century and by 1700 there were 11 water mills here, which were operated by the Incorporation of Baxters (the bakers' trade guild). One of the old mill buildings has been converted into flats, and the village is now an attractive residential area.

Several 17th-century houses and carved stones remain. On the parapet of the **old bridge** (18th-century) at the foot of Bell's Brae, there is a carving showing crossed 'peels' – long shovels for putting loaves into ovens – and the inscription 'Blesit be God for al His giftis'. On the door lintel of the house opposite is another carving of crossed peels with three loaves of bread, and the words 'God bless the Baxters of Edinbrugh uho bult this hous 1675'.

From the old bridge, you can follow the Water of Leith Walkway downstream to Stockbridge (10 minutes – see p93), or follow the signs upstream to the Scottish National Gallery of Modern Art (15 minutes).

DEAN GALLERY Map p217

☎ 624 6200; 73 Belford Rd; admission free except for special exhibitions; 10am-5pm Fri-Wed, 10am-7pm Thu; bus 13

Directly across Belford Rd from the Scottish National Gallery of Modern Art, another neoclassical mansion houses its adjunct, the Dean Gallery. The Dean holds the Gallery of Modern Art's collection of Dada and surrealist art, including works by Dali, Giacometti and Picasso, and a large collection of sculpture and graphic art created by the Edinburgh-born sculptor Sir Eduardo Paolozzi.

ROYAL BOTANIC GARDEN Map pp214–15

☎ 552 7171; www.rbge.org.uk; 20a Inverleith Row; admission free; 10am-7pm Apr-Sep, 10am-6pm Mar & Oct, 10am-4pm Nov-Feb; bus 8, 17, 23, 27, 37

A 10-minute walk northwards from Stockbridge along St Bernard's Row, Arboretum Ave and Arboretum Pl leads to the Royal Botanic

Garden. Founded near Holyrood in 1670 and moved to its present location in 1823, Edinburgh's Botanic Garden is the second oldest institution of its kind in Britain (after Oxford), and one of the most respected in the world. Seventy beautifully landscaped acres include splendid Victorian palm houses, colourful swathes of rhododendron and azalea, and a world-famous rock garden. The Terrace Cafe offers good views towards the city centre.

SCOTTISH NATIONAL GALLERY OF MODERN ART Map p217

☎ 624 6200; 75 Belford Rd; admission free, special exhibitions £1-5; 10am-5pm Fri-Wed, 10am-7pm Thu; bus 13

Set in a neoclassical building surrounded by a sculpture park, 500m west of Dean Village, is the Scottish National Gallery of Modern Art. The collection – housed in bright, modern galleries that belie the building's austere façade – concentrates on 20th-century art, with various European art movements represented by the likes of Matisse, Picasso, Kirchner, Magritte, Miro, Mondrian and Giacometti. American and English artists are also represented, but most space is given to Scottish painters – from the Scottish colourists of the early 20th century to contemporary artists, such as Peter Howson and Ken Currie. There's an excellent café downstairs and the surrounding park features sculptures by Henry Moore, Sir Eduardo Paolozzi and Barbara Hepworth among others.

Transport

Bus Nos 24, 29 and 42 run from Frederick St in the city centre to Raeburn Pl in Stockbridge. For Dean Village, take bus 13, 19, 37 or 41 from George St to Dean Bridge and walk down Bell's Brae.

Parking There is metered on-street parking in Stockbridge and Dean Village, but spaces are very limited; it's better not to bring a car.

Façades on Victoria Terrace

EDINBURGH WEST

Eating p110; Drinking p126; Shopping p153; Sleeping p165

This neighbourhood stretches from the western edge of the New Town to Dalry, taking in the new financial district called the Exchange, the shopping streets of the West End, and Haymarket, home to Edinburgh's other train station. There are no tourist attractions here, but you'll find some good places to stay (p165) and some excellent places to eat (p110).

The West End is an extension of the New Town, all Georgian elegance and upmarket shops, but the shiny new Exchange district to its south is a maze of chrome, glass and sandstone modernity, with people in suits striding purposefully between office blocks. Haymarket and Dalry were once working-class industrial areas – there are still two working breweries in the area – but the opening of new restaurants on Dalry Rd and the building of new luxury apartments in Dalry and Port Hamilton – the Edinburgh terminus of the Union Canal (see p97 and p178) – seem to point the way to the neighbourhood's future gentrification.

Transport

Bus Lothian Buses 3, 4, 12, 25, 26, 31, 33 and 44 head west from Princes St, along Shandwick Pl to Haymarket. Nos 3, 4, 25, 33 and 44 continue southwest on Dalry Rd, while 12, 26 and 31 head west towards Murrayfield Stadium and Corstorphine.

EDINBURGH SOUTH

Eating p111; Drinking p127; Shopping p153; Sleeping p166

Edinburgh South wraps around the southern edge of the Old Town from Lothian Rd and Bruntsfield to Holyrood Park, taking in the 19th-century tenement districts of Bruntsfield, Marchmont and Sciennes (pronounced 'sheens') and the elegant villa quarters of Morningside, Grange and Newington. Away from the main thoroughfares of Lothian Rd/Home St/Bruntsfield Pl and Clerk St/South Clerk St/Newington Rd, it's a peaceful residential neighbourhood of smart Victorian tenement flats and spacious garden villas, stretching south from the peaceful, green oasis of the Meadows. There's not much to see in the area, but there are many good restaurants (p111), pubs (p127) and places to stay (p166).

The eastern half of the neighbourhood, which includes Edinburgh University's main campus, centred on George Sq, and Pollock Halls of Residence, has a sizable student population, and the bookshops, bars, cafés and good-value restaurants that go along with it. Southside flats also became popular with the hundreds of nurses and doctors who work at the Edinburgh Royal Infirmary, but the hospital's move from Lauriston Pl to a new greenbelt site in 2003 means that they are now faced with a rather longer commute.

Transport

Bus The main bus routes south from the city centre are Nos 10, 11, 15, 16, 17, 23, 27 and 45 from the west end of Princes St to Tollcross (all except 10 and 27 continue south to Bruntsfield and Morningside); and Nos 3, 5, 7, 8, 29, 31, 37 and 49 from North Bridge to Newington. Buses 24 and 41 run from Princes St and Hanover St, respectively, to Melville Dr on the south side of the Meadows.

The southwestern part, around the Grange and Morningside suburbs, is characterised by garden villas built in the 19th century for Edinburgh's middle and upper classes. Morningside in particular became a byword for respectability; indeed, 'Morningside' is now often used as an adjective describing traditional Edinburgh middle-class respectability. Today this part of Edinburgh is still affluent but much more laid-back, its spacious villas and apartments much sought after by Edinburgh's urban professionals.

THE MEADOWS

Melville Dr; admission free; ☺ 24 hr; bus 5, 24, 41

This mile-long stretch of lush grass, criss-crossed with tree-lined walks, was once a shallow lake known as the Borough Loch. It was drained in the 1740s and converted into parkland for the newly emerging middle classes to enjoy – Melville Dr (now a main road) and Middle Meadow Walk were laid out as carriage drives and footpaths.

The park is a great place for a picnic or a quiet walk, away from the city bustle – in spring its walks lie ankle-deep in drifts of pink cherry blossom, and there are great views of Arthur's Seat. There are amateur cricket matches in summer, and impromptu football games in winter. Each year, on the first weekend in June, the park hosts the two-day **Meadows Festival** (www .meadowsfestival.co.uk), with fun-fair and live music.

WATERFRONT EDINBURGH

Eating p116; Drinking p129; Shopping p155; Sleeping p169

Edinburgh's waterfront stretches for 10 miles along the southern shore of the Firth of Forth, from the pretty riverside village of Cramond in the west to the seaside suburb of Portobello in the east, taking in the former fishing village of Newhaven and the redeveloped industrial docklands of Leith. The western part, from Cramond to Granton, is pleasantly rural, with a quiet, traffic-free promenade walk; the central part, from Granton to Leith, is lined up for a major redevelopment to take place over the next 10 years or so (see p18).

LEITH

Leith – located 2 miles northeast of the city centre – has been Edinburgh's seaport since the 14th century, and remained an independent burgh with its own town council until it was incorporated by the city during the 1920s. Like many of Britain's dockland areas, it fell into decay in the decades following WWII but has been undergoing a revival since the late 1980s. Old warehouses have been turned into luxury flats and a lush crop of trendy bars and restaurants has sprouted up right along the waterfront. The area was given an additional boost in the late 1990s when the Scottish Office (a government department, now renamed the Scottish Executive) relocated to a new building on Leith docks.

The city council has now formulated a major redevelopment plan for the entire Edinburgh waterfront from Leith to Granton, the first phase of which is **Ocean Terminal**, a shopping and leisure complex that includes the former Royal Yacht *Britannia* and a berth for visiting cruise liners. Parts of Leith are still a bit rough – Coburg St, for example, is a notorious red-light district – but it's a distinctive corner of the city and well worth exploring.

The most attractive part of old Leith is the **Shore**, where the Water of Leith runs into Leith Docks. Before the docks were built in the 19th century, this was Leith's original wharf. An iron plaque set into the quay in front of No 30 The Shore marks the **King's Landing** – the spot where King George IV (the first reigning British monarch to visit Scotland since Charles II in 1650) stepped ashore in 1822.

Located north of the bridge across the river is the circular **Signal Tower**, built in 1686, and originally a windmill; it now houses the excellent Fisher's seafood restaurant (see p116). Beyond is the 19th-century baronial façade and clock tower of the old Sailor's Home, now the Malmaison Hotel (see p169).

Leith Links, a public park located in the eastern part of Leith, was originally common grazing land, but is more famous as the home of the game of golf. Although golf has not been played on the links since the 19th century, the game has a very long history in Leith. The kirk Session Records of 1610 for the parish church of South Leith note that the Session agreed that there should be no 'public playing suffered on the Sabbath dayes. As playing at the valley bowles, at the penny stane, archery, gowfe etc'.

Transport

Bus Lothian Buses 10, 12, 16, and 22 run from Princes St down Leith Walk to the junction of Constitution and Great Junction Sts; from here 10 and 16 go west to terminate at Newhaven; 12 goes along Constitution St then east to Portobello; 22 goes north to The Shore and Ocean Terminal. Bus 35 runs from the Royal Mile (eastbound) to Ocean Terminal. Buses 1, 11, 34 and 36 also terminate at Ocean Terminal. Buses 7, 11, and 32 also go to Newhaven.

Parking There are large multistorey car parks at Ocean Terminal and Newkirkgate shopping centre. On-street parking is limited; your best bet is on Commercial St.

ROYAL YACHT BRITANNIA Map p216

☎ 555 5566; www.royalyachtbritannia.co.uk; Ocean Terminal, Leith; adult/child £8/4; ☾ 9.30am-6pm Apr-Sep, 10am-5pm Oct-Mar, 10am-4pm 24 & 31 Dec, last admission 1½ hrs before closing; bus 1, 11, 22, 34, 35, 36

One of Edinburgh's biggest tourist attractions is the former Royal Yacht *Britannia*. She was the Royal Family's floating home during their foreign travels from her launch in 1953 until her decommissioning in 1997, and is now moored permanently in front of Ocean Terminal.

The tour, which you take at your own pace with an audioguide (also available in French, German, Italian and Spanish), gives an intriguing insight into the Queen's private tastes – *Britannia* was one of the few places where the Royal Family could enjoy true privacy. The entire ship is a monument to 1950s' décor and technology, and the accommodation reveals Her Majesty's preference for simple, unfussy surroundings – the Queen's own bed is surprisingly tiny and plain. In fact, the initial interior design was rejected by the Queen for being too flashy.

There was nothing simple or unfussy about the running of the ship, though. When the Queen travelled, along with her went 45 members of the Royal Household, five tons of luggage and a Rolls-Royce that was carefully squeezed into a specially built garage on the deck. The ship's company consisted of an admiral, 20 officers and 220 yachtsmen. The decks (of Burmese teak) were scrubbed daily, but all work near the royal accommodation was carried out in complete silence and had to be finished by 8am. A thermometer was kept in the Queen's bathroom to make sure that the water was the correct temperature, and when in harbour one yachtsman was charged with ensuring that the angle of the gangway never exceeded 12 degrees. And note the mahogany windbreak that was added to the balcony deck in front of the bridge – it was put there to stop wayward breezes from blowing up skirts and inadvertently revealing the Royal Undies.

The Britannia Tour bus (see p49) runs from Waverley Bridge to *Britannia*.

TRINITY HOUSE Map p216

☎ 554 3829; 99 Kirkgate; adult/child £2.50/1; ☾ guided tours only, phone to book in advance; all Leith buses

Four hundred yards (364m) south of The Shore, hidden away in the incongruous surroundings of the modern Newkirkgate shopping centre, is a neoclassical building dating from 1816. It was the headquarters of the Incorporation of Masters and Mariners (founded in 1380), the nautical equivalent of a tradesmen's guild, and is a treasure house of old ship models, navigation instruments and nautical memorabilia relating to Leith's maritime history. The management of Trinity House was taken over

Royal Yacht Britannia

Golf on the Links

Although St Andrews claims seniority in having the oldest golf course in the world, it was at Leith Links in 1744 that the first official rules of the game were formulated by the Honorable Company of Edinburgh Golfers – these 13 rules formed the basis of the modern game. Rule No 9 gives some insight into the 18th-century game – 'If a ball be stop'd by any person, Horse, Dog or anything else, the Ball so stop'd must be played where it lyes'. The original document is in the National Library of Scotland and the Honorable Company is now the famous Muirfield Golf Club. A stone cairn on the western side of the links bears a plaque that describes how the game was played over five holes, each being around 400 yards. There are plans to re-create one of the original holes, along with a permanent exhibition.

by the Historic Scotland agency in 2001, but at the time of writing it was open for pre-booked guided tours only. A £2.65 million scheme to regenerate the Kirkgate area of Leith was approved in 2003, and the building may eventually be opened to the public.

NEWHAVEN

Immediately to the west of Leith, Newhaven was once a distinctive fishing community whose fishwives tramped the streets of Edinburgh's New Town selling 'caller herrin' (fresh herring) from wicker creels on their backs. Sadly, modern development has dispelled the fishing-village atmosphere, with ugly flats mixed in among the old cottages and terraces. The old fish-market building beside the little harbour now houses the Newhaven Heritage Museum, and the former church is now home to Alien Rock indoor climbing centre (p141).

NEWHAVEN HERITAGE MUSEUM

Map pp214–15

☎ 551 4165; 24 Pier Pl; admission free; ☽ noon-4.45pm; bus 7, 10, 11, 16, 32

The former fish-market on the eastern side of the harbour now houses a small museum decked out with tableaux celebrating the lives of Newhaven fishers, and the origins of Newhaven as a naval dockyard. A 15-minute video illustrates the hard-working lifestyle that survived here until the 1950s when overfishing put paid to the traditional source of income.

SEA.FARI ADVENTURES Map pp214–15

☎ 331 5000; www.seafari.co.uk; Newhaven Harbour; adult/child cruises from £15/12; ☽ 10am-5pm May-Sep; bus 7, 10, 11, 16, 32

During the summer you can take a tour around the Firth of Forth on a high-speed RIB (semi-rigid inflatable boat). Sea.fari runs cruises from Newhaven, weather permitting, to visit seal and seabird colonies around the islands of Inchkeith and Inchcolm. A one-hour cruise costs £15/12 per adult/child and a two-hour cruise costs £20/15 – telephone Sea.fari to check cruise times and book tickets. Waterproofs and lifejackets are provided, but dress warmly too.

CRAMOND

With its moored yachts, stately swans and whitewashed houses spilling down a hillside at the mouth of the River Almond, Cramond is Edinburgh's most picturesque village. It is also rich in history – it has long been known that the Romans built a fort here in the 2nd century AD (the village's name comes from *Caer Amon*, 'the fort on the River Almond'), but recent archaeological excavations have revealed evidence of a Bronze-Age settlement as long ago as 8500 BC, the oldest known site in the whole of Scotland.

Cramond, which was originally a mill village, has an historic, 17th-century church, a 15th-century tower house and some rather unimpressive Roman remains, but most visitors come to enjoy a walk along the river to the ruined mills or to take the rowing-boat ferry across the river to Dalmeny Estate.

Transport

Bus Lothian Buses 24 and 41 run to Cramond, the former from Lothian Rd and Princes St, the latter from George IV Bridge, the Mound and George St. From the Cramond bus stop, it's a 400m walk north along Cramond Glebe Rd to the village.

Ferry At the time of writing the Cramond Ferry (adult/child 50/10p; ☽ 9am-1pm & 2-7pm Sat-Thu Apr-Sep, 10am-1pm & 2-4pm Sat-Thu Oct-Mar) was closed 'until further notice', while the jetty is repaired; it should open again in summer 2004.

Parking There is a large car park off Cramond Glebe Rd, signposted on the right just as the road narrows. Do not continue past this turn-off – parking is not allowed beyond this point.

About a mile from the mouth of the river lies **Cramond Island**, uninhabited except for nesting seabirds. The gap between the island and the shore is spiked with a row of concrete teeth – a WWII barrier designed to prevent miniature submarines from creeping upstream to Rosyth naval base. You can walk out to the island at low tide – there are some small sandy beaches that make pleasant summer picnic sites. The walk takes about 20 minutes and the safe period for crossing lasts from two hours before to two hours after the time of low water.

To check on tide times call **Forth Coastguard** (☎ 01333-450666). Do *not* cross unless you are sure of the tides – every year dozens of people get caught out and have to be rescued.

There are a couple of good places in Cramond to stop for a drink, or even a meal. See p117.

DALMENY HOUSE Map pp214–15
☎ 331 1888; www.dalmeny.co.uk; Dalmeny Estate; adult/child £4/2; ⏱ 2-5.30pm Sun-Tue Jul & Aug; passenger ferry from Cramond

A leisurely 30-minute walk through the wooded grounds of the Dalmeny Estate, located on the far bank of the river from Cramond, leads to the stately home of Dalmeny House. Dalmeny is the seat of the earls of Rosebery, and a guided tour of the house – often conducted by the present Lord and Lady Rosebery themselves – takes in beautiful 18th-century furniture, tapestries, porcelain and paintings by Millais, Gainsborough, Reynolds and Raeburn. There is also a fascinating collection of Napoleon Bonaparte memorabilia assembled by the fifth earl of Rosebery.

You can also reach Dalmeny House by car from Edinburgh – head westwards on the A90, following the signs for the Forth Road Bridge, then leave the main road on the B924 to Dalmeny and Queensferry. The entrance to the house is signposted on the right, half a mile after leaving the A90.

THE MALTINGS Map pp214–15
☎ 312 6034; Cramond Village; admission free; ⏱ 2-5pm Sat & Sun Jun-Sep, daily during Edinburgh Festival

Located a wee bit further downstream from the ferry landing you will find the Maltings, which hosts a small exhibition on the hisory of Cramond.

The Cramond Lioness

In November 1996, ferryman Robert Graham, who ran the rowing-boat ferry across the River Almond at Cramond, noticed part of a carved stone sticking out of the mud at low tide. He started to dig it out, thinking it might make a nice ornament for his garden, but when he realised that he was uncovering a five-foot long Roman sculpture of a lioness gripping a man's head in its teeth, he decided he'd better let the experts take over. When the value of his find was realised, Mr Graham received a £50,000 reward for his efforts.

Archaeologists have dated the white sandstone sculpture to the late 2nd or early 3rd century AD, and have conjectured that it was a funerary monument – the 1800-year-old lioness is the only Roman statue of its kind ever found in Britain. At the time of writing it was on display in the Museum of Scotland (p63), but it may eventually be moved to a new interpretation centre that is planned for Cramond.

PORTOBELLO

The northeastern suburb of Portobello is fringed by a mile-long strand of clean, golden sand with expansive views along the Firth of Forth to the conical hill of North Berwick Law (see p183) and across to the rolling fields of Fife. Located 4 miles east of the city centre, Portobello was named after a cottage built there in the 1740s by a veteran of the Battle of Puerto Bello (a naval battle between the British and Spanish in 1739). It saw its first recreational bathers in 1795, when a local entrepreneur introduced bathing machines to the beach, and rapidly grew into a fashionable 19th-century seaside resort known as 'the Brighton of the North'. It was absorbed into Edinburgh in 1896.

Portobello once boasted a ¼-mile long steamer pier (demolished in 1917) and a huge outdoor swimming pool with wave machine (closed in 1980), but its fortunes fell into decline after the 1960s. In recent years, however, there has been much redevelopment, and Porty's popularity is on the

Transport
Bus Lothian bus 15 or 26 (eastbound) from Princes St, or 46 from St Andrew Sq.

rise again. The mile-long **promenade** provides a pleasant seaside walk (go west to east for the best views), the beach swarms with kids on warm summer days, and there are old-fashioned amusement arcades offering slot machines and bingo games. If it's too cold to swim in the sea, there's a restored Victorian **swimming pool** complete with old-fashioned Turkish baths (see p142).

A bronze plaque on a cream-coloured cottage at No 3 Bridge St commemorates the **birthplace of Sir Harry Lauder** (see p32), the famous music-hall entertainer. An attempt has been made to lure performers back to the seaside through the community arts project **Portobello Open Door** (www.the-pod.org); during the second week of August it brings a programme of children's events, music gigs and Festival Fringe acts to Portobello. **Golden Days** (second Saturday in June) is another event that harks back to the 1930s heyday of the seaside holiday, with pony rides on the beach, a sandcastle competition and jazz and swing bands playing in local pubs. And if the New Year's Eve party in the city centre seems too big to handle, Portobello has its own **Hogmanay** celebrations with plenty of fireworks and live music.

GREATER EDINBURGH

Eating p118; Shopping p156

As the city of Edinburgh expanded during the 19th and 20th centuries, it swallowed up several of the outlying villages and rural areas, many of which still preserve a distinct identity within the city today.

The Greater Edinburgh area is a suburban sprawl of villas, bungalows, gardens, parks and the occasional tower block, that encloses the odd hidden corner of history – from leafy Corstorphine to medieval Duddingston and bucolic Swanston to picturesque Queensferry.

CORSTORPHINE

Corstorphine, on the main road west out of the city, is a douce (sedate), middle-class suburb that takes its name from a medieval village – the early-15th-century parish church still survives on Kirk Loan. Its main feature is Corstorphine Hill, a low, wooded lump which is criss-crossed with footpaths, and much frequented by local dog-walkers. Its sunny southern slopes are home to Edinburgh Zoo, the main reason for visiting.

Opened in 1913, and located 2½ miles west of the city centre, Edinburgh Zoo is one of the world's leading conservation zoos. Edinburgh's captive breeding programme has saved many endangered species, including Siberian tigers, pygmy hippos and red pandas. The main attractions are the four species of penguin, kept in the world's biggest penguin pool, the sea lion and red panda feeding times, the animal handling sessions, and the Lifelinks 'hands on' zoology centre.

BLACKFORD HILL

Lying 1½ miles directly south of the city centre, Blackford Hill (164m) offers pleasant walking (see p96) and a splendid panorama of the castle, Old Town and Arthur's Seat. It is also home to the Royal Observatory.

Transport

Bus Lothian bus 12, 26 or 31 (westbound) from Princes St or Shandwick Pl, or Lothian bus 1 from Princes St or Lothian Rd.

Transport

Bus Lothian Bus 41 (southbound) from Hanover St, the Mound or George IV Bridge.

EDINBURGH ZOO Map pp214–15

☎ 334 9171; www.edinburghzoo.org.uk; 134 Corstorphine Rd; adult/child £8/5; ☼ 9am-6pm Apr-Sep; 9am-5pm Oct & Mar; 9am-4.30pm Nov-Feb; bus 12, 26, 31, 100

ROYAL OBSERVATORY OF EDINBURGH Map pp214–15

☎ 668 8404; www.roe.ac.uk; Blackford Hill; adult/child £2.60/1.85; ⏱ 7-8.45pm Fri Oct-Mar; bus 24, 38, 41

The Royal Observatory was built here in 1896 to replace the City Observatory (p70) on Calton Hill whose view of the night sky has been obscured by smoke from Waverley train station. The original dome still houses a 36-inch reflecting telescope, the largest in the UK. Today the observatory is principally an academic institution – its visitor centre closed in September 2003 – but it remains open to the public for observing the night sky on Friday evenings in winter. If the weather is bad, there is a multimedia gallery with computers and CD-ROMs on astronomy, and a shop selling books and gifts.

DUDDINGSTON

Nestling directly beneath the southeastern slopes of Arthur's Seat, the picturesque little village of Duddingston is a place of great antiquity – archaeologists have unearthed Bronze Age remains here. The village itself dates from the 12th century, though all that remains from that date are parts of **Duddingston Parish Church**, which sits on a promontory overlooking Duddingston Loch. The western door of the church is Norman, decorated with chevron patterns and carvings of Christ on the Cross and a soldier with a sword and axe. There are some interesting medieval relics at the kirkyard gate – the **Joug**, a metal collar that was used, like the stocks, to tether criminals and sinners; and the **Loupin-On Stane**, a stone step to help gouty and corpulent worshippers mount their horses. The early-19th-century **watch tower** inside the gate was built to deter body snatchers.

The village itself consists of only two streets – Old Church Lane and The Causeway. At the western end of the latter stands an 18th-century pub, the **Sheep Heid** (see p128), and at the eastern end is **Prince Charlie's Cottage**, where the Young Pretender held a council of war before the Battle of Prestonpans in 1745.

To climb **Arthur's Seat** (251m) from Duddingston, head westwards from the church to the parking area just inside the gate to Holyrood Park, then turn right and climb up the steep stairs known as Jacob's Ladder to another road. Turn right, and when you reach another parking area (200m), leave the road and take the path on the left to the summit (20 to 30 minutes total).

Transport

Bus Lothian Bus 42 (southbound) from Hanover St, the Mound or George IV Bridge.

SWANSTON

Huddled in the shadow of the Pentland Hills on the southern fringe of the city, the tiny hamlet of Swanston is an unlikely survivor – a village green, an old schoolhouse and a square of whitewashed cottages with reed-thatched roofs barely 500m from the roaring traffic of Edinburgh's ring-road. This picturesque spot is a favourite starting point for walks into the Pentland Hills, but is most famous as the childhood summer retreat of Robert Louis Stevenson. Stevenson's father leased the nearby 18th-century villa, **Swanston Cottage**, as a summer home from 1867 to 1880, hoping that the clean air would improve the health of his sickly son.

Transport

Bus Take bus 4 (westbound) from Princes St and get off at Oxgangs Rd, just past Hunter's Tryst, then walk 750m southwards on Swanston Rd.

QUEENSFERRY

Although Queensferry lies 8 miles (13km) west of the city centre, on the southern bank of the Firth of Forth, it falls within the official boundaries of the city of Edinburgh. Located at the narrowest part of the firth, it served as a port for the ferries that plied across the water to Fife from the earliest times, ceasing only in 1964 when the graceful **Forth Road Bridge** – now the fifth longest in Europe – was opened. The **Forth Bridge** predates the Forth Road Bridge by 74 years.

Queensferry is a lively and attractive village, with cobbled lanes, 17th- and 18th-century terraced houses and a picturesque little harbour. There are several good pubs

Water of Leith

Edinburgh's river is a modest stream, flowing only 20 miles (32km) from the northwestern slopes of the Pentland Hills through western and northern Edinburgh to enter the Firth of Forth at Leith. Rarely more than 9m across, it cuts a surprisingly rural swathe through the city, offering the chance to stroll along wooded riverbanks only 500m from Princes St.

Throughout history the river has served as a source of power for water-mills (see p71) and a convenient waste-disposal system, but it has now been cleaned up and provides an important wildlife habitat (you can see otters and kingfishers) and recreation resource for walkers and anglers. The **Water of Leith Walkway**, a project that started in the 1970s, is now nearing completion, offering an almost uninterrupted walking and cycling route along the river from Leith to the village of Balerno, on the southwestern edge of the city. There are access points and signposts throughout its length.

The **Water of Leith Visitor Centre** (Map pp214–15; ☎ 455 7367; www.waterofleith.org.uk; 24 Lanark Rd; adult/child £1.90/1.20; ☾ 10am-4pm daily Apr-Sept, 10am-4pm Wed-Sun Oct-Mar) has interactive displays on the river's wildlife and ecology, and underwater video cameras that allow you to watch aquatic creatures live.

To get to the visitor centre take bus No 28, 35, 44 or 66.

along the High St. One of them is the **Hawes Inn** (p118), famously mentioned in Robert Louis Stevenson's novel *Kidnapped*; it's opposite the Inchcolm ferry, beneath the railway bridge.

Transport

Bus Take First Edinburgh bus 43 (£1.80; 30 minutes) westbound from Princes St (eastern end) or Charlotte Sq; there's a bus every 20 minutes. It's a 10-minute walk eastwards from the bus stop to the Hawes Inn and the Inchcolm ferry.

Parking There is plenty of free parking along the seafront west of the Hawes Inn.

Train There are frequent trains (£2.90; 15 minutes) from Edinburgh Waverley and Haymarket to Dalmeny station. From the station exit, the Hawes Inn is a five-minute walk away along a footpath (across the road, behind the bus stop) that leads north beside the railway and under the bridge.

FORTH BRIDGE

The magnificent Forth Bridge – only outsiders ever call it the Forth Rail Bridge – is one of the finest engineering achievements of the 19th century. Completed in 1890 after seven years' work, its three huge cantilevers span 1447m and its construction took 59,000 tonnes of steel, eight million rivets, 254 tonnes of paint and the lives of 58 men. It has become an icon of Scottish engineering excellence, and has appeared in several films, most famously in the 1959 version of *The Thirty-Nine Steps*.

Maintaining the structure is a monumental undertaking – 'it's like painting the Forth Bridge' is a local phrase often used to describe a seemingly never-ending task. There was a furore in the Scottish parliament in 2003 when one member suggested that in view of the huge costs of maintenance, the bridge's demolition should be considered. In the same year an £11 million project began, with the intention of sand-blasting the structure back to bare steel and coating it with a modern glass-flake/epoxy paint that is expected to last at least 20 years.

HOPETOUN HOUSE Map pp214–15
☎ 331 2451; adult/child £6/3; ☾ 10am-5.30pm Apr-Sep, last admission 4.30pm; car

Two miles west of Queensferry lies one of Scotland's finest stately homes, in a superb location in lovely grounds beside the Firth of Forth. There are two parts, the older built to Sir William Bruce's plans between 1699 and 1702 and dominated by a splendid stairwell, the newer designed between 1720 and 1750 by three members of the Adam family, William and sons Robert and John. The highlights are the red-and-yellow Adam drawing rooms, lined in silk damask, and the view from the roof terrace.

The Hope family supplied a viceroy of India and a governor-general of Australia so the upstairs museum displays interesting reminders of the colonial life of the ruling class.

Britain's most elegant equine accommodation – where the marquis once housed his pampered racehorses – is now the stylish **Stables Tearoom** (mains £4-7; ☾ same as house), a delightful spot for lunch.

Interior of Hopetoun House (opposite) near Queensferry (p79)

Hopetoun House is located 2 miles west of Queensferry along the coast road. Driving from Edinburgh, turn off the A90 onto the A904 just before the Forth Bridge and follow the signs.

INCHCOLM ABBEY Map pp214–15
☎ 01383-823332; Inchcolm, Fife; adult/child £3/1;
9.30am-6.30pm Apr-Oct; ferry

The island of Inchcolm lies directly to the east of the Forth bridges, less than a mile off the coast of Fife. Only 800m in length, it is home to the ruins of Inchcolm Abbey, one of Scotland's best-preserved medieval abbeys, founded by Augustinian priors in 1123. In the well-tended grounds stand the remains of a 13th-century church as well as a remarkably well-preserved octagonal chapter house with a stone roof.

The ferry boat **Maid of the Forth** (☎ 331 4857) sails to the island of Inchcolm from Hawes Pier in Queensferry. There are two or three sailings daily during July and August, at weekends only from April to June and in September and October. The return fare costs £11/4.50 per adult/child, including admission to Inchcolm Abbey. It's a half-hour sail to Inchcolm and you get 1½ hours ashore. As well as the abbey, the trip gives you the chance to see the island's grey seals, puffins and other seabirds.

The Burry Man

If you happen to be visiting Edinburgh on the first Friday in August, head west to the village of Queensferry to see the Burry Man. As part of the village gala day festivities, a local man spends nine hours roaming the streets wearing a woolly suit which has been laboriously covered from head to toe in big, green, prickly burrs, and carrying two staves that are decorated with flowers. One glance at his costume – he looks like a child's drawing of a Martian, with added prickles – would make you think that he's suffering some form of bizarre medieval punishment. But the Burry Man is descended from an ancient fertility rite, and it is actually an honour to be selected. If you can't visit in August, there's a Burry Man costume on show in the Queensferry Museum.

QUEENSFERRY MUSEUM Map pp214–15

☎ 331 5545; 53 High St; admission free; ☉ 10am-1pm & 2.15-5pm Mon & Thu-Sat, noon-5pm Sun; First Edinburgh bus 43

This small town-hall museum on Queensferry's pretty, terraced High St contains some really interesting information on the building of the Forth bridges, along with some fascinating photographs of the railway bridge in various stages of construction. There is also a glass case containing a preserved Burry Man costume (see p81).

1 Old Chain Pier pub (p129)
2 Scott Monument and Christmas ferris wheel in Princes St Gardens (p68)
3 Hibs supporters, Easter Road Stadium (p141)
4 Old-style lamp, Edinburgh Castle (p52)

1 *Polar room, Our Dynamic Earth (p59)*
2 *Ocean Terminal shopping centre (p155)*
3 *Queen's Gallery, Palace of Holyroodhouse (p60)*
4 *Victoria Street and Victoria Terrace toward the Highland Tolbooth Kirk (p54)*

1 *National Monument, Calton Hill (p70)*
2 *Old College, University of Edinburgh (p63)*
3 *Statue of Allan Ramsay, Princes St Gardens (p68) and Edinburgh Castle (p52)*
4 *Bute House, Charlotte Square (p68)*

1 *Royal Scottish Academy (p68)*
2 *Tower restaurant (p103),*
Museum of Scotland (p63)
3 *Jazz night, Fairmile Inn (p139)*
4 *Folk-rock band, the Roods,*
Finnegan's Wake (p137)

1 Holyrood Park and Arthur's Seat (p58)
 2 Salisbury Crags, Holyrood Park (p58)
3 City Observatory, Calton Hill (p70) and Broughton (p71)
4 Governor's House, Calton Hill (p70)

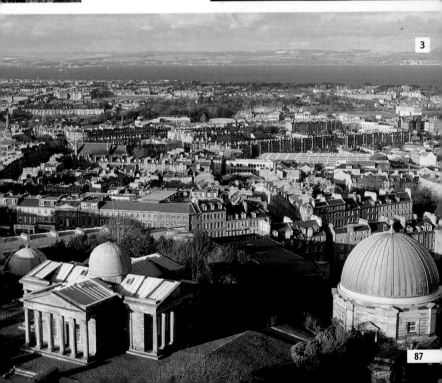

1 *Opal Lounge (p124)*
2 *Oloroso restaurant (p108) with Charlotte Square's West Register House (p68) in the background*
3 *Honeycomb club (p135)*
4 *Beluga Restaurant & Bar (p101)*

1 *Edinburgh Playhouse (p144)*
2 *Malmaison Hotel (p169)*
3 *Greensleeves shop window (p154)*
4 *21st Century Kilts (p156)*

1 *Melrose Abbey (p185)*
2 *Glasgow Cathedral (p176)*
3 *West Sands and the Royal &
Ancient Golf Club, St Andrews
(p181)*
4 *Stirling Castle (p187)*

Walking Tours

Walking Tours

Edinburgh's compact centre, with its winding streets and steep narrow closes, hidden corners and unexpected views, just begs to be explored on foot. Our selection of walking tours will lead you into many of those hidden corners, many of them – surprisingly – right in the middle of the busiest, most touristy parts of town.

If you'd prefer to take a guided walking tour, there's a broad range of choices listed in the Neighbourhoods chapter (see p50). Remember that Edinburgh is, in the words of Robert Louis Stevenson, 'a precipitous city' – wear good walking shoes and be prepared for a few steep climbs.

WALK 1: THE OLD TOWN

Edinburgh's Old Town spreads down the Royal Mile to the east of the castle and southwards to the Grassmarket and Greyfriars. This walk explores a few of the Old Town's many interesting nooks and crannies, and involves a fair bit of climbing up and down steep stairs and closes.

Begin on the **Castle Esplanade** 1 (p52), which provides a grandstand view southwards over the Grassmarket; the prominent quadrangular building with all the turrets is George Heriot's School, which you'll be passing later on. Head towards Castlehill and the start of the Royal Mile. The 17th-century house on the right, above the steps of North Castle Wynd, is known as **Cannonball House** 2 because of the iron ball lodged in the wall (look between, and slightly below, the two largest windows). It was not fired in anger, but instead marks the gravitation height to which water would flow naturally from the city's first piped water supply.

The low, rectangular building across the street (now a touristy tartan-weaving mill) was originally the reservoir that held the Old Town's water supply. On its western wall is the **Witches Well** 3, where a modern bronze fountain commemorates around 4000 people (mostly women) who were burnt or strangled in Edinburgh between 1479 and 1722 for suspicion of witchcraft.

Go past the reservoir and turn left down Ramsay Lane, and take a look at **Ramsay Garden** 4 – a most desirable address in Edinburgh – where late-19th-century apartments were built around the octagonal Ramsay Lodge, once home to poet Allan Ramsay. The cobbled street continues around to the right below student residences, to the towers of

Walk Facts

Start Castle Esplanade

End Greyfriars Kirkyard or Museum of Scotland

Distance 1½ miles

Duration 1–2 hours

Transport 28 (start bus); 2, 23, 27, 41, 42 (end buses)

the **New College** 5 – home to Edinburgh University's Faculty of Divinity. Nip into the courtyard to see the **statue of John Knox.**

Just past New College turn right and climb up the stairs into Milne's Court, a student residence that houses the public entrance to the temporary home of the Scottish Parliament. Exit into the Lawnmarket, cross the street (bearing slightly left) and duck into **Riddell's Court** 6 at No 322–8, a typical Old Town close. You'll find yourself in a small courtyard but the house in front of you (built in 1590) was originally the edge of the street (the building you just walked under was added in 1726 – check the inscription in the doorway on the right). The arch (with the inscription 'VIVENDO DISCIMUS', 'we live and learn') leads into the original 16th-century courtyard.

Go back into the street, turn right, and then right again down Fisher's Close, which ejects you onto the delightful Victoria Tce, strung above the cobbled curve of shop-lined Victoria St. Wander right, enjoying the view – **Maxie's Bistro** 7 (p102), at the far end of the terrace, is a great place to stop for a drink –

Tombstone incorporated into the façade of Greyfriars Kirk (p63)

Walking Tours – Walk 2: New Town & Stockbridge

then descend the stairs at the foot of Upper Bow and continue downhill to the Grassmarket (p62). At the east end, outside Maggie Dickson's pub, is the **Covenanters' Monument** 8 (p62); if you're feeling peckish, there are several good places to eat (p101) and a couple of good pubs – Robert Burns once stayed at the **White Hart Inn** 9 (p122).

At the west end of the Grassmarket, turn left up the flight of stairs known as The Vennel. At the top of the steps on the left you'll find the **Flodden Wall** 10 (p62). Follow its extension, the Telfer Wall, to Lauriston Pl and turn left along the impressive façade of **George Heriot's School** 11 (p62). Note that this is the back of the building – the front was designed to face the castle, and impress the inhabitants of the Grassmarket.

Turn left again at Forrest Rd, and if it's a Sunday afternoon pop into **Sandy Bell's** 12 (p138) for a pint and some Scottish folk music. Finish off your walk with a stroll through **Greyfriars Kirkyard** 13 (p62) or a visit to the **Museum of Scotland** 14 (p63).

WALK 2: NEW TOWN & STOCKBRIDGE

This perambulation probes the more interesting parts of the New Town and ends with a pleasant stroll along the wooded valley of the Water of Leith.

Begin on the east side of St Andrew Sq. Looking westwards along George St, you can see the dome of **West Register House** (p68) – formerly a church – at the far end. The original plans for New Town envisaged a matching Church of St Andrew on the eastern side of St Andrew Sq, but the rich and ambitious Sir Lawrence Dundas had other plans – he bought up the land, and had his own elaborate mansion, **Dundas House** 1 (p69) built on the site.

Go around the north side of the square, passing **Nos 23-26 St Andrew Sq** 2 (p68) – the oldest houses in the New Town – and pause to look up at the **Melville Monument** 3 (p69). Walk westwards along George St, past the **Church of St Andrew & St George** 4 (p69). Note the ostentatious temple to Mammon on your left that was once a bank and is now an impressive restaurant (**Dome** 5; see p106). Turn right at Hanover St, where a **statue of George IV** 6 commemorates his royal visit in 1822, and then left along Thistle St. This and its companion Rose St were built to house the servants, tradesmen and stables that catered to the needs of the New Town gentry; today it still serves a similar purpose, but with expensive restaurants and antique shops catering to

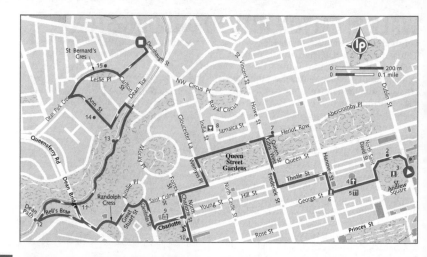

Walk Facts

Start St Andrew Square

End Deanhaugh St

Distance 2½ miles

Duration 1½–2½ hours

Transport 8, 10, 11, 15, 16, 17, 24, 28, 45 (start buses); 24, 29, 42 (end buses)

the wealthy professionals who now inhabit the Georgian town houses.

Turn right on Frederick St and continue downhill past Queen St and its gardens, and turn right into Heriot Row. A few doors along at **No 17 Heriot Row** 7 an inscription marks the house where Robert Louis Stevenson lived from 1857 to 1880. Retrace your steps and continue westwards along Heriot Row, a typical New Town Georgian terrace. If you're feeling thirsty, the delightful **Kay's Bar** 8 (p124) is just around the corner off India Pl.

Turn left at Wemyss Place (pronounced 'weems'), then go right and first left into North Charlotte St, which leads to **Charlotte Square** (p68). On the north side is the beautiful neoclassical façade of **Bute House** 9 (p68), while off the southeast corner is **16 South Charlotte St** 10 (p68), birthplace of Alexander Graham Bell.

After looking around the square, exit via Glenfinlas St in the northwestern corner, and bear left into Ainslie Pl. This elegant oval space, with its octagonal neighbour Moray Pl on one side and semicircular Randolph Cres on the other, constitute the Moray Estate (built between 1822 and 1850), perhaps the most beautiful part of the New Town.

Go left along Great Stuart St, bear right through Randolph Cres and cross busy Queensferry St, before turning right towards **Dean Bridge** 11 (p71). Go out into the middle of the bridge for a view over Dean Village, then return and descend the steep cobbled lane of Bells' Brae – before Dean Bridge was built, this was the main road from Edinburgh to Queensferry (p79). Just before the **old bridge** 12 (p71), turn right along Miller Row and follow the footpath along the Water of Leith. The buildings high up on the cliff above the private gardens on the right are the backs of the ones you saw earlier on Ainslie Pl. Five minutes' walk brings you to **St Bernard's Well** 13, a circular temple with a statue of Hygeia, the goddess of health, built in 1789. The sulphurous spring, similar to the ones in Harrogate, was discovered by schoolboys from George Heriot's School in 1760, and became hugely popular during the late-18th-century fad for 'taking the waters' – one visitor compared the taste to 'the washings of foul gun barrels'.

Where the footpath passes under an arch, climb the steps and cross the bridge over the Water of Leith. Turn left on Dean Tce, then right along **Ann St** 14 (p71). Having lusted after some of Edinburgh's most beautiful (and expensive) properties, turn right on Dean Park Crescent and continue through the tree-lined splendour of **St Bernard's Crescent** 15 (p71). At the far end, a left turn along Leslie Pl will deposit you in Deanhaugh St in the heart of Stockbridge, where various bars, cafés, shops and restaurants await.

WALK 3: CALTON HILL TO DUDDINGSTON

Edinburgh's city-centre hills provide superb views over the city and surrounding countryside. This walk is fairly strenuous, taking in the summits of both Calton Hill and Arthur's Seat.

Start at the eastern end of Princes St, at **Register House 1** (p67). Walk east along Waterloo Pl, pausing to explore the **Old Calton Burying Ground 2** (p70), and climb the stairs on the left (after Howie's restaurant). At the top of the steps, on the left, is an iron gate marked **Rock House 3**. This was once the home of David Octavius Hill, an early pioneer of portrait photography. Beyond the gate, turn right up another flight of steps and continue up the path to the top of Calton Hill.

The summit is scattered with the monuments that gave Edinburgh its nickname, Athens of the North – the **Monument to Dugald Stewart 4** (p70), the **Nelson Monument 5** (p70), the **National Monument 6** (p70) and the **City Observatory 7** (p70). On the northern side, the view extends from the Forth Bridges in the west, to the distant conical hill of North Berwick Law in the east.

Walk eastwards from the summit, and follow the road curving right and dropping down to Regent Rd. Cross the road and go left until you're opposite the Greek temple of the old **Royal High School 8** (p70).

Take a quick look at the nearby **Burns Monument 9**, then descend the footpath that drops down on the southern side of Regent Rd; halfway down, double-back to the left to reach Calton Rd. Follow Calton Rd east to the **Palace of Holyroodhouse 10** (p59), and finish the walk here if you're tired. If you need a refreshing drink, head for the **Tun 11** (p121).

Walk Facts

Start Register House
End Charlie's Cottage
Distance 4 miles
Duration 2–3 hours
Transport 1, 3, 8, 19, 29, 30, 31, 33, 34, 37 (start buses); 42 (end bus)

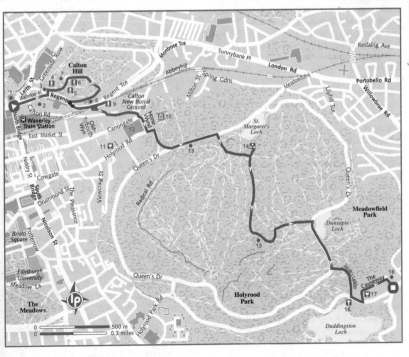

Follow Horse Wynd past the site of the new **Scottish Parliament Building** 12 (p60). Go left at the roundabout and cross the road to **St Margaret's Well** 13 (p58). Follow the path leftwards up the hillside towards the ruins of **St Anthony's Chapel** 14 (p59), then head south on the path that follows the floor of a shallow dip just east of Long Row crags. This eventually curves around to the left and climbs more steeply up some steps to a saddle; turn right here, and make the final short climb to the rocky summit of **Arthur's Seat** 15 (p58).

After taking in the view, descend eastwards to Queen's Dr at Dunsapie Loch. Turn right and follow the road for about 200m then descend to the left on the steep stairs known as Jacob's Ladder, and turn left along Old Church Lane into Duddingston village. Take a look around **Duddingston Parish Church** 16 (p79) before downing a pint at the **Sheep Heid** 17 (p128). On the way to the bus stop on Duddingston Rd, you'll pass **Prince Charlie's Cottage** 18 (p79).

WALK 4: BLACKFORD HILL

A countryside walk in the heart of the city – this route takes you along a peaceful, wooded valley beside a gurgling stream, then climbs to one of the city's best viewpoints.

Start at the southerly junction of Braid and Comiston Rds, near Buckstone Gdns at the southern edge of the city. From the Buckstone Gdns bus stop on Comiston Rd, walk back north along Braid Rd. Just past Buckstone Dr on the right-hand side of the road you will see a cobbled alcove in the wall, with a small sandstone pillar, about a metre high, at the back with a plaque above it. This is the **Buck Stane** 1, an ancient boundary marker that once stood 250m to the north – the long, straight stretch of Braid Rd and its continuation south on Comiston Rd follow the line of the old Roman road to the fort at Cramond (p76). Legend has it that in medieval times the king's hunting parties would unleash their buckhounds (ie deerhounds) at this marker as they rode out to hunt in the woods that once clothed the lower slopes of the Pentland Hills; a pole bearing the royal standard would be stuck in the hole on top of the stone to warn that the king was hunting in the area.

Continue north on Braid Rd, down past the Braid Hills Hotel and up again on the far side of the bridge over the Braid Burn. About 600m beyond the bridge, just past the junction with Comiston Tce and opposite No 66 Braid Rd, you will see two square slabs of sandstone set into the road, outlined in red brick; these are the **Hanging Stones** 2. These stone sockets once held the posts of a gallows, where the last execution for highway robbery in Scotland took place in 1812.

Retrace your step towards the bridge, and just before you reach it turn left through the gate to the footpath that leads through the **Hermitage of Braid** 3 nature reserve. The path meanders through a glen for three-quarters of a mile (with sunlight filtering through the leaves and the sound of birdsong all around, you'll feel miles from the city), crisscrossing the stream and passing an 18th-century mansion that now houses a visitor centre, **Hermitage House** 4 (☎ 447 7145; admission free; ☺ 2-5pm Mon-Thu & Sat, 2-4pm Fri, noon-5pm Sun). The centre explains the history and wildlife of the glen, and has details of nearby nature trails.

At the eastern end of the reserve you emerge from the trees and pass through a gate beside a bridge; turn left, here and head uphill on a broad, path that curves back to the left, following the upper edge of the woodland. As the path levels off and curves round to the right, with a stone wall and open fields on the left, look out for a hollow in the slope on your right. A steep path with a flight of wood and turf steps lead up to a radio mast – go around the far end of the fenced enclosure and back left to reach the trig point on the **summit of Blackford Hill** 5 (164m).

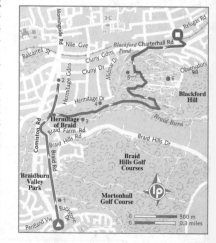

The view north from the summit offers a splendid panorama of the city. Straight ahead, beyond the villa gardens, parks and tenements of Edinburgh South, you can see the castle atop its rock, with the bristling spine of the Old Town straggling to its right; this view, seen at dawn, was described by Sir Walter Scott in his poem *Marmion*:

Such dusky grandeur clothed the height
Where the huge castle holds its state,
And all the steep slope down,
Whose ridgy back heaves to the sky,
Piled deep and massy, close and high,
Mine own romantic town!

To the right of the Old Town are the monuments on Calton Hill, the bold wedge of Salisbury Crags, and the 'sleeping lion' of Arthur's Seat (the summit lump is supposed to be its head, with the 'body' stretching to its right). On a clear day you'll see the Ochil Hills to the northwest, and even the Highland hills of Ben Vorlich and Stuc a'Chroin; and, far to the east, the conical hump of North Berwick Law (p183). The red-sandstone building with the domes on the hilltop to the east is the **Royal Observatory 6** (p79).

Descend the north slope of the hill below the trig point by one of several winding paths through the gorse to Blackford Pond, and pause to feed the ducks before heading for the gate at its eastern end. Turn right along Charterhall Rd, and then first left on Blackford Av; a bus stop here (on the left hand side of the road) will take you back into the city centre.

WALK 5: COLINTON DELL & THE UNION CANAL

This walk also treads a rural path through the midst of the city, past a pretty parish church, along a wooded river gorge, and then back towards the city centre via a canal towpath.

Start in Colinton, at the junction of Colinton Rd/Bridge Rd with Dreghorn Loan. Head west on the north side of Bridge Rd, and look out for the newsagent on the right, just before the Colinton Inn; turn right and descend the stairs (signpost for Colinton Parish Church) to Spylaw St. Uphill to your left is a terrace of picturesque cottages dating from 1900, but turn right and cross the bridge over the Water of Leith, then climb up Dell Rd to pretty little **Colinton Parish Church 1**. Although there has been a church here since 1095, it has been destroyed and re-built several times; the present building was originally 18th-century, but the Italian-style campanile (bell tower) dates from 1837, and much of the exterior was remodelled in 1907. Robert Louis Stevenson's grandfather was the minister here from 1823 to 1860 and is buried in the kirkyard, which has many interesting stones.

Follow Dell Rd past the church to where it ends, and descend a steep flight of stairs into the wooded ravine of **Colinton Dell 2**. The path follows the riverbank beside a mossy wall, with the scent of wild garlic wafting down from the slope above. This is one of Edinburgh's many rural retreats where the city feels very far away, although there's traffic whizzing past on Lanark Rd less than 200m to the west. When you reach a wooden footbridge over the river, don't cross it; instead, climb up the steep staircase to the left to join the **Water of Leith Walkway 3**, which follows the line of a disused railway. Follow this path for half a mile until it forks, then take the right-hand branch, which descends to the riverbank again. Cross the first bridge you come to and turn left along the far bank of the river. The path here winds up and down through a delightful stretch of woodland, before emerging onto Lanark Rd. Across the road and to the left is the **Water of Leith Visitor Centre 4** (see p80), with the Slateford Aqueduct rising behind it.

You can cut short your walk here (2 miles), and catch bus 28, 34 or 44 from Lanark Rd back into town. Otherwise, follow the walkway that begins at the visitor centre and turn right up the stairs to reach the bank of the Union Canal at the eastern end of Slateford Aqueduct.

The 31½-mile Union Canal opened in 1822 to take passengers and cargo between Edinburgh and Falkirk, where it linked up with the Forth and Clyde Canal (see p178). It was dug almost entirely by hand; among the thousands of navvies who laboured on its construction were the

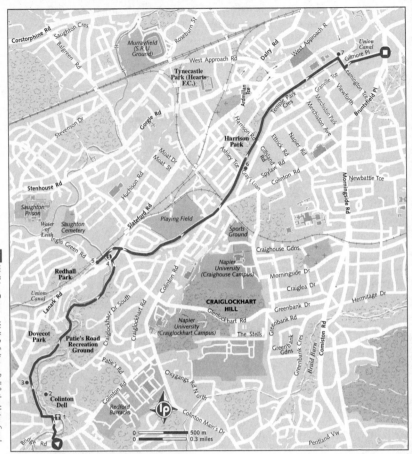

Walk Facts

Start Junction of Colinton Rd/Bridge Rd

End Bennet's Bar/Ndebele Café

Distance 4½ miles

Duration 2–3 hours

Transport 10, 16, 18, 45 (start buses); all Tollcross buses (end buses)

murderers Burke and Hare (see p44). The eight-arched, 153m-long **Slateford Aqueduct 5** carries the canal across the Water of Leith, and is the second-longest in Scotland (the longest is the Avon Aqueduct, near Linlithgow).

Continue along the canal towpath towards the city centre; keep an eye out for the milestones beside the path. This section of the canal is used by uni rowing clubs, and in term time you will often see sculls zipping along. After passing under the Gray's Loan bridge there's a pretty little **basin 6** with rowing boats belonging to the Union Canal Society, whose pavilion lies on the far bank; here, too, is the canal boat restaurant **Zazou** (p114).

The final reach of the canal cuts a peaceful swathe between the backs of residential flats and tenements (and a brewery) before reaching the **Leamington Lift Bridge 7**. The bridge was built in 1896, and was restored to full working order in 2002; the district to the east of the bridge is being redeveloped. Cross the bridge and turn left on Gilmore Place, which leads into Tollcross; head to **Bennet's Bar** (p128) or **Ndebele** (p113) for a revitalising refreshment.

Eating

Eating

In the last decade there has been a boom in the number of restaurants in Edinburgh – the city now has more restaurants per head of population than London. Eating out has become a commonplace event rather than something reserved for special occasions, and the choice of eateries ranges from stylish but inexpensive bistros and cafés to gourmet restaurants.

In addition, most pubs serve food, offering either bar meals or a more formal restaurant or both, but be aware that pubs without a restaurant licence are not allowed to serve children under the age of 16. See p119 for further information.

If you require more information than we provide here, the excellent *Edinburgh & Glasgow Eating & Drinking Guide* (£4.95; www.list.co.uk/ead), published annually by *The List* magazine, contains reviews of around 800 restaurants, cafés and bars.

Modern Scottish Cuisine

Although Scotland has never been celebrated for its national cuisine – in fact, from haggis to deep-fried Mars Bars, it has more often been an object of ridicule – a new culinary style known as Modern Scottish has emerged in the last decade or so. It's a style that should be familiar to fans of Californian Cuisine and Mod Oz.

Chefs take top-quality Scottish produce – from Highland venison, Aberdeen Angus beef and west-coast scallops to root vegetables, raspberries and Ayrshire cheeses – and prepare it in a way that enhances the natural flavours, often adding a French, Italian or Asian twist.

Classic Scottish dishes are often given a new slant – eg haggis wrapped in filo pastry parcels and served with a hoisin dipping sauce, or Cullen skink (a traditional soup of smoked haddock and potato) jazzed up with herbs and cream.

Opening Hours

In general, lunch is served from noon to 2.30pm, and dinner from 6pm to 10pm. Office workers generally break for lunch between 1pm and 2pm, and city centre restaurants are often very busy then.

Many places remain open in the afternoon, and a few (especially Indian, Italian and Chinese places) stay open till 11pm or midnight. Cafés generally open from 8am or 9am to 6pm.

The opening hours given in the restaurant reviews in this chapter are the times during which orders are taken, so if a listing says dinner is available from 7pm to 10pm, then as long as you're seated before 10pm you'll get a meal – it doesn't mean that you have to be out by 10pm!

How Much?

In an average, mid-range restaurant you can expect to pay around £10 to £15 a head for lunch, not including drinks, and £20 to £25 a head for dinner, including a bottle of wine between two. At Edinburgh's top tables, you can easily double that. Many places, including the more expensive restaurants, offer good lunch deals. Look out also for pre-theatre or 'early bird' specials (usually available between 5pm and 7pm).

The Cheap Eats options listed in this chapter have an average main-course price of less than £6.

The prices ranges for main courses ('mains') listed in the reviews are for dinner menus, unless otherwise indicated; prices for main courses at lunch are often considerably cheaper.

Top Five Modern Scottish Restaurants

- **Atrium** (p112)
- **Number One** (p107)
- **Restaurant Martin Wishart** (p116)
- **Rhubarb** (p113)
- **Tower** (p103)

Booking Tables

Eating out in Edinburgh is popular and booking a table is strongly recommended, especially in August (the Festival) and in December (lots of office parties and Christmas dinners).

The www.5pm.co.uk website lists last-minute offers from restaurants with tables to spare that evening. Using this service you can find a three-course dinner at one of Edinburgh's better restaurants for as little as £12 if you're prepared to eat early or late.

Tipping

Normal practice in Edinburgh is to leave a tip of around 10% unless the service was unsatisfactory. If the bill already includes a service charge (usually 10%), you needn't add a further tip. Note that some restaurants add a compulsory 10% service charge on large groups (usually eight or more people); if this is the case, it should be mentioned on the menu and on the bill.

Self-Catering

There are grocery stores and food shops all over the city, many of them open 9am to 10pm daily, while many petrol stations also have shops that sell groceries. There are several supermarkets spread throughout the city too. The most convenient are: **Marks & Spencer** (Map pp218–20; ☎ 225 2301; 54 Princes St; ✆ 9am-7pm Mon-Fri, 9am-8pm Thu, 8.30am-6pm Sat, 11am-5pm Sun); **Sainsbury's** (Map pp218–20; ☎ 225 8400; 9-10 St Andrew Sq; ✆ 7am-10pm Mon-Sat, 10am-8pm Sun); and **Tesco Metro** (Map pp218–20; ☎ 456 2400; 94 Nicolson St; ✆ 7am-midnight Mon-Sat, 9am-10pm Sun). There are also many excellent delicatessens where you can buy fresh produce from all over the world (see p145).

OLD TOWN

From cosy, vaulted cellars to stylish rooftop restaurants, the Old Town offers a wide range of appealing eateries.

BELUGA RESTAURANT & BAR

Map pp224–5 *International*

☎ 624 4545; 30a Chambers St; mains lunch £5.50-7.50, dinner £11-15; ✆ noon-3pm & 6-10pm; bus 35, 41

Hip Beluga caters to the 20-something clubbing crowd, and is stylish – all brown leather, slate and steel – and loud. The downstairs bar (food served noon to 9pm) offers booze-absorbing grub such as nachos (£5.25) or pork, sage and apple sausages with mash and gravy (£5.95), while the sophisticated ground-floor restaurant has intricate, culinary confections that take longer to read from the menu than to eat.

BLACK BO'S Map pp224–5 *Vegetarian*

☎ 557 6136; 57-61 Blackfriars St; mains £10.50-12.50; ✆ 6-10.30pm daily, noon-2pm Fri & Sat; bus 35

You can't accuse the chef at Black Bo's, a very popular vegetarian and vegan eatery located just off the Royal Mile, of being unadventurous in the slightest. The menu is always really interesting – veggie haggis and cream cheese filo parcels with a whisky and raspberry sauce, for example – and there are a couple of meat and fish options that might take your fancy too. There's a lively bar next door, which often has live music.

CAFÉ HUB Map pp224–5 *Bistro*

☎ 473 2067; Castlehill, Royal Mile; mains £9-15, two-course lunch £9.90; ⏰ 9.30am-9.30pm Tue-Sat, 9.30am-6pm Sun & Mon; bus 28

A Gothic hall beneath the Tolbooth Kirk – now home to the Edinburgh Festival offices – has been transformed into this bright and breezy bistro with some zingy yellow paint, cobalt-blue furniture and lots of imagination. Drop in for cake and cappuccino, or try something more filling – Thai crab cakes with pak-choi broth (£4.90) or a falafel and lime-chutney pitta (£3.65) – or linger over the good-value set lunch.

DAVID BANN Map pp224–5 *Vegetarian*

☎ 556 5888; 56-8 St Mary's St; mains £9-11; ⏰ 11-1am; bus 64

If you want to convince a carnivorous friend that cuisine à la veg can be every bit as tasty and inventive as a meat-muncher's menu, take them to David Bann's stylish new restaurant. Dishes such as Shepherdless Pie, with vegetables in a rich, red-wine gravy and parmesan-crusted mashed potato, are guaranteed to win converts. They also do a tasty veggie brunch from 11am to 5pm at weekends.

DORIC WINE BAR & BISTRO

Map pp224–5 *Scottish*

☎ 225 1084; 15-16 Market St; mains £8-15; ⏰ 11.30-1am Mon-Sat year round, noon-1am Sun mid-Apr–Sep; bus 64

Recent renovation has restored this 1st-floor bistro (entrance stairs to the right of the Doric Bar) to its former position as one of Edinburgh's favourite eateries, handy for both Princes St and the Royal Mile. Wooden floors, warm ochre walls and window tables with views of the Scott Monument and Balmoral Hotel complement a menu of fresh Scottish produce. The table d'hôte lunch (from £6.99) and dinner (two/three courses £17.50/21) menus change daily.

GORDON'S TRATTORIA Map pp224–5
Italian

☎ 225 7992; 231 High St; mains £8-16.50; ⏰ noon-midnight Sun-Thu, noon-3am Fri & Sat; bus 35

The aroma of garlic bread wafting into the street will guide you into this snug haven of chattering diners, wise-cracking waiters and hearty Italian comfort food. In summer you can chomp pizza and slurp wine at a pavement table on the Royal Mile, and the late-night opening means that Gordon's often develops something of a party atmosphere after midnight on Friday and Saturday.

HEIGHTS Map pp224–5 *Modern Scottish*

☎ 473 7156; Apex International Hotel, 31-5 Grassmarket; mains £11-18; ⏰ 7-10pm Mon-Sat; bus 2

Starkly elegant in red and grey, Heights' dining room is perched high above the Grassmarket – an entire wall of picture windows allows an uninterrupted view of Edinburgh Castle, which is spectacularly floodlit at night, and during the Edinburgh Festival you'll get a grandstand view of the Military Tattoo fireworks if you're still there around 10.30pm. Typical dishes include a modern version of Cullen skink (with added herbs and sautéed potatoes) and herb-crusted rump of Scottish lamb. You can dine à la carte, or opt for the fixed-price menu of three courses for £17.

IGG'S Map pp224–5 *Spanish*

☎ 557 8184; 15 Jeffrey St; mains £15-19; ⏰ noon-2.30pm & 6-10.30pm Mon-Sat; bus 64

A sumptuous dining room with dark wood furniture, crisp, white linen and rich, mustard-yellow walls make Igg's a good choice for a special night out. The menu is mostly Spanish, with tapas-style starters and interesting main courses such as pan-fried fillet of barracuda on a spicy plum risotto with spinach and red pepper coulis. You can get a set two-/three-course lunch for £11.50/14.50.

MAISON BLEUE Map pp224–5 *International*

☎ 226 1900; 36-8 Victoria St; mains £5-13; ⏰ noon-3pm & 5-10.15pm; bus 2

Eating at Maison Bleue is a comfortably laid-back affair, like having dinner at an old friend's house – albeit a rather stylish old friend. The intimate ground-floor dining room has woven straw chairs, chunky wooden tables, modern art on bare stone walls, candlelight and cool tunes; upstairs is brighter and more café-like. The menu lists *bouchées* (French for 'mouthfuls') – starter-size helpings of which you can have as many or as few as you wish. The food is an eclectic mix of European, North African and Far Eastern influences, from haggis balls in crispy batter and Vietnamese *nems* (crispy rice pancakes filled with crab and shrimp) to coriander-crusted salmon and Moroccan-style chicken brochettes.

MAXIE'S BISTRO & WINE BAR

Map pp224–5 *International*

☎ 226 7770; 5b Johnston Tce; mains £7-11; ⏰ bistro 11am-11pm, wine bar 11am-1am

Maxie's candle-lit cellar bistro, with its cushion-lined nooks set amid stone walls, cream plaster and wooden beams is a pleasant enough setting for a cosy dinner, but at summer lunch times people queue for the outdoor tables on Victoria Tce, with great views over Victoria St. The food is dependable – Maxie's has been around for over 20 years – ranging from pastas, steaks and stir-fries to superb seafood platters and daily specials, and there's an excellent selection of wines.

METRO BRASSERIE & CAFÉ BAR
Map pp224–5 *International*
☎ 474 3466; 31-5 Grassmarket; mains £8-10.50, 3-course dinner £14; 🕑 11am-11pm; bus 2

Depending on your tastes, minimalist Metro is either desperately stylish or just looks a little bit like a school canteen. Either way, the international menu is way better than anything you had at school – try tiger prawn and monkfish skewers followed by butternut squash and spinach lasagne – and there's a view of the castle from the window tables.

NEGOCIANTS
Map pp224–5 *International*
☎ 225 6313; 45-7 Lothian St; mains £7-12; 🕑 9-3am Mon-Sat, 10-3am Sun; bus 2, 41, 42

A student stalwart that's been around for 20 years – Edinburgh University's main campus is right across the street – Negociants is a café-bar-bistro that keeps the food coming till well

Stylish seating at Tower

into the wee hours of the morning (last orders for food 2.15am). It's pleasantly quiet during the day, but as the evening wears on it fills up with pre- and post-clubbers fuelling up on mountainous nachos, juicy burgers and sizzling fajitas.

PANCHO VILLA'S
Map pp224–5 *Mexican*
☎ 557 4416; 240 Canongate, Royal Mile; mains £8-11; 🕑 noon-2.30pm & 6-10.30pm Mon-Thu, noon-11pm Fri & Sat, 6-10pm Sun; bus 35

With a Mexican manager, plenty of Latin American staff, and freshly squeezed limes in the margaritas, it's not surprising that Pancho's is one of the most authentic-feeling Mexican restaurants in town. It's also the city's best-value Mexican, with a set lunch for £5, and it's often busy, so book ahead. The dinner menu includes tender steak fajitas and spicy spinach enchiladas.

PETIT PARIS
Map pp224–5 *French*
☎ 226 2442; 38-40 Grassmarket; mains £9-13; 🕑 noon-11pm, closed Sun Oct-Easter; bus 2

Like the name says, this is a little piece of Paris, complete with checked tablecloths, friendly waiters and good-value grub – the *moules-frites* (mussels and chips) are excellent. There's a lunch and afternoon deal of the *plat du jour* and a coffee for £5 (£6.90 during the Edinburgh Festival), available from noon to 5pm.

POINT RESTAURANT
Map pp218–20 *Modern Scottish*
☎ 221 5555; Point Hotel, 34 Bread St; 2-course lunch £8.90, 3-course dinner £14.90; 🕑 noon-2pm Mon-Fri, 6-10pm Mon-Thu, 6-11pm Fri & Sat, 6-9pm Sun; bus 2, 28

The Point Restaurant's now legendary lunch and dinner menus offer exceptional value – delicious Scottish/international cuisine served in an elegant room with dark-wood furniture, proper linen napkins and attentive, smartly clad staff. They must make their profit on the drinks, though the house wine costs only £10.95 per bottle. Reservations are strongly recommended.

TOWER
Map pp224–5 *Modern Scottish*
☎ 225 3003; Museum of Scotland, Chambers St; mains £13-20; 🕑 noon-11pm; bus 35, 41

A doorman guides you to a private elevator that whisks you up four floors to the trendy Tower, perched atop the Museum of Scotland building (see p63). Chic and sleek, attired in black leather, purple suede, oak and brushed aluminium, the Tower has played host to countless celebrities, from the Countess of Wessex to Catherine Zeta-Jones, attracted by the grand views of the castle, a superb wine list, and a menu of top-quality Scottish produce, simply prepared – try half a dozen Cumbrae rock oysters followed by a char-grilled Aberdeen Angus fillet steak. The theatre-supper menu, available 4pm to 6.30pm daily, costs only £12 for two courses.

WITCHERY BY THE CASTLE

Map pp224–5   Scottish/French

☎ 225 5613; Castlehill, Royal Mile; mains £15-22; ☺ noon-4pm, 5.30-11.30pm; bus 28

Edinburgh's most atmospheric restaurant has been a 25-year labour of love for owner and founder James Thomson. Set in a merchant's town house dating from 1595, the Witchery is a candlelit treasury of antique splendour, with oak-panelled walls, low ceilings, opulent wall hangings and red-leather upholstery. Stairs lead down to a second, even more romantic, dining room called the Secret Garden. But décor isn't everything – the menu, which ranges from *tourchon* of goose liver with rhubarb jelly to fillet of well-hung Aberdeen Angus steak, and the wine list (there are almost 1000 bins), are an epicurean's delight. The bargain two-course light lunches (noon to 4pm) and pre- or post-theatre dinners (5.30pm to 6.30pm and 10.30pm to 11.30pm) cost only £9.95. Book well in advance.

James Thomson

When James Thomson founded the Witchery by the Castle (this page) in 1979, at the age of 20, he became Scotland's youngest licensee. Today the Witchery is still renowned as one of Edinburgh's finest restaurants, and Mr Thomson is Edinburgh's best-known restaurateur. He expanded his empire in 1998 when he opened the Tower (p103), atop the new Museum of Scotland building. Its sleek modern lines and view of the castle were in complete contrast to the cosy, wood-panelled Old Town house of the Witchery, but the close attention to food and service were the same.

As a penniless student chef in Edinburgh in the 1970s, Thomson eked out his grant by working as a waiter at the prestigious Prestonfield House Hotel (p168). In 2003 he bought the place for several million pounds, and its new restaurant, Rhubarb (p113), is now the hottest table in town.

CHEAP EATS

CAFETERIA @ THE FRUITMARKET

Map pp224–5   Café

☎ 226 1843; 45 Market St; mains £4-5; ☺ 11am-5pm Mon-Sat, noon-5pm Sun; bus 64

After checking out the art in the Fruitmarket Gallery (see p61), check out the menu in its stylish café – fresh sandwiches, big crunchy salads and hot ciabatta melts – or settle down with a cappuccino (£1.40) to browse through the title you just bought in the adjacent art bookshop.

ELEPHANT HOUSE CAFÉ

Map pp224–5   Café

☎ 220 5355; 21 George IV Bridge; mains £4-6; ☺ 8am-11pm; bus 35, 41

Here you'll find counters at the front, tables with views of the castle at the back, and little effigies and images of elephants everywhere. Excellent cappuccino and home-made food – pizzas, quiches, pies, sandwiches and cakes – at reasonable prices make it deservedly popular with local students, shoppers and office workers.

FAVORIT Map pp224–5   Café

☎ 220 6880; 19-20 Teviot Pl; sandwiches £4, salads £4-5; ☺ 8-3am; bus 2, 23, 27, 41, 42

A stylish café-bar with a slightly retro feel, Favorit caters for everyone: workers grabbing breakfast on the way to the office, coffee-slurping students skiving off afternoon lectures, and late-night clubbers with an attack of the munchies. It also serves the best bacon butties in town – a warmed bap loaded with lots of crispy, streaky bacon, with a choice of HP sauce or tomato ketchup. Yum. There's a second **Favorit** (Map pp222–3; ☎ 221 1800; 30 Leven St; ☺ 8am-1am) in Tollcross.

KARIBA COFFEE Map pp224–5   Café

☎ 226 1214; 1 Parliament Sq, High St, Royal Mile; snacks £3-5; ☺ 8am-6pm Mon-Sat, 9am-6pm Sun; bus 35

A bright and appealing café with comfy sofas and a spacious sitting area, Kariba offers special deals on its excellent coffee – from 8am to 10am and 4.30pm to 6pm, Monday to Friday, a regular latte, cappuccino or Americano costs £1.20. Their largest cappuccino (£2.15) is big enough to bathe in. Also on the menu are freshly squeezed juices, fruit smoothies and sandwiches.

KEBAB MAHAL Map pp224–5   South Asian

☎ 667 5214; 7 Nicolson Sq; kebabs £3.25-5.50; ☺ noon-midnight Sun-Thu, noon-2am Fri & Sat

Sophisticated it ain't, but this is the Holy Grail of kebab shops – quality shish kebab and tandoori dishes washed down with chilled lassi for less than a fiver. It's a basic cafeteria-style place with a stainless-steel counter and glaring fluorescent lights, but the menu is 100% halal (the Edinburgh Mosque is just 100m along the road) and the kebabs and curries are authentic and delicious. Kebab Mahal? Kebab nirvana.

LOWER AISLE Map pp224–5   *Café*
☎ 225 5147; St Giles Cathedral, High St, Royal Mile; snacks £2-4; ☽ 8.30am-4.30pm Mon-Fri, 9am-2pm Sun; bus 35

Hidden in a vault beneath St Giles Cathedral (the entrance is on the Parliament Square side, opposite the Royal Mile), the Lower Aisle is a good place to escape from the crowds, except during weekday lunch hours when it becomes packed with lawyers, clerks and secretaries from the nearby courts. Known as the 'café in the crypt', it serves up some heavenly home baking – from quiche to carrot cake – plus a range of both salads and sandwiches.

MADE IN ITALY Map pp224–5   *Café*
☎ 622 7328; 42 Grassmarket; mains £3-5; ☽ 8am-11pm Mon-Thu, 8-1.30am Fri & Sat, 10am-11pm Sun; bus 2

Look out for this traditional-style café where you can sit inside at the counters or outside at the tables and enjoy real Italian coffee (large cappuccinos cost £1.75) and real gelati as you watch the world go by. If you're hungry, they do good pizzas and panini sandwiches too.

Late-Night Munchies

Edinburgh has more than a few places where it's possible to chow down after 10.30pm. Many of them are Italian, Indian and Chinese restaurants that accept sit-down customers until 11pm on weekdays and midnight on Fridays and Saturdays. The following places stay open until midnight or even later.

- **David Bann** (p102)
- **Favorit** (p104)
- **Gordon's Trattoria** (p102)
- **Kebab Mahal** (p104)
- **Negociants** (p103)

NEW TOWN

You can barely walk 20 paces along a New Town street without passing a restaurant. The elegant Georgian terraces to the north of Princes St are the epicentre of Edinburgh's fine dining scene, with lots of stylish restaurants offering a wide range of cuisines. The abundance of office workers means that there are lots of weekday lunch specials to look out for too.

BASEMENT Map pp218–20   *International*
☎ 557 0097; 10a-12a Broughton St; mains £5-8; ☽ food served noon-10pm; bus 8,17

The Basement is a groovy bar – check out the weird, welded tank-track and motorcycle-chain furniture – with a separate restaurant area, offering a two-course lunch for only £5.95 (noon to 3pm Monday to Friday). The grub is sort of international – bruschetta, nachos, spaghetti, chicken in orange and ginger sauce – but goes all Thai on Wednesdays and Mexican at the weekend.

BUFFALO GRILL Map p217   *American*
☎ 332 3864; Raeburn Pl; mains £7-13; ☽ 6-10.30pm Mon-Thu, 6-11pm Fri, 5-11pm Sat, 5-10.30pm Sun; bus 24, 49, 32

This Stockbridge incarnation is a bit more spacious than the original branch (see p112), but has the same Wild West décor and beefy, all-American menu. Unlike the Chapel St branch, this place is fully licensed, but they still allow you to BYOB if you prefer (£1 corkage charge).

CAFÉ MARLAYNE Map pp218–20   *French*
☎ 226 2230; 76 Thistle St; mains £12-14; ☽ noon-2pm & 6-10pm Tue-Sat; bus 13, 24, 29, 42

All scrubbed, weathered wood and warm yellow walls, little Café Marlayne is a cosy nook offering satisfying French farmhouse cooking – *escargot* with garlic and parsley, oysters with lemon and Tabasco, *boudin noir* (black pudding) with sautéed apples, peppered duck breast with balsamic vinegar – at very reasonable prices. It's only little, so book a table well in advance.

CAFÉ MEDITERRANEO Map pp218–20   *Café*
☎ 557 6900; 73 Broughton St; mains £8; ☽ 8am-6pm Mon-Thu, 8am-9pm Fri & Sat; bus 8, 17

Blonde-wood furniture in the bright, busy dining room behind the deli counter makes Café Med a favourite hang-out for local residents. The food, mostly inspired by Italy and the south of France, is tasty and good value, and the coffee is superb.

CAFÉ ROYAL OYSTER BAR

Map pp218–20   *French/Seafood*
☎ 556 4124; 17a West Register St; mains £16-20;
☻ noon-2pm & 7-10pm; all Princes St buses

Pass through the revolving doors on the corner of West Register St and you're transported back to Victorian times – a palace of glinting mahogany, polished brass, marble floors, stained glass, Doulton tiles, gilded cornices and table linen so thick that it creaks when you fold it. The menu is mostly classic seafood, from oysters on ice to succulent Coquilles St Jacques Parisienne (scallops in a cream and mushroom sauce) and lobster thermidor, augmented by a handful of beef and game dishes.

CIRCUS CAFÉ Map pp218–20   *Café*
☎ 220 0333; 15 Northwest Circus Pl; mains £7-10;
☻ 10am-11pm; bus 24, 29, 42

This upmarket café is just *so* Stockbridge – a former bank that's been given a designer makeover (think mahogany, mirrors, dark-chocolate suedette, and shimmering, opalescent modern chandeliers). More silver spoon than greasy spoon, this is a café where a cheese-and-ham sandwich becomes 'Joselito Gran Reserva ham and brie on a sourdough ficelle', and the soup of the day is likely to be langoustine and sage. There's a great deli downstairs where you can choose a bottle of wine and drink it in the café for no extra charge between 4pm and 7pm. It's child-friendly too.

DOME Map pp218–20   *International*
☎ 624 8624; 14 George St; mains £10-16; ☻ noon-10.30pm Sun-Thu, noon-11pm Fri & Sat; bus 24, 28, 45

Housed in the former headquarters of a bank, the Dome boasts one of the city's most impressive dining rooms. The lofty, domed ceiling and ornate decoration keep dragging your eyes away from your plate, which is probably just as well – the food, though decent, does not quite measure up to the surroundings, or to the prices. It's best to go there for lunch, when you can ogle the fittings without breaking the bank, as it were.

FISHERS IN THE CITY

Map pp218–20   *Seafood*
☎ 225 5109; 58 Thistle St; mains £12-19; ☻ noon-10.30pm Mon-Sat, 12.30-10.30pm Sun; bus 13, 19, 37, 41

A sleeker, more sophisticated version of the famous Leith restaurant (see p116), Fishers in the City is a busy, modern bar-restaurant with a nautical theme, serving up superior Scottish seafood.

Café Royal Oyster Bar

FORTH FLOOR RESTAURANT

Map pp218–20   *Modern Scottish*
☎ 524 8350; 30-4 St Andrew Sq; mains £14-19;
☻ noon-3pm Mon-Fri, noon-3.30pm Sat & Sun, 6-10pm Tue-Sat; all St Andrew Sq buses

The in-store restaurant at Harvey Nichols (see p150) has west-facing floor-to-ceiling windows overlooking St Andrew Sq, making it a great place to enjoy sunset views. The food has as much designer chic as the surroundings, with dishes such as braised lamb shank or seared scallops served with a stylish flourish.

HADRIAN'S BRASSERIE

Map pp218–20   *Scottish/French*
☎ 557 5000; Balmoral Hotel, 1 Princes St; mains £8-13;
☻ 7-10.30am, noon-2.30pm, 6-10.30pm Mon-Sat, 7.30-11am, 12.30-3pm, 6-10.30pm Sun; all Princes St buses

The Balmoral Hotel's brasserie has a 1930s Art Deco feel, with a décor of pale green walls and dark-wood furniture, and white-aproned, black-waistcoated waiters. The menu includes posh versions of Scottish favourites such as fish and chips (with peas and tartare sauce) and haggis, neeps and tatties (with whisky sauce), as well as more sophisticated offerings such as langoustine bisque and confit of pork with apple sauce and sage jus. There's a two-course lunch for £8 and a three-course set menu for £11.

Eating – New Town

HOWIE'S STOCKBRIDGE

Map pp218–20   *Modern Scottish*

☎ 225 5553; 4-6 Glanville Pl, Kerr St; 3-course lunch/dinner £8/15.50; noon-2.30pm & 6-10pm; bus 24, 29, 42

This branch of Howie's – all chrome, blonde wood and feng shui – is a trendier incarnation of their no-nonsense Bruntsfield restaurant, designed to pander to the fashionable New Town crowd. But the 'Scottish fusion' food is as tasty and as good value as ever. And who can resist a place with quaffable house wine at £7.90 a bottle?

LA P'TITE FOLIE
Map pp218–20   *French*

☎ 225 7983; 61 Frederick St; mains £8-10; noon-3pm Mon-Sat, 6-11pm daily; bus 13, 24, 29, 42

Breton-owned la P'tite Folie is a delightful little wood-panelled bistro whose menu takes in the French classics – *soupe à l'oignon* (French onion soup), *moules marinières* (mussels), Coquilles St Jacques (scallops) – as wells as steaks, seafood and a range of *plats du jour*. The two-/three-course lunch is a bargain at £5.90/6.90. The newer branch (p111) is on Randolph Pl.

MARRAKECH
Map pp218–20   *Moroccan*

☎ 556 4444; 30 London St; dinner £12; 6-10pm Mon-Sat; bus 8, 13, 17

A friendly and homely little Moroccan restaurant, in the basement of the Caravel Guest House (see p162), the Marrakech dishes up a delicious *tajine* (a slow-cooked casserole of lamb with almonds and dried fruit, usually prunes or apricots) accompanied by homebaked, caraway-scented bread. Round off the meal with a pot of mint tea.

MUSSEL INN
Map pp218–20   *Seafood*

☎ 225 5979; 61-5 Rose St; mains £6-15; noon-10pm Mon-Sat, 1.30-10pm Sun; all Princes St buses

Owned by shellfish farmers on the west coast, the Mussel Inn provides a direct outlet for fresh Scottish seafood. The busy restaurant is decorated with bright beech indoors, but tables spill out onto the pavement in summer. A kilogram pot of mussels with a choice of sauces – try leek, bacon, white wine and cream – costs £9.70, while a smaller platter of queen scallops costs £6.30.

NARGILE
Map pp218–20   *Turkish*

☎ 225 5755; 73 Hanover St; mains £9-12; noon-3pm & 5.30-10.30pm Mon-Thu, noon-3pm & 5.30-11pm Fri & Sat; bus 23, 27

Throw away any preconceptions about doner kebabs – this glitzy Turkish restaurant is a class act. Enjoy a spread of delicious *mezeler* (think Turkish tapas) followed by meltingly sweet, marinated lamb char-grilled to crispy perfection. Finish off with *baklava* (nut-filled pastry soaked in honey) and a Turkish coffee. If it weren't for the prices, you could almost be in Turkey.

NIJI Map pp218–20   *Japanese*

☎ 226 7657; 64 Thistle St; mains £14-19; noon-2.30pm & 7-10pm Tue-Fri, noon-3pm & 6-10pm Sat; bus 13, 24, 29, 42

Owner Katsuo Honjigawa has abandoned his famous Tampopo noodle bar, which once sat next to Henderson's at the east end of Thistle St, for the more upmarket delights of this stylish Japanese restaurant. The menu ranges from sea-fresh sushi to authentic Japanese classics such as *yakitori* (marinated and grilled kebab), teriyaki (marinated beef or fish, pan-fried) and tempura (battered and deep-fried pieces of meat, seafood or vegetable with a dipping sauce).

NO 3 ROYAL TERRACE

Map pp218–20   *Scottish/International*

☎ 477 4747; 3 Royal Tce; mains £9-15; noon-2pm & 5.30-10pm; bus 1, 5, 19, 34

Set in a spacious Georgian town house, No 3 has a homely bar and bistro, (complete with open fireplace) at street level, and a more formal restaurant decorated with Indonesian furniture and artwork upstairs. Traditional Scottish produce – beef, lamb, salmon and seafood – is complemented by more unusual offerings such as Balinese vegetable curry. One of the house specialities is top-quality Scottish beef steaks (£15 to £20), hung on the bone for a minimum of three weeks and cooked to order on a charcoal grill.

NUMBER ONE

Map pp218–20   *Modern Scottish*

☎ 557 6727; Balmoral Hotel, 1 Princes St; mains £22-24; noon-2pm Mon-Fri, 7-10pm Sun-Thu, 7-10.30pm Fri & Sat; bus 3, 8, 25, 31, 33

If the Pompadour (see below) is a grand old Scottish dame, then Number One – at the opposite end of Princes St – is a stylish and sophisticated chatelaine, all gold-and-velvet elegance, with a Michelin Star sparkling on her finger. The food is top-notch modern Scottish – choose from à la carte, a two-course lunch for £15.50, three-course dinner for £41, or six courses for

£55 – and the service is just on the right side of fawning. You'll need two of the waiters to pull you out of the opulent sofas that you sink into as you peruse the menu. Best to book ahead, and dress up a bit for dinner.

OLOROSO Map pp218–20 *Modern Scottish*
☎ 226 7614; 33 Castle St; mains £15-22, bar meals £5-9; ◷ restaurant noon-2.30pm & 6-10.30pm, bar 11-1am; bus 13, 19, 37, 41

Oloroso is one of Edinburgh's newest and most stylish restaurants, perched on a glass-encased New Town rooftop with views across a Mary Poppins chimney-scape to the Firth of Forth and the Fife hills. Swathed in sophisticated cream linen and charcoal upholstery enlivened with splashes of deep yellow, the dining room serves top-notch Scottish produce with Asian and Mediterranean touches. On a fine afternoon you can savour a snack and a drink on the outdoor roof terrace while soaking up the sun and a view of the castle.

PIZZA EXPRESS Map p217 *Italian*
☎ 332 7229; 1 Deanhaugh St; mains £6-8; ◷ 11.30am-11.30pm; bus 24, 29, 42

Trust Stockbridge to have a designer pizza place – housed in a former bank beneath a Baronial clock tower, it has a stylish interior on two levels overlooking the Water of Leith, and a decked outdoor terrace right on the riverbank. Their thin and crisp-crusted gourmet pizzas include such delights as the Veneziana (onions, capers, olives, pine kernels, sultanas) and the Prince Carlo (leeks, rosemary, parmesan).

POMPADOUR Map pp218–20 *French*
☎ 222 8888; Caledonian Hilton Hotel, Princes St; mains £14-24; ◷ 6.30-10.30pm Tue-Fri, noon-10.30pm Sat; bus 3, 4, 12, 26, 31, 33, 44

On the go since 1925, the Pompadour is the refined old lady of Edinburgh restaurants. The palatial décor includes red carpets (of course), delicate oriental murals and glittering mirrors, and there's a view of the castle. The food is French, the wine expensive, and the service attentive but discreet – just sit back and be pampered. Dress code requires that men wear a jacket.

RICK'S Map pp218–20 *International*
☎ 622 7800; 55a Frederick St; mains £8-10; ◷ 7am-10pm Sun-Wed, 7am-11pm Thu-Sat; bus 13, 24, 29, 42

Occupying a labyrinthine New Town basement, Rick's is hip to the power *n*. The daytime menu (served from 7am to 6pm) includes breakfast dishes, salads, sandwiches and pastas (£5 to £6.50), as well as grills and seafood, coffee and cakes. The eclectic evening menu (from 6pm) offers simple but tasty dishes with international influences, such as monkfish with mustard mash and port wine sauce, and Thai green vegetable curry with jasmine rice.

SONGKRAN II Map pp218–20 *Thai*
☎ 225 4804; 8 Gloucester St; mains £8-10; ◷ noon-2.30pm & 6-10.45pm Mon-Sat, 6-10.45pm Sun; bus 24, 29, 42

Dishes up the same fine food as the Stockbridge branch (p111), but in the more spacious and atmospheric dining room of a 17th-century town house.

STAC POLLY
Map pp218–20 *Modern Scottish*
☎ 556 2231; 29-33 Dublin St; mains £10-18; ◷ noon-2.30pm Mon-Fri, 6-11pm daily; bus 10, 11, 16, 17

Named after a mountain in northwestern Scotland, Stac Polly's kitchen adds sophisticated twists to fresh Highland produce. Meals such as garden pea and fresh mint soup with garlic cream and parmesan crouton, followed by pan-fried saddle of venison with orange, tarragon and green peppercorn sauce, keep the punters coming back for more. The restaurant's famous baked filo pastry parcels of haggis, served with plum sauce, are so popular they've almost become a national dish. What would Burns think?

The dining room, a cosy maze of stone-walled cellars, is formal but intimate; the original branch of Stac Polly (Map pp218–20; ☎ 229 5405; 8-10 Grindlay St) is less formal and easier to get a table at.

VALVONA & CROLLA CAFFÈ BAR
Map pp218–20 *Italian/Café*
☎ 556 6066; 19 Elm Row, Leith Walk; mains £9-13; ◷ 8am-6pm Mon-Sat, 11am-4.30pm Sun; all Leith Walk buses

The menu at this bright and cheerful café, tucked upstairs at the back of the famous deli (see p152), is based on the owners' family recipes from central and southern Italy, such as pasta with crab, chilli and white wine sauce, and fillet of sole baked with cream and parmesan. Fancy some wine with that? Choose a bottle from the deli on your way in and have it served at your table (£4 corkage). Breakfast is served from 8am to 11.30am Monday to Saturday, and lunch from noon to 3pm. During the Edinburgh Festival the café is open for dinner too, from Thursday to Saturday.

CHEAP EATS

BLUE MOON CAFÉ Map pp218–20   *Café*
☎ 557 0911; 1 Barony St; mains £6-7; ⏱ 11am-10pm
Mon-Fri, 9.30am-10pm Sat & Sun; bus 8, 17
The Blue Moon is the focus of Broughton
Street's gay social life – always busy, always
friendly, and serving up tasty nachos, salads,
sandwiches and baked potatoes. It's famous
for its brilliant, home-made hamburgers,
which come plain or topped with cheese or
chilli sauce, and delicious daily specials.

CUISINE D'ODILE Map p217   *French*
☎ 225 5685; Insitut Français, 13 Randolph Cres; mains
£5-6; ⏱ noon-2pm Tue-Sat; bus 19, 36, 37, 41
This unpretentious little restaurant is housed in
the French consulate and serves home-cooked
French food prepared by the eponymous chef,
Odile Pétré, including mouth-watering soups,
savoury tarts and a chocoholic's paradise of

desserts. There's a two-/three-course set lunch
menu (£6.65/7.35). Although Odile's is un-
licensed, you're free to bring your own wine.

GARDEN CAFÉ Map pp218–20   *Café*
☎ 624 8624; 17 Rose St; sandwiches £5-6; ⏱ 9am-
5.30pm Mon-Sat; all Princes St buses
This attractive, outdoor café is in a sunken
courtyard at the back of the Dome (see p106).
Littered with potted palms strewn beneath
the towering stained-glass windows of the
Dome's dining room, it becomes a lunch
time sun-trap in summer. Soups, salads and
sandwiches are on offer, along with excellent
coffee and tea.

HENDERSON'S SALAD TABLE
Map pp218–20   *Vegetarian*
☎ 225 2131; 94 Hanover St; mains £4.50-6; ⏱ 8am-
10.45pm Mon-Sat (plus Sun during the Edinburgh
Festival); bus 23, 27
Established in 1962, Henderson's is the grandmother of Edinburgh's vegetarian restaurants.
The food is mostly organic, guaranteed GM-free,
and special dietary requirements can be catered
for. The self-service restaurant still has something of a 1970s cafeteria feel to it (but in a good
way), and the daily salads (£1.50 a portion) and
hot dishes are as popular as ever. A two-course
lunch/dinner with coffee costs £7.95/8.95.

Valvona & Crolla Caffè Bar (opposite)

STARBUCKS Map pp218–20 *Café*
☎ 226 5881; 120b Princes St; snacks £2-4; ⊙ 7.30am-8pm Mon-Sat, 9.30am-6pm Sun; all Princes St buses
You may not approve of their plans for world domination, but there's no denying that Starbucks' Princes St flagship – reputedly the largest coffee shop in Scotland – enjoys what is probably the best view in the city. Settle down in an armchair with a large cappuccino (£2.15) and a panini (£3.85) and take in the breathtaking panorama of the castle and gardens across the street.

Top Five Breakfasts

- **Blue Moon Café** (p109) For £5.50 the Blue Moon will ply you with a full Scottish breakfast, or its tasty vegetarian equivalent.
- **Café Mediterraneo** (p105) Café Med serves a full Scottish fry-up for £5.95 or lighter meals, such as a smoked salmon and scrambled-egg croissant, for £3.95.
- **Hadrian's Brasserie** (p106) The regular breakfast menu includes everything from croissants to eggs Benedict, while the slap-up three-course Sunday brunch (£16.50) is accompanied by live jazz from noon till 4pm.
- **Montpeliers** (p113) Breakfast offerings (£3 to £7) – served from 9am all the way through to 6pm – include pancakes and maple syrup, French toast, eggs Benedict and yoghurt with fruit. The full Scottish fry-up (meat or veggie) costs £6.95.
- **Valvona & Crolla Caffè Bar** (p108) Brekkie with an Italian flavour – full *paesano* (meat) or *verdure* (veggie) fry-ups (both £5.95), or deliciously light and crisp *panettone* in *carrozza* (sweet brioche dipped in egg and fried; £3.75). There are also almond croissants, muesli, yoghurt and fruit, freshly squeezed orange juice and perfect Italian coffee.

EDINBURGH WEST

The gradual 'gentrification' of Haymarket and Dalry Rd has seen the area's long-established Indian and Chinese restaurants challenged by a rash of stylish new eateries, including the cosy bistro First Coast, and the refreshing bustle of La Partenope, now one of the city's best Italian eateries. Restaurants here are widely spaced, but the ones below are worth seeking out.

CHANNINGS RESTAURANT
Map p217 *Scottish/Mediterranean*
☎ 315 2225; 12-16 South Learmonth Gardens; mains £15-22, 2-course lunch £16; ⊙ 12.30-2pm & 7-10pm Tue-Sat; bus 19, 37, 41
Channings has a bit of a split personality. The dining room, with its dark wood, striped wallpaper and big, station waiting-room clock, is an elegant, Edwardian gentleman of vaguely military bearing, but the menu – fresh Scottish seafood and game served with a Mediterranean twist – is as modern as Madonna. Try this place for something unerringly superb.

FIRST COAST
Map p217 *Scottish/International*
☎ 313 4404; 99-101 Dalry Rd; mains £7-13; ⊙ noon-2pm Wed-Sat, 5-11pm daily; bus 2, 3, 4, 25, 33, 44
One of our favourite neighbourhood bistros, First Coast has a striking main dining area with stripped stone walls, painted wood panelling and original cornices, and a short and simple menu offering hearty comfort food such as sticky pork and noodle salad (with caramelised

pork in oriental spices), baked sea bass with creamy mash and mussel broth, and jam roly-poly with custard. At lunch, and from 5pm to 6.30pm, you can have any dish for £5.95, any two for £10, or any three for £12.50.

McKIRDY'S STEAKHOUSE
Map p217 *Scottish*
☎ 229 6660; 151 Morrison St; mains £11-17; ⊙ 5-10.30pm; bus 2
In 1999 the McKirdy brothers – owners of a butcher's business that was established in 1895 – decided to cut out the middleman and open their own restaurant. The result is one of Edinburgh's best steakhouses, with friendly staff serving starters such as haggis with Drambuie sauce, and juicy, perfectly cooked steaks from rump to T-bone, accompanied by mustard mash or crispy fries.

OMAR KHAYYAM Map p217 *Indian*
☎ 220 0024; 1 Grosvenor St; mains £8-12; ⊙ noon-2pm & 5-11pm Mon-Fri, noon-11pm Sat, 4.30-11pm Sun; all Haymarket buses

A mainstay of Edinburgh's curry house scene, the Omar Khayyam is an old-fashioned Punjabi restaurant with attentive, waistcoated waiters, plush décor and an ornate fountain trickling away in the middle of the dining room. The food is always fresh and flavourful, ranging from old favourites such as chicken tikka masala to more unusual dishes like Kabul chicken (with chick peas, cumin and coriander). If you enjoy curried seafood, try the Handi Fish Dopiaza – rich and spicy without overwhelming the flavour of the fish.

LA PARTENOPE Map p217 *Italian*
☎ 347 8880; 96 Dalry Rd; mains £8-14; ☽ noon-2pm Tue-Sat, 5-10.30pm daily; bus 2, 3, 4, 25, 33, 44

A family from Naples set up this homely, unpretentious restaurant serving superb southern Italian cuisine, especially seafood. Go for the daily specials – if the smoked swordfish is on the menu, don't miss it. Genial, bespectacled Rosario works the stoves behind the counter, rustling up delectable dishes with his signature sauce of sweet cherry tomatoes, white wine and garlic.

LA P'TITE FOLIE Map p217 *French*
☎ 225 8678; 9 Randolph Pl; mains £8-10; ☽ noon-3pm Mon-Sat, 6-11pm daily; bus 13, 19, 37, 41

La P'tite Folie's new branch is completely different in character, housed in an unusual, Tudor-lookalike building tucked behind West Register House. The upstairs dining room has a pleasantly clubbish feel, with green walls and dark-stained wood – try to grab the table in the little corner turret, with a view along Melville St to the spires of St Mary's Cathedral. The original branch (p107) is located on Frederick St.

RINCÓN DE ESPAÑA Map p217 *Spanish*
☎ 313 3334; 63 Dalry Rd; tapas £2-8; ☽ noon-3pm & 5.30-9.30pm Mon-Sat; bus 2, 3, 4, 25, 33, 44

Like the name says, this is a warm, welcoming 'corner of Spain' with a splendid menu of traditional tapas, ranging from a dish of small, tart Catalonian olives and mouth-watering

embutidos (a spread of cured meats, including Serrano ham, chorizo and *salchichón*) to a hearty *fabada Asturiana* (a rich stew of fava beans, chorizo and black pudding) and probably the best *gambas pil-pil* (prawns in garlic and chilli) that you will find north of Santander.

SONGKRAN Map p217 *Thai*
☎ 225 7889; 24a Stafford St; mains £8-10; ☽ noon-2.30pm & 5.30-11pm Mon-Sat; all West End buses

You'd better book a table and be prepared for a squeeze to get into this tiny basement. The reason for the crush is some of the best Thai food in Edinburgh – try the tender *yang* (marinated and barbecued beef, chicken or prawn), the crisp and tart orange chicken, or the chilli-loaded warm beef salad. Choose Stafford St for lunch, the Stockbridge branch (p108) for dinner.

TASTE GOOD Map p221 *Chinese*
☎ 313 5588; 67-9 Slateford Rd; mains £5-8; ☽ 4.30pm-midnight; bus 4, 28, 35, 38, 44

The downstairs dining area, with its clean lines in pale wood and stainless steel, makes a refreshing change from the usual Chinese restaurant décor. The food matches the interior design in style and taste – the aromatic crispy duck is meltingly sweet, and the beef in black bean sauce has just enough chilli to be pleasantly hot.

Top Five Vegetarian

Many Edinburgh restaurants, of all descriptions, offer vegetarian options on the menu – some good, some bad, some indifferent. The places listed below are all 100% veggie (with vegan options), and all fall into the 'very good' category.
- Ann Purna (p112)
- David Bann (p102)
- Henderson's Salad Table (p109)
- Kalpna (p113)
- Susie's Diner (p115)

EDINBURGH SOUTH

Edinburgh South's eating options range from the mixed bag of upmarket restaurants and Italian and Chinese places in the theatre district of Lothian Rd and Tollcross, to the good-value bistros, cafés and vegetarian places in the student stronghold of Southside, between George Sq and Clerk St. And don't miss the recently opened Rhubarb at Prestonfield House Hotel, one of Edinburgh's most talked-about new restaurants.

ANN PURNA

Map pp218–20   *Indian/Vegetarian*

☎ 662 1807; 45 St Patrick's Sq; mains £5-8; ⏲ noon-2pm & 5.30-11pm Mon-Fri, 5.30-11pm Sat & Sun; bus 42

This little gem of a restaurant serves exclusively vegetarian dishes from southern India, in a bright, unfussy dining room enlivened by a few homely decorations. If you're new to this kind of food, opt for a *thali* (£10.50) – a self-contained platter that contains two starters, four different curry dishes, rice, puri (puffed bread) and a dessert.

APARTMENT Map pp222–3   *International*

☎ 228 6456; 7-13 Barclay Pl; mains £6-9; ⏲ 5.45-11pm Mon-Fri, noon-3pm & 5.45-11pm Sat & Sun; all Bruntsfield buses

Effortlessly cool and classy, and almost always full, the Apartment is just too popular – fantastic bistro food and a buzzy, youthful atmosphere make it hard to get a table. Book in advance – by at least three weeks, preferably – and don't be surprised if you still have to wait. But it's worth being patient for treats such as marinated lamb meatballs with merguez and basil-wrapped goat's cheese, or roasted monkfish marinated in yoghurt with sweet red chilli, served up by the friendly and all-too-gorgeous waiting staff.

ATRIUM Map pp218–20   *Modern Scottish*

☎ 228 8882; 10 Cambridge St; mains £16-20; ⏲ noon-2pm & 6-10pm Mon-Sat; all Lothian Rd buses

Elegantly draped in cream linen and candlelight, the Atrium is one of Edinburgh's most fashionable restaurants, counting Mick Jagger and Jack Nicholson among its past guests. The cuisine is modern Scottish with a Mediterranean twist, with the emphasis on the finest of fresh, seasonal produce – fillet of sea bass with spinach and aubergine caviar, or wild mushroom risotto with truffle and tarragon. The entrance is to the left of the foyer in the Traverse Theatre.

BAR ITALIA Map pp218–20   *Italian*

☎ 228 6379; 100 Lothian Rd; mains £6-8; ⏲ noon-midnight Mon-Thu, noon-1am Fri & Sat, 5pm-midnight Sun; all Lothian Rd buses

A classic Italian restaurant of the old school, Bar Italia comes complete with candles in Chianti bottles and pepper-mills the size of California redwoods wielded by smartly dressed, wise-cracking waiters who occasionally burst into song. Good-value Italian nosh and a lively atmosphere make it a popular venue for birthdays

and office parties, but you'll almost always get a walk-in table.

BLONDE Map pp222–3   *Modern Scottish*

☎ 668 2917; 75 St Leonard's St; mains £8-10; ⏲ noon-2.30pm Tue-Sun, 6-10pm daily; all Newington buses

Well off the beaten tourist track, Blonde is very Edinburgh, catering to a clientele of students, academics and young professionals who appreciate the informal, Southside apartment décor and the exquisite but reasonably priced food. A basket of home-baked bread and a jug of water appear smartly on your table while you peruse a menu that includes the likes of sole fillet stuffed with a seafood, lime and dill mousseline.

BLUE BAR CAFÉ

Map pp218–20   *Modern Scottish*

☎ 221 1222; 10 Cambridge St; mains £11-14; ⏲ noon-2.30pm & 6-10.30pm Mon-Sat; all Lothian Rd buses

Set above the foyer of the Traverse Theatre, this cool, white, minimalist space is a lighter and less formal alternative to the Atrium (see above). The food is simple but skilfully cooked and presented, and the atmosphere loud and chatty with all those luvvies from the theatre downstairs.

BUFFALO GRILL Map pp218–20   *American*

☎ 667 7427; 12-14 Chapel St; mains £7-13; ⏲ noon-2.30pm & 6-10.30pm Mon-Fri, noon-4pm & 5-11pm Sat, noon-4pm & 5-10.30pm Sun; bus 42

The Buffalo Grill is cramped, noisy, fun and always busy, so book ahead. An American-style menu offers burgers, steaks and side orders of fries and onion rings, along with fish and chicken dishes, prawn tempura and a vegetarian burger, but steaks are the main event. This place is not licensed, but you can BYOB for a corkage charge of £1 per bottle of wine, or 50p per beer.

HUMAN BE-IN

Map pp218–20   *Mediterranean*

☎ 662 8860; 2-8 West Crosscauseway; mains £6-8; ⏲ bar 11-1am, food served noon-9pm; bus 42

A stylish café-bar with a choice of tables, comfy booths or chill-out sofas, the Be-In has an inventive Mediterranean menu with good vegetarian options (how about grilled goat's cheese with roasted fennel, tomato and basil?). The weekend brunch menu, served noon to 3pm, includes interesting variations like smoked salmon, poached egg and Hollandaise sauce on grilled muffins.

KALPNA Map pp222–3   *Indian/Vegetarian*
☎ 667 9890; 2-3 St Patrick Sq; mains £5-7; 🕙 noon-2pm & 5.30-11pm Mon-Fri, 5.30-11pm Sat; all South Bridge buses

Another long-standing Edinburgh favourite, Kalpna is one of the best Indian restaurants in the country, vegetarian or otherwise. The cuisine is mostly Gujarati, with a smattering of dishes from other parts of India – try the *khoya kaju* (vegetables, cashew nuts, sultanas and pistachios in a cream sauce with coriander and nutmeg, served with coconut rice and puri). Specials include the buffet lunch (£4.50) and the Kalpna thali (£8.50), which includes samosas, two curry dishes, rice, puri and a dessert.

MARQUE CENTRAL
Map pp218–20   *Modern Scottish*
☎ 229 9859; 30b Grindlay St; mains £11-15; 🕙 11.45am-2pm & 5.30-10pm Tue-Thu, 11.45am-2pm & 5.30-11pm Fri, noon-2pm & 5.30-11pm Sat; all Lothian Rd buses

Tucked between the Lyceum Theatre and the Usher Hall, this split-level bistro (go for an upstairs table if you have the choice) is perfectly positioned to catch the theatre-going crowds. The menu is top-notch modern Scottish, with dishes such as cod strips in a light and crispy batter, breast of wood pigeon with wild mushroom and black pudding tagliatelle, and there are nice little touches like home-baked bread and a complimentary *amuse-gueule* of wild mushroom cappuccino. The pre-/post-theatre special of two/three courses for £12.50/15 is available from 5.30pm to 7pm and 9pm to 10pm Tuesday to Thursday, and 9.30pm to 11pm Friday and Saturday.

MONTPELIERS Map p221   *International*
☎ 229 3115; 159-61 Bruntsfield Pl; mains £8-10; 🕙 food served 9am-10pm; all Bruntsfield buses

Montpeliers is a popular and stylish bar (see p127) with a separate restaurant area done up in cheerful chocolate and orange colours, offering good food all day long. It has a pleasant, laid-back buzz – the place is rarely empty, at any time of day – and the menu wanders the globe from French onion soup to duck pancakes with hoisin sauce to wild mushroom and parmesan risotto to Thai green chicken curry.

NAMASTE Map pp222–3   *Indian*
☎ 466 7061; 41-2 West Preston St; mains veg £5-7, meat & fish £9-11; 🕙 5.30-11pm; bus 3, 8, 31, 37

The food at this cosy little place is from the North Indian frontier, and the atmosphere has a chilled, hippie-trail-to-Kathmandu feel with incense, candlelight and scattered cushions. Dishes range from curried dhal (lentils) and *bhindi* (okra) to butter chicken and prawn *jhal-frezie* (cooked with herbs, green pepper and chillis), but our favourite is the fantastically flavoursome *malai kofta* – little cutlets of paneer (cheese), potato and nuts in a rich, creamy, spice-laden sauce. The restaurant serves beer and soft drinks – if you prefer wine, then BYOB (no corkage charge).

NDEBELE Map pp222–3   *South African*
☎ 221 1141; 57 Home St; mains £6-7; 🕙 10am-10pm; all Tollcross buses

This South African café is hidden deep in darkest Tollcross, but is worth seeking out for the changing menu of unusual African dishes (including at least one veggie option) – try a boerewors sandwich (sausage made with pork, beef and coriander). Before you leave, pop downstairs for a look a their gallery of African art.

ORIGINAL KHUSHI'S Map pp224–5   *Indian*
☎ 667 0888; 30 Potterrow; mains £7; 🕙 11am-midnight Mon-Fri, 5-10pm Sat & Sun; bus 2, 41, 42

Established in 1947, Khushi's is an authentic Punjabi canteen and something of an Edinburgh institution – it recently moved from Drummond St to shiny new premises next to Edinburgh University's George Sq campus. Its speciality is basic Indian dishes, marinated and cooked in the traditional way, served with no frills at reasonable prices. It's not licensed but you can bring your own booze (no corkage).

RAINBOW ARCH Map pp218–20   *Chinese*
☎ 221 1288; 8-16 Morrison St; mains £7-11; 🕙 noon-11.30pm; all Lothian Rd buses

It's always a sign of a good Chinese restaurant when you see members of the local Chinese community eating there, and you'll see plenty of them enjoying the excellent dim sum at the Rainbow Arch. The menu is more adventurous than most and even the standard dishes, such as lemon chicken, are a cut above the usual.

RHUBARB Map pp214–15   *Modern Scottish*
☎ 225 1333; Prestonfield House Hotel, Priestfield Rd; mains £14-24; 🕙 noon-3pm & 6-11pm; taxi

James Thomson's latest restaurant (see p104 and p168), set in the splendid 17th-century Prestonfield House, is as much a feast for the eyes as for the taste buds. From the floodlit façade, glowing like a ruby in the night, to the striped and swirling scarlets, burgundies and vermilions that deck the walls, curtains, carpets and upholstery, the décor flaunts a full palette of rich reds set off with black and gold. The air of decadence is enhanced by the flicker of diptyque-scented candlelight, and the sensuous surfaces – damask, brocade, marble, gilded leather – make you want to touch everything. The over-the-top décor is matched by the intense flavours and rich textures of the food – pungent smoked haddock soup with a silky, raw quail's egg plopped on top; plump, pink fillet steak with chewy roast garlic and wild mushrooms; voluptuous rhubarb *crème brûlée* – and the wine list runs to 500 bins. Don't miss the opportunity to take your postprandial coffee and brandy upstairs to the sumptuous fireside sofas in the Tapestry Room. A set-menu lunch and dinner (£12.95) is available from noon to 3pm, 6pm to 7pm, and 10pm to 11pm.

ROGUE Map pp218–20 *Modern Scottish*
☎ 228 2700; 67 Morrison St; mains £6-15; ☽ noon-3pm & 6-11pm Mon-Sat; bus 2
Hidden in the heart of the city's new financial district (the far-from-obvious doorway is next to the main entrance to the Scottish Widows insurance company building), fashionable Rogue has a definite theatrical feel – a sweeping, curved banquette backed by diaphanous curtains encloses an oval dining area; the décor is all in cream, the waiters all in black. It pulls in a mixed clientele ranging from students trying to impress their dates to chief executives trying to impress their bankers. The menu likewise ranges from comfort food (posh pizza and bangers and mash) to haute cuisine (fillet steak and lobster). Be sure to check out the toilets, if you can find them – the doors are cunningly disguised as blank walls.

SANTINI Map pp218–20 *Italian*
☎ 221 7788; 8 Conference Sq; mains £18-22; ☽ noon-2.30pm Mon-Fri, 6.30-10.30pm Mon-Sat; all Lothian Rd buses
Tucked away at the back of the Sheraton Grand Hotel, Santini is one of a small family of select restaurants with branches in London and Milan. This is a cut (two cuts, even) above your average Italian restaurant – the dining area is draped in white muslin and linen, with flagstone floors,

mosaic panels and cinnamon-coloured armchair seats, and the waiting staff are dressed just as elegantly in Versace and Gucci. The quality of the food matches the surroundings, from the starter of garganelli with duck ragout and pistachios to the main event of scallops with asparagus and Sicilian oranges.

SUKHOTHAI Map pp222–3 *Thai*
☎ 229 1537; 23 Brougham Pl; mains £7-8; ☽ noon-2.30pm & 6-11pm; bus 24
This unassuming but attractive Tollcross restaurant serves up authentic, good-value Thai food, including a fiery *tom yum goong* (hot and sour soup with prawns) and a creamy, coconutty *gaeng phed* (mild, red curry). The Sunday lunch time buffet – all you can eat for £9.95 – is excellent value.

SURUCHI Map pp224–5 *Indian*
☎ 556 6583; 14a Nicolson St; mains £7.50-11; ☽ noon-2pm & 5.30-11pm Mon-Sat, 5.30-11pm Sun; all South Bridge buses
A laid-back Indian eatery with handmade turquoise tiles, lazy ceiling fans and chilled-out jazz guitar, the Suruchi offers a range of exotic dishes as well as the traditional tandoori standards. Try *shakuti* from Goa (lamb or chicken with coconut, poppy seeds, nutmeg and chilli), or vegetarian *kumbhi narial* (mushrooms, coconut and coriander). An amusing touch is provided by the menu descriptions – they're translated into broad Scots ('a beezer o' a curry this…gey nippie oan the tongue').

THAI LEMONGRASS Map pp222–3 *Thai*
☎ 229 2225; 40-1 Bruntsfield Pl; mains £7-12; ☽ 5-11.30pm Mon-Thu, noon-11.30pm Fri-Sun; all Bruntsfield buses
From the waiter's prayer-like gesture of greeting (known as a *wâi*) to the rich and varied flavours of the food – fiery chilli, fragrant lemongrass, tangy lime leaves and sweet coconut – everything about this restaurant feels authentically Thai. The rustic décor of terracotta tiles, yellow walls, dark-stained wood and cane table-mats makes for a relaxing ambience, enlivened by a constant buzz of conversation – it's a popular place, so book ahead if possible.

ZAZOU Map p221 *Scottish/French*
☎ 669 3294; Union Canal, Ogilvie Tce, Polwarth; 3-course dinner £25; ☽ by advance booking only; bus 38
How's this for dinner with a difference – hire a whole canal-boat and cruise along the Union Canal as you dine. The menu varies, but offers

a choice of four starters and four main courses, including one fish and one vegetarian option. Book at least seven days in advance; groups of six or more (maximum 12) can have the boat to themselves.

CHEAP EATS
CHINESE HOME COOKING
Map pp222–3 *Chinese*
☎ 668 4946; 34 West Preston St; mains £4-7; ⏰ noon-2pm Mon-Fri & 5-11pm daily; bus 42

This long-established, no-nonsense eatery has been serving up good-value, authentic Chinese food for around 25 years now. Menus in Chinese and Japanese, as well as English, show that the place is favoured by people who really know oriental food.

FILMHOUSE CAFÉ BAR
Map pp218–20 *Café*
☎ 229 5932; 88 Lothian Rd; mains £4-6; ⏰ 10am-11.30pm Sun-Thu, 10-12.30am Fri & Sat; all Lothian Rd buses

This is the place to peruse the Filmhouse's cinema programme while slumped on a sofa watching trailers on the big-screen TV and slurping soup or munching nachos. The coffee and hot chocolate (lots of cream and flaky chocolate) are good, as are the cakes, sandwiches and soup of the day (£1.85; the soup is always vegan).

HO HO MEI NOODLE SHACK
Map pp218–20 *Chinese*
☎ 221 1288; 8-16 Morrison St; mains £4.50-8.50; ⏰ 5.30pm-1.30am Mon-Sat; all Lothian Rd buses

The Ho Ho Mei, upstairs from the Rainbow Arch (see p113) and under the same management, is a popular late-night eatery serving big bowls of noodles and tasty Chinese hot-pot dishes to eat in or take away.

SUSIE'S DINER Map pp218–20 *Vegetarian*
☎ 667 8729; 51-3 West Nicolson St; mains £3-6; ⏰ 9am-8pm Mon, 9am-9pm Tue-Sat; bus 2, 41, 42

Susie's is a down-to-earth, self-service, veggie restaurant with scrubbed wooden tables, rickety chairs and a friendly atmosphere. The menu changes daily but includes things such as tofu, aubergine and pepper casserole, and Susie's famous falafel plates. Billed as 'the best falafel in the Western world', these crunchy, cumin-laced chick-pea patties are well worth trying.

> ## Top Five Romantic Restaurants
> - Café Marlayne (p105)
> - Rhubarb (p113)
> - Santini (p114)
> - Stac Polly (p108)
> - Witchery by the Castle (p104)

Witchery by the Castle (p104)

WATERFRONT EDINBURGH

Edinburgh has not made too much of its waterfront in the past, but the recent regeneration of Leith has seen the Shore (on the banks of the Water of Leith) and Dock Pl (just to the west of the Shore) develop a sizable enclave of gourmet restaurants, many with appealing historic settings. There is also a handful of long-established waterfront pubs serving excellent bar lunches and suppers.

LEITH

BRASSERIE DE MALMAISON

Map p216   *French*

☎ 468 5000; 1 Tower Pl; mains £11-15; ☺ 7-10am Mon-Fri, 7-11am Sat & Sun, noon-2.30pm & 6-11pm daily; bus 16, 22, 35, 36

Clean-cut, contemporary design and wholesome French cooking are the distinguishing features of the Malmaison, set in the hotel of the same name (see p169). The à la carte menu includes dishes such as *pithivier* (puff pastry tart) of artichoke, goat's cheese and spinach, grilled lemon sole with lobster butter, and creamy, caramelly *crème brûlée*. The *prix fixe* three-course dinner menu costs £15.95.

BRITANNIA SPICE Map p216   *Asian*

☎ 555 2255; 150 Commercial St; mains £8-15; ☺ noon-11.45pm; bus 1, 11, 22,34, 35, 36

No, not Geri Halliwell's latest incarnation, but a multi-award-winning curry house with nautical, ocean-liner décor, serving a wide range of dishes from northern India, Bangladesh, Nepal, Thailand and Sri Lanka. The waist-widening, all-you-can-eat buffet lunch costs £7.95.

DANIEL'S BISTRO Map p216   *French*

☎ 553 5933; 88 Commercial St; mains £8-12; ☺ noon-10pm; bus 16, 22, 35, 36

The eponymous Daniel comes from Alsace, and his all-French kitchen staff combine top Scottish and French produce with Gallic know-how to create a wide range of delicious dishes. The fish soup is richly flavoured, and main courses range from slow-cooked knuckle of pork to hearty Alpine *tartiflette* (potato, onion and bacon baked in cream and topped with cheese). You can nip in for coffee and cake in the afternoon too.

FISHERS Map p216   *Seafood*

☎ 554 5666; 1 The Shore; mains £12-19; ☺ noon-10.30pm; bus 16, 22, 35, 36

This cosy little bar-turned-restaurant, tucked beneath a 17th-century signal tower, is one of the city's best seafood places. Fishers' fishcakes are an Edinburgh institution, and the rest of the hand-written menu (you might need a calligrapher to decipher it) rarely disappoints. Booking is recommended – if you can't get a table here, try their more sophisticated New Town branch, Fishers in the City (p106).

KHUBLAI KHAN Map p216   *Mongolian*

☎ 555 0005; 43 Assembly St; 3-course lunch £7.95, dinner £15.95; ☺ 6-10.30pm daily, 12.30-2.30pm Fri & Sun; bus 12, 16, 35

How many cities outside Ulan Baator can boast a Mongolian restaurant? OK, the authenticity may be questionable but it certainly makes a change from curry or pizza. Choose from a buffet of raw meat, seafood and vegetables, flavoured with oils, spices and sauces of your choice, and have it cooked to order on a Mongolian-style barbecue (veggies have their own grills). The cost of dinner includes three courses and all you can eat from the buffet – as the menu says: 'You may repeat the experience as often as any tight-fitting clothing you may be wearing will allow.'

THE RAJ Map p216   *Indian*

☎ 553 3980; 91 Henderson St, The Shore; mains £7-11; ☺ noon-2.30pm daily, 5.30-11.30pm Sun-Thu, 5.30pm-midnight Fri & Sat; bus 16, 22, 35, 36

Run by celebrity chef Tommy Miah (author of *True Taste of Asia*), the Raj is an atmospheric curry house overlooking the Water of Leith and serving Indian (including Goan) and Bangladeshi cuisine. Specialities include the tongue-tingling green Bengal chicken (marinated with lime juice, mint and chilli) and spicy Goan lamb garam fry. If you want to eat at home or in your hotel room, try their **Curry-in-a-Hurry** (toll-free ☎ 0800 073 1983; www.curry-in-a-hurry.org) delivery service, available 5.30pm to 11pm.

RESTAURANT MARTIN WISHART

Map p216   *French*

☎ 553 3557; 54 The Shore; mains £20-25; ☺ noon-2pm & 7-10pm Tue-Fri, 7-10pm Sat; bus 16, 22, 35, 36

In 2001 this restaurant became the first in Edinburgh to win a Michelin star. The eponymous chef has worked with Albert Roux, Marco Pierre White and Nick Nairn, and brings a modern

French approach to the finest Scottish produce, from fillet of halibut to roast saddle of lamb. The dining room is crisply elegant, the service professional and discreet, and the food beautifully presented. A set three-course lunch costs £18, and a six-course tasting menu is £45; book ahead as far as possible.

WATERFRONT Map p216   *Scottish/Seafood*
☎ 554 7427; 1c Dock Pl; mains £12-17; ✆ noon-9.30pm Mon-Thu, noon-10.30pm Fri & Sat, 12.30-9.30pm Sun; bus 16, 22, 35, 36
Housed in a single-storey, red-brick building that was once a waiting room for ferries across the Forth, the Waterfront is a cosy warren of timber-lined nooks and corners with a gorgeous conservatory out the back. The menu is dominated by seafood, from succulent scallops and pan-fried squid to seared tuna and sweet-fleshed lobster, with an added Asian zing supplied by spices such as ginger or Sichuan pepper.

NEWHAVEN

OLD CHAIN PIER Map pp214–15   *Pub Grub*
☎ 552 1233; 1 Trinity Cres; mains £4-8; ✆ food served noon-8pm; bus 16, 32
The Old Chain Pier is a lovely little pub overlooking – nay, overhanging – the Firth of Forth on the waterfront east of Granton Harbour; grab a window table and enjoy a view across the Firth to the hills of Fife. The excellent bar menu includes soup of the day, a creamy and filling mussel and smoked haddock stew, rich

Top Five Seafood Restaurants

- **Café Royal Oyster Bar** (p106)
- **Fishers** (p116)
- **Fishers in the City** (p106)
- **Mussel Inn** (p107)
- **Waterfront** (below)

prawn curry, and succulent steak and onion baguette with chips. The menu of real ales is no less enticing than the food.

CRAMOND

CRAMOND GALLERY BISTRO   *Scottish*
☎ 312 6555; 5 Cramond Village; 2-course lunch £7; ✆ 10am-6pm May-Sep, 10am-5pm Oct-Apr; bus 24, 41
This little bistro has a delightful setting beside the river – there are outdoor tables in summer – and serves good fish dishes as well as coffee, cakes and pastries.

CRAMOND INN   *Scottish*
☎ 336 2035; 30 Cramond Glebe Rd; mains £7-12; ✆ bar 11am-11pm Mon-Thu, 11am-midnight Fri & Sat, 12.30-11pm Sun; food served 11am-2.30pm & 6-9.30pm Mon-Fri, 11am-9.30pm Sat & Sun; bus 24, 41
The picturesque Cramond Inn is a welcoming, traditional pub with lots of wood-panelled nooks and cosy fireplaces. It serves a good range of filling food, from a chunky Cullen skink (smoked haddock and potato soup) to steaks, seafood and vegetarian dishes.

Top Five Fish and Chips

Most of Edinburgh's best fish and chip shops are owned by members of the city's sizable Scots-Italian community. The sign of good fish is a light, crispy batter that stays crispy to the end; Scots prefer haddock rather than cod, the English favourite.

In Scotland a take-away portion of fish and chips is called a 'fish supper'; a piece of fish without the chips is a 'single fish'. And in an Edinburgh chip shop you will be asked if you want 'salt and sauce' on your food. The latter is a runny, brown concoction, a bit like diluted, vinegary HP sauce; if you'd prefer salt and vinegar (or nothing at all), say so.

L'Alba D'Oro (Map pp218–20; ☎ 557 2580; 5-9 Henderson Row, New Town; ✆ 11.30am-2.30pm & 5pm-midnight Mon-Fri, 5pm-midnight Sat & Sun; bus 23, 27, 36) One of the few places where you can pick up a bottle of decent wine along with your fish and chips.

L'Aquila Bianca (Map p217; ☎ 332 8433; 17 Raeburn Pl, Stockbridge; ✆ 11.30am-1.30pm Mon-Fri, 4.30pm-12.30am Tue-Sun; bus 24, 29, 42)

Deep Sea (☎ 557 0276; 2 Antigua St, New Town; all Leith Walk buses)

Hadrian's Brasserie (see p106) Excellent, upmarket fish and chips for the sit-down crowd (no take-aways).

Rapido (☎ 556 2041; 79 Broughton St, New Town; ✆ 10.30am-2pm Mon-Fri, 4.30pm-1am Sun-Thu, 4.30pm-2am Fri & Sat; bus 8, 17) Not only fish and chips, but also baked potatoes, pizzas, sandwiches and Ben and Jerry's ice cream.

GREATER EDINBURGH

There are not too many memorable eating places outside the city's central districts, but Queensferry has a handful of decent pubs where you can get a good bar lunch or supper.

QUEENSFERRY

HAWES INN   Scottish/International

☎ 331 1990; Newhalls Rd; mains £4-8; ☻ bar 11am-11pm Mon-Sat, 12.30-10.30pm Sun; food served noon to 10pm; First Edinburgh bus 43

This 350-year-old coaching inn, famously mentioned in *The Antiquary* by Sir Walter Scott and also in Robert Louis Stevenson's *Kidnapped*, is an atmospheric warren of rustic rooms tucked beneath the southern end of the Forth Bridge. It's a child-friendly place serving excellent pub grub – there are outdoor tables in summer – with a main menu ranging from fresh sandwiches to haggis, steaks and seafood, and a kids' menu with the likes of spaghetti hoops, fish fingers, and mini-chicken Kiev.

Drinking

Drinking

Edinburgh has always been a drinker's city. The 18th-century poets Robert Fergusson and Robert Burns spent much of their time in – and often drew inspiration from – Edinburgh's public houses, and rather than attend his law lectures at Edinburgh University, the young Robert Louis Stevenson preferred to haunt the city's many howffs (drinking dens) – a practice perpetuated by many Edinburgh students to this day.

Although many city-centre pubs have been 'themed' or converted into vast drinking halls catering to office workers unwinding at the end of the day, the neighbourhood bar is still a social centre where you can meet friends, watch the football on TV, listen to live music or take part in the weekly quiz night. Edinburgh has over 700 pubs – more per square mile than any other city in the UK – and they are as varied and full of character as the people who drink in them... from Victorian palaces to stylish pre-club bars, and from real-ale howffs to trendy cocktail bars.

Trad vs Trendy

At one end of Edinburgh's broad spectrum of hostelries lies the traditional 19th-century bar, which has preserved much of its original Victorian decoration and generally serves cask-conditioned real ales and a staggering range of malt whiskies. At the other end is the modern 'style bar', with a cool clientele and styling so sharp you could cut yourself on it. The bar staff here are more likely to be serving cocktails. Here are some suggestions from each end of the range:

Top Five Traditional Pubs

- Abbotsford (p123)
- Athletic Arms (The Diggers) (p126)
- Bennet's Bar (p128)
- Café Royal Circle Bar (p123)
- Sheep Heid (p128)

Pubs generally open from 11am to 11pm Monday to Saturday and 12.30pm to 11pm on Sunday. Many open later on Friday and Saturday, when they stay open till midnight or 1am, while those with a food or music licence can party on until 3am. The bell for last orders rings about 15 minutes before closing time, and you're allowed 15 minutes' drinking-up time after the bar closes.

For more pubs check out the Eating (p99) and Entertainment (p131) chapters.

OLD TOWN

The pubs on the Royal Mile are – not surprisingly – aimed mainly at the tourist market, but there are still some good old-fashioned drinking dens hidden up the closes and along the side streets.

Many Grassmarket pubs have outdoor tables on sunny summer afternoons, but in the evenings they are often favoured by boozed-up lads on the pull. Cowgate – Grassmarket's extension to the east – leads into Edinburgh's club land.

ROYAL MILE

BAR KOHL Map pp224–5

☎ 225 6939; 54 George IV Bridge; ☽ 4pm-1am Mon-Sat, 5.30pm-1am Sun; bus 2, 23, 27, 41, 42

One of the city's original style bars, Communism-themed Bar Kohl is crammed with old wooden furniture and awash with booming hip-hop and varicoloured vodka – it stocks some 250 different vodkas from around the world, including 54 flavoured Finlandias, from bubblegum to red hot chilli pepper.

CITY CAFÉ Map pp224–5

☎ 220 0125; 19 Blair St; ☽ 11-1am; bus 35

Dating from the 1980s, the City Café is Edinburgh's original pre-club bar, with a 1950s-American-diner retro look, great munchies, and a downstairs DJ spinning hip-hop, R&B, ragga and funk. It's a place of pilgrimage for

Irvine Welsh fans – the bar was mentioned in *Trainspotting*.

ENSIGN EWART Map pp224–5
☎ 225 7440; 225 Lawnmarket; ⏱ 11am-11.30pm Mon-Thu, 11am-midnight Fri & Sat, 12.30pm-midnight Sun; bus 28

The nearest pub to the castle, the Ensign Ewart trades on its historic setting and military associations. A mix of tourists, students from the university residences in Milne's Court and journalists, covering events at the Scottish Parliament's temporary home next door, drop in to enjoy real ale and good bar food. There's live folk music on Friday, Saturday and Sunday evenings. .

JOLLY JUDGE Map pp224–5
☎ 225 2669; 7a James Court; ⏱ noon-midnight Mon & Thu-Sat, noon-11pm Tue & Wed, 12.30-11pm Sun; bus 28

Tucked away down an Old Town close, the Judge exudes a cosy 17th-century ambience with its low, timber-beamed ceilings and numerous nooks and crannies, and has the added attraction of a cheering log fire in cold weather.

LOGIE BAIRD'S BAR Map pp224–5
☎ 556 9940; 1 South Bridge; ⏱ 9-1am; all South Bridge buses

Yet another former bank that has been converted into a bar and hotel, the Logie Baird has an imposing mahogany island bar, a balcony area and outdoor tables in summer. It also serves good bar meals, including breakfast.

MALT SHOVEL Map pp224–5
☎ 225 6843; 11-15 Cockburn St; ⏱ 11am-midnight Mon-Thu, 11-1am Fri & Sat, 12.30pm-midnight Sun; bus 64

A traditional-looking pub, with dark wood and subdued tartanry, the Malt Shovel offers a go od range of real ales and over 100 malt whiskies, and is famed for its regular Tuesday night jazz from Swing 2004 (or 2005, or 2006, depending what year it is).

ROYAL MILE TAVERN Map pp224–5
☎ 557 9681; 127 High St; ⏱ 11am-midnight Mon-Fri, 11-1am Sat, 12.30-11pm Sun; bus 35

An elegant, traditional Edinburgh bar lined with polished wood, mirrors and brass, the Royal Mile serves real ale, good wines and fine food – *moules marinières* and crusty bread is a lunch time speciality.

TRON Map pp224–5
☎ 226 0931; 9 Hunter Sq; ⏱ 11.30-1am Mon-Sat, 12.30pm-1am Sun; all South Bridge buses

A popular place with the student crowd, the lower floors of The Tron (part of the nationwide It's A Scream pub chain) form a horror-theme pub (oooh, scary) with wild discos on Friday and Saturday only. The slightly more staid street-level bar is open the rest of the week.

TUN Map pp218–20
☎ 557 9297; The Tun Building, Holyrood Rd; ⏱ 11am-11pm Sun-Thu, 11-1am Fri & Sat; bus 64

Set among the modern coloured-glass and steel architecture of the redeveloped Holyrood district next to the brand new Scottish Parliament building, the Tun is a funky fishtank of a place, with chunky leather sofas, steel bar stools and a sloping back wall that looks like a sample page from a floor-tile catalogue. It is much frequented by media people from the neighbouring BBC studios and the *Scotsman* newspaper offices just across the road.

WORLD'S END Map pp224–5
☎ 556 3628; 4 High St; ⏱ 11-1am Mon-Sat, 12.30pm-1am Sun; bus 35

So named because this part of the High St once lay next to the Old Town's eastern limit – part of the 16th-century Flodden Wall can still be seen in the basement – the World's End is an old local pub, with plenty of regulars as well as tourists. They do good bar food, including excellent fish and chips.

GRASSMARKET

BEEHIVE INN Map pp224–5
☎ 225 7171; 18-20 Grassmarket; ⏱ 11am-midnight Mon-Thu, 11-1am Fri & Sat, 11am-10pm Sun; bus 2

Formerly a real-ale haven, the historic Beehive has changed tack and is now a big, buzzing party pub, with extremely cheesy disco music on Friday and Saturday nights. You can

Drinking – Old Town

get reasonable grub during the day, but the main attraction is sitting out the back in the Grassmarket's only beer garden, with grand views up to the castle. The Beehive is the starting point for the Edinburgh Literary Pub Tour (see p50).

BOW BAR Map pp224–5
☎ 226 7667; 80 West Bow; ☼ noon-11.30pm Mon-Sat, 12.30-11pm Sun; bus 2, 23, 27, 41, 42

A busy, traditional pub, unspoilt by touristy trappings despite its nearness to the Royal Mile, the Bow Bar serves a range of excellent real ales and a vast selection of malt whiskies – this is not the sort of place to go asking for Bacardi Breezers. There are snug window seats and leather benches, but you'll find it's often standing-room only on Friday and Saturday evenings.

GREYFRIARS BOBBY'S BAR Map pp224–5
☎ 225 8328; 34 Candlemaker Row; ☼ 11am-midnight Mon-Sat, 12.30pm-midnight Sun; bus 2, 23, 27, 41, 42

Bobby's is a pleasant, old-fashioned Edinburgh bar that is much frequented by students (it serves inexpensive food and is on the way to the fleshpots of the Cowgate) and handy for tourists sheltering from the rain after trying to photograph the statue of the eponymous wee pup outside.

THE LAST DROP Map pp224–5
☎ 225 4851; 74 Grassmarket; ☼ 11-1am Mon-Sat, 12.30pm-1am Sun; bus 2

The Last Drop is an 18th-century inn with low, timbered ceilings and lots of hidden corners. The name commemorates the gallows that used to stand nearby, but far from being morose it's a swinging (har har) party pub, popular with students and backpackers.

THREE SISTERS Map pp224–5
☎ 622 6800; 39 Cowgate; ☼ 9-1am; bus 64

This huge pub is actually three bars – one American, one Irish and one Gothic – with a big cobbled courtyard for outdoor drinking in summer. It's a bit of a mad party place but you can come back the morning after and soothe your hangover with a big, fried breakfast – and a free Bloody Mary if you order before 11am.

WHITE HART INN Map pp224–5
☎ 226 2806; 34 Grassmarket; ☼ 11-1am; bus 2

A brass plaque outside this pub proclaims: 'In the White Hart Inn Robert Burns stayed during his last visit to Edinburgh, 1791.' Claiming to be the city's oldest pub in continuous use (since 1516), it also hosted William Wordsworth in 1803. Not surprisingly, it's a traditional, cosy, low-raftered place with folk music sessions every night except Friday and Saturday.

White Hart Inn

Drinking – Old Town

NEW TOWN

George St, once the city's most prestigious business address, has changed enormously in the last decade. Many of the offices are now shops and all the grand old bank buildings have been turned into bars, allowing city wags to make lots of lame jokes about liquid assets and standing orders. Most of the city's most fashionable new bars are on or near George St.

Rose St was once a famous pub crawl, where generations of students, sailors and rugby fans would try to visit every pub on the street (around 17 of them) and down a pint of beer in each one. These days shopping, not boozing, is Rose St's *raison d'être*, but there are still a few pubs there that are worth visiting.

Bohemian Broughton, at the eastern end of the New Town, is the centre of Edinburgh's gay scene, and has an eclectic mixture of traditional real-ale pubs, modern pre-club bars and all-out gay bars.

Drinking in Stockbridge, on the other hand, is mostly a relaxed, traditional affair, involving comfy seats, conversation and real ale, wine or whisky – if it's a wild time you're after, look elsewhere.

GEORGE STREET

ABBOTSFORD Map pp218–20
☎ 225 5276; 3 Rose St; ⏱ 11am-11pm Mon-Sat; all Princes St buses

One of the few pubs in Rose St that has retained its Edwardian splendour, the Abbotsford has long been a hang-out for writers, actors, journalists and media people and has many loyal regulars. Dating from 1902 and named after Sir Walter Scott's country house, the pub's centrepiece is a splendid, mahogany island bar.

BAR 38 Map pp218–20
☎ 220 6180; 126-8 George St; ⏱ 11-1am Mon-Sat, 11am-midnight Sun; bus 13, 19, 37, 41

Unisex toilets with a sofa and a fountain? In Bar 38, trendiness extends right into the plumbing. This is a big, busy bar with an excellent range of snack foods that fills up with suits from the surrounding offices in the early evening.

CAFÉ ROYAL CIRCLE BAR Map pp218–20
☎ 556 1884; 17 West Register St; ⏱ 11am-11pm Mon-Wed, 11am-midnight Thu, 11-1am Fri & Sat, 12.30-11pm Sun; all Princes St buses

Perhaps *the* classic Edinburgh bar, the Café Royal's main claims to fame are its magnificent oval bar and the series of Doulton tile portraits of famous Victorian inventors. Check out the bottles on the gantry – staff line them up to look as if there's a mirror there, and many a drink-befuddled customer has been seen squinting and wondering why they can't see their reflection.

CUMBERLAND BAR Map pp218–20
☎ 558 3134; 1-3 Cumberland St; ⏱ 11-1am Mon-Sat, 12.30pm-1am Sun; bus 13

Under the same management as the Bow Bar in Victoria St (see p122), the Cumberland pays the same attention to serving well-looked-after, cask-conditioned ales. Though relatively modern, the bar has an authentic, traditional wood-brass-and-mirrors look and there's a nice little beer garden outside.

FRAZER'S COCKTAIL BAR Map pp218–20
☎ 624 8624; 14 George St; ⏱ noon-11pm Sun-Wed, noon-midnight Thu, noon-12.30am Fri & Sat; bus 24, 28

Frazer's is the bar at the Dome (see p106), formerly a temple to Mammon (it was originally a bank's head office) and now a shrine to Dionysus – stand in the foyer for a moment and be impressed. The gleaming bar (to your left) is a beautiful Art Deco masterpiece and serves fine real ales as well as pukka cocktails.

GREAT GROG WINE BAR Map pp218–20
☎ 225 1616; 43 Rose St; ⏱ 10am-11pm Sun-Thu, 10-1am Fri & Sat; all Princes St buses

A chilled-out haven in the middle of bustling Rose St, Great Grog is the ideal place to kick back in a leather sofa and choose from a list of more than 30 wines available by the glass (if you want to go for a whole bottle, the choice increases to over 100 varieties).

GUILDFORD ARMS Map pp218–20
☎ 556 4312; 1 West Register St; ⏱ 11am-11pm Mon-Thu, 11am-midnight Fri & Sat, 12.30pm-midnight Sun; all Princes St buses

Located next door to the Café Royal, the Guildford is another classic Victorian pub full of polished mahogany, brass and ornate cornices. The bar lunches are good – try to get a table in the unusual upstairs gallery, with a view over the sea of drinkers down below.

KAY'S BAR Map pp218–20

☎ 225 1858; 39 Jamaica St; 🕑 11am-midnight Mon-Thu, 11-1am Fri & Sat, 12.30-11pm Sun; bus 13, 24, 29, 42

Housed in a former wine-merchant's office, tiny Kay's Bar is a cosy haven with red-leather benches, a coal fire and a fine range of real ales. Good food is served in the back room at lunch time but you'll have to book a table – Kay's is a small but popular place.

KENILWORTH Map pp218–20

☎ 226 4385; 152-4 Rose St; 🕑 9.30am-11pm Mon-Thu, 9.30am-12.45pm Fri & Sat, 12.30-11pm Sun; all Princes St buses

A gorgeous, Edwardian drinking palace, complete with original fittings – from the tile floors, mahogany circle bar and gantry, to the ornate mirrors and gas lamps – the Kenilworth was Edinburgh's original gay bar back in the 1970s. Today it attracts a mixed crowd of all ages and serves a good range of real ales and malt whiskies.

NEW TOWN BAR Map pp218–20

☎ 538 7775; 26b Dublin St; 🕑 noon-1am Mon-Thu, noon-2am Fri & Sat, 12.30pm-1am Sun; all York Pl buses

Dark and smoky, with a suspiciously sticky carpet, the New Town is a gay bar that attracts mainly older males and lots of leather. The cellar bar has a disco (10pm to 2am) on Friday and Saturday.

OLOROSO LOUNGE BAR Map pp218–20

☎ 226 7614; 33 Castle St; 🕑 11-1am Mon-Sat, 12.30pm-1am Sun; bus 13, 19, 37, 41

The roof-top lounge at the much hyped Oloroso restaurant (see p108) is currently Edinburgh's place to see and be seen – this bar would be at home in New York, Paris or London. Sleek leather sofas and floor-to-ceiling windows allow comfortable views across the city to Arthur's Seat, and – if the weather deigns to allow use of the outdoor terrace – the castle.

OPAL LOUNGE Map pp218–20

☎ 226 2275; 51 George St; 🕑 noon-3am; bus 24, 41, 42

One of Edinburgh's newest style bars, the Opal is jammed at weekends with affluent 20-somethings who've spent £200 and two hours in front of the mirror to achieve that artlessly scruffy look. During the week, when the

air-kissing, cocktail-sipping crowds thin out, it's a good place to relax with a fruit smoothie (or one of those expensive, but excellent, cocktails) and sample the tasty Asian food on offer. Expect to queue on weekend evenings.

OXFORD BAR Map pp218–20

☎ 539 7119; 8 Young St; 🕑 11-1am Mon-Sat, 12.30pm-1am Sun; bus 13, 19, 37, 41

The Oxford is that rarest of things these days – a real pub for real people, with no 'theme', no music, no frills and no pretensions. Immortalised by regular Ian Rankin, author of the Inspector Rebus novels, the Ox is a place to meet people and have genuine conversations.

PO NA NA Map pp218–20

☎ 226 2224; 43b Frederick St; 🕑 9pm-3am; bus 13, 24, 29, 42

This bar is one of a UK-wide chain, which makes the North African souk-style décor seem more contrived than imaginative. Still, the DJs play great party music and the place opens till 3am every night, so... rock the casbah, rock the casbah...

ROBERTSONS 37 Map pp218–20

☎ 225 6185; 37 Rose St; 🕑 11am-11pm Mon-Sat; all Princes St buses

No 37 is to malt whisky connoisseurs what The Diggers once was to real-ale fans. Its long gantry sports a choice of more than 100 single malts, and the bar provides a quiet and elegant environment in which to sample them.

STANDING ORDER Map pp218–20

☎ 225 4460; 62-6 George St; 🕑 10-1am; bus 24, 41, 42

One of several converted banks on George St, the Standing Order is a cavernous beer hall with a fantastic vaulted ceiling and some cosy rooms off to the right – look for the one with the original 27-tonne safe. Despite its size, it can be standing-room only at the weekend, with crowds pulled in by the cheap drinks – as little as £1.50 for a pint.

TILES BAR-BISTRO Map pp218–20

☎ 558 1507; 1 St Andrew Sq; 🕑 8am-midnight Mon-Fri, 11am-midnight Sat & Sun; all Princes St buses

A regular haunt of city lawyers and accountants, Tiles is a smart and stylish bar in yet another converted bank, with live jazz on Sunday evenings at 6.30pm. It takes its name from the lovely Victorian tiles inside.

TONIC Map pp218–20
☎ 225 6431; 34a North Castle St; ☽ 3pm-1am Mon-Sat, 5pm-1am Sun; bus 13, 24, 29, 42

As cool and classy as a perfectly mixed martini, Tonic prides itself on the authenticity of its cocktails, of which there are many – the menu goes on forever. Check out those Philippe Starck bar stools – do you sit on them or use them as ashtrays?

YO! BELOW Map pp218–20
☎ 220 6040; 66 Rose St; ☽ 5pm-midnight Mon-Thu, 5pm-1am Fri & Sat, 3pm-1am Sun; all Princes St buses

Tucked below the Yo! Sushi restaurant, this Japanese-themed bar has metered, serve-yourself beer taps on each table and offers free tarot readings and a range of oriental massages. DJs play house grooves on Friday and Saturday nights, while Wednesday is karaoke night and Sunday is comedy night.

BROUGHTON

CASK & BARREL Map pp218–20
☎ 556 3132; 115 Broughton St; ☽ 11-12.30am Sun-Thu, 11-1am Fri & Sat; bus 8, 17

At the foot of Broughton St, the spit-and-sawdust style Cask & Barrel is a beer-drinker's delight, with a selection of up to 10 real ales, as well as Czech and German beers.

CLAREMONT BAR Map pp214–5
☎ 556 5662; 133-5 East Claremont St; ☽ 11-1am Mon-Sat, 12.30pm-1am Sun; bus 13

Scotland's only sci-fi theme pub (no, you have to see it), the Claremont is a friendly, gay-owned bar and restaurant. The first and third Saturdays of the month are men-only nights, when leather, rubber and skinheads are the order of the evening. If that's not your bag, Monday nights see the weekly meeting of the Edinburgh Doctor Who Appreciation Society (honest!).

CLARK'S BAR Map pp218–20
☎ 556 1067; 142 Dundas St; ☽ 11am-11pm Mon-Wed, 11am-11.30pm Thu-Sat, 12.30-11pm Sun; bus 23, 27

A century old and still going strong, Clark's caters to a clientele of real-ale aficionados and regulars, who appreciate an old-fashioned, no-frills pub.

MATHERS Map pp218–20
☎ 556 6754; 25 Broughton St; ☽ 11-12.30am Mon-Thu, 11-1am Fri & Sat, 12.30-11pm Sun; bus 8, 17

Cocktail at Tonic

Mathers is the 40-something generation's equivalent of the 20-something's Basement bar (p105) across the street – a friendly, relaxed pub with Edwardian décor serving real ales and good pub grub.

PIVO CAFFÈ Map pp218–20
☎ 557 2925; 2-6 Calton Rd; ☽ noon-1am; all Leith St buses

Aiming to add a little taste of Bohemia to Edinburgh's bar scene, Pivo (Czech word for beer) serves goulash and dumplings, bottled and draught Czech beers – the Staropramen is God in a glass – and two-pint cocktails. Try a 'long absinthe' (absinthe with lemonade and lime).

POP ROKIT Map pp218–20
☎ 556 4272; 2 Picardy Pl; ☽ 10-1am Mon-Sat, 11-1am Sun; bus 8, 17

A shrine to chrome, steel, concrete and glass – even part of the floor is made of glass – Pop Rokit is style with a capital yessss. Full-length glass walls mean you can ogle the passers-by outside, that is if you can tear your eyes away from the beautiful people inside. Down in the basement, resident DJs pump out groove, funk and disco for the pre-club crowds.

STAG & TURRET Map pp218–20
☎ 661 6443; 1-7 Montrose Tce; ☽ noon-1am; buses 15, 35

This is a pleasant, gay local with karaoke from 8.30pm on Wednesday, Friday and Sunday. It's good for cruising – as the locals say: 'If ye're gaggin' fur it, try the Stag and Turret.'

STOCKBRIDGE

THE ANTIQUARY Map pp218–20
☎ 225 2858; 72-8 St Stephen St; ◷ 11.30-12.30am Mon-Wed, 11.30-1am Thu-Sun; bus 24, 29, 42
A dark, downstairs den of traditional beersmanship, the long-established Antiquary has lively open folk-music sessions on Thursday night, when all comers are welcome to perform.

BAILIE BAR Map pp218–20
☎ 225 4673; 2 St Stephen St; ◷ 11am-midnight Mon-Thu, 11-1am Fri & Sat, 12.30-11pm Sun; bus 24, 29, 42
Tucked down in a basement, the Bailie is an old Stockbridge stalwart, a dimly lit, warm and welcoming nook where you can enjoy good coffee as well as real ales and malts.

BERT'S BAR Map p217
☎ 332 6345; 2 Raeburn Pl; ◷ 11am-midnight Mon-Thu, 11-1am Fri & Sat, 12.30pm-1am Sun; bus 24, 29, 42
Under the same management as its namesake in the West End (see below), Bert's is a welcoming womb of warm wood and leather, a good place to linger over a pint of real ale and a decent pie.

HECTOR'S Map p217
☎ 332 5328; 47 Deanhaugh St; ◷ noon-midnight Sun-Wed, noon-1am Thu-Sat; bus 24, 29, 42
A trendy café-bar with good food and an excellent range of wines, Hector's is a popular meeting place, whether for breakfast, afternoon coffee or an evening meal and a drink.

EDINBURGH WEST

The West End and Haymarket are home to a handful of good old-fashioned pubs, plus a smattering of newer places.

WEST END & HAYMARKET

ATHLETIC ARMS (THE DIGGERS)
Map p221
☎ 337 3822; 1-3 Angle Park Tce; ◷ noon-midnight Mon-Thu, noon-1am Fri & Sat, 12.30-6pm Sun; bus 1, 28, 34
Named for the cemetery across the street – the grave-diggers used to nip in and slake their thirst after a hard day's interring – the Diggers dates from the 1890s. Its heyday as a real-ale drinker's Mecca has gone, but it's still staunchly traditional – the décor has barely changed in 100 years – and it's packed to the gills with football and rugby fans on match days.

BERT'S BAR Map p217
☎ 225 5748; 29-31 William St; ◷ 11am-11pm Mon-Wed, 11-1am Thu-Sat; all Shandwick Pl buses
A classic re-creation of a 1930s-style pub – complete with a jar of pickled eggs on the bar – Bert's is a good place to sample real ale and down-to-earth pub grub such as Scotch pies and bangers and mash.

CALEY SAMPLE ROOM Map p221
☎ 337 7204; 58 Angle Pk Tce; ◷ 11am-midnight Mon-Thu, 11-1am Fri & Sat, 12.30pm-midnight Sun; bus 4, 28, 34, 35, 44
Owned by the nearby Caledonian Brewery, the Sample Room is a big, lively pub with a wide range of excellent real ales. It's popular with sports fans too, who gather to watch football and rugby matches on the large-screen TVs.

CUBA NORTE Map p217
☎ 221 1430; 192 Morrison St; ◷ noon-midnight Sun-Wed, noon-1am Thu-Sat; all Haymarket buses
Swagger in, order a Cuba libre and prepare to salsa. Cuba Norte provides a little touch of Latino levity in the cold, northern winters, dishing up good Cuban tapas, Havana cigars and hip-swaying salsa beats. You can hone your technique at one of their regular salsa classes.

GOLDEN RULE Map p221
☎ 622 7112; 30 Yeaman Pl; ◷ 11am-11.30pm Mon-Sat, 12.30-11pm Sun; bus 10, 27
Hard to find but worth the hunt, the Golden Rule is a great wee local with a lively atmosphere and up to eight real ales on tap.

INDIGO YARD Map p217
☎ 220 5603; 7 Charlotte Lane; ◷ 8.30-1am; bus 13, 19, 36, 37, 41

Set around an airy, stone-floored and glass-roofed courtyard, Indigo Yard is a *très* fashionable West-End watering hole that has been patronised by the likes of Liam Gallagher, Pierce Brosnan and Kylie Minogue. Good food – including open-air barbecues during the summer months – just adds to the attraction.

RYAN'S BAR Map pp218–20

☎ 226 6669; 2 Hope St; ⏱ 7.30-1am Mon-Sat, 12.30pm-1am Sun; bus 13, 19, 36, 37, 41

Housed in a former fruit market, Ryan's has retained its original vaulted ceiling but is best known as a lively bar where office workers gather at the end of the day. In summer there are outdoor tables, and good food is served all day.

EDINBURGH SOUTH

Southside's large student population is well served by lots of stylish pre-club bars and café-bars clustered around Edinburgh University's George Sq and Old College buildings.

Tollcross, formerly a working-class industrial district, has a good range of traditional, real-ale pubs, though designer bars are beginning to make inroads, especially in the trendier suburbs of Bruntsfield and Morningside to the south.

BRUNTSFIELD & MORNINGSIDE

CANNY MAN'S Map p221

☎ 447 1484; 237 Morningside Rd; ⏱ 11.30am-11pm Mon-Wed, 11.30am-midnight Thu-Sat, 12.30-11pm Sun; bus 11, 15, 16, 17, 23

A lovably eccentric pub, the Canny Man's is a crowded warren of tiny rooms crammed with a bizarre collection of antiques and curiosities (a description that could apply to some of the regulars) where the landlord regularly refuses entry to anyone who looks scruffy, inebriated or vaguely pinko/commie/subversive. If you can get in, you'll find it serves excellent real ale, vintage port and Cuban cigars.

GOLF TAVERN Map pp222–3

☎ 229 5040; 30 Wright's Houses; ⏱ noon-midnight Sun-Thu, noon-1am Fri & Sat; all Bruntsfield buses

The Golf occupies a 19th-century building overlooking the pitch-and-putt course on Bruntsfield Links, though there have been licensed premises on this spot since the 15th century. It's an attractively old-fashioned bar, with polished wood and luxurious leather sofas, that pulls in a young, studenty crowd at the weekends.

MONTPELIERS Map p221

☎ 229 3115; 159-61 Bruntsfield Pl; ⏱ 9-1am; all Bruntsfield buses

The 'in' place to down a pint in Bruntsfield, Monty's is packed at weekends with rugby-playing, public-school-educated financial analysts chasing sun-tanned, blonde Emmas and Carolines just back from skiing in St Moritz or villa-hunting in Tuscany. The food (see p113) and the beer are good, though.

SOUTHSIDE

ASSEMBLY BAR Map pp224–5

☎ 220 4288; 41 Lothian St; ⏱ 9-1am; bus 2, 41, 42

Assembly originally opened in 1996 (as Iguana), making it positively prehistoric for a style bar, but a combination of timeless décor, cool sounds and a recent facelift and relaunch have kept it popular. There's a relaxed crowd of mostly students topping up on coffee during the day, but the atmosphere heats up as pre-clubbers pour in during the evening.

BAM BU Map pp224–5

☎ 556 0200; 67 South Bridge; ⏱ 11-1am; all South Bridge buses

Bam Bu is all, well… bamboo, candlelight and mock-oriental décor. You can get tanked on Japanese sake cocktails, and snack on sushi and dim sum, and there's DJs spinning drum'n'bass on Friday and hip-hop on Saturday.

BOROUGH Map pp222–3

☎ 668 2255; 72-80 Causewayside; ⏱ 11-1am; bus 42

The Borough Hotel's (see p167) bar brings a whiff of the *Sex and the City* lifestyle to the Southside, with its broad expanses of timber floor, deep leather sofas, expertly assembled cocktails and a menu of vintage champagnes at up to £99 a bottle. The Borough Mary cocktail has no less than 10 perfectly judged ingredients, and could just as easily create a hangover as cure one.

OXYGEN Map pp224–5

☎ 557 9997; 3 Infirmary St; ⏱ 10-1am; all South Bridge buses

When this place first opened, Czech beer and Morgans Spiced weren't the only things that came in bottles – it was so breathtakingly cool

The Other National Drink...

What do Scotland and Peru have in common?

Answer: They are the only countries in the world where a locally manufactured soft drink outsells Coca Cola. In Peru it's Inca Cola but in Scotland it's Barr's Irn-Bru, which commands 25% of the Scottish fizzy-drinks market (Coke has 24%). A Barr's advertising campaign in the 1980s promoted Irn-Bru as 'Scotland's other national drink'.

Barr's have been making soft drinks in Scotland since 1880, but it was in 1901 that they launched a new beverage called 'Iron-Brew' (labelling regulations forced a change of spelling to 'Irn-Bru' in 1946). As with Coke, the recipe (32 ingredients, including caffeine and ammonium ferric citrate – the source of the iron in the name) remains a closely guarded secret known by only two people. Scots swear by its efficacy as a cure for hangovers, which may account for its massive sales. You can even get Irn-Bru along with your Big Mac in Scottish branches of McDonald's.

In recent years Barr's have begun to build their brand overseas, exporting the quirky, humorous and award-winning advertising campaign that positions Irn-Bru drinkers as mischievous and rascally. Irn-Bru is hugely popular in Russia, where it is the third-favourite soft drink after Coke and Pepsi (maybe it's that hangover thing again), and in the Middle East, but it has yet to challenge Coke and Pepsi in the USA. Big Red, beware!

Tasting notes:

Colour is a rusty, radioactive orange. Nosing reveals a bouquet of bubble gum, barley sugar and something vaguely citrus, maybe tangerine? Carbonation is medium, and mouth-feel... well, you can almost feel the enamel dissolving your teeth.

---

that they served bottled oxygen to keep you from passing out. The potential fire hazard soon put paid to that gimmick, but Oxygen is still a popular pre-club venue with industrial-chic décor, cool tunes and a tempting food menu.

PEAR TREE HOUSE Map pp218–20
☎ 667 7533; 38 West Nicolson St; 11am-midnight Mon-Thu, 11-1am Fri & Sat, 12.30pm-midnight Sun; bus 2, 41, 42
The Pear Tree is another student favourite, with comfy sofas and board games inside, plus the city centre's biggest beer garden outside. There's live music in the garden on Sunday afternoons in summer.

SHEEP HEID Map pp214–5
☎ 656 6951; 43-5 The Causeway, Duddingston; 11am-11pm Mon-Wed, 11am-midnight Thu-Sat, 12.30-11pm Sun; bus 42
Possibly the oldest licensed premises in Edinburgh – dating back to 1360 – the Sheep Heid is more like a country pub than a city bar. Set in the semi-rural shadow of Arthur's Seat, it's famous for its 19th-century skittles alley and lovely beer garden. The name comes from an ornamental snuff box in the form of a sheep's head that was presented to the inn by James VI in 1580, commemorated in a carving above the bar.

SOUTHSIDER Map pp224–5
☎ 667 2003; 3-7 West Richmond St; 11am-midnight Mon-Wed, 11-1am Thu-Sat, 12.30pm-midnight Sun; all Newington buses

Always busy with students and locals, the South-sider is a big and welcoming old-fashioned pub that pulls in people from further afield with a good selection of real ales, including Maclay's, one of Scotland's excellent small breweries.

TOLLCROSS

BENNET'S BAR Map pp222–3
☎ 229 5143; 8 Leven St; 11-12.30am Mon-Wed, 11-1am Thu-Sat, 12.30-11.30pm Sun; all Tollcross buses
Bennet's has managed to retain almost all of its beautiful Victorian fittings, from the leaded, stained-glass windows and ornate mirrors to the wooden gantry and brass water taps on the bar – if whisky is your poison, there are over 100 malts to choose from.

BLUE BLAZER Map pp218–20
☎ 229 5030; 2 Spittal St; 11-1am Mon-Sat, 12.30pm-1am Sun; bus 2, 35
With its bare wooden floors, cosy fireplace and efficient bar staff, the Blue Blazer is a down-to-earth antidote to the designer excess of Monboddo (see following) across the road, catering to a loyal clientele of real-ale enthusiasts, pie eaters and Saturday horse-racing fans.

CLOISTERS Map pp218–20
☎ 221 9997; 26 Brougham St; noon-midnight Sun-Thu, noon-12.30am Fri & Sat; bus 24
Housed in a converted manse (minister's house) that once belonged to the next-door church, and furnished with well-worn, mismatched wooden

tables and chairs, Cloisters now ministers to a mixed congregation of students, locals and real-ale connoisseurs. It has decent grub and coffee, and a nice, warm fireplace in winter.

MONBODDO BAR Map pp218–20
☎ 221 5555; 34 Bread St; ⏱ 11am-midnight Mon-Thu, 11-1am Fri & Sat, noon-midnight Sun; bus 2, 35

Tollcross is better known for its traditional pubs than for the sleek, designer looks of the Monboddo, part of the Point Hotel (see p160). The polished steel bar, spindly chairs, chocolate leather banquettes and modern artworks are complemented by efficient, friendly staff who know how to mix a superb champagne cocktail.

WATERFRONT EDINBURGH

As befits a dockland area, Leith and Newhaven are well supplied with old-fashioned pubs, once the haunts of shore-going sailors but now increasingly gentrified for the district's new upmarket residents.

LEITH

CAMEO BAR Map p216
☎ 554 9999; 23 Commercial St; ⏱ noon-1am; bus 16, 22, 35, 36

How's this for bar-room games one-upmanship? Forget table football, darts or pool; this pub has its own six-hole putting green out the back. When you're not practising your golfing skills, the bright red Cameo offers a warm, relaxing bar with open fire in winter, good food, live music and a giant-screen TV for sporting occasions.

CARRIERS QUARTERS Map p216
☎ 554 4122; 42 Bernard St; ⏱ 11am-11pm Sun-Wed, 11am-midnight Thu, 11-1am Fri & Sat; bus 16, 22, 35, 36

With a low, wooden ceiling, stone walls and a fine old fireplace, the Carriers has all the historic atmosphere that its 18th-century origins would imply. It serves real ales and malt whiskies, and traditional Scottish bar meals such as stovies and haggis.

KING'S WARK Map p216
☎ 554 9260; 36 The Shore; ⏱ noon-11pm Mon-Thu, noon-midnight Fri & Sat, 11am-11pm Sun; bus 16, 22, 35, 36

Set in a fine old 17th-century building, the King's Wark is a very cosy, candlelight-and-fireplace sort of a pub, with an upmarket clientele and excellent food and wine.

OLD DOCK BAR Map p216
☎ 555 4474; 3-5 Dock Pl; ⏱ 11am-11pm Mon-Thu, 11am-midnight Fri & Sat, 12.30-11pm Sun; bus 16, 22, 35, 36

Like the Old Chain Pier (following), this place is owned by legendary Edinburgh pub landlord and real-ale enthusiast Drew Nicol. Although it has been through several incarnations since it opened in 1813, Drew has returned it to its original role of a convivial, traditional Leith bar. Also like its sister pub, it serves excellent food as well as a good range of quality beers and wines.

PORT O'LEITH Map p216
☎ 554 3568; 58 Constitution St; ⏱ 9-12.45am Mon-Sat, 12.30pm-12.45am Sun; bus 12, 16, 35

A good, old-fashioned, friendly local boozer, the Port is swathed with flags and cap bands left behind by visiting sailors – the harbour is just down the road. Pop in for a pint and you'll probably stay till closing time.

NEWHAVEN
OLD CHAIN PIER Map pp214–5
☎ 552 1233; 32 Trinity Cres; ⏱ 11am-11pm Mon-Thu, 11am-midnight Fri & Sat, 12.30-11pm Sun; bus 16, 32

As well as being a great place to eat (see p117), the Old Chain Pier is an award-winning real ale pub, full of polished wood, brass and nautical paraphernalia – the building was once the 19th-century booking office for steamers across the Firth of Forth. The pier from which it takes its name was washed away in a storm in 1898.

STARBANK INN Map pp214–5
☎ 552 4141; 64 Laverockbank Rd; ⏱ 11am-11pm Mon-Wed, 11am-midnight Thu-Sat, 12.30-11pm Sun; bus 16, 32

Along with the Old Chain Pier (see previous), the Starbank is an oasis of fine ales and good, home-made food on Edinburgh's wind-swept waterfront. In summer there's a sunny conservatory at the back, and in winter there's a blazing fire to toast your toes in front of.

How to Be a Malt Whisky Buff

'Love makes the world go round? Not at all! Whisky makes it go round twice as fast.' From *Whisky Galore,* by Compton Mackenzie (1883–1972).

Whisky-tasting today is almost as popular as wine-tasting was in the yuppie heyday of the late 1980s. Being able to tell your Ardbeg from your Edradour is *de rigueur* among the whisky-nosing set, so here are some pointers to help you impress your friends.

What's the difference between malt and grain whiskies?

Malts are distilled from malted barley – that is, barley that has been soaked in water, then allowed to germinate for around 10 days until the starch has turned into sugar – while grain whiskies are distilled from other cereals, usually wheat, corn or unmalted barley.

So what is a single malt?

A single malt is a whisky that has been distilled from malted barley and is the product of a single distillery. A pure (vatted) malt is a mixture of single malts from several distilleries, and a blended whisky is a mixture of various grain whiskies (about 60%) and malt whiskies (about 40%) from many different distilleries.

Why are single malts more desirable than blends?

A single malt, like a fine wine, somehow captures the essence of the place where it was made and matured – a combination of the water, the barley, the peat smoke, the oak barrels in which it was aged, and (in the case of certain coastal distilleries) the sea air and salt spray. Each distillation varies from the one before, like different vintages from the same vineyard.

How should a single malt be drunk?

Either neat, or preferably with a little water added. To appreciate the aroma and flavour to the utmost, a measure of malt whisky should be cut (diluted) with one-third to two-thirds as much spring water (still, bottled spring water will do). Ice, tap water – except for Edinburgh's exceptionally clean-tasting tap water – and (God forbid) mixers are for philistines. Would you add lemonade or ice to a glass of Chablis?

Give me some tasting tips!

Go into a bar and order a Lagavulin (Islay) and a Glenfiddich (Speyside). Cut each one with half as much again of still, bottled spring water. Taking each one in turn, hold the glass up to the light to check the colour; stick your nose in the glass and take two or three short, sharp sniffs. By now, everyone in the pub will be giving you funny looks, but never mind.

For the Lagavulin you should be thinking: amber colour, peat-smoke, iodine, seaweed. For the Glenfiddich: pale white-wine colour, malt, pear drops, acetone, citrus. Then taste them. Then try some others. Either you'll be hooked, or you'll never touch whisky again.

Where's the cheapest place to buy Scotch whisky?

A French supermarket, unfortunately. In the UK, where a bottle of single malt typically costs £25 to £35, taxes account for around 72% of the price, making Scotland one of the most expensive places in Europe to enjoy its own national drink.

If you're serious about spirits, the **Scotch Malt Whisky Society** (☎ 554 3451; www.smws.com) runs an intensive one-day Whisky School that covers the basics of whisky-tasting and evaluation. The cost is £210, including lunch, canapés and drinks. Membership of the society costs from £75 per year and includes use of members' rooms in Edinburgh and London.

Drinking – Waterfront Edinburgh

PORTOBELLO

BEDFORD HOUSE HOTEL Map pp214–5

☎ 454 4500; 77 The Promenade; ☾ bar 11am-midnight Mon-Thu, 11-1am Fri & Sat, 12.30-11pm Sun; food served noon-2pm & 6-9pm Mon-Fri, noon-7pm Sat, 12.30-7pm Sun; bus 15, 26

A welcoming, traditional pub set in a Victorian hotel (see p169), the family-friendly Bedford House Hotel has a spacious beer-garden right next to the promenade beside Portobello beach, and hosts live music on Friday and Saturday evenings. It's only a 15-minute bus ride from the city centre.

Entertainment

Entertainment

Glasgow folk have a colourful expression – 'all fur coat and nae knickers' – that they apply to Edinburgh, suggesting that it projects an air of middle-class respectability on the surface but is cheap and dirty underneath. There's an element of truth there – the city that inspired the story of Jekyll and Hyde certainly has its seamier side – and the high culture epitomised in the Edinburgh Festival finds its counterpoint in the city's reputation as a pub-crawler's paradise.

Edinburgh has a number of fine theatres and concert halls, and there are independent art-house cinemas as well as mainstream movie theatres. Many pubs offer entertainment ranging from live Scottish folk music to pop, rock and jazz to karaoke and quiz nights, while the new generation of style bars purvey house, dance and hip-hop to the pre-clubbing crowd (see the Drinking chapter p119 for more information).

What's On

Edinburgh's most comprehensive source of what's-on information is *The List* (£2.20; www.list.co.uk), an excellent, fortnightly listings and reviews magazine (also covering Glasgow), available from most newsagents. *The Gig Guide* (www.gigguide.co.uk) is a free, monthly leaflet that advertises regular music gigs under the headings 'Rock, Pop & Blues', 'Jazz' and 'Folk & World'; you can pick it up in bars, cafés and music venues. The free monthly booklet *What's On Edinburgh & Lothians* (www.whatson-scotland.co.uk) is produced by the Edinburgh and Lothians Tourist Board. It covers a wide range of events and exhibitions, including art galleries and museums. The *Edinburgh Evening News* newspaper has daily reviews and listings of cinema, music, theatre, clubs, comedy and arts events.

Online ticket agencies which serve a range of Edinburgh venues and events, from rock gigs to rugby matches, include:

Ticketline (☎ 0870 100 0000; www.ticketline.co.uk)

Ticketmaster (☎ 0870 060 0800; www.ticketmaster.co.uk)

Ticketweb (☎ 0870 060 0100; www.ticketweb.co.uk)

Way Ahead (☎ 0870 122 2106; www.wayahead.com)

CINEMA

Film buffs will find plenty to keep them happy in Edinburgh's art-house cinemas, the Filmhouse and the Cameo, while popcorn munchers can choose from a range of multiplexes. Most offer concessions for school kids, students, the unemployed and senior citizens, and most have wheelchair access and induction loops for hearing-impaired customers.

You can check cinema listings in the *Edinburgh Evening News* newspaper and *The List*.

CAMEO Map pp222–3
box office ☎ 228 4141, info ☎ 228 2800; 38 Home St; adult/child £5.50/3.50; bus 10, 11, 1, 16, 17

The independently owned, three-screen Cameo cinema is a good, old-fashioned cinema showing an imaginative mix of mainstream as well as art-house movies. There is a good programme of midnight movies, late-night double bills and Sunday matinees, and the seats in Screen 1 are big enough for you to get lost in.

DOMINION Map p221
box office ☎ 447 4771, info ☎ 447 2660; 18 Newbattle Tce; adult/child £5.90/3.70; bus 11, 15, 16, 17, 23

The much-loved Dom is a delightful, independent, family-run four-screener in a 1938 Art Deco building. The programme is unashamedly mainstream awnd family-oriented.

FILMHOUSE Map pp218–20
box office ☎ 228 2688, info ☎ 228 2689; 88 Lothian Rd; adult/child £5.50/4; all Lothian Rd buses

The Filmhouse screens a full programme of art-house, classic, foreign and second-run films, with lots of themes, retrospectives and 70mm screenings, and is the main venue for the International Film Festival. It has wheelchair access to all screens. Matinees and early evening screenings are cheaper, and the bargain Friday matinees (starting before 4pm) cost only £2.50/1.20 per adult/child.

ODEON Map pp218–20
☎ 0870 505 0007; 118 Lothian Rd; adult/child £5.80/4.60; all Lothian Rd buses
This five-screen multiplex shows mainstream, first-run films and special children's matinees. All screens have wheelchair access.

UGC FOUNTAINPARK Map p221
☎ 0870 902 0417; 130 Dundee St; adult/child £5.50/3.50; bus 1, 28, 34, 35
The UGC is a massive 12-screen multiplex, complete with café-bar, movie-poster shop and scarily overpriced popcorn.

VUE CINEMA Map pp218–20
☎ 0870 240 6020; Omni Centre, Greenside Pl; adult/child £5.60/3.30; all Leith Walk buses
Another 12-screen multiplex, with three 'Gold Class' screens (tickets cost £7.50) where you can watch your movie of choice from the comfort of a luxurious leather reclining seat complete with sidetable for your drink and complementary snacks.

COMEDY

Stand-up comedy has come to dominate the Fringe in the last decade, and its popularity has spun off a couple of decent comedy clubs and countless comedy nights in various pubs – check the Comedy listings in *The List*.

BEDLAM THEATRE Map pp224–5
☎ 225 9893; www.bedlamtheatre.co.uk; 11b Bristo Pl; admission £3; bus 2, 23, 27, 41, 42
The Bedlam hosts a long-established (10 years), weekly improvisation slot, The Improverts, which is hugely popular with local students – shows kick off at 10.30pm every Friday, and you're guaranteed a robust and entertaining evening. See also Theatre p144.

JONGLEURS Map pp218–20
☎ 0870 787 0707; www.jongleurs.com; Omni Centre, Greenside Pl; admission £12-16; all Leith Walk buses
This nationwide chain of comedy clubs has finally opened a venue in Edinburgh, in the gleaming new Omni Centre at the top of Leith Walk. There are shows on Thursday, Friday and Saturday year round, with four in-house stand-ups, and occasional gigs by big-name UK comics.

THE STAND COMEDY CLUB
Map pp218–20
☎ 558 7272; www.thestand.co.uk; 5 York Pl; admission £1-7; all York Pl buses
The Stand, founded in 1995, is Edinburgh's main comedy venue. It's a cabaret bar – you can eat and drink as well as laugh – with shows every night (doors open 7.30pm), plenty of big-name appearances, and a free improv show at Sunday lunch time.

CLUBBING

Edinburgh's club scene took a nose dive in 2002, with attendances falling as the huge crowds and huge venues that characterised the late 1990s were deserted in favour of more intimate DJ sessions in late-night style bars. In response, Edinburgh's clubs have become more diverse and stage a wider mix of cultural events, including live gigs, comedy and even art exhibitions.

Most of the venues are concentrated in and around the twin sumps of Cowgate and Calton Rd, to either side of the Royal Mile – so it's downhill all the way...

Club nights are fickle things, coming and going with the seasons; for details check the latest issue of *The List* and look for flyers in pre-club bars and record shops – Underground Solush'n (see p149) in Cockburn St is a good place for information.

> ## Top Five Pre-Club Bars
> - **Assembly Bar** (p127)
> - **Borough** (p127)
> - **Pivo Caffè** (p125)
> - **Opal Lounge** (p124)
> - **Oxygen** (p127)

reggae night **Messenger Sound System** (admission £7; 🕙 11pm-3am, 1st & 3rd Sat of month).

CABARET VOLTAIRE Map pp224–5
☎ 220 6176; www.cabaret-voltaire.co.uk; 36 Blair St; bus 35

An atmospheric warren of stone-lined vaults houses Edinburgh's newest 'alternative' club, which eschews huge dance floors and egotistical DJ-worship in favour of a 'creative crucible' hosting an eclectic mix of DJs, live acts, comedy, theatre, visual arts and the spoken word. Well worth a look.

CAVENDISH/DIVA Map pp218–20
☎ 228 3252; 3 West Tollcross; all Tollcross buses

It's been around for decades and once had a reputation as a grab-a-granny meat market, but the Cav has undergone a refit and is now a stylish, split-level club with a big, bouncy dance floor. It still packs them in on Fridays (admission free before 11pm, £5 after; 🕙 4pm-3am) and Saturdays (admission £6; 🕙 10pm-3am) with a policy of over-25s only and smart dress code (no trainers, no jeans) – the main arena plays mainstream chart tracks, while the upper-level Diva churns out cheesy party hits from the '60s, '70s and '80s. Tuesdays, Wednesdays and Sundays are student nights (admission £2; 🕙 10pm-3am).

CC BLOOMS Map pp218–20
☎ 556 9331; 23 Greenside Pl; 🕙 6pm-3am Mon-Sat, 8pm-3am Sun; all Leith St buses

The raddled old queen of the Edinburgh gay scene, CC's offers two floors of deafening dance and disco. It's a bit overpriced and often overcrowded but still worth a visit – if you can get past the bouncers and the crowds of drunks looking for a late drink.

COMMPLEX Map p216
☎ 555 5600; www.thecommplex.co.uk; 39-40 Commercial St; bus 16, 22, 35, 36

The Commplex is an intimate new club venue housed in a converted church in Leith. Events range from Cuban club nights with Latino bands, dancers and salsa classes to live bands to monthly open-mic nights when wannabe rockers get to strut the stage for an evening. Regular club nights include **Velvet** (www.club-velvet.co.uk; admission £6; 🕙 10pm-2am, every 4th Sat), a women's club night, advertised as being 'for gay girlies and their specially invited gay boyfriends' (men only admitted if accompanied by a woman).

Opal Lounge (p124)

EL BARRIO Map pp218–20
☎ 229 8805; www.elbarrio.co.uk; 104 West Port; admission free; 🕙 8pm-3am; bus 2, 35

Edinburgh's sizable Spanish-speaking community congregates at this lively Latino bar to clink Cuba libres, slurp minty *mojitos* and get down to some naughty Latin American rhythms. There's a club session every night except Sunday, from the flamenco of Monday's Spanish Fiesta to the salsa and merengue of Friday's Mambo Juice. If you're not sure of your moves, there are salsa classes between 8pm and 10pm Tuesday to Saturday (see Dance p136).

BONGO CLUB Map pp218–20
☎ 558 8844; www.thebongoclub.co.uk; Moray House, Paterson's Land, 37 Holyrood Rd; bus 64

The weird and wonderful Bongo Club has moved to new premises east of the Cowgate. During the day, the Bongo serves as a café-bar and exhibition space, and transforms at night into one of the city's best clubs; it also hosts live music, theatre cabaret, and 'any other artform'. It's still famous for the hip-hop, funk and breakbeat night **Headspin** (admission £7; 🕙 10pm-3am, 2nd Sat of month). Also worth checking out is the booming bass of roots-and-dub

EGO Map pp218–20
☎ 478 7434; 14 Picardy Pl; bus 8, 17

A glitzy two-floor venue in a former casino, Ego dishes up everything from the hard house, trance and techno of **NuklearPuppy** (admission £8; ⊗ 11pm-5am, 2nd & 4th Fri of month) to the glammy cheese-fest of **Disco Inferno** (admission £8; ⊗ 10.30pm-3am, 3rd Sat of month).

GAIA Map pp218–20
☎ 229 9438; 28 Kings Stables Rd; admission £4; ⊗ 10pm-3am Tue & Thu-Sat; bus 28

Gaia pulls in a pissed-up, studenty, dance-till-you-puke crowd, gamely thrashing away to a soundtrack of pop, funk, disco and house while trying not to barf up the gallon of cheap promo drinks they just downed. On Mondays you pay £10 to get in, then it's free drinks all night. Grand fun.

HONEYCOMB Map pp224–5
☎ 556 2442; www.the-honeycomb.com; 15-17 Niddry St; bus 35

Tucked away in the vaults beneath the South Bridge, Honeycomb is one of Edinburgh's hottest clubs. It is home to **Manga** (admission £10; ⊗ 11pm-3am, 3rd Fri of month), Edinburgh's unmissable drum'n'bass club, as well as the consistently crowded classics night **Motherfunk** (admission free; ⊗ 10.30pm-3am Tue).

LIQUID ROOM Map pp224–5
☎ 225 2564; www.liquidroom.com; 9c Victoria St; bus 2, 23, 27, 41, 42

Set in a subterranean vault deep beneath Victoria St, the Liquid Room is a superb club venue with a thundering sound system. There are weekly club nights Wednesday to Friday and Sunday – the long-running **Evol** (admission £5; ⊗ 10.30pm-3am Fri, weekly) caters to the indie-kid crowd, and is regularly voted as Scotland's top club night out, while the gay-friendly garage and house night **Taste** (admission £5-8; ⊗ 11pm-5am Sun, weekly) is always packed out.

MAMBO CLUB Map pp218–20
☎ 228 3252; 3 West Tollcross; admission £5; ⊗ 10pm-3am Sat; all Tollcross buses

Just upstairs and yet a thousand miles away from the Cavendish/Diva (see p134), the long-established Mambo Club provides a regular Saturday-night fix of reggae, ragga, R&B and hip-hop.

MASSA Map pp224–5
☎ 226 4224; 36-9 Market St; bus 64

Club Mercado has undergone a radical facelift and re-emerged as the slick, amphitheatre-like Massa, with a sunken, elliptical dance floor. Despite the name change, the most popular club nights remain: At house night **Eye Candy** (admission £10; ⊗ 11pm-3am, 2nd & 4th Sat of month) the dress code is 'dress glam or scram' – an outrageous costume will get you in the door for only £6 – while the **Time Tunnel** (admission £5; ⊗ 10pm-3am Fri) carries jaded office workers back to the 1960s, '70s and '80s. Drawing a mixed gay and straight crowd, the ever-popular **Tackno** (admission £6; ⊗ 10.30pm-3am, last Sun of month) thrives on cheesy music and themed fancy dress – who could resist dressing up for Tackno at the Beach, Tackno in Space, Eurovision Tackno or Tackno Down Under.

OPIUM Map pp224–5
☎ 225 8382; 71 Cowgate; bus 2, 64

This traditionally grungy venue (formerly The Attic/Legends) in the tunnel-like trench of central Cowgate has been re-vamped as the dark and stylish Opium, now the city's top rock club. Saturday night is a thrash-fest of rock, metal, nu-metal and indie, while the popular **Toxik** (admission free; ⊗ 11pm-3am Wed) describes itself as 'the sinister side of all things metal'. **Nu:Order** (admission £5; ⊗ 5-9.30pm Fri) is an alcohol-free club for 14- to 17-year-olds, playing metal, grunge, rock and alternative.

PLANET OUT Map pp218–20
☎ 524 0061; 6 Baxter's Pl; ⊗ 4pm-1am Mon-Fri, 2pm-1am Sat & Sun; all Leith St buses

Planet Out is a stylish gay bar and club that pulls in a younger crowd than CC Bloom's and has a better party atmosphere at the weekends – it's a bit quieter through the week, when you can chill out on the sofas and blether.

STUDIO 24 Map pp218–20
☎ 558 3758; 24 Calton Rd; bus 35

Studio 24 has two levels, with an intimate, relaxed drinking area above the main, sweaty dance floor. The programme covers all bases, from house to Goth to nu-metal. The **Mission** (admission £5; ⊗ 11pm-3am Sat, weekly) is the city's classic Goth and metal night, but the big session for serious clubbers is the hard house and techno of **Dogma** (admission £9; ⊗ 10.30pm-3am, 2nd Fri of month). **Mingin'** (admission £5; ⊗ 10.30pm-3am, every 4th Sat)

Gay & Lesbian Edinburgh

Edinburgh has a small – but perfectly formed – gay and lesbian scene, centred on the area around Broughton St (known affectionately as 'The Pink Triangle') at the eastern end of the New Town. Although not as mad, bad and dangerous to know as the Glasgow scene, there are enough pubs and clubs to keep the boozing and cruising crowd happy. You can find out what's happening through the listings in *Scotsgay* magazine (www.scotsgay.com) and *The List*. For community contacts see p195.

There are several club nights that are gay- or lesbian-only or that attract a large gay contingent. A few of the more permanent fixtures are mentioned in the Clubbing section of this chapter, but as club nights and venues change often, it's best to check *Scotsgay* or *The List* for the latest details.

is a gay-friendly club night pumping out hard house, sexy trance and techno. In Scotland, mingin' means 'dirty'; it also means 'drunk'. That's all you need to know really.

THE VENUE Map pp218–20
☎ 557 3073; www.edinvenue.com; 17-23 Calton Rd; bus 35

Spread out over three floors, the Venue is an old-school club of the sticky floors and scuffed furniture variety, a vast, wooden-panelled venue with an air of faded grandeur. Try **Majestica** (admission £10; 🕑 10pm-3am, every 4th Sat) for dark-and-dirty house, or **3D** (admission £5; 🕑 11pm-3am Fri), which offers three big-name clubs in the one venue

for one bargain cover charge. The Venue is also home to **Joy** (www.clubjoy.co.uk; admission £10; 🕑 11pm-3am, every 4th Fri), Edinburgh's longest-running and most upfront gay club night.

WEE RED BAR Map pp218–20
☎ 229 1442; Edinburgh College of Art, Lauriston Pl; bus 23, 27, 35, 45

The Wee Red Bar has been around so long there's a danger the authorities will slap a blue plaque on it and declare it a national monument. Wee, red and frequented, hardly surprisingly, by lots of art students, it's famous for **The Egg** (admission £4.50; 🕑 11pm-3am Sat), a weekly smorgasbord of classic punk, ska, northern soul, indie etc.

WHY NOT? Map pp218–20
☎ 624 8633; 14 George St; admission £3-7.50; 🕑 10pm-3am Fri & Sat; all St Andrew Sq buses

Located downstairs to the right of the Dome (see p106), Why Not? is a sophisticated club playing mainstream chart sounds to a well-heeled, 30-something, New Town crowd. Dress smart and be sure to raid a cash machine on the way.

Top Five Gay Venues

- **Blue Moon Café** (p109)
- **Massa** (p135)
- **Planet Out** (p135)
- **Studio 24** (p135)
- **The Venue** (see above)

DANCE

Whether you prefer to watch a performance, or get up and perform yourself, Edinburgh has a varied and invigorating selection of dance venues. The Edinburgh International Festival (p22) hosts dance performances from around the globe.

EL BARRIO Map pp218–20
☎ 229 8805; www.elbarrio.co.uk; 104 West Port; £4 per session; 🕑 8.15-10pm Tue-Thu, 9-10pm Fri & Sat; bus 2, 35

Perfect your dips and hone those merengue moves at El Barrio's salsa classes before burning up the dance floor at the ensuing Latino club night. Beginners' classes run 8.15pm to 9pm Tuesday to Thursday and 9pm to 10pm Friday and Saturday; improvers are 9.15pm to 10pm Tuesday to Saturday. See also Cuba Norte (p126).

DANCE BASE Map pp224–5
☎ 225 5525; www.dancebase.co.uk; 14-16 Grassmarket; 🕑 8am-9.30pm Mon-Fri, 10am-5.45pm Sat; bus 2

Opened in late 2001, Scotland's National Centre for Dance is a complex of dance studios housed in a spectacular modern building in the shadow of the castle; it's worth a visit for the architecture alone. The centre runs courses in all kinds of dance – from ballroom to belly, hip-hop to Highland, and tango to tap – as well as hosting workshops and performances.

EDINBURGH FESTIVAL THEATRE

Map pp224–5

☎ 529 6000; www.eft.co.uk; 13-29 Nicolson St; tickets £6-46; ⓨ box office 10am-6pm Mon-Sat, till 8pm on show nights; all South Bridge buses

The curving glass-and-steel façade of the Festival Theatre houses the city's main venue for ballet, contemporary dance and opera; it also stages musicals, concerts, drama and children's shows. Performances by the critically acclaimed **Scottish Ballet** (www.scottishballet .com) are a regular feature of the programme. Based in Dundee, the **Scottish Dance Theatre** (www.scottishdance theatre.com) occasionally performs in Edinburgh, usually at the Edinburgh Festival Theatre.

THISTLE HOTEL Map pp218–20

☎ 0870 333 9153; edinburgh@thistle.co.uk; 107 Leith St; show & dinner £43.50, show only £25; ⓨ 6.45pm Apr-Oct; all Leith St buses

The Thistle Hotel stages 'Jamie's Scottish Evening', a night of Scottish country dancing, music, songs and comedy accompanied by a four-course dinner (including the chance to try some haggis).

MUSIC

It's not only at Festival time that Edinburgh comes alive with the sound of music – the city has a wide range of venues offering classical, rock, folk and jazz all year round.

CLASSICAL MUSIC, OPERA & BALLET

Edinburgh is home to the **Scottish Chamber Orchestra** (SCO; www.sco.org.uk), one of Europe's finest and well worth hearing. Their performances are usually held at the Queen's Hall and Usher Hall.

Scottish Opera (www.scottishopera.org.uk) and the **Royal Scottish National Orchestra** (RSNO; www.rsno.org.uk) are based in Glasgow but regularly perform in Edinburgh, at the Edinburgh Festival Theatre (see above) and Usher Hall (see below) respectively.

GREYFRIARS KIRK Map pp224–5

☎ 226 5429; Greyfriars Pl; tickets £6-12; buses 2, 23, 27, 41, 42

The Edinburgh Symphony Orchestra, established in 1963 and composed of amateur musicians, performs concerts here. There are regular organ recitals and concerts throughout the year – contact the Edinburgh and Scotland Information centre (see p199) for details.

QUEEN'S HALL Map pp222–3

☎ 668 2019; www.queenshalledinburgh.co.uk; Clerk St; tickets £7-22; ⓨ box office 10am-5.30pm, or till 15 minutes after show begins; all Newington buses

The Queen's Hall is home to the Scottish Chamber Orchestra, but it also hosts jazz concerts and a whole range of other events.

ST GILES CATHEDRAL Map pp224–5

☎ 225 9442; www.stgiles.net; High St, Royal Mile; tickets free-£7; bus 35

The big kirk on the Royal Mile hosts a regular and varied programme of classical music, including popular lunch time and evening concerts and organ recitals, notably at 6pm on Sundays; check the website for full details. The cathedral choir sings at the 10am and 11.30am Sunday services.

USHER HALL Map pp218–20

☎ 228 1155; www.usherhall.co.uk; Lothian Rd; tickets £7.50-27; ⓨ box office 10.30am-5.30pm, till 8pm on show nights

Built in 1914 with money donated by the brewery magnate Andrew Usher, the architecturally impressive, 2900-seat Usher Hall hosts concerts by the RSNO and performances of popular music.

FOLK

The capital is a great place to hear traditional Scottish (and Irish) folk music, with a mix of regular spots and impromptu sessions. The following bars mentioned in other chapters also have regular folk sessions: the Ensign Ewart (p121), West End Hotel (p166) and the White Hart Inn (p122).

FINNEGAN'S WAKE Map pp224–5

☎ 226 3816; 9b Victoria St; admission free; ⓨ 5pm-1am Mon-Thu, 1pm-1am Fri-Sun; bus 2, 23, 27, 41, 42

Finnegan's is a cavernous – and often raucous – Irish theme pub with a stage where you can catch a live band (mostly Irish and Scottish folk and folk-rock) seven nights a week.

HEBRIDES BAR Map pp224–5

☎ 220 4213; 17 Market St; admission free; ⏰ 11am-midnight Mon-Thu, 11-1am Fri & Sat, 12.30pm-midnight Sun; bus 64

Friendly, welcoming and handy for Waverley train station, the Hebrides offers a taste of Highland hospitality in the heart of the city. There's live Scottish and Irish folk, Celtic and bluegrass on Thursday, Friday and Saturday evenings at 9pm and on Sunday afternoons at 4pm.

PLEASANCE CABARET BAR Map pp224–5

☎ 650 2349; 60 The Pleasance; admission £6-8; ⏰ 8-11pm Wed; bus 64

The Pleasance is home to the Edinburgh Folk Club – voted Folk Club of the Year 2003 – which runs a programme of visiting bands and singers at 8pm on Wednesdays; there's no advance booking, so buy your ticket at the door. The bar is a major Fringe venue, so there are no concerts here during the Festival period.

ROYAL OAK Map pp224–5

☎ 557 2976; 1 Infirmary St; admission free; ⏰ 11-2am Mon-Sat, 12.30pm-2am Sun; all South Bridge buses

The ever-popular Royal Oak rivals Sandy Bell's (see next) as Edinburgh's most popular folk venue, with music every night in both public bar and lounge. Admission to the downstairs lounge, with its tiny bar and space for only 30 punters, is free but by ticket only, so get there early (9.30pm start) if you want to be sure of a place. On Saturday nights there's a gig (6pm) followed by a sing-along session (9.30pm) – bring your own instruments (or a good singing voice). Sunday night gigs organised by the Wee Folk Club cost £3.

SANDY BELL'S Map pp224–5

☎ 225 2751; 25 Forrest Rd; admission free; ⏰ 11.30-12.45am Mon-Sat, 12.30-11pm Sun; bus 2, 23, 27, 41, 42

This unassuming bar has been a stalwart of the traditional music scene in Edinburgh since The Corrs were in nappies. There's folk music almost every evening at 9pm, from 3pm on Saturdays and pretty much all day on Sundays.

THE SHORE Map p216

☎ 553 5080; 3-4 The Shore; admission free; ⏰ 11am-midnight Mon-Sat, 12.30-11pm Sun; bus 16, 22, 35, 36

This is a snug, wood-panelled, traditional bar on the waterfront in Leith, complete with open fire and upright piano, that hosts lively informal folk sessions on Wednesday nights at 9pm.

THE TASS Map pp224–5

☎ 556 6338; 1 High St, Royal Mile; admission free; ⏰ 11am-midnight Mon-Thu, noon-1am Fri & Sat, 12.30pm-midnight Sun; bus 35

Royal Oak

This Royal Mile pub takes Scotland's national bard Robert Burns as its theme, and is a great place for an impromptu song or six – there are regular folk sessions on Tuesday, Wednesday and Friday, but musicians are welcome to bring along their instruments any time.

Top Five Lazy Sunday Afternoons

- Sunday matinee double bill at the **Cameo Cinema** (p132)
- Jazz Brunch at **Hadrian's Brasserie** (p106)
- Hydrotherapy in a rooftop pool at **One Spa** (p143)
- A stroll along the towpath of the **Union Canal** (see p143 and p97)
- Sweating in the steam room at **Portobello Turkish Baths** (p142)

JAZZ

The climax of Edinburgh's jazz calendar is the week-long International Jazz & Blues Festival in late July/early August, but there are plenty of regular gigs throughout the year advertised in *The Gig Guide* and in the free quarterly Jazz booklet. Visiting jazz bands often play at the Queen's Hall (see p137).

Several restaurants, including Hadrian's Brasserie (p106) and Oloroso (p108) have Sunday afternoon jazz sessions. Henderson's (p109), a popular vegetarian restaurant, has live music (mainly jazz and classical guitar) at 7.30pm most evenings.

EIGHTY QUEEN STREET Map pp218–20

☎ 226 5097; 80 Queen St; admission free; ⏰ noon-11pm Mon-Wed, noon-midnight Thu, noon-1am Fri & Sat; bus 13, 19, 37, 41

The clubbish Cellar Bar at Eighty Queen Street, with its polished mahogany and wicker chairs and sofas, provides a traditional setting for live jazz from 9pm to midnight three nights a week. There's a jam session on Mondays, a guest band on Fridays and the house band on Saturdays.

FAIRMILE INN map pp214–15

☎ 445 2056; 44 Biggar Rd; admission £4-7; ⏰ noon-11pm Mon-Thu, noon-midnight Fri & Sat, 12.30-11pm Sun; bus 4, 11, 15, 18

This Art Deco, 1930s-style pub, right on the southern edge of the city, is home to the Edinburgh Jazz'n'Jive Club. The Friday night gigs

put the emphasis on traditional jazz, from ragtime to New Orleans to swing.

HARRY'S BAR Map p217

☎ 539 8100; 7b Randolph Pl; admission free; ⏰ 11am-midnight Mon-Thu, 11-1am Fri & Sat, 12.30-11pm Sun; bus 13, 19, 36, 37, 41

Harry's is a laid-back basement bar with an American theme, with free jazz sessions at 3.30pm on Saturday afternoons.

HENRY'S JAZZ BAR Map pp218–20

☎ 538 7385; 8a Morrison St; admission £5-7; ⏰ 8.30pm-3am Tue-Sun; all Lothian Rd buses

Edinburgh's hottest jazz joint, Henry's is a dark, smoky basement bar dripping with candle-wax and cool. There's something going on nearly every night, from traditional and contemporary jazz to soul, funk, hip-hop and drum'n'bass.

ROCK, BLUES & POP

In the last decade many of Edinburgh's live-music venues have closed down or been converted into clubs and bars, and the capital's live-music scene today is not a patch on Glasgow's. There are occasional rock gigs at clubs such as the Bongo Club (see p134), Cabaret Voltaire (see p134), the Commplex (p134), and The Venue (see p136).

Big-name bands and solo artists tend to play at the SECC in Glasgow these days; those that include Edinburgh usually appear at the Edinburgh Playhouse (see p144). In summer, promoters take advantage of the seating installed for the Military Tattoo to stage a few spectacular concerts on the Castle Esplanade. These shows are atmospheric but potentially cold and wet.

Tickets to major gigs are usually sold at Virgin Megastore (Map pp218–20; ☎ 220 3234; 125 Princes St) and Ripping Records (Map pp224–5; ☎ 226 7010; 91 South Bridge), as well as through the online agencies mentioned in What's On (p132).

BANNERMAN'S Map pp224–5

☎ 556 3254; 212 Cowgate; admission free; ⏰ noon-1am; bus 2

A long-established favourite, Bannerman's bar straggles through a warren of old vaults beneath South Bridge, and pulls in a lively crowd of local students and backpackers. The beer is good, and there is live music (mostly indie/rock) in a crowded cavern-like space every night except Tuesday.

Entertainment – Music

EDINBURGH CORN EXCHANGE
Map pp214–15

☎ 443 0404; www.ece.uk.com; 10 Newmarket Rd; ticket prices vary; ☺ gigs only; bus 35

Opened by Blur in 1999, and home to the annual 'T on the Fringe' and Blues festivals, the Corn Exchange is a 3000-seat hall in a converted market building in the west of the city.

LIQUID ROOM Map pp224–5

☎ 225 2564; www.liquidroom.com; 9c Victoria St; tickets £9-15; ☺ gigs only; bus 2, 23, 27, 41, 42

One of the city's top live-music venues, boasting a superb sound system, the Liquid Room

stages all kinds of gigs from local bands to big names like Moby, Coldplay, Smashing Pumpkins and The Damned. It's also a great clubbing venue (see p135).

WHISTLE BINKIE'S Map pp224–5

☎ 557 5114; www.whistlebinkies.com; 4-6 South Bridge; admission free; ☺ 7pm-3am; all South Bridge buses

This crowded cellar bar found just off the Royal Mile has live music, including rock, blues and folk, every night of the week. Open mic night, from 9pm on Mondays, showcases new talent.

READINGS

The tradition of Edinburgh's many poets and storytellers is kept alive in the following two venues.

SCOTTISH POETRY LIBRARY
Map pp218–20

☎ 557 2876; www.spl.org.uk; 5 Crichton's Close, Canongate; tickets free-£3; ☺ 11am-6pm Mon-Fri, 11am-4pm Sat; bus 35

Housed in an award-winning modern building close to the new Scottish Parliament, the Scottish Poetry Library holds a huge collection of contemporary and historic poetry in Scots, Gaelic and English. Check the website for details of regular poetry readings and other events.

SCOTTISH STORYTELLING CENTRE
Map pp224–5

☎ 557 5724; www.scottishstorytellingcentre.co.uk; 43-5 High St, Royal Mile; tickets £3-5; bus 35

The Scottish Storytelling Centre was founded in 1992 to encourage and support the ancient art of storytelling, and to help preserve the oral culture of Scotland. It operates a programme of storytelling performances both at the centre and at other venues throughout Edinburgh.

SPORT & FITNESS

Edinburgh has plenty of places where you can pamper yourself or perk up those sagging muscles with a spot of healthy exercise.

Football and rugby fans can shout themselves hoarse at one of the city's three major stadiums, and golfers can take their pick from around 90 courses within easy reach of the city.

CLIMBING

Although there's an impressive, cliff-bound mini-mountain in the form of Arthur's Seat, bye-laws make it illegal to climb on Salisbury Crags and other rock outcrops in Holyrood Park. The nearest natural rock-climbing is at Traprain Law, near Haddington (20 miles east of Edinburgh) and at Aberdour on the Fife coast (15 miles north). There are, however, two excellent indoor climbing centres.

ADVENTURE CENTRE Map pp214–15

☎ 333 6333; www.adventurescotland.com; South Platt Hill, Ratho; admission £7-10 per day, adult/child

beginners lessons from £20/10; ☺ climbing arena 10.30am-10.30pm Mon-Fri, 9.30am-8pm Sat & Sun, fitness centre 6.30am-10pm Mon-Fri, 8am-8pm Sat & Sun

Opened in December 2003 when it hosted the finals of the UIAA-ICC World Cup climbing competition, this is the largest covered climbing arena in the world, offering both artificial walls and natural rock crags. Attractions include an aerial adventure course, fitness centre, health spa and sauna, mountain bike trails, running and walking trails and a scuba-diving school The centre is located in a former quarry on the banks of the Union Canal, 8 miles (13km) west of Edinburgh. It can be reached by car via the M8 motorway, or on foot or bicycle via the Union Canal towpath. Waverley Travel (☎ 317 7697) runs bus No 67 (£1.80, 30 min, hourly) which leaves from Waterloo Pl in the city centre to Ratho village.

ALIEN ROCK Map pp214–15

☎ 552 7211; www.alienrock.co.uk; 8 Pier Pl, Newhaven; adult/child £5.50/3; ☿ noon-11pm Mon-Thu, noon-10pm Fri, 10am-9pm Sat & Sun; bus 7, 10, 16, 32
A converted church overlooking Newhaven harbour provides excellent indoor climbing facilities, with a range of walls up to 20m high, and a separate, extensive bouldering area. There are off-peak rates (before 4pm weekdays and after 5pm weekends) of £4/3, and boots and harness can be hired for £3.

CYCLING

Edinburgh and surroundings offer many excellent opportunities for cycling (see also Bicycle p191).

FOOTBALL

Edinburgh has two rival football (soccer) teams playing in the Scottish Premier League – Heart of Midlothian (a.k.a. Hearts, nicknamed the Jam Tarts or Jambos), founded in 1874, and Hibernian (a.k.a. Hibs, Hibbies or Hibees), founded in 1875. The domestic football season lasts from August to May and most matches are played at 3pm on Saturday or 7.30pm on Tuesday or Wednesday.

EASTER ROAD STADIUM Map pp218–20

☎ 661 2159; www.hibs.co.uk; 12 Albion Pl; tickets £17-25; bus 1, 35
Hibernian's home ground is northeast of the city centre. Hibs – who have not won the Scottish Cup since 1902 – came close in 2001, making it to the final only to lose 3-0 to Glasgow Celtic. The last trophy they won was the Skol Cup in 1991, beating Dunfermline 2-0.

TYNECASTLE STADIUM Map p221

☎ 200 7200; www.heartsfc.co.uk; Gorgie Rd; tickets £16-20; bus 1, 2, 3, 25, 33
Hearts – winners of the Scottish Cup in 1998 – have their ground southwest of the centre in Gorgie. The future of Tynecastle hangs in the balance as the club has put forward controversial plans to move to a new stadium outside the city.

GOLF

There are 19 golf courses in Edinburgh, and another 70 within 20 miles of the city. For details of other courses in and around Edinburgh, check out www.scotlands-golf-courses.com.

Famous Links Courses

Some of the most famous links courses in the world lie within an hour's drive, including **Muirfield** (☎ 01620-842 123; Gullane; green fees per round £85; ☿ visitors Tue & Thu only) and **Gullane No 1** (☎ 01620-842 255; West Links Rd, Gullane; green fees £60; ☿ visitors 10.30am-noon & 2.30-4pm Mon-Fri) in East Lothian; and **St Andrews Old Course** (☎ 01334-476 666; www.standrews.org.uk; Pilmour House, St Andrews; green fees in high/low season £85/56; ☿ visitors Mon-Sat) in Fife. To play on these courses you will have to book at least a month in advance.

The Old Course at St Andrews is 55 miles north of Edinburgh across the Firth of Forth (see p179). The Alfred Dunhill Cup, the world's most prestigious international team tournament, takes place here in mid-October. The British Open Championship is also held here regularly.

BRAID HILLS GOLF COURSE

Map pp214–15

☎ 447 6666; Braid Hills Approach; weekday/weekend green fees £14/16; bus 11, 15
This challenging public course is only 10 minutes' drive south of the city centre, spread across gorse-clad ridges and heath land with great views of the Old Town and Arthur's Seat.

LOTHIANBURN GOLF COURSE

Map pp214–15

☎ 445 2206; www.lothianburngolfclub.com; 106a Biggar Rd, Fairmilehead; weekday/weekend green fees £16.50/22.50; bus 4, 15
Historic Lothianburn Golf Course, dating from the 1890s, enjoys a scenic setting at the foot of the Pentland Hills.

MELVILLE GOLF CENTRE Map pp214–15

☎ 663 8038; www.melvillegolf.co.uk; Lasswade, Midlothian; 9-hole green fee £9-11, range (50 balls) £3; ☿ 9am-10pm Mon-Fri & 9am-8pm Sat & Sun; bus 3
This golfing centre on the southern edge of the city offers a nine-hole course, floodlit driving range, putting green, equipment hire, professional tuition and a golf shop.

GYMS

MEADOWBANK SPORTS CENTRE

Map pp214–15

☎ 661 5351; 139 London Rd; admission varies;
⏱ 9am-10pm; bus 4, 5, 15, 26, 44, 45

Public facilities at Scotland's main sports arena include a fitness studio, gym, free weights room, squash courts, athletics track and a children's soft play area.

NEXT GENERATION Map pp214–15

☎ 554 5000; www.nextgenerationclubs.co.uk;
Newhaven Harbour; admission by membership;
⏱ 6.30am-11pm; bus 7, 10, 11, 16, 32

This fitness centre on the western breakwater of Leith Harbour has a large gym, indoor and outdoor swimming pools, tennis courts, sauna and steam room. The gym overlooks the sea, and you can jog on a running machine while enjoying a spectacular view along the Firth to the Forth Bridges.

HORSE RACING

MUSSELBURGH RACECOURSE

Map pp214–15

☎ 665 2859; www.musselburgh-racecourse.co.uk;
Linkfield Rd, Musselburgh; admission £10-15; bus 15

Horse-racing enthusiasts should head 6 miles east to Scotland's oldest racecourse (founded 1816), where meetings are held throughout the year.

RUGBY UNION

Each year, from January to March, Scotland's national rugby team takes part in the **Six Nations Rugby Union Championship** (www .6nations.net). The most important fixture is the clash against England for the Calcutta Cup, which takes place in Edinburgh every second year (next one: 2006). At club level, the season runs from September to May.

MURRAYFIELD STADIUM Map pp214–15

☎ 346 5000; www.scottishrugby.org; 112 Roseburn
St; tickets from £15; bus 2, 12, 26, 31, 36, 63, 69, 100

Murrayfield Stadium, about 1½ miles west of the centre, is the venue for international rugby matches. Most tickets for Six Nations games are allocated through rugby clubs; any that remain go on sale at the **Ticket Centre** (☎ 0870 040 1925) in Murrayfield Stadium about two weeks before the competition begins.

SAUNA

PORTOBELLO TURKISH BATHS

Map pp214–15

☎ 669 6888; Portobello Swim Centre, 57 Promenade;
admission £5.80; ⏱ women only 3-9pm Mon & 9am-
9pm Wed, men only 9am-9pm Tue & Thu, mixed 9am-
9pm Fri, 9am-4pm Sat & Sun; bus 12, 15, 19, 32, 42, 49

The big draw at Portobello's municipal swimming pool is not the pool itself, but the beautifully restored, 19th-century Turkish baths, where you can sweat away the aches and pains of a hard day's sightseeing.

TOWNHOUSE SAUNA & GYM

Map pp218–20

☎ 556 6116; 53 East Claremont St; admission £4-9;
⏱ noon-11pm Sun-Thu, noon-midnight Fri & Sat;
bus 8, 17

Gay-owned and -operated, the Townhouse is Scotland's biggest gay sauna, spread over four floors of a Georgian town house. Facilities include two sauna cabins, steam room, Jacuzzi, gym, video lounge and bar.

SKIING & SNOWBOARDING

Skiing in Edinburgh? Yup – Europe's longest dry ski slope lies on the northern slopes of the Pentland Hills at the southern edge of the city.

MIDLOTHIAN SKI CENTRE Map pp214–15

☎ 445 4433; Biggar Rd, Hillend; adult/child £8.50/5.60
per 2 hr; ⏱ 9.30am-9pm Mon-Fri, 9.30am-7pm Sat &
Sun May-Aug; 9.30am-9pm Mon-Sat, 9.30am-7pm Sun
Sep-Apr; bus 4, 15

You can punish your thighs in preparation for winter via the two button tows and chairlift that serve the 400m long artificial slope (100m vertical difference), two nursery areas and fun jump slope, all floodlit in winter. Admission includes ski hire, but snowboard and boot rental costs £2 extra for two hours.

SPA & MASSAGE

A TOUCH OF ZEN Map pp218–20

☎ 557 5159; www.atouchofzen.co.uk; 7 Dundonald
St; massage from £10 per 15 min; ⏱ noon-8pm Mon;
noon-7pm Tue; 10am-8pm Wed & Fri; 11am-8pm Thu;
noon-4pm Sat; bus 13

This New Town clinic specialises in shiatsu massage, but other treatments such as craniosacral therapy, therapeutic massage and acupuncture are also available.

EDINBURGH FLOATARIUM Map pp218–20

☎ 225 3350; www.edinburghfloatarium.co.uk; 29 NW Circus Pl; floating £25 per hr; ☻ 9am-8pm Mon-Fri, 9am-6pm Sat, 9.30am-4pm Sun; bus 24, 29, 42

Escape from the bustle of the city centre in a warm, womb-like flotation tank, or take advantage of the many other therapies on offer, including aromatherapy massage, reflexology, shiatsu and Indian head massage. There's a sweet-scented shop, too, where you can buy massage oils, incense, candles, homeopathic remedies, CDs and so on.

ONE SPA Map pp218–20

☎ 221 7777; www.one-spa.com; Sheraton Grand Hotel, 8 Conference Sq, Lothian Rd; £55-65 per hr; ☻ 6.30am-10pm Mon-Fri, 7am-9pm Sat & Sun; all Lothian Rd buses

Voted Condé Nast Traveller's 'Favourite Hotel Spa of the Year' in 2003, this gorgeous rooftop spa offers a wide range of pampering treatments from reflexology and reiki to facials and hot-stone therapy. The setting is unbeatable, with a beautiful, oval indoor pool, rooftop hydrotherapy pool, rustic sauna and curvaceous, mosaic-tiled 'aroma grotto'. You can book individual treatment sessions, or splash out on a half/full-day package (£115/220), which combines a programme of treatments with free use of the spa facilities.

SWIMMING

The Firth of Forth is a bit on the chilly – and polluted – side for enjoyable swimming, but there are several indoor alternatives on offer.

DALRY SWIM CENTRE Map p221

☎ 313 3964; 25-9 Caledonian Cres; ☻ 8am-10pm Mon-Fri, 9am-3.40pm Sat & Sun; bus 2, 3, 4, 25, 33, 44

A recently re-furbished Victorian baths with 25m pool and gym.

GLENOGLE SWIM CENTRE Map p217

☎ 343 6376; Glenogle Rd; ☻ 8am-10pm Mon-Thu, 8am-10.30pm Fri, 7.45am-3.40pm Sat & Sun; bus 36

An atmospheric Victorian swimming baths also with 25m pool and gym.

ROYAL COMMONWEALTH POOL

Map pp222–3

☎ 667 7211; 21 Dalkeith Rd; adult/child £3.10/1.80; ☻ 9am-9.30pm Mon, Tue, Thu & Fri, 10am-9.30pm Wed, 10am-4.30pm Sat & Sun; bus 2, 14, 30, 33

The city's main facility is the Royal Commonwealth Pool, which was built for the 1970 Commonwealth Games. It has a 50m Olympic pool, diving pool, children's pool, flumes and fitness centre.

WARRENDER SWIM CENTRE

Map pp222–3

☎ 447 0052; 55 Thirlestane Rd; ☻ 7.30am-9.30pm Mon-Fri, 9am-3.40pm Sat & Sun; bus 24, 41

Traditional Victorian pool with modern facilities, including gym, sauna and yoga classes.

WALKING

Edinburgh is lucky to have several good walking areas within the city boundary, including Arthur's Seat, Calton Hill, Blackford Hill, Hermitage of Braid, Corstorphine Hill and the coast and river at Cramond. The Pentland Hills, which rise to over 500m, stretch south-westwards from the city for 15 miles (25km), offering excellent high- and low-level walking.

You can follow the Water of Leith Walkway from the city centre to Balerno (8 miles), and continue across the Pentlands to Silverburn (6½ miles) or Carlops (8 miles), and return to Edinburgh by bus. Another good option is to walk along the towpath of the Union Canal, which begins in Fountainbridge (Map p221), and runs all the way to Falkirk (31 miles). You can return to Edinburgh by bus at Ratho (8½ miles) and Broxburn (12 miles), and by bus or train from Linlithgow (21 miles).

See the Walking Tours chapter for more information (p91).

Out for a walk on Arthur's Seat (p58)

WATERSPORTS

The Firth of Forth provides sheltered waters for all kinds of sailing and watersports.

PORT EDGAR MARINA & SAILING SCHOOL Map pp214–15

☎ 331 3330; www.portedgar.co.uk; Shore Rd, Queensferry; ✆ boat rental sessions 10am-noon & 2-4pm year round, plus 7-9pm Mon-Fri Apr-Oct; First Edinburgh bus 43

A council-operated yachting marina in the shadow of the Forth Road Bridge, Port Edgar rents out Topper/420/Wayfarer sailing dinghies at £9.80/18.20/25.40 for a two-hour session. It also offers canoeing, power-boating and sailing courses.

YOGA

UNION YOGA Map pp218–20

☎ 558 3334; www.union yoga .co.uk; 25 Rodney St; from £10/class; ✆ 6.30am-9pm Mon-Fri, 8.30am-noon Sat; bus 8, 13, 17

The bamboo-floored studio here is one of Europe's largest. As well as eight-week courses in Ashtanga yoga, it offers a 'drop-in' one-hour **introductory session** (£10; ✆ 6pm Wed) for people who have never tried yoga before, and an intensive **weekend course** (£75) for beginners.

THEATRE

Despite the huge international popularity of the Edinburgh Festival and Fringe, theatre audiences during the rest of the year have been falling, prompting much doom and gloom regarding the future funding of Edinburgh's theatres. For more theatres see Dance (p136).

BEDLAM THEATRE Map pp224–5

☎ 225 9893; www.bedlamtheatre.co.uk; 11b Bristo Pl; tickets £3-4; ✆ box office open for performances only; bus 2, 12, 23, 27, 41, 42

Situated at the southern end of George IV Bridge in a converted church, the much-loved Bedlam is home to the Edinburgh University Theatre Company (EUTC), and also serves as a popular Fringe venue. In 2002 the university tried to sell off the building to developers, but it was saved from closure when the city council refused planning permission. The theatre company remains in residence for the time being, but may have to move in the future. As well as staging EUTC productions, it hosts performances by visiting theatre companies. See also Comedy (p133).

EDINBURGH PLAYHOUSE Map pp218–20

☎ 524 3301, bookings ☎ 0870 606 3424; www .edinburgh-playhouse.co.uk; 18-22 Greenside Pl; tickets £7-26; ✆ box office 10am-6pm Mon-Sat, till 8pm on show nights; all Leith Walk buses

This restored theatre at the top of Leith Walk stages Broadway musicals, dance shows, opera and popular-music concerts.

KING'S THEATRE Map pp222–3

☎ 220 4349; 2 Leven St; tickets £7-18; ✆ box office open 1 hr before show; all Tollcross buses

The King's is a traditional theatre with a programme of musicals, drama, comedy and its famous annual Christmas pantomime.

NETHERBOW THEATRE Map pp224–5

☎ 556 9579; 43-5 High St; tickets £4-6; bus 35

This small theatre on the Royal Mile features modern Scottish and international drama, and is also home to the Scottish Storytelling Centre (see p140). At the time of writing it was undergoing a major renovation and expansion, and was due to reopen in summer 2005.

ROYAL LYCEUM THEATRE Map pp218–20

☎ 248 4848; www.lyceum.org.uk; 30b Grindlay St; tickets £7-20; ✆ box office 10am-6pm Mon-Sat, till 8pm on show nights; all Lothian Rd buses

A grand Victorian theatre located beside the Usher Hall, the Lyceum stages drama, concerts, musicals and ballet.

TRAVERSE THEATRE Map pp218–20

☎ 228 1404; www.traverse.co.uk; 10 Cambridge St; ✆ box office 10am-6pm Mon, 10am-8pm Tue-Sat, 4pm-8pm Sun; all Lothian Rd buses

The Traverse Theatre is the main focus for new Scottish writing and stages an adventurous programme of contemporary drama and dance.

Shopping

Shopping

Shopping in Edinburgh offers everything from muzak-lulled mall-crawling to rubbing shoulder-bags with fussing fashionistas in Harvey Nicks, from traditional department stores to cutting-edge designer boutiques. And all in a compact city centre that you can cover without blowing the bank on taxis or getting blisters from your Blahniks.

Princes St is Edinburgh's principal shopping street, lined with all the big high-street stores, from Marks & Spencer to Dixons to Virgin Megastore, with many smaller shops along pedestrianised Rose St. There are also two big shopping centres – Princes Mall, at the eastern end of Princes St next to the Balmoral Hotel, and the nearby St James Centre, at the top of Leith St.

A brand new shopping complex with a flagship Harvey Nichols (see p150) store opened on the eastern side of St Andrew Square in 2002, but Ocean Terminal in Leith, anchored by Debenhams and BHS department stores, is the biggest shopping centre in Edinburgh.

Other central shopping streets include South Bridge, Nicolson St and Lothian Rd. For more off-beat shopping – including fashion, music, crafts, gifts and jewellery – head for the cobbled lanes of Cockburn, Victoria and St Mary's Sts, all near the Royal Mile in the Old Town; William St in the West End; or Stockbridge.

Opening Hours

Most shops are open from 9am to 5.30pm Monday to Wednesday, Friday and Saturday, and till 7pm or 8pm on Thursday. Plenty of shops open on Sunday too, but with shorter hours, generally from noon until 4pm or 5pm.

Consumer Taxes

Value-added tax (VAT) is a 17.5% sales tax that is levied on all goods and services in the UK except fresh food, children's clothes, books and newspapers.

Non-European Union (EU) citizens can sometimes claim a VAT refund paid on goods bought within the EU, which makes for a considerable saving.

The VAT refund scheme is voluntary and not all shops participate. Different shops will have different minimum-purchase conditions (normally around £40).

On request, participating shops give you a special form/invoice (called VAT 407); they'll need to see your passport. This form must be presented with the goods and receipts to customs when you depart (VAT-free goods can't be posted or shipped home). After customs has certified the form, it should be returned to the shop for a refund, less an administration fee.

Several companies offer a centralised refunding service to shops. Participating shops carry a sign in their window. You can avoid bank charges for cashing a sterling cheque by using a credit card for purchases and asking to have your VAT refund credited to your credit card account. Cash refunds are sometimes available at major airports.

For further details, check out the HM Customs & Excise website at www.hmce.gov.uk or pick up the leaflet *Notice 704/1 – Tax Free Shopping – VAT Refunds for Travellers Departing from the European Community*, available from all customs arrival points throughout the UK.

Top Five Shopping Areas

- Cockburn St (p147)
- George St (p149)
- Princes St (p149)
- Stockbridge (p152)
- Victoria St/West Bow (p147)

OLD TOWN

The top end of the Royal Mile, from the castle down to the Lawnmarket, is infested with tacky, tartan tourist shops, but there are many good shops further downhill, and on nearby Victoria, Cockburn and St Mary's Sts.

AHA HA HA Map pp224–5 *Toys & Gifts*
☎ 220 5252; 99 West Bow; 🕑 10am-6pm Mon-Sat, noon-4pm Sun Aug & Dec; bus 2

The guys at Aha Ha Ha have enough plastic poo, fake vomit, stink bombs and electronic farting machines to keep your average Dennis the Menace (or Uncle Ian) happy for at least a month. It's also a good place to go if you're looking for Halloween masks, costumes and practical jokes.

ARMSTRONG'S Map pp224–5 *Fashion*
☎ 220 5557; 83 Grassmarket; 10am-6pm Mon-Sat, noon-6pm Sun; bus 2

Armstrong's is an Edinburgh fashion institution, a second-hand clothes emporium offering everything from elegant 1940s dresses to funky 1970s flares. As well as retro fashion, it's a great place to hunt for a 'previously owned' kilt or to seek inspiration for that fancy dress party.

AVALANCHE RECORDS
Map pp218–20 *Music*
☎ 228 1939; 28 Lady Lawson St; 🕑 9.30am-6pm Mon-Sat, noon-6pm Sun; bus 2, 35

Along with Fopp (see p148), Avalanche is a sacred place of pilgrimage for music fans in search of good-value CDs – especially indie, rock and punk.

BAUERMEISTER Map pp224–5 *Books*
☎ 226 5561; 19 George IV Bridge; 🕑 9am-8pm Mon-Fri, 9am-5.30pm Sat, noon-5pm Sun; bus 2, 23, 27, 41, 42

Bauermeister is a good general bookshop and newsagent, with a fair selection of Scottish titles, travel guides and reference books, and a sizable stationery department located downstairs.

BIG IDEAS Map pp224–5 *Fashion*
☎ 226 2532; 96 & 116 West Bow; 🕑 10am-5.30pm Mon-Sat; bus 2, 23, 27, 41, 42

This boutique stocks a wide range of designer fashion for women sized 16 and above, with labels including Elena Grunert, Almia, Bittie Kai Rind, Wille, Laurie, Sahara, Head Over Heels and others.

Carson Clark Gallery

CARSON CLARK GALLERY
Map pp218–20 *Antique Maps*
☎ 556 4710; 181-3 Canongate; 🕑 10.30am-6pm Mon-Sat; bus 35

This shop near the foot of the Royal Mile has an interesting range of original and facsimile antique maps, charts and plans of Scotland, Europe and the rest of the world, as well as some gorgeous antique globes.

CASEY'S Map pp224–5 *Confectionery*
☎ 556 6082; 52 St Mary's St; 🕑 9am-5.30pm Mon-Sat; bus 35, 64

In the USA it's candy, in Australia it's lollies, but in Scotland it's always been sweeties. Casey's is a good, old-fashioned sweetie shop where the shelves are lined with glass jars full of glorious, tooth-dissolving delicacies. You can buy Scottish childhood favourites such as soor plooms, kola kubes, butter nuts and Carluke balls (don't ask) by the quarter-pound (OK then, 125g).

CASHMERE STORE Map pp224–5 *Fashion*
☎ 226 1577; 2 St Giles St, Royal Mile; 🕑 9.30am-6pm Mon-Sat; bus 35

This shop stocks a wide range of traditional and modern knitwear, in over 30 colours, plus a big choice of cashmere accessories such as scarves and shawls.

COOK'S BOOKSHOP Map pp224–5 *Books*
☎ 226 4445; 118 West Bow; 🕑 10.30am-5.30pm Mon-Sat; bus 2

This tiny, Old-Town bookshop, owned by Clarissa Dickson-Wright of TV's *Two Fat Ladies* fame, stocks all manner of books on cookery, Scottish cuisine and food and drink in general.

CORNICHE Map pp224–5 *Fashion*
☎ 556 3707; 2 Jeffrey St; ⌚ 10am-5.30pm Mon-Sat; bus 35, 64

A major stockist of designer clothes for women, with a selection of big-name labels such as Jean-Paul Gaultier, Vivienne Westwood, Anna Sui, Ghost and Alexander McQueen. The next-door branch concentrates on designer menswear.

CRUISE Map pp224–5 *Fashion*
☎ 556 2532; 14 St Mary's St; ⌚ 10am-6pm Mon-Fri, 9.30am-6pm Sat, noon-5pm Sun; bus 35, 64

This branch of Cruise stocks men's casual wear. The other branch is located on George St (see p149).

DESIGNS ON CASHMERE
Map pp224–5 *Fashion*
☎ 556 6394; 28 High St; ⌚ 10am-5.30pm Mon-Sat; bus 35

A good place to shop for top-quality cashmere clothing for both men and women, along with cashmere scarves, hats, gloves, snoods and capes.

EDINBURGH FARMERS MARKET
Map pp218–20 *Food & Drink*
☎ 652 5940; Castle Tce; ⌚ 9am-2pm, lst & 3rd Sat of month; bus 28

Held on the first and third Saturday of the month, this colourful event attracts stallholders selling everything from wild boar, venison and home-cured pedigree bacon to organic bread, free-range eggs and handmade soap. There are plans to relocate the market to the Grassmarket, and make it a weekly event – check the 'Farmers Markets' link on the www.edinburghcc.com website for the latest news.

FOPP Map pp224–5 *Music*
☎ 220 0133; 55 Cockburn St; ⌚ 9.30am-7pm Mon-Sat; 11am-6pm Sun; bus 35, 64

Fopp is a good place to hunt for cheap CDs and vinyl – prices are much better than Virgin and HMV – and the friendly staff really know what they're talking about. There's a second branch of Fopp (p150) in the New Town.

FUDGE HOUSE OF EDINBURGH
Map pp218–20 *Confectionery*
☎ 556 4172; 197 Canongate, Royal Mile; ⌚ 10am-5.30pm; bus 35

Another monument to the Scots' sweet tooth, this shop has acres of fudge to die for, including chocolate and peppermint, rum and raisin, hazelnut, and tasty Highland cream. Mmmmm. There's a coffee shop too.

GEOFFREY (TAILOR) INC
Map pp224–5 *Scottish*
☎ 557 0256; 57-9 High St, Royal Mile; ⌚ 9am-5.30pm Mon-Wed, Fri & Sat, 9am-7pm Thu, 10am-5pm Sun; bus 35

Geoffrey can fit you out in traditional Highland dress, run up a kilt in your own clan tartan, or just hire out the gear for a wedding or other special event. Their offshoot, 21st Century Kilts (see p156), offers modern fashion kilts in a variety of fabrics.

IAN MELLIS Map pp224–5 *Food & Drink*
☎ 226 6215; 30a Victoria St; ⌚ 10am-6pm Mon-Fri, 9.30am-6pm Sat; bus 2, 23, 27, 41, 42

Mr Mellis is a cheesemonger, and there's not much that he doesn't know about the stuff. This is the place to purchase the best Scottish cheeses, from creamy Lanark Blue (the Scottish Roquefort) to sharp Isle of Mull Cheddar There's another branch (p153) in Stockbridge.

JOYCE FORSYTH DESIGNER
KNITWEAR Map pp224–5 *Fashion*
☎ 220 4112; 42 Candlemaker Row; ⌚ 11am-5.30pm Tue-Thu & Sat, 11am-4.45pm Fri; bus 2, 23, 27, 41, 42

The colourful designs on show at this intriguing little shop will drag your ideas about woollens firmly into the 21st century.

MR WOOD'S FOSSILS Map pp224–5 *Gifts*
☎ 220 1344; 5 Cowgatehead; ⌚ 10am-5.30pm Mon-Sat; bus 2

This fascinating speciality shop has a wide range of minerals, gems, fossils and other geological gifts.

PALENQUE Map pp224–5 *Jewellery*
☎ 557 9553; 56 High St, Royal Mile; ⌚ 10am-5.30pm Mon-Sat; bus 35

Palenque is a treasure trove of contemporary silver jewellery and hand-crafted accessories made using ceramics, textiles and metalwork. There's a second branch (p151) in the New Town.

ROYAL MILE WHISKIES

Map pp224–5   *Whisky*

☎ 225 3383; 379 High St, Royal Mile; ☺ 10am-6pm
Mon-Sat, 12.30-6pm Sun; bus 35

If it's a drap of the cratur ye're after, this place
stocks a vast selection of single malts, in miniature and full-size bottles. There's also a range of
blended whiskies, Irish whiskey and bourbon.

SCOTTISH GEMS Map pp224–5   *Jewellery*

☎ 557 5731; 24 High St, Royal Mile; ☺ 9.30am-
5.30pm Mon-Sat; bus 35

Scottish Gems sources its jewellery and crafts
from top Scottish artisans, specialising in gold
and silver jewellery in both traditional – mostly
Celtic – and modern designs. Items range from
intricate Celtic interlace designs and traditional
Scottish thistles to delicate butterflies in silver
and enamel, pewter goods and turned wooden
bowls in the form of traditional silver quaichs.

UNDERGROUND SOLUSH'N

Map pp224–5   *Music*

☎ 226 2242; 9 Cockburn St; ☺ 10am-6pm Mon-Wed
& Sat, 10am-7pm Thu & Fri, 1-5pm Sun; bus 35, 64

A paradise for those in search of new and
second-hand vinyl, this place has thousands
of records – techno, house, jungle, hip hop,
R&B, funk, soul and 45s – plus t-shirts, videos,
books and merchandise. They also have a
(smaller) selection of CDs.

WEST PORT BOOKS

Map pp218–20   *Second-hand Books*

☎ 229 4431; 147 West Port; ☺ 10.30am-5.30pm
Mon, Thu & Fri, noon-5.30pm Tue, Wed & Sat; bus 2, 35

A long-established second-hand bookshop,
West Port has a good range of material covering Scottish history and has published its own
edition of *An Atlas of Old Edinburgh*, a collection of facsimile antique maps of the city from
1544 to the 19th century. It also specialises in
titles covering Indian and Himalayan history
and art.

> ### Top Five Designer Knitwear
>
> - Arkangel (p153)
> - Cashmere Store (p147)
> - Designs on Cashmere (p148)
> - Jenners (p150)
> - Joyce Forsyth Designer Knitwear (p148)

NEW TOWN

The New Town is the city centre's main shopping area, with bag-toting crowds milling
along Princes St and pouring in and out of the shopping centres of Princes Mall and the
St James Centre.

Princes St, with its department stores and high-street chains, and George St, lined
with designer boutiques, are the high-rent heart of Edinburgh's retail trade. The area
surrounding Broughton St has good browsing potential, especially if you are into
second-hand bookshops. It's also a good place to pick up deli food for a picnic or
barbecue.

Stockbridge is a good place to shop for gifts, crafts and jewellery. The main shopping
areas are on Raeburn Pl, on the main drag west of the Water of Leith, and St Stephen St,
which has a selection of boutiques selling everything from jewellery to second-hand books
to retro furniture.

GEORGE & PRINCES STS

AITKEN & NIVEN Map pp218–20   *Scottish*

☎ 225 1461; 77-9 George St; ☺ 9am-5.30pm Mon-
Sat; bus 13, 19, 37, 41

Aitken & Niven, founded in 1905, is another
independent Scottish shop with a good
range of quality tartans and tweeds. They
also stock a wide selection of rugby shirts
and accessories – if you happen to be looking for a Scotland rugby shirt, this is the place
to go.

CRUISE Map pp218–20   *Fashion*

☎ 226 3524; 94 George St; ☺ 10am-6pm Mon-Fri,
9.30am-6pm Sat, noon-5pm Sun; bus 13, 19, 37, 41

An ornately corniced and pilastered foyer
leads into three floors of white-painted, minimalist art-gallery-like décor showing off the
best of mainstream designer labels for men
and women, including Paul Smith, Jasper
Conran, Hugo Boss, Joseph Tricot, Armani and
Dolce e Gabbana. There's also a branch of
Cruise in the Old Town (p148), which stocks
men's casual wear.

EDINBURGH WOOLLEN MILL

Map pp218–20   *Woollens*

☎ 226 3840; 139 Princes St; ⏰ 9am-7pm Mon-Fri, 9am-6pm Sat, 11am-5pm Sun; all Princes St buses

The Edinburgh Woollen Mill is a stalwart of the tourist trade with a good selection of traditional jerseys, cardigans, scarves, shawls and rugs, and Pringle knitwear.

FOPP Map pp218–20   *Music*

☎ 220 0310; 7 Rose St; ⏰ 9.30am-7pm Mon-Sat; 11am-6pm Sun; all Princes St buses

There's another branch located in the Old Town (p148). Both are good places to hunt for cheap CDs and vinyl.

HARVEY NICHOLS

Map pp218–20   *Department Store*

☎ 524 8388; 32-4 St Andrew Sq; ⏰ 10am-6pm Mon-Wed, 10am-8pm Thu, 10am-7pm Fri & Sat, noon-6pm Sun; all St Andrew Sq buses

The newest addition to Edinburgh's shopping scene is the four floors of designer labels and eye-popping price tags at Harvey Nicks, which dominates the east side of St Andrew Sq.

JENNERS Map pp218–20   *Department Store*

☎ 225 2442; 48 Princes St; ⏰ 9am-6pm Mon & Wed-Sat, 9.30am-6pm Tue, 11am-5pm Sun; all Princes St buses

Founded in 1838 (and with a brand new shop sign prominently visible from the fourth floor of young upstart Harvey Nichols), Jenners is the grande dame of Edinburgh shopping, and the oldest independently owned department store in the world. Its labyrinthine five floors stock a wide range of quality goods, both classic and contemporary – it's especially strong on designer shoes and handbags, hats, knitwear and oriental rugs – food hall, hairdresser, gift-wrapping service and four cafés.

JO MALONE Map pp218–20   *Fashion*

☎ 478 8555; 93 George St; ⏰ 10am-6pm Mon-Wed, 10am-7pm Thu, 9.30am-6pm Fri & Sat; bus 13, 19, 37, 41

This is a sweet-smelling palace of perfumery and posh cosmetics, where the in-store experts will provide a 'fragrance-combining' consultation that allows you to choose your perfect perfume, along with a range of other scents to 'layer' over it. Try the original nutmeg and ginger bath oil that made Ms Malone famous, or newer combinations such as lime, basil and mandarin, or amber and lavender.

JOHN LEWIS

Map pp218–20   *Department Store*

☎ 556 9121; St James Centre; ⏰ 9am-5.30pm Mon-Wed & Fri, 9am-7.30pm Thu, 9am-6pm Sat; all Leith St buses

A sprawling department store in the St James Centre, this is the place to go for good-value clothes and a huge selection of household goods, including a computer and electronics department and good-value kitchenware.

LIME BLUE Map pp218–20   *Jewellery*

☎ 220 2164; 107 George St; ⏰ 10am-6pm Mon-Wed & Fri, 10am-7pm Thu, 9.30am-5.30pm Sat, noon-4pm Sun; bus 13, 19, 37, 41

Put on those shades and tighten your grip on that purse – you'll be dazzled by both the merchandise and the price tags in this elegant and clean-cut emporium of diamond jewellery – earrings for £1300, silver necklaces for £15,000 plus. They also stock more affordable silver jewellery, crystal ware and other luxury goods.

MAPPIN & WEBB Map pp218–20   *Jewellery*

☎ 225 5502; 88 George St; ⏰ 9.30am-5.30pm Mon-Sat; bus 13, 19, 37, 41

Mappin & Webb are jewellers to HM the Queen, no less, and stock a range of jewellery, watches and silverware of the highest quality,

Jenners shop window

including silver-plated tableware, crystal and silver whisky decanters, and diamond rings.

MARKS & SPENCER

Map pp218–20 *Department Store*
☎ 225 2301; 54 Princes St; 🕑 9am-6pm Mon-Wed & Fri, 9am-8pm Thu, 8.30am-6pm Sat, 11am-5pm Sun; all Princes St buses
This city centre branch of Britain's best-known store has a wide range of men's, women's and children's clothing, homewares, cosmetics, and an excellent food hall.

ONE WORLD SHOP

Map pp218–20 *Arts & Crafts*
☎ 229 4541; St John's Church, cnr Princes St & Lothian Rd; 🕑 10am-5.30pm Mon-Wed, Fri & Sat, 10am-7pm Thu; all Princes St buses
The One World Shop sells a wide range of handmade crafts from developing countries, including paper goods, rugs, textiles, jewellery, ceramics, accessories, food and drink, all from accredited Fair Trade suppliers. During the Festival period there's a good crafts fair in the churchyard at St John's Church, with a wide range of jewellery, ceramics and leather goods.

ORTAK Map pp218–20 *Jewellery*

☎ 557 4393; Unit 29, Princes Mall, 3 Princes St; 🕑 9am-6pm Mon-Wed, Fri & Sat, 9am-7pm Thu, 11am-5pm Sun; all Princes St buses
Ortak's workshop in the Orkney Islands produces beautiful gold and silver jewellery based on Celtic and Art Nouveau designs, as well as pieces inspired by Charles Rennie Mackintosh.

OTTAKAR'S Map pp218–20 *Books*

☎ 225 4495; 57 George St; 🕑 9am-6pm Mon, Wed, Fri & Sat, 9.30am-6pm Tue, 9am-8pm Thu, 11.30am-5.30pm Sun; bus 13, 19, 37, 41
Formerly James Thin's bookshop, this large bookshop has a good selection of Scottish books and a large children's department, as well as a decent coffee shop upstairs.

PALENQUE Map pp218–20 *Jewellery*

☎ 225 7194; 99 Rose St; 🕑 10am-5.30pm Mon-Sat; all Princes St buses
There's also a branch in the Old Town. See the review p148.

SAMARKAND GALLERIES

Map pp218–20 *Rugs*
☎ 225 2010; 16 Howe St; 🕑 10am-5.30pm Mon-Sat; bus 13, 24, 29, 42

This clean-lined modern gallery-shop exhibits a colourful display of contemporary rugs, runners, flat-weaves and tribal weavings from Turkey, the Caucasus, Iran, Afghanistan and Central Asia. There is also a limited stock of antique rugs, flat weaves and salt bags, and some gorgeous Nepalese silver jewellery.

SCOTTISH GALLERY Map pp218–20 *Art*

☎ 558 1200; www.scottish-gallery.co.uk; 16 Dundas St; 🕑 10am-6pm Mon-Fri, 10am-4pm Sat; bus 23, 27
Home to Edinburgh's leading art dealers, Aitken Dott, this private gallery exhibits and sells paintings by contemporary Scottish artists and by masters of the late-19th and early 20th centuries, as well as a wide range of ceramics, glassware, jewellery and textiles.

TISO Map pp218–20 *Outdoor Sports*

☎ 225 9486; 123-5 Rose St; 🕑 9am-7pm Mon-Wed, Fri & Sat, 9am-8pm Thu, 9am-6pm Sun; all Princes St buses
Edinburgh's biggest outdoor equipment store has four floors of camping, hiking, climbing, canoeing, skiing and snowboarding gear. See also Tiso Outdoor Experience p156.

VIRGIN MEGASTORE Map pp218–20 *Music*

☎ 220 2230; 125 Princes St; 🕑 9am-6pm Mon-Wed, Fri & Sat, 9am-8pm Thu, 11am-6pm Sun; all Princes St buses
The Virgin Megastore is, well, a megastore, with wall-to-wall racks of mostly mainstream CDs, DVDs, cassettes and a bit of vinyl, plus computer games, t-shirts and posters. It also has a Ticketmaster outlet (see p132) where you can buy tickets for major music gigs.

WATERSTONE'S Map pp218–20 *Books*

☎ 226 2666; 128 Princes St; 🕑 8.30am-8pm Mon-Sat, 10.30am-7pm Sun; all Princes St buses
Waterstone's flagship Princes St branch has four floors of books, with a good Scottish section on the ground floor and lots of travel guides and a coffee shop on the second floor; it also hosts frequent book signings and author events. There are other branches at the **East End** (Map pp218–20; ☎ 556 3034; 13 Princes St; 🕑 9am-8pm Mon-Fri, 9am-7.30pm Sat, 10am-7pm Sun) and **George St** (Map pp218–20; ☎ 225 3436; 83 George St; 🕑 9.30am-9pm Mon-Fri, 9.30am-8pm Sat, 11am-6pm Sun).

WHISTLES Map pp218–20 *Fashion*

☎ 226 4398; 97 George St; 🕑 10am-6pm Mon-Wed & Fri, 10am-7pm Thu, 9am-6pm Sat; bus 13, 19, 37, 41

Crisp white and hot pink décor sets off the racks of designer clothes for women in this branch of the well-known London-based store. Lots of little black dresses here – just the place if you're looking for something a little more formal and dressy for that special occasion.

BROUGHTON

CROMBIE'S Map pp218–20   Butcher
☎ 557 0111; 97-101 Broughton St; ✆ 8am-6pm Mon-Fri, 8am-5pm Sat; bus 8, 17

Crombie's is a top-quality butcher shop where the good folk of Edinburgh go to stock up on superb home-made haggis. It's also famous for its gourmet sausages, with almost three dozen varieties ranging from wild boar and apricot to duck and ginger.

McNAUGHTAN'S BOOKSHOP
Map pp218–20   Second-hand Books
☎ 556 5897; 3a-4a Haddington Pl; ✆ 9.30am-5.30pm Tue-Sat; all Leith Walk buses

The maze of shelves found at McNaughtan's basement bookshop houses a broad spectrum of general second-hand and antiquarian books.

OUT OF THE BLUE
Map pp218–20   Gay & Lesbian
☎ 478 7048; 1 Barony St; ✆ noon-7pm Sat-Wed, noon-8pm Thur & Fri; bus 8, 17

Set in the basement beneath the Blue Moon Café (see p109), Out of the Blue is a gay and lesbian shop selling books, mags, videos, toys and so on.

SECOND EDITION
Map pp218–20   Second-hand Books
☎ 556 9403; 9 Howard St; ✆ 11am-4.30pm Tue-Sat; bus 8, 17, 23, 27

This is a place for serious collectors buying and selling rare editions, with a good range of titles on Scottish subjects. It's at the far northern edge of Broughton, just past the Canonmills roundabout.

TROON Map pp218–20   Fashion
☎ 557 4045; 1 York Pl; ✆ 10am-5pm Mon, 10am-5.30pm Tue-Sat; all York Pl buses

Troon is a cool little nook crammed with desperately desirable designer gear from lesser-known names like Ally Cappellino and Betty Jackson.

VALVONA & CROLLA
Map pp218–20   Delicatessen
☎ 556 6066; 19 Elm Row; ✆ 8am-6.30pm Mon-Sat, 11am-5pm Sun; all Leith Walk buses

The acknowledged queen of the Edinburgh delicatessens, established during the 1930s, Valvona and Crolla's is packed with Mediterranean goodies, including an excellent choice of fine wines. It also has a good café (see p108).

STOCKBRIDGE

ADAM POTTERY
Map pp218–20   Arts & Crafts
☎ 557 3978; 76 Henderson Row; ✆ 10am-6pm Mon-Sat; bus 36

This small, independent pottery produces its own colourfully glazed ceramics, both decorative and functional, in a wide range of styles.

ANNIE SMITH Map p217   Jewellery
☎ 332 5749; 20 Raeburn Pl; ✆ 10am-5.30pm Mon-Sat, noon-5pm Sun; bus 24, 29, 42

Annie Smith's back-of-the-shop studio creates beautiful and original jewellery to contemporary designs in silver and 18-carat gold, with beaten and worked surfaces that reflect natural textures such as rock, ice and leaves. If there's nothing in the shop that takes your fancy, you can commission Ms Smith to make something to order.

BLACKADDER GALLERY Map p217   Gifts
☎ 332 4605; 5 Raeburn Pl; ✆ 10am-5.30pm Mon-Sat, 1-5pm Sun; bus 24, 29, 42

This is a great place for girly gifts, from colourful, handmade cards and giftwrap, to copper and silver jewellery, scented candles, art prints and accessories.

GALERIE MIRAGES Map p217   Gifts
☎ 315 2603; 46a Raeburn Pl; ✆ 10am-5.30pm Mon-Sat, 1-5pm Sun; bus 24, 29, 42

A narrow lane located between two houses (beside Peckham's deli) leads to this Aladdin's Cave packed with jewellery, textiles and handicrafts from all over the world. It's best known for its silver, amber and gemstone jewellery in both ethnic and contemporary designs, but you will also find things like scented sandalwood boxes, handmade paper goods, colourful cushions and gorgeous throws.

GLADRAGS Map pp218–20 *Fashion*

☎ 557 1916; 17 Henderson Row; 🕙 11am-6pm
Tue-Sat; bus 36

Gladrags sports an elegant range of second-hand and retro clothes, shoes and jewellery, from Victorian petticoats to 1950s suits and dresses.

HERBIE'S Map p217 *Delicatessen*

☎ 332 9888; 66 Raeburn Pl; 🕙 9.30am-7pm Mon-Fri,
9am-6pm Sat; bus 24, 29, 42

Head down to Herbie's to load up your picnic basket with delicious fresh bread (including bagels), French cheeses and charcuterie, plump olives and home-made hummus.

IAN MELLIS Map pp218–20 *Food & Drink*

☎ 225 6566; 6 Bakers Pl, Kerr St; 🕙 9.30am-6pm
Mon-Wed, 9.30am-6.30pm Thu, 9.30am-7pm Fri, 9am-6pm Sat, 11am-5pm Sun; bus 24, 29, 42

There's also a branch in the Old Town. See the review on p148.

Top Five Scottish Jewellery

- Annie Smith (p152)
- Galerie Mirages (p152)
- Ortak (p151)
- Palenque (p148)
- Scottish Gems (p149)

EDINBURGH WEST

Edinburgh's West End has a string of high-street chain stores on the main drag of Shandwick Pl, but there's also a hidden enclave of decadent designer shops clustered around the junction of William and Stafford Sts.

ARKANGEL Map p217 *Fashion*

☎ 226 4466; 4 William St; 🕙 9.30am-6pm Mon-Sat;
all Shandwick Pl buses

Owners Janey and Lulu will help you pick out a glamorous outfit from their carefully selected wardrobe of off-beat European chic – look out for the superb cashmere knitwear by Scots designer Hillary Rohde.

HELEN BATEMAN Map p217 *Shoes*

☎ 220 4495; 16 William St; 🕙 9.30am-6pm Mon-Sat;
all Shandwick Pl buses

From sparkly stilettos and sleek satin pumps to 1950s-style open-sided court shoes and soft suede loafers, Helen Bateman's shop has every kind of handmade shoe and boot you could ever wish for. You can even order customised satin shoes – slingbacks, court shoes, pumps or kitten heels – dyed to any colour and decorated with whatever your heart desires.

SAM THOMAS Map p217 *Fashion*

☎ 226 1126; 18 Stafford St; 🕙 9.30am-6pm Mon-Wed, Fri & Sat, 9.30am-7pm Thu, 12.30-5pm Sun; all
Shandwick Pl buses

This William St boutique has a good range of affordable designer gear, from casual to evening wear, as well as reasonably priced jewellery, bags, boots and shoes.

EDINBURGH SOUTH

Eclectic Edinburgh South offers a broad range of retail therapy, including the crafts and antique shops on Causewayside, the bookshops clustered around the university, and the trendy fashion and design shops in Morningside.

ANOTHER PLANET Map p221 *Toys & Gifts*

☎ 337 0072; 34 Ashley Tce; 🕙 10am-6pm Mon-Sat;
bus 38

Another Planet – named so that the owner could answer the phone with 'Hello, this is Tom from Another Planet' – sells things that fly, sail, spin or are otherwise operated by the breeze – from £1.50 plastic boomerangs to £1500 Blokarts (mini land yachts; the latest, ultracool, big boys' toys). There's also lots of animated toys and kits of the kind that 11-year-olds (of all ages) drool over.

BACKBEAT Map pp218–20 *Music*

☎ 668 2666; 31 East Crosscauseway; 🕙 10am-5.30pm Mon-Sat; bus 42

If you're hunting for second-hand vinyl from way back, Backbeat has a stunning collection of jazz, blues, rock and soul, plus lots of '60s and '70s stuff.

BLACKWELL'S BOOKSHOP

Map pp224–5   *Books*

☎ 622 8222; 53-62 South Bridge; ☼ 9am-8pm Mon & Wed-Fri, 9.30am-8pm Tue, 9am-6pm Sat, 11am-5pm Sun; all South Bridge buses

James Thin's, founded in 1848, was the city's principal home-grown bookstore and Edinburgh University's main supplier. Taken over by Blackwell's of Oxford in 2002, its four floors still have an admirable selection of reading matter, and are particularly strong on academic books.

BOARDWISE

Map pp218–20   *Outdoor Sports*

☎ 229 5887; 4 Lady Lawson St; ☼ 10am-6pm Mon-Sat; bus 2, 35

Boardwise supplies all the gear – and the cool threads – you'll need for any board-based sports, be it snow, skate or surf.

COURTYARD ANTIQUES

Map pp222–3   *Antiques*

☎ 662 9008; 108a Causewayside; ☼ 10am-5pm Mon-Sat; bus 42

Hidden down a lane, the Courtyard has two crowded floors of wooden furniture (19th century to the 1970s), toys and militaria, including some fascinating bric-a-brac that ranges from 78rpm records to a home-made canvas canoe.

FLIP Map pp224–5   *Fashion*

☎ 556 4966; 60-2 South Bridge; ☼ 9.30am-5.30pm Mon-Wed, 9.30am-6pm Thu-Sat; all South Bridge buses

Flip is a vast American emporium purveying all things denim, canvas, cowboy and retro to (mainly) students and skaters at marked-down prices.

FORBIDDEN PLANET Map pp224–5 *Fashion*

☎ 225 8613; 40-1 South Bridge; ☼ 10am-5.30pm Mon-Wed, Fri & Sat, 10am-6pm Thu, noon-5pm Sun; all South Bridge buses

This place stocks a wide range of sci-fi comics, videos and t-shirts, as well as Star Trek, Simpsons and South Park merchandise. It's also the place to shop for your Rocky Horror Show gear.

GREENSLEEVES Map p221   *Fashion*

☎ 447 8042; 203 Morningside Rd; ☼ 10am-5.30pm Mon-Sat; bus 5, 11, 15, 16, 17, 23

If you would like to buy a designer dress without breaking the bank, search the rails at Greensleeves which specialises in high-quality second-hand clothes, handbags and shoes, including many with designer labels.

Shopping – Edinburgh South

Clothing Sizes

Measurements approximate only, try before you buy

Women's Clothing

Aus/UK	8	10	12	14	16	18
Europe	36	38	40	42	44	46
Japan	5	7	9	11	13	15
USA	6	8	10	12	14	16

Women's Shoes

Aus/USA	5	6	7	8	9	10
Europe	35	36	37	38	39	40
France only	35	36	38	39	40	42
Japan	22	23	24	25	26	27
UK	3½	4½	5½	6½	7½	8½

Men's Clothing

Aus	92	96	100	104	108	112
Europe	46	48	50	52	54	56
Japan	S		M	M		L
UK/USA	35	36	37	38	39	40

Men's Shirts (Collar Sizes)

Aus/Japan	38	39	40	41	42	43
Europe	38	39	40	41	42	43
UK/USA	15	15½	16	16½	17	17½

Men's Shoes

Aus/UK	7	8	9	10	11	12
Europe	41	42	43	44½	46	47
Japan	26	27	27½	28	29	30
USA	7½	8½	9½	10½	11½	12½

JONATHAN AVERY DESIGN

Map p221   *Kitchen Equipment*

☎ 447 1000; 7-9 Church Hill Pl; ☼ 9.30am-5pm Mon-Fri, 10am-5.30pm Sat; bus 11, 15, 16, 17, 23

Avery is a designer of customised non-fitted kitchen furniture, and this beautifully arranged shop lets you imagine the kitchen of your dreams while browsing their range of desirable kitchen accessories, ceramics, books and gifts.

KILBERRY BAGPIPES

Map pp222–3   *Scottish*

☎ 221 9925; 38 Lochrin Bldgs, Gilmore Pl; ☼ 9am-5pm Mon-Fri, 9am-1pm Sat; bus 10, 27

Makers and retailers of traditional Highland bagpipes; Kilberry also sell piping accessories, snare drums, CDs and learning materials.

MCALISTER MATHESON MUSIC

Map pp218–20   *Music*

☎ 228 3827; 1 Grindlay St; ☼ 9.30am-7pm Mon-Fri, 9am-5.30pm Sat; bus 2, 35

This is Scotland's biggest specialist shop dealing in classical music CDs and books, and is also the place to head for Scottish folk and Celtic music.

MEADOWS POTTERY Map pp222–3 *Crafts*
☎ 662 4064; 11a Summerhall Pl; ☺ 10.30am-5.30pm Mon-Sat; bus 42
This little shop sells a range of colourful, high-fired oxidised stoneware, both domestic and decorative, all hand-thrown on the premises.

PECKHAM'S Map p221 *Delicatessen*
☎ 229 7054; 155-9 Bruntsfield Pl; ☺ 8am-midnight Mon-Sat, 9am-11pm Sun; all Bruntsfield buses
Peckham's is a busy neighbourhood deli selling all the usual deli stuff – smoked salmon, gravadlax and kippers, all kinds of cheeses, freshly made bread and sandwiches, and organic veggies. There's also a great selection of wines and whiskies, and you can buy booze here until midnight, seven days a week.

STATIONERY OFFICE BOOKSHOP
Map pp218–20 *Books*
☎ 606 5566; 71 Lothian Rd; ☺ 9am-5pm Mon-Fri, 10am-5pm Sat; all Lothian Rd buses

The Stationery Office has a good selection of books on business, Scottish history, travel (including travel guides) and computers, and probably the widest range of Ordnance Survey maps in town.

WONDERLAND Map pp218–20 *Toys*
☎ 229 6428; 97-101 Lothian Rd; ☺ 9.30am-6pm Mon-Fri, 9am-6pm Sat; all Lothian Rd buses
Wonderland is a classic, kids-with-their-noses-pressed-against-the-window toy shop that is filled with model aircraft, spaceships and radio-controlled cars, but it also caters to the serious train-set and model-making fraternity.

WORD POWER Map pp218–20 *Books*
☎ 662 9112; 43 West Nicolson St; ☺ 10am-6pm Mon-Fri, 10.30am-6pm Sat; all South Bridge buses
Word Power is a radical, independent bookshop that supports both small publishers and local writers. It stocks a wide range of political, gay and feminist literature, as well as non-mainstream fiction and non-fiction.

WATERFRONT EDINBURGH

Apart from the huge mall of Ocean Terminal and the high-street stores on Great Junction St and Leith Walk, Leith itself is not a major shopping area, but there are several good specialist shops scattered among its streets.

EDINBURGH ARCHITECTURAL
SALVAGE YARD Map p216 *Antiques*
☎ 554 7077;31 West Bowling Green St; ☺ 9am-5pm Mon-Fri, noon-5pm Sat; bus 14, 21, 36
A happy hunting ground for house renovators, this is a rich source of period features where you can find everything from original Georgian and Victorian cast-iron fireplaces and kitchen ranges to roll-top baths and gleaming chrome, Art Deco bathroom fittings.

FLUX Map p216 *Arts & Crafts*
☎ 554 4075; 55 Bernard St; ☺ 9am-5pm Mon & Tue, 9am-7pm Wed-Fri, 11am-7pm Sat & Sun; bus 16, 22, 35, 36
Flux is an outlet for contemporary Scottish arts and crafts, including stained glass, metalware, jewellery and ceramics.

GEORGIAN ANTIQUES Map p216 *Antiques*
☎ 553 7286; 10 Pattison St; ☺ 8.30am-5.30pm Mon-Fri, 10am-2pm Sat; bus 12, 16, 35
With 50,000 sq ft of floor space, this place has the largest selection of antiques in Scotland with three floors of Victorian and Edwardian

Ocean Terminal shopping centre

A Kilt Above the Rest

The kilt, as it is worn today, is a relatively modern invention. In the 17th century the traditional garb of the Highlander was the *plaid* (Gaelic for 'blanket'), a long piece of material that was pleated and then wrapped around the body and held with a belt at the waist, with the upper part drawn over the shoulders. (Check out the Highlanders in the film *Rob Roy* – their dress is pretty authentic.) A cut-down version of the plaid – involving the lower, skirt-like part only – was known as the *feileadh beag* (phillibeg, or 'little wrap'), in contrast to the full plaid or *feileadh mor* (phillimore, or 'big wrap').

All manner of Highland dress was made illegal after the Jacobite rebellion of 1745, and in the following decades the Highlanders were drafted into the British army. The Highland regiments proved to be courageous fighters, and in order to foster a sense of identity and national pride, a formalised Highland dress, based around the phillibeg, was reintroduced as a regimental uniform after 1782.

Aided by Sir Walter Scott's tireless promotion of all things Scottish, Highland dress soon became all the rage in high society; even King George IV and the lord mayor of London wore kilts during the royal visit to Scotland in 1822. It is this formal version of Highland dress that gets worn to countless weddings, Burns suppers and clan gatherings today. Dedicated followers of fashion, however, have not ignored the kilt – everyone from Siouxsie of the Banshees to Madonna have donned the tartan in the name of chic. But there is one Edinburgh designer who has gone a step further and has made the kilt a cult fashion item.

Howie Nicholsby, of **21st Century Kilts** (see Geoffrey (Tailor) Inc p148; www.21stcenturykilts.co.uk), has targeted the style-conscious market with his fashion kilts, retaining the traditional design and cut but experimenting with different fabrics and accessories. Choose a plain black barathea kilt – the most popular model – or try on one made from denim, imitation leather, stretchy black PVC, or even camouflage material. Who knows, he might develop a kilt following...

furniture, clocks, brass, porcelain, mirrors, light fittings and paintings.

KINLOCH ANDERSON Map p216 *Scottish*
☎ 555 1390; 4 Dock St; ☺ 9am-5pm Mon-Sat; bus 16, 22, 35, 36

Founded in 1868 and still family-run, Kinloch Anderson is the main supplier of kilts and Highland dress to the Royal Family. They can find out your tartan and kit you out in formal or semi-formal Highland dress, or even tartan trousers.

TISO OUTDOOR EXPERIENCE
Map p216 *Outdoor Sports*
☎ 554 0804; 41 Commercial St; ☺ 9am-6pm Mon, Tue & Sat, 9am-5pm Wed, 10am-5pm Sun, closed Thu; bus 16, 22, 35, 36

Outdoor Experience is the macho cousin of Tiso's flagship city centre store (see p151), where you can try before you buy with their Goretex-testing shower, boot-bashing footpath, rock-climbing wall, ice-climbing wall and stove-testing area.

GREATER EDINBURGH

There are several large shopping malls on the edge of the city, and a couple of other places that might tempt you away from the Princes St shops.

MACSWEEN OF EDINBURGH *Food*
☎ 440 2555; www.macsween.co.uk; Bilston Glen Industrial Estate, Dryden Rd, Loanhead; ☺ 8.30am-5pm Mon-Fri; bus 37

MacSween – the most famous haggis-makers in Edinburgh – closed their Morningside butcher shop a few years ago to concentrate on making and selling haggis. You can buy direct from the factory, by mail order via their website, or from Jenners (see p150). MacSween haggis is also stocked by Harrods, Selfridges and Fortnum & Mason stores.

INGLISTON MARKET *Market*
☎ 333 3801; Ingliston Showground Car Park, Glasgow Rd; ☺ 10am-4pm Sun; First Edinburgh bus 12, 16

The Sunday flea-market at Ingliston, located close to the airport 8 miles west of the city centre, sells household goods, clothes and bric-a-brac; there's also a car boot sale. Beware of pirated CDs, videos and computer software, though – £10 million worth of pirated goods was seized here in December 2003.

Sleeping

Sleeping

A boom in hotel building has seen Edinburgh's tourist capacity swell markedly in recent years, but you can guarantee that the city will still be packed to the gills during the Festival and Fringe period (August) and over Hogmanay (New Year). If you want a room during these periods, book as far in advance as possible. In general, it's best to book ahead at Easter and between mid-May and mid-September. Accommodation might also be in short supply during the Royal Highland Show (late June) and over the weekends when international rugby matches are being played at Murrayfield (two or three weekends from January to March).

Accommodation Styles

Edinburgh offers a wide range of accommodation options, from moderately priced guest houses set in lovely Victorian villas and Georgian town houses to expensive and stylish boutique hotels. There are also plenty of international chain hotels, and a few truly exceptional hotels housed in magnificent historic buildings. At the budget end of the range, there is no shortage of youth hostels and independent backpacker hostels, which often have inexpensive double and twin rooms available.

Apartments

There's plenty of self-catering apartment accommodation in Edinburgh. The minimum stay is usually one week in the summer peak season; three nights or less at other times.

The Scottish Tourist Board and the Edinburgh and Scotland Information Centre (see Tourist Information p199) can provide listings of self-catering accommodation in Edinburgh and the Lothians. Depending on facilities, location and time of year, prices range from £150 to £750-plus per week. At the more expensive end of the market are serviced apartments, which can be let by the night and include a daily cleaning service and house manager.

The following prices are for a one-bedroom apartment (sleeping two or three).

Edinburgh Central Apartments (Map pp218–20; ☎ 622 7840; www.edinburgh-central-apartments.co.uk; Home St; apt per week £250-350) ECA provides basic but comfortable flats in centrally located Tollcross.

Fountain Court Apartments (Map p217; ☎ 622 6677; www.fountaincourtapartments.com; 123 Grove St; apt per night £80-95; Ⓟ) These places close to Haymarket come with well-equipped kitchens (microwave, dishwasher, washing machine) and free private parking.

Glen House Apartments (Map pp218–20; ☎ 228 4043; www.edinburgh-apartments.co.uk, 101 Lauriston Pl; apt per week £300-550) This is a large agency that can provide flats of all sizes and categories throughout Edinburgh.

Price Ranges

Rates at a typical mid-range hotel or guest house start at around £50 for a double room. In the following reviews, places listed under Cheap Sleeps cost £25 or less per person, based on two people sharing.

Long-Term Rentals

The Edinburgh rental market has boomed in recent years and there are plenty of rooms, apartments and houses to let. Rates for a single or double room in a shared flat start at around £220 per calendar month in central districts such as Tollcross and Marchmont, though £250 to £350 is more common. A one-bedroom flat in the highly desirable New Town would cost at least £500 per month, but you can get a flat with two double bedrooms in Bruntsfield for around £750. If you don't mind travelling into the city, it's possible to find a two-bedroom house or cottage within an hour's drive of Edinburgh for £500 per month.

The minimum lease on long-term rental properties is usually six months, but there are also many short-term lettings available (usual minimum three nights), especially during the summer and the festival period. Most landlords will demand a security deposit (normally one month's rent) plus a month's rent in advance; some will also ask for some sort of reference.

If you want to search for long-term accommodation yourself, check out the property section in the Thursday edition of the *Scotsman* newspaper, or the Flatshare section in *The List* magazine (see p198). Hostel noticeboards area also a good place to look.

When you inspect a flat it's wise to take someone else with you, both for safety reasons and for help in spotting any shortcomings. A few things to check before signing a tenancy agreement include: the cost of gas, electricity, phone, TV and how they're to be paid for; whether there's street parking and/or how convenient is public transport; the arrangements for cleaning the house or flat; and whether the lease allows you to have friends to stay.

Reservations

If you arrive in the city without a room, there are several agencies that can help. The Edinburgh and Scotland Information Centre's **booking service** (☎ 473 3800) will try and find a room to suit, and will charge you a £4 fee if successful. If you have the time, get hold of its free accommodation brochure (see p199) and ring round yourself.

You can also try the Scottish Tourist Board's **booking hotline** (☎ 0845-2255 121 within UK, +44 1506-83212 outside UK), which has a £3 surcharge, or search for accommodation on the **Edinburgh & Lothians Tourist Board** (www.edinburgh.org) or **VisitScotland** (www.visitscotland.com) websites.

If you are having trouble finding a vacant room for the Festival period, try **Festival Beds** (☎ 225 1101; www.festivalbeds.co.uk), which specialises in matching visitors with B&Bs during August only.

Top Five Hotels with a History...

A number of Edinburgh's most atmospheric hotels are housed in interesting historic buildings. Here are our top five:

- Bank Hotel (p160)
- Malmaison Hotel (p169)
- Point Hotel (p160)
- Prestonfield House Hotel (p168)
- Scotsman Hotel (p161)

OLD TOWN

Staying in the Old Town puts you in the heart of Edinburgh's historical heritage, within easy walking distance of the castle and Holyroodhouse. But there's a dearth of decent mid-range options – most accommodation here is in hostels or expensive hotels; anything in between is mostly in characterless chain hotels.

APEX INTERNATIONAL HOTEL

Map pp224–5   *Hotel*

☎ 300 3456; www.apexhotels.co.uk; 31-5 Grassmarket;
r £120-160; bus 2; **P**

Centrally located and with good business facilities, the modern, 175-room Apex has great views towards the castle and an excellent rooftop Heights restaurant (see p102).

BANK HOTEL Map pp224–5   *Hotel*

☎ 622 6800; www.festival-inns.co.uk; 1 South Bridge;
s/d £90/110; all South Bridge buses

The Bank Hotel, on the corner of the Royal Mile and the North Bridge, is in an imposing, neo-classical building dating from 1923. Formerly a bank (surprise, surprise), it has nine elegant rooms themed around famous Scots, including Robert Burns, Robert Louis Stevenson and Charles Rennie Mackintosh.

CARLTON HOTEL Map pp224–5   *Hotel*

☎ 472 3000; www.paramount-hotels.co.uk; 19 North
Bridge; r £140-225; all South Bridge buses; **P** **R**

The Carlton has recently undergone a £10-million renovation, complete with swimming pool and leisure complex, and is now one of the city's most luxurious hotels. Comfort and convenience are the main draws – the hotel is only a few minutes' walk from both Waverley train station and the Royal Mile.

EDINBURGH (CITY CENTRE) PREMIER
LODGE Map pp224–5   *Chain Hotel*

☎ 0870 700 1370; www.premierlodge.com; 94
Grassmarket; r £52; bus 2

The Premier Lodge is a budget chain hotel with a great Old Town location. Rooms are small but comfy, and the rate includes up to two adults and two children. Breakfast is not included.

KNIGHT RESIDENCE

Map pp218–20   *Apartments*

☎ 622 8120; www.theknightresidence.co.uk; 12
Lauriston St; d apt £125-160; bus 2

Works by contemporary artists adorn the 19 one- and two-bedroom apartments (available by the night) that make up the Knight Residence. Each has a fully equipped kitchen (including washing machine and dryer) and a comfortable lounge with cable TV, video and stereo (and an extension speaker in the bathroom). You can even order specific CDs and videos to be waiting in your rooms when you arrive. The Knight has a good central location in a quiet street only a few minutes' walk from Grassmarket.

The James Watt room at the Bank Hotel

HOLYROOD HOTEL Map pp218–20   *Hotel*

☎ 550 4500; www.macdonaldhotels.co.uk; 81
Holyrood Rd; r £90-170; bus 64

A new luxury hotel with a traditional feel, the Holyrood sits at the foot of Salisbury Crags, alongside the site of the new Scottish Parliament and only minutes from Our Dynamic Earth and the Palace of Holyroodhouse. Facilities include a 14m pool, gym, sauna and steam room. Check the website for special offers.

IBIS HOTEL Map pp224–5   *Chain Hotel*

☎ 240 7000; www.ibishotel.com; 6 Hunter Sq;
r £50-70; bus 35

A spruce, modern chain hotel just off the Royal Mile, the Ibis offers a flat room rate that includes a self-service breakfast buffet.

POINT HOTEL Map pp218–20   *Hotel*

☎ 221 5555; www.point-hotel.co.uk; 34 Bread St;
s/d from £95/105

Housed in the beautiful former showrooms of the St Cuthbert Co-operative Association (built in 1937), the Point is famous for its striking contemporary interior design. Some rooms have stunning castle views.

RADISSON SAS Map pp224–5   *Hotel*
☎ 557 9797; www.radissonsas.com; 80 High St, Royal Mile; s/d from £155/180; all South Bridge buses; **P** **⟨⟩**
This luxury hotel was built in the 1990s, but blends in nicely with the Royal Mile's 17th-century architecture. The interior is, nonetheless, as modern as you would expect. Check the website for cheaper deals on rooms.

ROYAL MILE RESIDENCE
Map pp224–5   *Apartments*
☎ 226 5155; www.royalmileresidence.com; 65 Cockburn St; apt per week £175-300; bus 35, 64
Contemporary interior design combined with a classic Old Town location place these flats among the most desirable serviced apartments in Edinburgh. There are six two-bedroom flats (each sleeping up to four people); those at the rear have views over the city to the Firth of Forth, while those at the front overlook the Royal Mile. The lowest rates apply from September to June (excluding New Year and rugby weekends), and the price includes free use of the adjacent fitness club.

SCOTSMAN HOTEL Map pp224–5   *Hotel*
☎ 556 5565; www.thescotsmanhotelgroup.co.uk; 20 North Bridge; r from £150; all South Bridge buses; **⟨⟩**
The former offices of the *Scotsman* (opened in 1904 and hailed as 'the most magnificent newspaper building in the world') are now home to Edinburgh's finest luxury hotel. Standard rooms – those on the northern side enjoy superb views over New Town and Calton Hill – come with coffee machine, DVD player, wide-screen TV and computer with Internet, while the Penthouse Suite (£950) has its own library and sauna.

TAILOR'S HALL HOTEL Map pp224–5   *Hotel*
☎ 622 6801; www.festival-inns.co.uk; 139 Cowgate; s/d/tw £90/110/130; bus 2
The Tailor's Hall, with bright, modern rooms decorated in blue, pink and natural pine wood, is located bang in the middle of Edinburgh's clubland, and has three big bars of its own downstairs. Great for partying, but not really a place for the quiet life.

TRAVELODGE EDINBURGH CENTRAL
Map pp224–5   *Chain Hotel*
☎ 557 6281; www.travelodge.co.uk; 33 St Mary's St; r £70; bus 35
Yet another centrally located budget hotel, convenient for the Royal Mile and Cowgate's pubs and clubs, the Travelodge's twin rooms accommodate up to two adults and two kids.

WITCHERY BY THE CASTLE
Map pp224–5   *Suites*
☎ 225 5613; www.thewitchery.com; Castlehill, Royal Mile; ste £225; bus 28
The ultimate in self-indulgent decadence, the Witchery's seven themed suites (and atmospheric restaurant; see p104) are regularly mentioned in magazine roundups of the world's most romantic places to stay. And with good reason – set in a 16th-century Old Town house just two minutes' walk from the castle, these lavish rooms are extravagantly furnished with antiques, oak panelling, tapestries, open fires and roll-top baths, and supplied with flowers, chocolates and complimentary champagne. Our favourite is the Gothic Library Suite, overlooking the Royal Mile – the book-lined bathroom has its own log fire and a bath big enough for two. Book at least six months in advance.

Top Five Rooms with a View

- Balmoral Hotel (p162)
- Bedford House Hotel (p169)
- Glasshouse (p163)
- Point Hotel (p160)
- Scotsman Hotel (see opposite)

CHEAP SLEEPS
The following hostels are right in the heart of things, and all are close to pubs and clubs.

BRODIE'S BACKPACKER HOSTEL
Map pp224–5   *Hostel*
☎ 556 6770; www.brodieshostels.co.uk; 12 High St, Royal Mile; dm £10-16; bus 35
Brodies is a small (50 beds), friendly place with four dorms (three mixed and one women-only) and seriously comfy hotel-quality mattresses and duvets. It has a kitchen and a cosy lounge area with a fireplace. There is no TV, which makes for good socialising, though it can be a little cramped and smoky for some tastes. Top location bang in the middle of the Royal Mile.

CASTLE ROCK HOSTEL
Map pp224–5   *Hostel*
☎ 225 9666; castlerock@scotlands-top-hostels.com; 15 Johnston Tce; dm £12-13; bus 28
With its bright, spacious, single-sex dorms, superb views and friendly staff, the 200-bed

Castle Rock has prompted plenty of positive feedback from travellers. It has a great location only a minute's walk from the castle (but a fair uphill trek from train and bus stations), a games room, reading lounge, and big-screen video nights; it's a shame the beds aren't as comfortable as those at Brodies.

EDINBURGH BACKPACKERS HOSTEL

Map pp224–5   *Hostel*
☎ 220 1717; www.hoppo.com; 65 Cockburn St; dm £13-15.50; bus 35, 64

Just a short walk up the hill from Waverley train station, Edinburgh Backpackers is clean, bright and friendly. It's right in the heart of Edinburgh's pub culture, which makes it great for partying but not so good for a peaceful night's sleep.

HIGH STREET HOSTEL Map pp224–5 *Hostel*
☎ 557 3984; high-street@scotlands-top-hostels.com; 8 Blackfriars St; dm £12-13; bus 35

This long-established and well-equipped hostel is housed in a 17th-century building. It has a reputation as a party place, so if you're not in the party mood you might find it noisy.

ST CHRISTOPHER'S INN

Map pp224–5   *Hostel*
☎ 226 1446; www.st-christophers.co.uk; 9-13 Market St; dm £10-19; bus 64

The St Christopher's is just across from the Market St entrance to Waverley station, with accommodation in four- to 14-bed dorms, each with toilet and shower. It's a real party joint, with two bars and a good-value restaurant, so don't some here to catch up on your beauty sleep.

NEW TOWN

The New Town offers a range of accommodation options, from elegant Georgian guest houses to gleaming boutique hotels, all within easy reach of the city's main shopping and restaurant areas. Many places are also within walking distance of the bus and train stations.

19 ST BERNARD'S CRESCENT

Map p217   *Guest House*
☎ 332 6162; balfourwm@aol.com; 19 St Bernard's Cres; s/d £90/110; bus 36

This magnificent Georgian town house, packed with antiques and original period features, sits near the middle of St Bernard's Cres (see p71). Both guest bedrooms are decked out in Regency elegance – if you have a choice, go for the Balfour room with its four-poster bed. Note that the quoted room rate is £10 less per night for stays of two nights or more.

AILSA CRAIG HOTEL Map pp218–20 *Hotel*
☎ 556 1022; www.townhousehotels.co.uk; 24 Royal Tce; r £65-100; all London Rd buses

The Ailsa Craig is a grand Georgian town house dating from 1820, set on a peaceful, tree-lined terrace overlooking Royal Tce Gardens. Many of its elegantly furnished rooms have grand views across the city rooftops to the Firth of Forth.

BALMORAL HOTEL Map pp218–20 *Hotel*
☎ 556 2414; www.thebalmoralhotel.com; 1 Princes St; s £190-230, d £220-280, ste £450-1200; all Princes St buses; 🔁

Built in 1902 as the North British Station Hotel for the railway company of the same name, the Balmoral (renamed in 1990 after a major refurbishment) is a major city landmark rising directly above Waverley train station. Its sumptuous rooms offer some of the most comfortable accommodation in Edinburgh, including suites with 18th-century décor, marble bathrooms and stunning sunset views of Princes St and the Scott Monument. There's a spa and gym with 20m pool in the basement.

CALEDONIAN HILTON HOTEL

Map pp218–20   *Hotel*
☎ 222 8888; www.hilton.com; 4 Princes St; r £150-225; all Princes St buses; 🔁

An Edinburgh institution, the 'Caley' is a vast, red-sandstone palace of Edwardian pomp and splendour dating from 1903, one of two grandiose hotels at opposite ends of Princes St built by competing railway companies at the turn of the 20th century (the other is the Balmoral). It has a spa, swimming pool and gym, and full business and conference facilities.

CARAVEL GUEST HOUSE

Map pp218–20   *Guest House*
☎ 556 4444; caravelguest@hotmail.com; 30 London St; r £40-60; bus 13

The friendly, family-run Caravel is handy for the New Town and for Broughton St nightlife. There's an excellent Moroccan restaurant in the basement (see Marrakech p107).

CASTLE GUEST HOUSE

Map pp218–20   *Guest House*

☎ 225 1975; www.castleguesthouse.com; 38 North Castle St; s £30-40, d £60-80; all Princes St buses

Dark, polished wood and deep-red walls characterise the traditional décor in this lovely Georgian town house in the heart of the New Town. Rose St pubs and Thistle St restaurants are just minutes away, and you can walk to the castle in a quarter of an hour.

CHRISTOPHER NORTH HOUSE HOTEL

Map pp218–20   *Boutique Hotel*

☎ 225 2720; www.christophernorth.co.uk; 6 Gloucester Pl; r £90-190; bus 24, 29, 42

This is a small, elegant boutique hotel set in a lovely Georgian building, with an appealing blend of contemporary décor and original architectural features. It's handy for the shops and restaurants in Stockbridge and walks along the Water of Leith, and the city centre is a short walk uphill.

DENE GUEST HOUSE

Map pp218–20   *Guest House*

☎ 556 2700; www.deneguesthouse.com; 7 Eyre Pl; s £20-35, d £40-70; bus 23, 27, 36

The Dene is a friendly and informal guesthouse set in a charming Georgian town house, with 11 bright and cheerful rooms (only three en suite). Children and (unusually for Edinburgh guest houses) dogs are welcome.

GEORGE INTERCONTINENTAL HOTEL

Map pp218–20   *Hotel*

☎ 225 1251; www.edinburgh.interconti.com; 19-21 George St; s £90-185, d £120-240; bus 24, 28, 45

With its elegant, Robert Adam façade and sophisticated Le Chambertin restaurant, the George is a very traditional hotel in the middle of the New Town. Red leather armchairs in the marble-floored lobby, a Corinthian-columned dining room, comfortably old-fashioned décor and extensive conference facilities draw in a clientele of wealthy tourists and business people.

GLASSHOUSE

Map pp218–20   *Boutique Hotel*

☎ 525 8200; www.theetoncollection.com; 2 Greenside Pl; r £160-300, ste £230-390; all Leith Walk buses

Floor-to-ceiling windows, a two-acre roof garden, Egyptian cotton sheets, leather sofas, glass and marble bathrooms – Edinburgh's newest luxury hotel is a palace of cutting-edge design perched atop the Omni Centre

at the foot of Calton Hill. Entered through the preserved Tudoresque façade of a mid-19th-century church, the granite-and-marble lobby has a bold spiral staircase leading to the hotel's own art gallery. Rooms have views over garden or city; there are four adapted for wheelchair users.

HANOVER HOTEL
Map pp218–20   *Hotel*

☎ 226 7576; www.thehanoverhotel.com; 40 Rose St; r from £90; all Princes St buses

Location, location, location – the bland but welcoming 96-room Hanover is a modern hotel on pedestrianised Rose St, bang in the middle of Edinburgh's main shopping district. No parking, but it's only a few minutes' stroll from Waverley train station, and there are dozens of good restaurants and pubs within a 500m radius.

HOWARD
Map pp218–20   *Boutique Hotel*

☎ 315 2220; www.thehoward.com; 34 Great King St; s £108-145, d £157-295, ste £270-475; bus 13; P

Pampering is perhaps too weak a word for the service you get at this small (18 rooms) but beautifully turned out Georgian hotel. On arrival, each guest is assigned a personal 'butler' who will do everything from unpacking your bags and polishing your shoes to 'organising your social itinerary' and serving dinner in your room – or even breakfast in bed. Gorgeous period décor, including striped Regency wallpaper and roll-top baths, is complemented by high-tech features such as email-TV and Internet access in all rooms.

OLD WAVERLEY HOTEL

Map pp218–20   *Hotel*

☎ 556 4648; www.oldwaverley.net; 43 Princes St; s/d from £75/130; all Princes St buses

This traditional tourist hotel with crisp, clean-cut accommodation has a prime location opposite the Scott Monument and only two minutes' walk from Waverley train station. Many rooms have superb views – ask for a 'premier' corner room whose bow windows look out over Princes St Gardens towards the castle.

PARLIAMENT HOUSE HOTEL

Map pp218–20   *Hotel*

☎ 478 4000; www.parliamenthouse-hotel.co.uk; 15 Calton Hill; s/d £110/160; all Leith Walk buses

Tucked away in a quiet corner of Calton Hill, the cosily traditional Parliament House is only five minutes' walk from Princes St, albeit with a bit of an uphill hike. There's a welcoming lounge with an open fire and plaid upholstery, which contrasts with the jazzy bistro, which has bright modern décor and a Mediterranean menu.

RICK'S Map pp218–20 *Boutique Hotel*
☎ 622 7800; www.ricksedinburgh.co.uk; 55a Frederick St; r £118; buses 13, 24, 29, 42

Describing itself as 'not a hotel', but a 'restaurant with rooms' (10 of them), Rick's was voted one of the world's coolest places to stay by *Condé Nast Traveller* magazine (for details of the restaurant, see p108). Designer fabrics and DVD players in the bedrooms, plus friendly service and cracking cocktails in the bar attract a young and fashion-conscious clientele.

ROXBURGHE HOTEL Map pp218–20 *Hotel*
☎ 240 5500; www.macdonald-hotels.co.uk; 38 Charlotte Sq; r £145-265; buses 13, 19, 36, 37, 41; 🛒

With one of Edinburgh's most prestigious locations and a recent £12 million facelift (including a 12m pool, sauna and steam room), the very elegant, Georgian-era Roxburghe is simply *the* place to stay, dahhling. The most splendid rooms, complete with period wainscot walls, marble-lined fireplaces and ornate cornices, are those overlooking Charlotte Sq; the modern rooms viewing George St have less character.

ROYAL GARDEN APARTMENTS
Map pp218–20 *Apartments*
☎ 621 8000; www.royal-garden.co.uk; York Bldgs, Queen St; 1-bedroom apt per night £130-175; all York Pl buses

The family-friendly Royal Garden has 30 luxurious, centrally located one- and two-bedroom apartments with daily maid service, business facilities, a private garden (with access to private Queen St Gardens) and use of the Scotsman Hotel's health club and pool. The penthouse apartments (£265 to £365 per night) sleep up to six people, and have rooftop balconies with superb views towards the Firth of Forth and the Fife hills.

ROYAL TERRACE HOTEL
Map pp218–20 *Hotel*
☎ 557 3222; www.theroyalterracehotel.co.uk; 18 Royal Tce; s/d £115/175; all London Rd buses; 🛒

This is one of the swishest hotels in Edinburgh – in a frilly, flouncy, valanced four-poster sort of way – with rooms full of fine furnishings. It also has a delightful terraced garden, swimming pool and sauna.

A room at - Rick's

SIX MARY'S PLACE Map p217 *Guest House*
☎ 332 8965; www.sixmarysplace.co.uk; 6 Mary's Pl, Raeburn Pl; r £60-100; bus 24, 29, 42

Six Mary's Place is an attractive Georgian town house, fully refurbished with a designer mix of period features, contemporary furniture and modern colours. It serves vegetarian breakfasts in the garden conservatory, and has some nice touches such as free coffee and newspapers, and Internet facilities in the lounge.

STUART HOUSE Map pp218–20 *Guest House*
☎ 557 9030; www.stuartguesthouse.com; 12 East Claremont St; s £30-50, d £65-100; bus 13, 23, 27

A readers' favourite, the eight-room Stuart House is a welcoming late-Georgian town house with many period features, including the open, three-storey staircase (no lift), cast-iron fireplaces and ornate cornices.

WAYFARER GUEST HOUSE
Map pp218–20 *Guest House*
☎ 556 3025; www.wayfarerguesthouse.co.uk; 5 Eyre Pl; s/d £44/77; bus 23, 27, 36

A renovated Georgian-style town house with 12 colourful, well-kept rooms (all en suite, with TV and DVD), the Wayfarer is only 10 minutes' walk from Princes St. Breakfast comes in the form of a sumptuous buffet with free newspapers in an idiosyncratic dining room dominated by a mural of Antarctic explorer Ernest Shackleton – give the resident cat a stroke on the way in.

CHEAP SLEEPS

CITY CENTRE TOURIST HOSTEL

Map pp218–20   *Hostel*

☎ 556 8070; www.edinburghhostels.com; 3rd fl, 5 West Register St; dm £12-20; all Princes St buses

The City Centre Tourist Hostel is a small (around 40 beds), clean and relatively quiet hostel, with pine-wood bunks and comfy mattresses in four-, six-, eight- and 10-bed dorms. There's a small kitchen (with microwave oven) and TV lounge, plus a laundry where you can do your ironing. The location is great – just two minutes' walk from train and bus stations.

Top Five Romantic Hideaways

- **Channings** (see below) Unwind in an Edwardian slipper bath or modern Jacuzzi.
- **Dundas Castle** (p170) Really get away from it all in the secluded Boathouse.
- **Howard** (p163) Where your personal butler will serve breakfast in bed.
- **Scotsman Hotel** (p161) The hotel's Vermilion restaurant is perfect for dinner *à deux*.
- **Witchery by the Castle** (p161) Themed Gothic suites let your imagination run riot, and the baths are big enough for two.

EDINBURGH WEST

The West End and Haymarket offer a good selection of mid-range hotels, many in spacious Georgian and Victorian villas and town houses. If you're arriving by rail from the direction of Glasgow, you should get off at Haymarket station for hotels in this area.

BONHAM Map p217   *Boutique Hotel*

☎ 226 6050; www.thebonham.com; 35 Drumsheugh Gdns; s £108-165, d £127-225; bus 19, 36, 37, 41

Bonham is one of the few Edinburgh hotels that manages a successful fusion of Victorian interiors with bold modern colours and contemporary design – check out the crimson spiral sofa in the lobby. Cool, crisp bed linen, luxury bathrooms and friendly but unobtrusive service make for a memorable stay. Though set in a quiet, West End backstreet, the Bonham is only five minutes' walk from Princes St.

CHANNINGS Map p217   *Boutique Hotel*

☎ 315 2226; www.channings.co.uk; 12-16 South Learmonth Gdns; s £101-155, d £131-205; bus 19, 36, 37, 41

Channings is a charming, Edwardian-style hotel with the feel of a private club – the lounges to the left of reception are lined with polished wood panelling, and there's huge, comfy sofas, fine artworks, vases of fresh flowers and open fires. The rooms are tailored in rich fabrics such as silk, velvet and suede, and the more expensive ones have black-and-white tiled bathrooms with roll-top slipper baths. The setting is peaceful – rooms at the front have views to the Forth and the spires of Fettes College, and those at the back overlook a private garden.

DUNSTANE HOUSE HOTEL

Map p217   *Hotel*

☎ 337 6169; www.dunstanehousehotel.co.uk; 4 West Coates; s £35-55, d £67-98; bus 12, 26, 31, 100; Ⓟ

Readers have recommended the friendly Dunstane House Hotel, a large Victorian villa dating from 1850 with many original features including beautiful rooms with four-poster beds, a good seafood restaurant and cosy bar.

EDINBURGH CITY TRAVEL INN

Map p217   *Chain Hotel*

☎ 228 9819; www.travelinn.co.uk; 1 Morrison Link; r £50; all Haymarket buses

Part of the Travel Inn budget chain, this place is sleek, modern and comfortable, and is only three minutes' walk from Haymarket train station. Rooms take up to two adults and two children, but breakfast is not included.

ORIGINAL RAJ Map p217   *Hotel*

☎ 346 1333; originalrajhotel@aol.com; 6 West Coates; r £70-110; bus 12, 26, 31, 100

Enjoy some oriental splendour at the Original Raj – Edinburgh's only Indian-themed hotel, founded by Tommy Miah, owner of the famous Raj restaurant (see p116). Its 17 spacious bedrooms are filled with colourful Indian fabrics and furniture, and it must be the only hotel in the city where you can get samosas for breakfast.

ROTHESAY HOTEL Map p217   *Hotel*

☎ 225 4125; www.rothesay-hotel.com; 8 Rothesay Pl; s/d £70/90; bus 19, 36, 37, 41

Located in a quiet, central street, this elegant, Victorian hotel has 36 pleasant, spacious rooms, all en suite. It's a little lacking in character, but the price and location make for excellent value.

WEST END HOTEL Map p217   *Hotel*
☎ 225 3656; www.rooms-in-edinburgh.co.uk; 35 Palmerston Pl; s/d from £40/60; bus 13
Renowned as a home-from-home for city-bound Highlanders, the West End has eight spacious and comfortable rooms above a lively lounge bar. It's only five minutes' walk from Haymarket train station, and a similar distance from the Scottish Gallery of Modern Art.

CHEAP SLEEPS

BELFORD HOSTEL Map p217   *Hostel*
☎ 225 6209; www.edinburghhostels.com; 6 Douglas Gdns; dm £12-17, d £40-52; bus 13

The Belford is a bit different from your average backpacker hostel – it's housed in a converted 19th-century church. Although some readers have complained of noise – there are only thin partitions between the rooms, and no ceilings – it's well run and cheerful with good facilities.

EGLINTON YOUTH HOSTEL
Map p217   *Hostel*
☎ 337 1120; www.syha.org.uk; 18 Eglinton Cres; dm £12-16; all Haymarket buses
This recently refurbished SYHA hostel is housed in an imposing Victorian terrace, just a few minutes' walk north of Haymarket train station, and a mile west of Waverley. The entrance hall is flanked by a spacious and elegant lounge and kitchen area, with upstairs dorms overlooking garden areas at both front and back.

EDINBURGH SOUTH

Edinburgh South has the city's greatest concentration of good, mid-range guest houses and B&Bs, as well as several excellent hotels. If you're hunting for vacancies on foot, the best strips are Newington Rd, Minto St, Mayfield Gdns and Craigmillar Park in Newington, and Gilmore Pl in Tollcross.

AMARYLLIS GUEST HOUSE
Map pp222–3   *Guest House*
☎ 229 3293; www.amaryllisguesthouse.com; 21 Upper Gilmore Pl; s £25-40, d £36-80; bus 10, 27; P
The gay-friendly Amaryllis is a cute little Georgian town house with a luxuriant garden. It has five rooms, all with TV and most with en suite facilities, and there's private parking out the front. Princes St is only 15 minutes' walk away.

BALLARAT GUEST HOUSE
Map pp222–3   *Guest House*
☎ 229 7024; ballarathouse@yahoo.com; 14 Gilmore Pl; s £20-35, d £40-70; bus 10, 27
The Ballarat is a small (five rooms) and friendly family guest house, one of several in this attractive Victorian terrace only a few minutes' walk from Tollcross' bars and restaurants.

EDINBURGH CITY HOTEL
Map pp218–20   *Hotel*
☎ 622 7979; www.bestwesternedinburghcity.co.uk; 79 Lauriston Pl; s £80-95, d £95-130; bus 23, 27, 45
Dating from 1879, and now tastefully restored and redecorated, the Edinburgh City Hotel was originally the Edinburgh Royal Maternity

Hospital. The refurbished rooms are spacious, bright and modern – some retain original features such as bay windows and turrets – and the hotel is only 15 minutes' walk from Edinburgh Castle.

HERALD HOUSE HOTEL Map p217   *Hotel*
☎ 228 2323; www.heraldhousehotel.co.uk; 70 Grove St; s/d £74/118; bus 1, 28, 34, 35
This place has good-value en suite rooms, is close to Haymarket train station and the theatre district and is only a 10 minute walk from Grassmarket.

SHERATON GRAND HOTEL
Map pp218–20   *Hotel*
☎ 229 9131; www.sheraton.com/grandedinburgh; 1 Festival Sq; r £105-270; all Lothian Rd buses; ♿
Rising glumly opposite the Usher Hall on Lothian Rd, the Sheraton looks a little bland on the outside, but is all elegance and finery within. The upper rooms at the front have superb views of Edinburgh Castle.

TOWN HOUSE Map pp222–3   *Guest House*
☎ 229 1985; www.thetownhouse.com; 65 Gilmore Pl; s £30-40, d £60-80; bus 10, 27

The four-room Town House is a plush little place, offering the sort of quality and comfort you might expect from a much larger and more expensive hotel. It's an elegant Victorian terraced house with big bay windows, spacious bedrooms (all en suite) and a breakfast menu that includes salmon fishcakes and kippers alongside the more usual offerings.

BRUNTSFIELD

AARON GUEST HOUSE

Map p221   *Guest House*
☎ 229 6459; www.aaronguesthouse.co.uk; 16 Hartington Gdns; s £40-60, d £60-120; bus 11, 15, 16, 17, 23; P
Located at the end of a quiet cul-de-sac, this comfortable and friendly 10-room guesthouse has spacious, high-ceilinged Victorian rooms. It is nonsmoking, caters to vegetarians and has private off-street parking.

BRUNTSFIELD HOTEL Map pp222-3   *Hotel*
☎ 229 1393; www.thebruntsfield.co.uk; 69 Bruntsfield Pl; s £85-130, d £100-195; all Bruntsfield buses; P
The 73-room Bruntsfield Hotel occupies three adjoining, 19th-century Scottish Baronial villas overlooking the pleasant parkland of Bruntsfield Links. It is close to the trendy restaurants of Morningside and Tollcross, and has its own lively bar and free private parking.

GREENHOUSE Map p221   *Guest House*
☎ 622 7634; www.greenhouse-edinburgh.com; 14 Hartington Gdns; s £55-75, d £60-80; bus 11, 15, 16, 17, 23
The six-room Greenhouse is a wholly vegetarian and vegan, nonsmoking guesthouse that uses organic and GM-free foods as much as possible; even the soap and shampoo are free of animal products. It's set in an attractively refurbished Victorian terrace, with traditional styling and brightly coloured bed quilts; room No 3, with its bay window and wing-back armchairs, is our favourite.

NOVA HOTEL Map pp222-3   *Hotel*
☎ 447 6437; fax 452 8126; 5 Bruntsfield Cres; s £35-55, d £60-90; all Bruntsfield buses
The Nova is set in a quiet, three-storey Victorian terrace, with views over Bruntsfield Links at the front and to the Pentland Hills at the back. The en suite rooms are large and high-ceilinged – some are big enough to sleep five, offering a good deal for families.

ROBERTSON GUEST HOUSE

Map p221   *Guest House*
☎ 229 2652; www.robertson-guesthouse.com; 5 Hartington Gdns; s £23-50, d £46-70; all Bruntsfield buses
Set in a Victorian terrace tucked away down a quiet backstreet, the homely, six-room Robertson Guest House offers a good range of food in the mornings including yoghurt, fresh fruit and a cooked vegetarian breakfast.

NEWINGTON

32 GRANBY ROAD

Map pp222-3   *Guest House*
☎ 667 9078; www.barbara-kellett.com; 32 Granby Rd; r from £75; bus 42
This elegant Edwardian terraced house is located on a quiet backstreet and has three sumptuous en suite bedrooms, all beautifully decorated in different styles. Our choice would be the spacious Drawing Room, with its period fireplace, big bay window and view of Arthur's Seat.

AVONDALE GUEST HOUSE

Map pp222-3   *Guest House*
☎ 667 6779; avondalehouse@aol.com; 10 South Gray St; s £20-29, d £40-60; all Newington buses; P
Readers have recommended the friendly, family-run Avondale, which is in a quiet, residential street with private parking, close to a main bus route into town.

BOROUGH HOTEL Map pp222-3   *Hotel*
☎ 668 2255; www.boroughhotel.com; 72-80 Causewayside; r £70-150; bus 42
Modern art and minimalist décor characterise the 12 smallish bedrooms, designed by Ben Kelly (best known for designing bars like Manchester's Hacienda), in this appealing boutique hotel. Though outside the main tourist areas, it's only 15 minutes' walk south of the Royal Mile.

FAIRHOLME GUEST HOUSE

Map pp222-3   *Guest House*
☎ 667 8645; www.fairholme.co.uk; 13 Moston Tce; s £25-45, d £50-80; bus 42
A pleasant, family-run Victorian villa with four rooms (three en suite), the gay- and vegetarian-friendly Fairholme has been recommended by several readers. It's on a quiet street close to a main bus route into the city centre.

HOPETOUN Map pp222-3   *B&B*
☎ 667 7691; www.hopetoun.com; 15 Mayfield Rd; r £50-60; bus 42

Travellers have recommended the warm welcome and friendly advice at the two-room Hopetoun, a homely Victorian terrace about 10 minutes by bus from the city centre.

KENVIE GUEST HOUSE
Map pp222–3   *Guest House*
☎ 668 1964; www.kenvie.co.uk; 16 Kilmaurs Rd; r £40-70; bus 2, 14, 30, 33
A Victorian town house with some attractive period features, the bright and welcoming Kenvie is situated in a quiet side street close to a main bus route.

PRESTONFIELD HOUSE HOTEL
Map pp214–15   *Boutique Hotel*
☎ 668 3346; www.prestonfield.com; Priestfield Rd; r £195-250; taxi; P
If the blonde wood, brown leather and brushed steel of modern boutique hotels leave you cold, then this is the place for you. A 17th-century mansion set in 20 acres of parkland (complete with peacocks and Highland cattle), Prestonfield House has undergone a £2m makeover at the hands of James Thomson (see p104) to become the 'ultimate retort to minimalism'. Draped in damask, packed with antiques and decorated in red, black and gold, the interior is opulent, decadent, extravagant – look out for original tapestries, 17th-century embossed leather panels, £500-a-roll hand-painted wallpaper, and pert-buttocked putti twanging arrows from 200-year-old moulded plaster ceilings. Despite their antique splendour, the hotel's 30 rooms are supplied with all mod cons, including Internet access, Bose sound systems, DVD players and flat-screen TVs.

SALISBURY GUEST HOUSE
Map pp222–3   *Guest House*
☎ 667 1264; www.salisbury-guest-house.co.uk; 45 Salisbury Rd; r £23-35 per person; all Newington buses; P
A semi-detached Georgian villa with eight bedrooms, large gardens and private parking, the Salisbury is quiet, comfortable and nonsmoking. It's closed over Christmas and New Year.

SHERWOOD GUEST HOUSE
Map pp222–3   *Guest House*
☎ 667 1200; www.sherwood-edinburgh.com; 42 Minto St; s £40-65, d £55-75; all Newington buses; P
One of the most attractive guesthouses on Minto St, the Sherwood is a refurbished Georgian terraced house decked out with hanging baskets and shrubs. Inside are six en suite rooms that combine Regency-style striped wallpaper with modern fabrics and pine furniture. It is wholly nonsmoking and has TV in all rooms, and there are two private, off-road parking spaces.

SOUTHSIDE GUEST HOUSE
Map pp222–3   *Guest House*
☎ 668 4422; fionasouthside@aol.com; 8 Newington Rd; s £40-50, d £70-100; all Newington buses
Although it occupies a traditional late-Georgian terrace, the Southside stands out from other Newington guesthouses through the clever use of bold colours and modern furniture – its eight stylish rooms just ooze interior design.

CHEAP SLEEPS
ARGYLE BACKPACKERS
Map pp222–3   *Hostel*
☎ 667 9991; www.argyle-backpackers.co.uk; 14 Argyle Pl; dm £10-15, d & tw £34-40; bus 41
The Argyle is a hostel with a slightly upmarket feel, housed in a Victorian terrace on the south side of the Meadows. The dorms and doubles are well kept, and there is a comfortable lounge, a conservatory and a pleasant walled garden at the back where you can sit outside in summer.

BRUNTSFIELD YOUTH HOSTEL
Map pp222–3   *Hostel*
☎ 0870 004 1114; www.syha.org.uk; 7 Bruntsfield Cres; dm £12-16; bus 11, 16
Situated in an attractive location overlooking Bruntsfield Links, about 2½ miles south of Waverley train station, this hostel has spick and span four- to 12-bed dorms, some with castle views, a canteen-style dining room, large-screen TV, two Internet terminals and resident cat.

LINDEN HOUSE Map pp222–3   *B&B*
☎ 667 9050; lindenhousegh@aol.com; 13 Mayfield Rd; s/d from £25/40; bus 42
Readers have recommended the Linden for its well-appointed rooms with en suite bathroom, TV and coffee-making facilities, and friendly, helpful owners.

MENZIES GUEST HOUSE
Map pp222–3   *Guest House*
☎ 229 4629; www.menzies-guesthouse.co.uk; 33 Leamington Tce; s £15-30, d £30-60; all Bruntsfield buses
This is a clean, friendly and well-run place, with seven rooms over three floors. Some of the rooms are a bit cramped (and some of the décor a bit flowery!) but the price and location are good.

WATERFRONT EDINBURGH

Pilrig St, halfway down the western side of Leith Walk, has a concentration of guest houses, and there are new hotels popping up in Leith itself. Accommodation here is a bit out of the mainstream, but is handy for the Royal Yacht *Britannia* and Leith's excellent restaurant scene (see p116). Portobello, with its sandy beach, is a good place for kids.

LEITH & PILRIG

ARDMOR HOUSE Map p216 *Guest House*
☎ 554 4944; www.ardmorhouse.com; 74 Pilrig St;
s £45-60, d £60-100; bus 11
The gay-owned, straight-friendly Ardmor is a stylishly renovated Victorian house with five gorgeous en suite bedrooms, and all those little touches that make a place special – an open fire, thick towels, crisp white bed linen and free newspapers at breakfast.

BALMORAL GUESTHOUSE
Map p216 *Guest House*
☎ 554 1857; bookings@balmoralguesthouse.co.uk;
32 Pilrig St; r £36-66; bus 11
Travellers have recommended this five-room guesthouse located in an elegant Victorian terrace. The bedrooms have an old-fashioned atmosphere (only one is en suite), and the breakfast room is graced by a large, antique kitchen table and dresser, and period black marble fireplace.

BALQUHIDDER GUEST HOUSE
Map p216 *Guest House*
☎ 554 3377; www.balquhidderedinscot.com;
94 Pilrig St; s £25-30, d £50-60; bus 11
This is a large, detached Victorian house, formerly a manse (church minister's house), set in its own grounds towards the northern end of Pilrig St. There are six fair-sized bedrooms (five en suite) and a relaxing residents' lounge.

EXPRESS BY HOLIDAY INN
Map p216 *Chain Hotel*
☎ 555 4422; www.hiex-edinburgh.com; Britannia
Way, Ocean Dr; r £75-89; bus 1, 11, 22, 34, 35, 36; P
Close to Ocean Terminal and the Scottish Executive, the Express is a big, modern, comfortable hotel with ample free parking. Rooms accommodate up to two adults and two children.

MALMAISON HOTEL Map p216 *Hotel*
☎ 468 5000; www.malmaison.com/edinburgh;
1 Tower Pl; r from £125; bus 16, 22, 35, 36; P
This stylish, award-winning hotel, housed in a former 19th-century Seaman's Mission in Leith, has an attractive waterfront location and an excellent French brasserie (see p116).

TRAVEL INN EDINBURGH LEITH
Map pp214–15 *Chain Hotel*
☎ 555 1570; www.travelinn.co.uk; 51-3 Newhaven Pl;
r £46; bus 7, 10, 16, 32; P
This hotel overlooks Newhaven Harbour, about 20 minutes by bus from the city centre. It has good parking facilities.

PORTOBELLO
BEDFORD HOUSE HOTEL
Map pp214–15 *Hotel*
☎ 454 4500; harrower@btconnect.com; 77 The Promenade; s £25-50, d £50-80; bus 15, 26; P
The recently refurbished Bedford House Hotel is a grand Victorian villa right on the seafront, with superb views over the Firth of Forth. The en suite bedrooms are spacious and comfortable – ask for one with a sea view – and the hotel is child-friendly, with a broad sandy beach just outside the front door. See also Drinking p130.

Room at the Malmaison Hotel

A Scotsman's Home is...

...his castle but a Scottish castle can also be your home – at least for a couple of days. There are a number of castles around Edinburgh that offer accommodation to visitors.

Borthwick Castle (☎ 01875-820514; borthwickcastle@hotmail.com; North Middleton, Gorebridge; r £115-195) Fifteenth-century Borthwick Castle stands foursquare on a hillside overlooking the Gore Water. At 110ft tall, it is one of the tallest and most impressive tower-houses in Britain. Mary Queen of Scots sought refuge here in 1567, and the castle walls still bear the scars of cannon fire from the time in 1650 when it was besieged by Oliver Cromwell's forces. Today it is a luxury hotel with 10 'bedchambers', five of them with four-poster beds; dinner in the vaulted Great Hall, complete with log fire and candlelight, is a memorable experience. Borthwick Castle is 12 miles southeast of Edinburgh, near North Middleton on the A7 road to Galashiels.

Dalhousie Castle (☎ 01875-820153; www.dalhousiecastle.co.uk; Bonnyrigg; s £115-140, d £155-190) Situated on the bank of the River South Esk just 7 miles southeast of Edinburgh city centre, Dalhousie Castle was built in the 15th century for the Ramsay family; it was converted to a hotel in 1972. The castle's 29 rooms include 10 with historical themes – the De Ramseia Suite (double £255 to £305) has an 18th-century carved oak bed, a stone alcove containing the 500-year-old castle well, and an oak-panelled bathroom with a (considerably more recent) double Jacuzzi. The hotel also has a luxurious spa.

Dundas Castle (☎ 319 2039; www.dundascastle.co.uk; South Queensferry; r from £300) Built in 1818 to the design of William Burn, and incorporating a 15th-century keep, Dundas Castle was originally the seat of the Dundas family. Now the home of Sir Jack Stewart-Clark and his family, you can rent out the castle for a wedding or the ultimate dinner party. There are nine luxurious twin/double rooms with en suite, but you have to take a minimum of four at once – for £1600 per night all in, including free run of the castle for a day. A gourmet dinner will cost from £35 per guest. Alternatively, you can rent the double room in the Boathouse for a romantic hideaway at £300 per night. Dundas Castle is 8 miles west of Edinburgh city centre, just south of South Queensferry.

ROBERT BURNS GUEST HOUSE

Map pp214–15   *Guest House*

☎ 669 5678; www.robertburnshotel.co.uk;
41 Abercorn Tce; r £32-80; bus 15, 26

The Robert Burns is an attractive, semi-detached Victorian villa close to Portobello Beach, run by a New York couple. It has six bright, comfortable rooms with modern pine furniture (five en suite), and the Scottish breakfast menu is complemented by American hash browns. The owner is a keen golfer, and can help you arrange a round of golf on local courses.

CHEAP SLEEPS

HOTEL BAR JAVA Map p216   *Hotel*

☎ 553 2020; www.hotelbarjava.com; 48-52 Constitution St; s/d £35/50; bus 16, 22, 35, 36

Bar Java is a popular drinking spot close to Leith's popular pub and restaurant district – you can't miss the gaudy orange and purple façade – with nine simple rooms (none en suite) upstairs. The price is right if you're in party mood, but don't count on a quiet and peaceful night – the bar can be pretty noisy.

Excursions

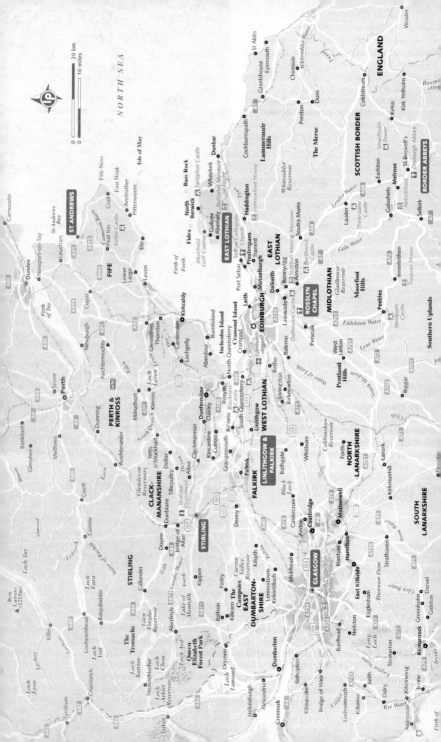

Excursions

If you have the time, it's worth getting out of Edinburgh to get a taste of the surrounding regions – the beaches and castles of East Lothian, the majestic border abbeys, the golfing capital of St Andrews, and of course Glasgow, Scotland's biggest city – and Edinburgh's great rival.

CASTLES

Connoisseurs of castles should head for **East Lothian** (p182) where you can explore the bottle dungeon at **Dirleton Castle** (p183), and patrol the airy, clifftop parapet of **Tantallon Castle** (p183). **Stirling** (p186) has a crag-bound castle that rivals Edinburgh's own, and to the south of the city there's **Thirlestane Castle** (p184), more country home than fortress.

FINE DINING

Scottish seafood is famed throughout Europe, and **St Andrews** (p179) offers a couple of top-notch restaurants where you can enjoy fish and shellfish fresh from the sea.

GOLF

There are two areas within easy reach of Edinburgh that will be well known to any keen golfer. **St Andrews** (p179) is home not only to the world-famous Old Course, but also to several other courses that are open to the public, and to the **British Golf Museum** (p181). Then there's East Lothian where, on the road between Prestonpans and North Berwick, you'll find the Muirfield championship course at **Gullane** (p141).

NATURE

There are several places on the **East Lothian** (p182) excursion that will be of interest to bird-watchers, notably the low-tide feeding grounds of **Aberlady Bay** (p182) and the remote-control cameras at the **Scottish Seabird Centre** (p183). The towpath of the **Union Canal** (p97) is another place where walkers will get the opportunity to spot wildlife, especially in spring and early summer when the waterfowl are nesting.

GLASGOW

☎ 0141

With twice the population of Edinburgh, and a radically different history rooted in industry and trade rather than politics and law, Glasgow is the most Scottish of cities, with a unique blend of friendliness, energy, dry humour and urban chaos. The city also boasts excellent art galleries and museums, most of them free – including the famous Burrell Collection – as well as numerous good-value restaurants, countless pubs, bars and clubs, and a lively performing arts scene.

Glasgow's major sights are fairly evenly dispersed around the city with the most important found along the River Clyde (the focus of a major regeneration programme) the leafy cathedral precinct in the East End and the museum-rich South Side. The city centre itself also contains a variety of attractions, notably the trendy **Merchant City**, a planned 18th-century civic development that has been restored and is now home to many fine shops, pubs and restaurants.

The exit from Queen St train station leads into George Square, dominated by the grand **City Chambers**, the seat of local government built in the 1880s at the high point of the city's wealth. The interior is even more extravagant than the exterior, and locals highly recommend a visit. A block south of the square is Scotland's most popular contemporary art gallery, the **Gallery of Modern Art**, a graceful neoclassical building featuring modern works from artists worldwide.

GLASGOW

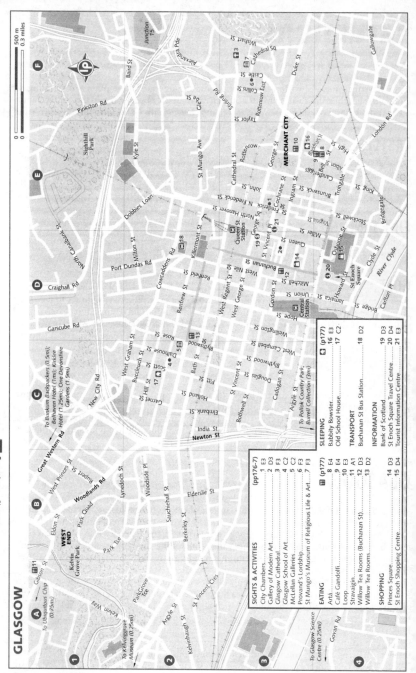

SIGHTS & ACTIVITIES (pp196-7)
City Chambers....................................1 E3
Gallery of Modern Art...........................2 D3
Glasgow Cathedral..............................3 F3
Glasgow School of Art..........................4 C2
McLellan Galleries................................5 C2
Provand's Lordship..............................6 F3
St Mungo's Museum of Religious Life & Art...7 F3

EATING (p177)
Artá...8 E4
Café Gandolfi.......................................9 E4
Loop...10 E3
Stravaigin...11 A1
Willow Tea Rooms (Buchanan St)............12 D3
Willow Tea Rooms................................13 D2

SHOPPING
Princes Square....................................14 D3
St Enoch Shopping Centre....................15 D4

SLEEPING (p177)
Babbity Bowster...................................16 E3
Old School House.................................17 C2

TRANSPORT
Buchanan St Bus Station.......................18 D2

INFORMATION
Bank of Scotland.................................19 D3
St Enoch Square Travel Centre..............20 D4
Tourist Information Centre.....................21 E3

Transport

Distance from Edinburgh 55 miles

Direction West

Travel time 1hr

Car From Haymarket, follow West Coates and Corstorphine Rd west, then take the M8 motorway.

Train There are trains from Waverley and Haymarket stations to Glasgow Queen St (50 minutes, leaving every 15 minutes); a standard single fare is £9, but a cheap day return – with outward travel after 9.30am, and returning the same day – is only £7.90.

A 10-minute walk northwest from Queen St station, along the city's main shopping strip of Sauchiehall St, leads to the 19th-century **McLellan Galleries**, which houses a selection of some of the finest treasures from Kelvingrove Museum (closed for refurbishment until 2006). There are also displays covering the work of Charles Rennie Mackintosh, whose greatest building, the **Glasgow School of Art**, lies a block to the northwest. It's hard not to be impressed by the thoroughness of the design; the architect's pencil seems to have shaped even the smallest detail of the building. The interior design is strikingly austere, with simple colour combinations (often just black and cream) and lots of those uncomfortable-looking high-backed chairs for which he is famous. Another Mackintosh masterpiece, the **Willow Tea Rooms** (1903; just east of the McLellan Galleries), is good place to break for tea and cakes.

A 10-minute walk east from Queen St train station leads to the imposing bulk of **Glasgow Cathedral**. The dimly lit and echoing interior conjures up an aura of medieval might and can send a shiver down your spine. It's a shining example of Gothic architecture, and the only mainland Scottish cathedral to have survived the Reformation. Most of the current building dates from the 15th century, and only the western towers were destroyed in the turmoil.

The entry is through a side door into the nave. The wooden roof above has been restored many times since its original construction, but some of the timber dates from the 14th century. Many of the cathedral's stunning, stained-glass windows are modern – to your left you'll see Francis Spear's 1958 work *The Creation*, which fills the west window.

The cathedral is divided by a late-15th-century stone rood screen, decorated with seven pairs of figures representing the Seven Deadly Sins. Beyond is the choir; the four stained-glass panels of the east window, depicting the apostles and also by Spear, are particularly effective.

The most interesting part of the cathedral, the lower church, is reached by a stairway. Its forest of pillars creates a powerful atmosphere around the tomb of St Mungo (who founded a monastic community here in the 5th century), the focus of a famous medieval pilgrimage that was believed to be as meritorious as a visit to Rome. Sunday services are at 11am and 6.30pm.

At the entrance to the cathedral grounds is **St Mungo's Museum of Religious Life & Art**, an audacious attempt to capture the world's major religions in an artistic nutshell. Its attraction is twofold: firstly, as impressive art that blurs the lines between religion and culture; and secondly as an opportunity to delve into different faiths, an experience that can be as deep or shallow as you wish. There are three galleries, representing religion as art, religious life and, on the top floor, religion in Scotland. In the main gallery Dali's *Christ of St John of the Cross* hangs beside statues of the Buddha and Hindu deities. Outside, you'll find Britain's only Zen garden.

Across the road from St Mungo's Museum is **Provand's Lordship**, the oldest house in Glasgow. It's a rare example of 15th-century domestic Scottish architecture, built in 1471 as a manse for the chaplain of St Nicholas Hospital. The ceilings and doorways are low and the rooms are sparsely furnished with period artefacts, except for an upstairs room, which has been furnished to reflect the living space of an early-16th-century chaplain. The building's best feature is its authentic feel – if you ignore the tacky imitation-stone linoleum covering the ground floor.

Scotland's flagship millennium project, the superb, ultra modern **Glasgow Science Centre** will keep the kids entertained for hours (and that includes middle-aged kids too). It brings science and technology alive through hundreds of interactive exhibits on four floors; look out for the illusions (like rearranging your features through a 3D head scan), and the cloud chamber, showing the tracks of atomic particles. There's also a futuristic, rotating observation tower 127m high. Two recent additions to the science centre are the Space Theatre – a planetarium, bringing the night sky to life – and a Virtual Science Theatre, treating visitors to a 3D molecular journey.

Excursions – Glasgow

One of Glasgow's top attractions is the **Burrell Collection**, a treasure house of art amassed by wealthy industrialist Sir William Burrell and donated to the city in 1944; it's housed in an outstanding museum, 3 miles south of the city centre. This idiosyncratic collection includes everything from Chinese porcelain and medieval furniture to paintings by Renoir and Cézanne. It's not so big as to be overwhelming, and the stamp of the collector lends an intriguing coherence.

Most visitors will find a favourite part of this museum, but the exquisite tapestry galleries are outstanding. Intricate European stories are woven into staggering, wall-sized pieces dating from the 13th century, capturing life in Europe. The massive *Triumph of the Virgin* exemplifies the complexity in nature and theme of this medium while posing the serious question: 'How long must this have taken?'

Floor-to-ceiling windows admit a flood of natural light, and the trees and landscape outside only enhance the effect created by the exhibits. Within the truly spectacular interior it feels as though you are wandering around a huge tranquil greenhouse. Carved-stone Romanesque doorways are incorporated into the structure so you actually walk through them.

There are occasional guided tours. Numerous buses pass the park gates (including Nos 45, 47, 48 and 57 from the centre), and there's a twice-hourly bus service between the gallery and the gates (a pleasant 10-minute walk). Alternatively, catch a train to Pollokshaws West from Central Station (four per hour; you want the second station on the line for East Kilbride or Kilmarnock).

The Genius of Charles Rennie Mackintosh

Great cities have great artists, designers and architects who remain faithful to the cultural and historical roots of their urban setting while expressing its soul and individuality. Charles Rennie Mackintosh was all three. The quirky linear and geometric designs of this famous Scottish architect and designer have had almost as much influence on the city as have Gaudí's on Barcelona. Many of the buildings Mackintosh designed in Glasgow are open to the public, and you'll see his tall, thin, Art Nouveau typeface reproduced in many places.

Born in 1868, Mackintosh studied at the Glasgow School of Art. In 1896, when he was only 27, his design won a competition for the School of Art's new building. The first section was opened in 1899 and is considered to be the earliest example of Art Nouveau in Britain, as well as Mackintosh's supreme architectural achievement. The building demonstrates his skill in combining function and style.

Although Mackintosh's genius was quickly recognised on the Continent, he did not receive the same encouragement in Scotland. His architectural career there lasted only until 1914 when he moved to England to concentrate on furniture design. He died in 1928, but it was only in the last decades of the 20th century that Mackintosh's contribution became widely recognised.

If you want to know more about the man and his work, contact the **Charles Rennie Mackintosh Society** (☎ 0141-946 6600; www.crmsociety.com; Queen's Cross Church, 870 Garscube Rd, Glasgow G20 7EL). From April to October the society runs weekend tours of his buildings (once or twice a month); the cost is £270/452 for one/two people, including B&B for two nights, lunches, coach, guide and admission.

Sights & Information

Burrell Collection (☎ 287 2550; Pollok Country Park; admission free, parking £1.50; ☺ 10am-5pm Mon-Thu & Sat, 11am-5pm Fri & Sun)

City Chambers (Map p174; ☎ 287 4018; George Sq; admission free; guided tours 10.30am & 2.30pm Mon-Fri)

Gallery of Modern Art (Map p174; ☎ 229 1996; Queen St; admission free; ☺ 10am-5pm Mon-Thu & Sat, 11am-5pm Fri & Sun)

Glasgow Cathedral (Map p174; ☎ 552 6891; Cathedral Sq; admission free; ☺ 9.30am-6pm Mon-Sat & 1-5pm Sun Apr-Sep, 9.30am-4pm Mon-Sat & 1-4pm Sun Oct-Mar)

Glasgow School of Art (Map p174; ☎ 353 4526; 167 Renfrew St; adult/child £5/4; guided tours only, 11am & 2pm Mon-Fri, 10.30am & 11.30am Sat, also 1pm Sat & Sun Jun-Aug)

Glasgow Science Centre (☎ 420 5000; 50 Pacific Quay; Science Mall adult/child £6.95/4.95, IMAX £5.95/4.45, combined ticket £9.95/7.45; ☺ 10am-6pm Sun-Wed, 11am-8pm Thu-Sat)

Glasgow TIC (Map p174; ☎ 204 4400; www.seeglasgow .com; 11 George Sq; ☺ 9am-6pm Mon-Sat Oct-May, 9am-7pm Jun & Sep, 9am-8pm Jul & Aug; 10am-6pm Sun Easter-Sep) Charges £2/3 for local/national accommodation bookings.

Felipe Linores' Seven Deadly Sins, *Gallery of Modern Art (p176)*

Glasgow TIC branch (☎ 848 4440; Glasgow International Airport; ⏱ 7.30am-5pm Mon-Sat year round, 8am-3.30pm Sun Jan-Easter & Oct-Dec, 7.30am-5pm Sun Easter-Sep)

McLellan Galleries (Map p174; ☎ 565 4100; 270 Sauchiehall St; admission free; ⏱ 10am-5pm Mon-Thu & Sat, 11am-5pm Fri & Sun)

Provand's Lordship (Map p174; ☎ 552 8819; 3 Castle St; admission free; ⏱ 10am-5pm Mon-Thu & Sat, 11am-5pm Fri & Sun)

St Enoch Square Travel Centre (Map p174; ☎ 226 4826; St Enoch Sq; ⏱ 8.30am-5.30pm Mon-Sat) Dishes out travel information only.

St Mungo's Museum of Religious Life & Art (Map p174; ☎ 553 2557; 2 Castle St; admission free; ⏱ 10am-5pm Mon-Thu & Sat, 11am-5pm Fri & Sun)

Eating

Artà (Map p174; ☎ 552 2101; 13 Walls St; tapas £3-6, mains £7.50-16; ⏱ Wed-Sun) An extraordinary Spanish hacienda-style place, with a mock-baroque ground-floor bar and elegant upstairs restaurant.

Café Gandolfi (Map p174; ☎ 552 6813; 64 Albion St; mains £5.50-12) Once part of the old cheese market, this is a friendly bistro and upmarket coffee shop – book a medieval-inspired, designer table in advance.

Loop (Map p174; ☎ 572 1472; 64 Ingram St; starters £4.24-5.50, mains £8.50-14.50) A bright and modern bistro-style place with an excellent Scottish and international menu.

Stravaigin (Map p174; ☎ 334 2665; 28 Gibson St; 2-course dinner £21.95) A foodie's delight with a menu constantly pushing the boundaries of originality, with a buzzing café-bar upstairs.

Ubiquitous Chip (☎ 334 5007; 12 Ashton Lane; 2-/3-course dinner £32.50/37.50) Excellent Scottish cuisine, fresh seafood and game dishes (which are accompanied by wild vegetables), and a lengthy wine list. There's a cheaper alternative here, **Upstairs at the Chip** (starters £3.45-5.75, mains £7.65-11.45).

Willow Tea Rooms (Map p174; ☎ 332 0521; 217 Sauchiehall St; light meals £4-6; ⏱ 9am-5pm Mon-Sat & 11am-4.30pm Sun) At lunch- and tea-time the queues can extend into the gift shop downstairs. Arrive early and splash out on a cracking breakfast of smoked salmon, scrambled eggs and toast. There's another **branch** (Map p174; ☎ 204 5242; 97 Buchanan St).

Sleeping

Babbity Bowster (Map p174; ☎ 552 5055; babbity bowster@gofornet.co.uk; 16-18 Blackfriars St; s/d £35/50) A lively bar/restaurant with six bedrooms (each with attached bathroom) bang in the heart of the trendy Merchant City.

Belhaven Hotel (☎ 339 3222; www.belhavenhotel .com; 15 Belhaven Tce; s £35-45, d £40-60) An amicable hotel just off Great Western Rd with spacious Art-Nouveau-meets-Renaissance rooms; one has been modified for disabled access. It has nonsmoking rooms available.

Bunkum Backpackers (☎ /fax 581 4481; www.bunkum glasgow.co.uk; 26 Hillhead St; dm/tw £11/30) A hostel with a great vibe in a terrific house with massive dorms and spotless bathrooms.

Kirklee Hotel (☎ 334 5555; fax 339 3828; 11 Kensington Gate; s/d £52/68) Combines the luxury of a classy hotel with the warmth of staying in someone's home. For families there is an excellent downstairs room with enormous bathroom.

Old School House (Map p174; ☎ 332 7600; oschoolh@ hotmail.com; 194 Renfrew St; s/d £35/52) A beautiful, listed building with renovated rooms in contemporary style – fresh, clean and well-furnished. All rooms except one have attached bathroom. There are nonsmoking rooms available.

One Devonshire Gardens (☎ 339 2001; www.one devonshiregardens.com; 1 Devonshire Gardens; s/d £100/225) Set in a terrace of four sumptuously decorated Georgian town houses, with the atmosphere of a luxurious country mansion, this is reputedly the best hotel in Glasgow. As one might expect, there's also an excellent restaurant here.

LINLITHGOW & FALKIRK

The **Union Canal** (p97) wends its way west from Edinburgh through the rural landscape of West Lothian to Falkirk, where it joins the Forth & Clyde Canal. Built 200 years ago and abandoned in the 1960s, both canals were restored and reopened to navigation in 2002 as a recreational waterway. There are many points of interest along its length, which can be visited by car, by train, or even by walking or cycling along the towpath.

Just 8 miles west of Edinburgh is the village of **Ratho**. Since the reopening of the canal, the village has developed into a centre for canal-boating; the **Bridge Inn** offers sightseeing cruises west to the impressive Almond Aqueduct, and lunch and dinner cruises on a restaurant barge. A 15-minute walk west along the towpath leads to the spectacular new **Adventure Centre** (see p140).

The ancient royal burgh of **Linlithgow** is one of Scotland's oldest towns, though much of it dates 'only' from the 15th to 17th centuries. Its centre retains a certain charm, except for a few ugly modern buildings and occasional traffic congestion. Just 150m south of the town centre lies the Union Canal and the pretty **Linlithgow Canal Centre**, where a little museum records the history of the canal.

The town's main attraction is the magnificent ruin of 15th-century **Linlithgow Palace**. It was a favourite royal residence – James V was born here in 1512, as was his daughter Mary (later Queen of Scots) in 1542, and Bonnie Prince Charlie briefly visited in 1745. Legend has it that a cooking fire left by retreating Jacobite soldiers caused the blaze that gutted the palace in 1746.

Beside the palace is the Gothic **St Michael's Church**. Built between the 1420s and 1530s, it is topped by a controversial aluminium spire that was added in 1964. The church is said to be haunted by a ghost that foretold King James IV of his impending defeat at Flodden in 1513.

The town of Bo'ness, 4 miles north of Linlithgow on the shores of the Firth of Forth, is the starting point for the vintage steam train that shuttles to and fro on the **Bo'ness & Kinneil Railway**. At the far end of the line, 130 steps lead down in the gorge of the River Avon, where you can take a guided tour of the **Birkhill Fireclay Mine**.

Falkirk, a large, formerly industrial town about 10 miles southeast of Stirling, is home to the famous **Falkirk Wheel** – an astounding and beautiful example of modern engineering at its best. Watching it spin its boat-bound occupants around is becoming a major tourist attraction. Designed to replace the flight of locks that once linked the two canals at Falkirk, it is the world's first rotating boat lift, raising vessels (plus almost 300 tons of water) 35m in one steel caisson, while descending boats are carried down in the second caisson on the opposite side of the wheel.

Boat trips leave every half hour from the visitor centre, travelling via the wheel to the Union Canal and through the eerie Roughcastle Tunnel before returning the same way.

Transport

Distance from Edinburgh 31 miles (to Falkirk)

Direction West

Travel time 30 mins

Car From the city centre, follow West Coates and Corstorphine Rd west, then take the M8 motorway. At junction 2 switch to the M9, then exit at junction 3 for Linlithgow, junction 5 for Falkirk.

Train There are trains every 15 minutes from Waverley and Haymarket stations to Glasgow Queen St, stopping at Linlithgow and Falkirk. The journey to Falkirk takes 26 minutes and a cheap day return – with outward travel after 9.30am, and returning the same day – is £6; to Linlithgow, it's 20 minutes and £5.

Bicycle You can cycle from Edinburgh to Linlithgow (21 miles) and Falkirk (31 miles) along the Union Canal towpath – it begins at Leamington Tce, just off Gilmore Pl in Tollcross (Map pp222–3). If the return trip seems too much, you can cycle there and take the train back.

Anyone with an interest in engineering shouldn't miss this ride – the kids will love it too. The visitor centre explains the workings of the mighty wheel – it consumes the electrical power of only eight toasters to make a full rotation!

Detour: Blackness Castle

The seaside hamlet of Blackness lies 3 miles northwest of Linlithgow, at the end of a dead-end road. It is dominated by the dramatic outline of **Blackness Castle** (☎ 01506-834807; Blackness, West Lothian; adult/child £2.20/75p; 9.30am-6.30pm Apr-Sep, 9.30am-4.30pm Mon-Wed & Sat, 9.30am-1pm Thu, 2pm-4.30pm Sun Oct-Mar), a massive ship-shaped artillery fortress jutting into the sea, built in the 15th and 16th centuries. It was used as a location in the movies *Hamlet* (starring Mel Gibson) and *The Bruce* (starring Oliver Reed) – a stroll around the battlements offers superb views over the Firth of Forth.

Sights & Information

Bo'ness & Kinneil Railway (☎ 01506-822298; Bo'ness Station, Union St, Bo'ness; adult/child return £4.50/2; including admission to Birkhill Fireclay Mine £7/4; 4 departures Tue-Sun Jul-Aug, Sat & Sun Apr-Jun, Sep & Oct)

Falkirk Wheel (☎ 0870 050 0208; www.thefalkirkwheel .co.uk; Falkirk; free admission to visitor centre, car park £2, boat trip child/adult/family £4/8/21; 9.30am-5pm)

Falkirk TIC (☎ 01324-620244; 2-4 Glebe St, Falkirk; 9.30am-5pm)

Linlithgow Canal Centre (☎ 01506-671215; www.lucs .org.uk; Manse Road Canal Basin, Linlithgow; admission free; 2-5pm Sat & Sun Easter-Sep, also 2-5pm Mon-Fri Jul & Aug)

Linlithgow Palace (☎ 01506-842896; Church Peel, Linlithgow; adult/child £3/1; 9.30am-6.30pm Apr-Sep, 9.30am-4.30pm Mon-Sat & 2pm-4.30pm Sun Oct-Mar)

Linlithgow TIC (☎ 01506-844600; Burgh Halls, The Cross, Linlithgow; 10am-5pm Apr-Oct)

St Michael's Church (☎ 01506-842188; Church Peel, Linlithgow; admission free; 10am-4.30pm Mon-Sat, 12.30-4.30pm Sun May-Sep; 10am-3pm Mon-Fri Oct-Apr)

Eating

Bridge Inn (☎ 0131-333 1320; www.bridgeinn.com; 27 Baird Rd, Ratho; mains £7-14; bar 11am-11pm Mon-Sat, 12.30-11pm Sun, food served noon-2.30pm & 6.30-9pm) A cosy, 19th-century coaching inn on the banks of the Union Canal, with lots of toys and stuff to keep the kids amused.

Champany Inn (☎ 01506-834532; Champany; mains £10-20; 12.30-2pm Mon-Fri, 7-10pm Mon-Sat) A country restaurant famous for its excellent Aberdeen Angus steak and Scottish lobster. The neighbouring **Chop and Ale House** (mains £6-13) is a less expensive alternative to the main dining room. The inn is 2 miles northeast of Linlithgow on the A803/A904 road towards Bo'ness and Queensferry.

Four Marys (☎ 01506-842171; 65-76 High St, Linlithgow; mains £4-8; food served noon-3pm & 5-9pm Mon-Fri, noon-9pm Sat & Sun) An attractive traditional pub (opposite the palace entrance) that serves real ales and excellent pub grub, including haggis, neeps and tatties.

Marynka (☎ 01506-840123; 57 High St, Linlithgow; mains lunch £6-8, 2-course dinner £19.50; noon-2pm & 6-11.30pm Tue-Sat) A pleasant little gourmet restaurant.

ST ANDREWS

☎ 01334

The reverence in which golf is held in this pretty, prosperous seaside town is one of Scotland's more endearing eccentricities. St Andrews is the headquarters of golf's governing body, the Royal & Ancient Golf Club, and the location of the world's most famous golf links, the St Andrews Old Course.

Even if belting little white balls with sticks isn't your thing, it's still well worth the trip. St Andrews boasts an impressive collection of medieval ruins and university buildings, there's some idyllic coastal scenery nearby. Exploring the streets on foot is easy and rewarding, with lots of cobbled lanes and alleys, and an inviting choice of shops, pubs and restaurants.

You'll hear just as many English accents around town as you will Scottish; it's home to an ancient university where wealthy English undergraduates (including Prince William) rub shoulders with Scottish theology students.

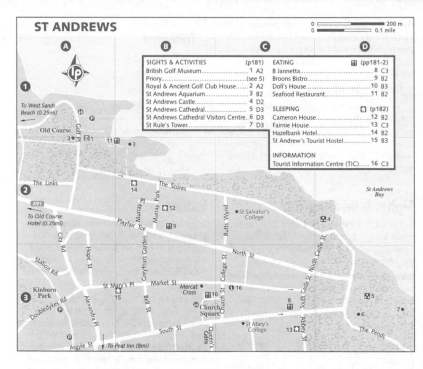

ST ANDREWS

0 ———————————— 200 m
0 ———————————— 0.1 mile

SIGHTS & ACTIVITIES	(p181)
British Golf Museum	1 A2
Priory	(see 5)
Royal & Ancient Golf Club House	2 A2
St Andrews Aquarium	3 B2
St Andrews Castle	4 D2
St Andrews Cathedral	5 D3
St Andrews Cathedral Visitors Centre	6 D3
St Rule's Tower	7 D3

EATING	(pp181-2)
B Jannetta	8 C3
Broons Bistro	9 B2
Doll's House	10 B3
Seafood Restaurant	11 B2

SLEEPING	(p182)
Cameron House	12 B2
Fairnie House	13 C3
Hazelbank Hotel	14 B2
St Andrew's Tourist Hostel	15 B3

| INFORMATION | |
| Tourist Information Centre (TIC) | 16 C3 |

St Andrews is said to have been founded by St Regulus, who arrived from Greece in the 4th century bringing important relics, including some of the bones of St Andrew, Scotland's patron saint. The town soon grew into a major pilgrimage centre and later became the ecclesiastical capital of the country. The university was founded in 1410, the first in Scotland; King James I received part of his education here, as did James III.

Golf was being played here as long ago as the 15th century, and the Old Course dates from the 16th. The Royal & Ancient Golf Club was founded in 1754 and the imposing clubhouse was built 100 years later. The British Open Championship, which was first held in 1860 in Prestwick, near Glasgow, has taken place regularly at St Andrews since 1873.

At the eastern end of North St is the ruined western façade of what was once the largest and one of the most magnificent cathedrals in the country. Although founded in 1160, **St Andrews Cathedral** wasn't consecrated until 1318 and remained a focus of pilgrimage until it was pillaged during the Reformation, in 1559. Many of the town's buildings were constructed using stones from the ruined cathedral.

The bones of St Andrew lay under the high altar; until the cathedral was built, they had been enshrined in the nearby Church of St Regulus (St Rule). All that remains of the church is **St Rule's Tower** (admission is included in the cathedral ticket), which is well worth the climb for the view over the town. In the same area are parts of the ruined 13th-century priory.

The visitors centre includes the calefactory, the only room where the monks could warm themselves by a fire. Masons' marks on the red-sandstone blocks, identifying who shaped each block, can still clearly be seen. There's also a collection of Celtic crosses and gravestones that have been found on the site.

Not far from the cathedral, with dramatic coastline views, **St Andrews Castle** is mostly in ruins, but the site itself is evocative. The most intriguing feature is the complex of siege tunnels, said to be the best surviving example of siege engineering in Europe. You can walk along the damp, mossy tunnels, now lit by electric light – but be warned, it helps if you're short! The castle was founded around 1200 as the fortified home of the bishop. A visitor centre gives a good audiovisual introduction and also has a small collection of Pictish stones.

In 1654, part of the castle was pulled down to provide building materials for re-building the harbour wall and pier. Enough survives to give you an idea of what each of the chambers was used for. After the execution of Protestant reformers in 1545, other reformers retaliated by murdering Cardinal Beaton and taking over the castle. The cardinal's body was hung from a window in the Fore Tower before being tossed into the bottle-shaped dungeon. The reformers then spent almost a year besieged in the castle.

From the castle, follow the Scores to the west past St Salvator's College to **St Andrews Aquarium**, where the exhibits include sharks, seals and an interesting sea-horse display; kids will enjoy hunting for the clownfish tanks, an activity promoted in the wake of the film *Finding Nemo*. Nearby is the **British Golf Museum**, a surprisingly interesting and modern museum with good audiovisual displays and touch screens as well as golfing memorabilia.

Opposite the museum is the clubhouse of the **Royal and Ancient Golf Club** (not open to the public); beyond stretches the **Old Course** and beside it the **West Sands**, the long, long beach made famous by the film *Chariots of Fire*.

Transport

Distance from Edinburgh 62 miles

Direction Northeast

Travel time 1½hr

Bus Stagecoach Fife operates a bus service from Edinburgh to St Andrews via Kirkcaldy (£5.50, two hours, hourly).

Car From Queensferry St in Edinburgh city centre, follow signs for the Forth Road Bridge (toll 80p, northbound only), then continue north on the M90 motorway. Exit at junction 8 and follow the A91 to St Andrews.

Train There is no train station in St Andrews itself, but you can take a train (one hour) from Edinburgh to Leuchars, 5 miles to the northwest. Ask for a railbus ticket – a standard return fare is £15, a cheap day return £12.60 – which includes travel on bus 94, 94A, 96, 99 or 99A between the station and St Andrews town centre.

Sights & Information

British Golf Museum (Map p180; ☎ 460046; Bruce Embankment; adult/child £4/2; ☾ 9.30am-5.30pm Easter–mid-Oct, 11am-3pm Thu-Mon mid-Oct–Easter)

St Andrews Aquarium (Map p180; ☎ 474786; The Scores; adult/child £5.50/3.75; ☾ 10am-6pm Easter-Oct)

St Andrews Castle (Map p180; ☎ 477196; North Castle St; adult/child £4/1.25 including admission to cathedral, ☾ 9.30am-6.30pm Apr-Oct, 9.30am-4.30pm Nov-Mar)

St Andrews Cathedral (Map p180; ☎ 472563; North St; adult/child £4/1.25 including admission to castle, £2.50/75p for cathedral only; ☾ 9.30am-6.30pm Apr-Oct, 9.30am-4.30pm Nov-Mar)

St Andrews TIC (Map p180; ☎ 472021; 70 Market St; ☾ 9.30am-8pm Mon-Sat & 11am-6pm Sun Jul-Aug; 9.30am-7pm Mon-Sat & 11am-6pm Sun Jun, Sep & early Oct; 9.30am-6pm Mon-Sat & 11am-4pm Sun Apr & May; 9.30am-5.30pm Mon-Fri & 9.30am-12.30pm Sat mid-Oct–Mar)

Eating

B Jannetta (Map p180; ☎ 473285; 31 South St; 2-dip cone from £1.50) A St Andrews institution – on a hot weekend there is a constant stream of people outside the place feverishly licking a delicious ice-cream cone before it melts to a puddle. Choose from 52 flavours.

Broons Bistro (Map p180; ☎ 478479; 119 North St; lunch mains £4.50-6.50, dinner mains £9-12; ☾ lunch & dinner) Housed in part of an old cinema, this is a friendly, hum-ming bar-bistro with a smoky atmosphere, students, busy waiters and kicking cocktails.

Doll's House (Map p180; ☎ 477422; 3 Church Sq; mains £8.50-12.45; ☾ lunch & dinner) A relaxed, informal and child-friendly restaurant with changing menu of French and Scottish cuisine – the two-course lunch at £6.95 is unbeatable value, and the early evening two-course deal for £11.95 isn't bad either.

Peat Inn (☎ 840206; by Cupar; 3-course lunch/dinner £19.50/30; ☾ lunch & dinner Tue-Sat) Run by master chef and wine expert David Wilson, this is one of the best res-taurants in Scotland. Housed in a rustic country inn about 6 miles west of St Andrews, its Michelin Rosette–winning menu includes such delights as medallions of monkfish and lobster with mushrooms and artichoke hearts. To get there, head south for 5 miles on the A915 then turn right on the B940 for another 1½ miles.

Seafood Restaurant (Map p180; ☎ 479475; The Scores; mains lunch £8-12, dinner £14-17.50; ☾ noon-4pm & 6pm-late) St Andrews' finest restaurant, set in a stylish, glass-walled room built out over the sea, with panoramic views of St Andrews Bay. Offers top class seafood and an excellent wine list.

Sleeping

Cameron House (Map p180; ☎ 472306; www.cameron house-sta.co.uk; 11 Murray Park; r per person £30) A soft and cuddly guesthouse that makes you feel right at home, right down to the teddy bears hanging off the bed posts.

Fairnie House (Map p180; ☎ 474094; www.fairniehouse .freeserve.co.uk; 10 Abbey St; r per person £18-35) A relaxed and friendly B&B in a Georgian townhouse, with one double and two twin rooms.

Hazelbank Hotel (Map p180; ☎ 472466; www.hazelbank .com; 28 The Scores; s £50-100, d £70-118) The elegant Hazelbank is a small (10 rooms) but comfortable, family-run hotel in a fine 1898 Victorian townhouse. The rooms have king-size beds and the four sea-view rooms are delightful.

Old Course Hotel (☎ 474371; www.oldcoursehotel .co.uk; rooms from £225) This imposing resort hotel and spa overlooking the Old Course has resident golf pros and a squad of therapists and beauticians providing massage for both body and ego.

St Andrews Tourist Hostel (Map p180; ☎ 479911; lee@ eastgatehostel.com; Inchcape House, St Mary's Pl; dm £12; ⏱ 7am-11pm year round) Only five minutes' walk from the bus station, and the only backpacker accommodation in town, so it fills up quickly.

EAST LOTHIAN

The fertile farmland of East Lothian stretches eastward from Edinburgh along the southern shores of the Firth of Forth to the seaside resort of North Berwick and the seabird colonies of the Bass Rock. The region is packed with interesting places to visit, ranging from fascinating industrial and aircraft museums to spectacular castles and sandy beaches, plus lots of great bird-watching opportunities.

At the junction where the A198 leaves the A1 is the village of **Prestonpans**. A simple monument on the eastern edge of the village marks the site of the Battle of Prestonpans, where the Jacobite army of Bonnie Prince Charlie defeated the government forces of Sir John Cope in 1745; a battlefield walk is held each year on 21 September, the anniversary of the encounter. Beside the shore road on the western outskirts is **Prestongrange Industrial Heritage Museum**, on the site of a former coal mine – coal has been dug from this site since monks first exploited the surface seams 800 years ago. The museum's pride and joy is the massive Cornish beam engine that once pumped water from the mine shafts; built in 1874, it continued in operation until 1954.

Two miles east of Prestonpans is the hidden gem of **Seton Collegiate Church**, dating from the 15th century and, like Rosslyn Chapel (see p186), having Templar associations. The interior has starkly beautiful Gothic vaulting and window tracery, the tombs of members of the Seton family, and the church's bell, cast in Holland and dating from 1577.

The attractive village of Aberlady sits at the head of the broad expanse of **Aber-lady Bay**. When the tide goes out it exposes

Transport

Distance from Edinburgh 24 miles (to North Berwick)

Direction East

Travel time 1hr

Bus First Edinburgh bus 124 runs hourly between Edinburgh and North Berwick, stopping at Preston-pans, Aberlady, Gullane and Dirleton. Buses X6 and X8 run from Edinburgh to Haddington every 30 minutes; a return ticket costs £6.80.

Car Follow the A1 east from Edinburgh city centre, to the junction at Tranent, then take A198 to North Berwick.

Train There are hourly trains between Edinburgh and North Berwick, stopping at Prestonpans; a return ticket costs £7.30, and the journey takes 35 minutes.

around 400 hectares of sand and mud flats, part of a nature reserve that provides excellent bird-watching opportunities. In autumn and winter, vast flocks of up to 10,000 waders, mostly lapwings and golden plovers, and 15,000 pink-footed geese fly in to feed, and in spring there's a good chance of seeing ospreys.

Haddington, straddling the River Tyne 5 miles south of Aberlady, was made a royal burgh by David I in the 12th century. Most of the modern town, however, dates from the 17th to

19th centuries during the period of prosperity that followed the Agricultural Revolution. **St Mary's Parish Church**, built in 1462, is the largest parish church in Scotland and one of the finest pre-Reformation churches in the country. Nearby **Lennoxlove House**, a lovely country house dating originally from around 1345, contains fine furniture and paintings, and memorabilia relating to Mary, Queen of Scots.

North Berwick is an attractive Victorian seaside resort with long sandy beaches, three golf courses and a picturesque little harbour, overlooked by the prominent conical hill of **North Berwick Law** (184m); a short steep path leads to the summit, marked by a pair of whale's jaw bones. When the weather is fine you'll find there are great views to the spectacular **Bass Rock**, iced white in spring and summer with the guano from thousands of nesting gannets.

It is possible to sail around the Bass Rock on boat trips leaving from North Berwick harbour. Alternatively, just walk to the eastern end of the harbour and visit the **Scottish Seabird Centre**, an ornithologist's paradise that uses remote-controlled video cameras sited on the Bass Rock and other islands to relay live images of nesting gannets and other seabirds – you can even control the cameras yourself, and zoom in on scenes of gannet domesticity.

There are two contrasting castles within easy reach of North Berwick. Two miles to the west is **Dirleton Castle**, an impressive medieval fortress with massive round towers, a drawbridge and a horrific pit dungeon, surrounded rather incongruously by beautiful, manicured gardens. Perched on a sea-cliff 3 miles to the east is the spectacular ruin of **Tantallon Castle**. Built around 1350, it was the fortress residence of the Douglas Earls of Angus, defended on one side by a series of ditches and on the other by an almost sheer drop into the sea.

In the countryside a few miles to the south of North Berwick (take the B1347) is the former RAF airfield at East Fortune that is now home to the superb **National Museum of Flight**. The huge collection of aircraft ranges from Percy Pilcher's 'Hawk' glider – dating from 1896 – to classic fighters such as the Spitfire and English Electric Lightning, and to the more recent Phantom and Harrier. Each July it hosts Scotland's biggest air show, and in 2003 it acquired one of the seven remaining Concordes when the supersonic plane went out of service.

Sights & Information

Dirleton Castle (☎ 01620-850330; Dirleton; adult/child £3/1; ☼ 9.30am-6.30pm Apr-Sep, 9.30am-4.30pm Mon-Sat & 2.30pm-4.30pm Sun Oct-Mar)

Lennoxlove House (☎ 01620-823720; Lennoxlove Estate; adult/child £4/2; guided tours 2-4.30pm Wed, Thu & Sun Easter-Oct)

National Museum of Flight (☎ 01620-880308; East Fortune Airfield; adult/child £3/free; ☼ 10am-5pm Apr-Oct, 11am-4pm Sat & Sun Nov-Mar)

North Berwick TIC (☎ 01620-892197; Quality St; ☼ 9am-6pm Mon-Sat, 11am-4pm Sun)

Prestongrange Industrial Heritage Museum (☎ 0131-653 2904; Morrison's Haven, Prestonpans; admission free; ☼ 11am-4pm Apr-Oct)

St Mary's Parish Church (☎ 01620-823109; Sidegate, Haddington; admission free; ☼ 11am-4pm Mon-Sat, 2-4.30pm Sun Apr-Sep)

Scottish Seabird Centre (☎ 01620-890202; www .seabird.org; The Harbour, North Berwick; adult/child £4.95/3.50; ☼ 10am-6pm daily Apr-Oct; 10am-4pm Mon-Fri & 10am-5.30pm Sat & Sun Nov-Jan; 10am-5pm Mon-Fri & 10am-5.30pm Sat & Sun Feb & Mar)

Seton Collegiate Church (☎ 01875-813334; Port Seton; adult/child £1.80/50p; ☼ 9.30am-6.30pm Apr-Sep)

Tantallon Castle (☎ 01620-892727; adult/child £3/1; ☼ 9.30am-6.30pm Apr-Sep; 9.30am-4.30pm Sat-Wed & 9.30am-1pm Thu Oct-Mar)

Eating & Sleeping

Beach Lodge (☎ 01620-892257; 5 Beach Rd, North Berwick; r per person £25) A friendly B&B offering sea views and vegetarian breakfasts.

Deveau's Brasserie (☎ 01620-850241; Open Arms Hotel, Dirleton; mains £9-11) A delightful brasserie serving French and Scottish food, with a convivial country pub next door.

Grange Restaurant (☎ 01620-893344; 35 High St; 3-course lunch/dinner £8/16) Bistro-style place serving good quality Scottish food.

Scottish Seabird Centre (☎ 01620-893342; mains £4-6; ☼ 10am-5.30pm Apr-Oct, 10am-4pm Nov-Mar) The centre contains an excellent café with views of the Bass Rock.

Waterside Bistro & Restaurant (☎ 01620-825764; 1-5 Waterside, Nungate, Haddington; bistro mains £7-9, restaurant £15-18) A lovely riverside spot, and a great to have lunch on a summer's day, watching the swans and ducks go by.

BORDER ABBEYS

South from Edinburgh lies the lovely Tweed Valley, and the rolling hills, forests, castles, ruined abbeys and sheltered towns of the Borders, which have a romance and beauty of their own. The region survived centuries of war and plunder and was romantically portrayed by Sir Walter Scott. This excursion is best by car, which lets you visit all three of the great border abbeys – Melrose, Dryburgh and Jedburgh – in a day.

On your way south stop at the village of Lauder to visit the fairytale towers and turrets of **Thirlestane Castle**. Perhaps more than in most stately homes, the narcissism and folly of aristocracy is evident here. Notice that many of the family portraits adorning the walls look similar – this is the result of the common practice of mass-production used by portrait painters at the time; the same sitter was used for most of the portraits, with individual faces and hands being superimposed later. Thirlestane is also home to some of the finest Restoration plasterwork ceilings in Europe. And don't miss Henry the Ram (a snuff box) in the dining room – kitsch beyond kitsch!

Charming **Melrose** is a polished little village running on the well-oiled wheels of tourism. Sitting at the foot of the three heather-covered Eildon Hills, it's popular with walkers and cyclists, but its main attraction is majestic **Melrose Abbey**. Perhaps the most interesting of all the great border abbeys, it was repeatedly destroyed by the English in the 14th century, and rebuilt by Robert the Bruce, whose heart is buried here. The remaining broken shell is pure Gothic and the ruins are famous for their decorative stonework – see if you can glimpse the pig gargoyle playing the bagpipes on the roof. You can climb to the top of the walls for tremendous views.

Dryburgh Abbey, 5 miles southeast of Melrose, is the most beautiful and complete of the Border abbeys, conjuring images of 12th-century monastic life more successfully than its counterparts in Melrose and Jedburgh. Dating from about 1150, it belonged to the Premonstratensians, a religious order founded in France. The pink-hued stone ruins were chosen as the burial place for Sir Walter Scott. Pack a picnic as there are some beautiful grassy spots here.

Transport

Distance from Edinburgh 49 miles (to Jedburgh)

Direction Southeast

Travel time 1–2hr

Bus First bus 62 runs from Edinburgh to Melrose (via Peebles) for £8 return (2¼ hours, hourly Mon-Sat). Munro's bus 29 runs from Edinburgh to Jedburgh (via Lauder) for £9.50 return (two hours, up to eight buses Mon-Sat, five on Sun).

Car From Edinburgh city centre follow Old Dalkeith Rd southeast to Dalkeith and then take the A68, signposted Jedburgh.

Fans of Sir Walter Scott can drop by **Abbotsford**, 2 miles west of Melrose, the country house that was built to his own design in the 1820s and is still in the possession of his descendants. Scott was an avid collector of historical curiosities, and the house is crammed with fascinating odds and ends, including Rob Roy McGregor's purse and musket, a lock of Bonnie Prince Charlie's hair, a sword that belonged to the Earl of Montrose, and the door of the old Tolbooth prison in Edinburgh (see St Giles Cathedral p57). You can poke around his study, where many of his famous novels were written, linger in the library with its 20,000 books, and stroll in the great man's gardens.

Jedburgh is a compact little town, where many of the old buildings and wynds (narrow alleys) have been intelligently restored, inviting exploration by foot. It is constantly busy with tourists, but if you wander into some of the pretty side streets you won't hear a pin drop! Dominating the town skyline, **Jedburgh Abbey**, founded in 1138 by David I as a priory for Augustinian canons, was the first of the great border abbeys to be passed into state care, and it really does show – there are numerous audio and visual interpretations scattered throughout the carefully preserved ruin, telling the abbey's story in great detail. The red-sandstone ruins are roofless but relatively intact and the ingenuity of the master mason can be seen in some of the rich (if somewhat faded) stone carvings found in the nave.

The ruins of Dryburgh Abbey, dating from around 1150

Sights & Information

Abbotsford (☎ 01896-752043; adult/child £4.50/2.25; ☉ 9.30am-5pm Mon-Sat late-Mar–Oct; 2-5pm Sun late-Mar–May & Oct, 9.30am-5pm Sun Jun-Sep)

Dryburgh Abbey (☎ 01835-822381; adult/child £3/1; ☉ 9.30am-6.30pm Apr-Sep, 9.30am-4pm Mon-Wed & Sat, 9.30am-noon Thu & 2pm-4pm Sun Oct-Mar)

Jedburgh Abbey (☎ 01835-863925; Abbey Bridge End; adult/child £3.50/1.20; ☉ 9.30am-6.30pm Apr-Sep, 9.30am-4pm Mon-Wed & Sat, 9.30am-noon Thu & 2pm-4pm Sun Oct-Mar)

Jedburgh TIC (☎ 0870 608 0404; Murray's Green; ☉ 9.30am-5pm Mon-Sat, 10am-5pm Sun)

Melrose Abbey (☎ 01896-822562; adult/child £3.30/1.20; ☉ 9.30am-6.30pm Apr-Sep, 9.30am-4pm Mon-Wed & Sat, 9.30am-noon Thu & 2pm-4pm Sun Oct-Mar)

Melrose TIC (☎ 0870 608 0404; Abbey House, Abbey St; ☉ 10am-5pm Mon-Sat year round, 10am-2pm Sun Apr-Oct)

Thirlestane Castle (☎ 01578-722430; Lauder; castle & grounds adult/child £5.50/3, grounds only £2/1; ☉ 10.30am-4.30pm Sun-Fri May–early Oct)

Eating & Sleeping

Burts Hotel (☎ 01896-822285; www.burtshotel.co.uk; Market Sq, Melrose; s/d £52/94) Set in an early 18th-century house, Burt's retains much of its period charm – room No 5 is the best. The hotel bar serves excellent meals.

Marmion's Brasserie (☎ 01896-822245; Buccleuch St, Melrose; mains £13.50-15.50) An atmospheric, oak-panelled nook serving snacks (from £3 to £5) throughout the day; the lunch and dinner menus include gastronomic delights such as roast quail, braised lamb and sweetbreads.

Russell's Restaurant (☎ 01896-822335; Market Sq, Melrose; mains £3.50-7.50; ☉ 9.30am-4.30pm Mon-Thu, 9.30am-5pm Fri, noon-5pm Sun) A traditional Scottish tearoom/restaurant with a large range of cakes, snacks and more substantial offerings.

Simply Scottish (☎ 01835-864696; 6-8 High St, Jedburgh; mains £7-12, 3-course dinner £11.95; ☉ all day) A buzzing bistro-style place serving good-value snacks all day, plus an interesting set dinner or à la carte menu in the evenings.

ROSSLYN CHAPEL

Rosslyn Chapel, Scotland's most beautiful and enigmatic church, was built in the mid-15th century for William St Clair, third earl of Orkney. The ornately carved interior – at odds with the architectural fashion of its time – is a monument to the mason's art, and rich in symbolic imagery. As well as flowers, vines, angels and biblical figures, the carved stones include many examples of the pagan 'Green Man'; other figures are associated with Freemasonry and the Knights Templar. Intriguingly, there are also carvings of plants from the Americas that predate Columbus' voyage of discovery. The symbolism of these images has led some researchers to conclude that Rosslyn is some kind of secret Templar repository, and it has been claimed that hidden vaults beneath the chapel could conceal anything from the Holy Grail or the head of John the Baptist to the body of Christ himself. The chapel is owned by the Episcopal Church of Scotland and services are still held here on Sunday mornings.

Just south of the chapel are the ruins of **Roslin Castle** (not open to the public), the former seat of the St Clair family. You can descend the path below the castle into **Roslin Glen**, where a path leads along the riverbank to a cave where 13th-century Scottish freedom fighter William Wallace is said to have hidden.

Sights & Information

Rosslyn Chapel (☎ 0131-440 2159; www.rosslyn-chapel .com; Roslin; adult/child £4/1; ☼ 10am-5pm Mon-Sat, noon-4.45pm Sun)

Eating & Sleeping

Roslin Glen Hotel (☎ 0131-440 2029; www.roslin-glen .co.uk; 2 Penicuik Rd, Roslin; s/d £60/75; mains £7-15) An appealing, Victorian town house hotel with eight rooms with attached bathroom, and a welcoming bar and restaurant, just a few minutes' walk from Rosslyn Chapel.

Transport

Distance from Edinburgh 7 miles

Direction South

Travel time 20-30 min

Bus Lothian Bus 15a runs from St Andrew Square in Edinburgh to Roslin village (£1 each way, 30 minutes, hourly on weekdays, every two hours on Saturday, and twice a day on Sunday).

Car From Edinburgh city centre follow Causewayside and Mayfield Rd south, and continue beyond the ring road on the A701 (signposted Penicuik and Peebles). Two miles on, at Bilston roundabout, turn left on the B7006 to Roslin village.

STIRLING

If you enjoy exploring medieval castles, you'll enjoy a trip to Stirling. Like Edinburgh in miniature, this lively town is dominated by a splendid fortress perched atop a crag, with an atmospheric old town filled with winding cobblestone streets clinging to the slopes beneath.

Throughout Scotland's history, Stirling has occupied a strategically important position – hold Stirling and you control the country. This simple truth has ensured that a castle has existed here since prehistoric times. Commanding superb views, you cannot help drawing parallels with Edinburgh's grand fortress – but **Stirling Castle** is better. The location, architecture and historical significance combine to make it one of the grandest of all Scottish castles. This means it also attracts visitors like bees to honey, so we'd advise you visit in the afternoon; most of the tour buses have buzzed off by 4pm.

There has been a fortress of some kind here for several thousand years, but the current building dates from the late-14th to the 16th centuries, when it was a residence of the Stuart monarchs. The Great Hall and Gatehouse were built by James IV, and the spectacular palace was constructed in the reign of James V (r 1540–42); French masons were responsible for the stonework. James VI remodelled the Chapel Royal and was the last king to live here. In the Great Kitchens there is an excellent depiction of 16th-century culinary techniques; apparently only men used to work in the kitchen.

The **Royal Burgh of Stirling Visitor Centre** on the Esplanade has an audiovisual presentation and exhibition about Stirling, including the history and architecture of the castle. There's a car

Transport

Distance from Edinburgh 35 miles

Direction Northwest

Travel time 1hr

Car From Edinburgh city centre, follow West Coates and Corstorphine Rd west, then take the M8 motorway. At junction 2 switch to the M9, then exit at junction 9 or 10 for Stirling.

Train There are trains from Edinburgh to Stirling (standard/cheap day return £9.40/6, 55 minutes, at least twice hourly Monday to Saturday, hourly Sunday).

park next to the castle (£2 for two hours); visitors with wheelchairs should contact HS for a courtesy vehicle to assist entry into the castle.

Close by the castle at the top of Castle Wynd is spectacular **Argyll's Lodging**, the most impressive 17th-century town house in Scotland. It's the former home of William Alexander, earl of Stirling and noted literary figure. It has been tastefully restored and gives an insight into the lavish aristocratic lifestyle of the 17th century. **Mar's Wark**, also on Castle Wynd, is the ornate façade of what was once a Renaissance-style town house commissioned in 1569 by the wealthy earl of Mar, regent of Scotland during James VI's minority.

Below the castle, the **Old Town** has cobblestone streets that are packed with fine examples of 15th- to 17th-century architectural gems. Its growth began when Stirling became a royal burgh, around 1124, and in the 15th and 16th centuries rich merchants built their houses here. The steep slopes ensure you'll be ready for a refreshment in a nearby café or pub after exploring for a couple of hours.

Stirling has the best surviving city wall in Scotland, built around 1547 when Henry VIII of England began the 'Rough Wooing' (see p41); the **Back Walk** follows the line of the wall from Dumbarton Rd (near the TIC) to the castle, continuing around Castle Rock and back to the old town.

The **Church of the Holy Rude** has been the town's parish church for 500 years; James VI was crowned here in 1567. The nave and tower date from 1456 and the church features one of the country's few surviving medieval, open-timber roofs.

Two miles north of Stirling is the impressive **Wallace Monument**, a Victorian tower raised in memory of Sir William Wallace, the Scottish freedom fighter who was hung, drawn and quartered by the English in 1305. The view from of the tower, which takes in no less than seven battlegrounds, is as breathtaking as the 67m climb to the top; the monument also contains interesting displays including Wallace's mighty two-handed sword (clearly the man was no weakling).

Another great Scottish hero is celebrated at the **Bannockburn Heritage Centre**, south of the city centre. On 24 June 1314, the greatest victory in the history of Scotland's struggle to remain independent took place at the Battle of Bannockburn. Robert the Bruce overcame superior numbers and sent Edward II's English force running for their lives. This victory turned the tide of fortune in favour of the Scots for the following 400 years. The heritage centre tells the story in a simple and eloquent exhibition, including a 12-minute audiovisual display. Outside is the eerie Borestone site, said to have been Robert the Bruce's command post before the battle. Check out his grim-looking statue, dressed in full battle gear and mounted on a charger.

Sights & Information

Bannockburn Heritage Centre (☎ 01786-812664; Glasgow Rd; adult/child £3.50/2.60; ⏰ 10am-5.30pm Apr-Oct, 10.30am-4pm Feb, Mar, Nov & Dec)

Church of the Holy Rude (☎ 01786-475275; St John St; admission free; ⏰ 10am-5pm May-Sep)

Royal Burgh of Stirling Visitor Centre (☎ 01786-479901; Castle Esplanade; admission free; ⏰ 9.30am-6pm Apr-Oct, 9.30am-5pm Nov-Mar)

Stirling Castle (☎ 01786-450000; adult/child including Argyll's Lodging £7.50/2; ⏰ 9.30am-6pm Apr-Oct, 9.30am-5pm Nov-Mar)

Stirling TIC (☎ 0870 720 0620; stirlingtic@aillst.ossian.net; 41 Dumbarton Rd; ⏰ 9am-7pm Jul & Aug, 9am-5pm May, Jun, Sep & Oct, 10am-5pm Mon-Sat Nov-Apr)

Wallace Monument (☎ 01786-472140; Abbey Craig, Causewayhead; adult/child/family £5/3.25/13.25; ⏰ 10am-5pm Mar-May & Oct, 10am-6pm Jun, 9.30am-6.30pm Jul & Aug, 9.30am-5pm Sep, 10.30am-4pm Nov-Feb)

Excursions – Stirling

Eating & Sleeping

Cambio (☎ 01786-461041; 1 Corn Exchange; mains £5; ⊙ 11am-8pm) A trendy, minimalist bar-restaurant serving Mexican food.

Darnley Coffee House (☎ 01786-474468; 18 Bow St; snacks £3.50-5) Just down the hill from the castle, offering home baking and speciality coffees.

Munro Guest House (☎ 01786-472685; www.munro guesthouse.co.uk; 14 Princes St; s £26-30, d £30-44) A luxurious, family-run guesthouse, 10 minutes' walk from the castle.

Olivia's (☎ 01786-446277; 5 Baker St; mains £12-17, 2-/3-course pre-theatre menu £12.95/14.95) A candlelight and crisp white linen kind of place, boasting an excellent menu.

Stirling Highland Hotel (☎ 01786-272727; www.para mount-hotels.co.uk/stirling; Spittal St; r per person £49-59) The smartest hotel in town, housed in the refurbished Victorian high school building, dating from 1854. Very convenient for the castle and old town.

Willy Wallace Backpackers Hostel (☎ 01876-446773; www.willywallacehostel.com; 77 Murray Place; dm/tw/d per person £11/12/13) an excellent, clean and friendly hostel in the middle of town.

Directory

Directory

TRANSPORT

Warning

The information in this section is particularly vulnerable to change: prices for international travel are volatile, routes are introduced and cancelled, schedules change, special deals come and go, and rules and visa requirements are amended. In addition, the travel industry is highly competitive and there are many lurks and perks.

Get opinions, quotes and advice from as many airlines and travel agents as possible before you part with your hard-earned cash and double-check you understand how a fare (and any ticket you may buy) works. The details given in this chapter should be regarded as pointers and are not a substitute for your own careful, up-to-date research into the current situation.

AIR

There are direct flights to Edinburgh (and Glasgow) airports from England, Wales, Ireland, USA, Canada, Scandinavia and several countries in western and central Europe.

From the rest of the world you will probably have to fly into a major European hub and catch a connecting flight to Edinburgh – London, Amsterdam, Frankfurt and Paris have the best connections with Edinburgh.

Airlines

Airlines serving Edinburgh and Glasgow airports include:

Aer Lingus (☎ 0845 973 7747; www.aerlingus.com)

Air Canada (☎ 0870 524 7226; www.aircanada.ca)

Air France (☎ 0845 084 5111; www.airfrance.com)

Air Malta (☎ 0141-847 1111; www.airmalta.com)

Air Scotland (☎ 0141-848 4990; www.air-scotland.com)

Air Transat (☎ 1866 847 112; www.airtransat.com)

American Airlines (☎ 0345 789789; www.aa.com)

British Airways (☎ 0845 773 3377; www.britishairways.co.uk)

British European/FlyBe (☎ 0870 567 6676; www.flybe.com)

British Midland (bmi; ☎ 0870 607 0555; www.flybmi.com)

Continental Airlines (☎ 0800 776464; www.continental.com)

Czech Airlines (☎ 0870 4443 747; www.czechairlines.co.uk)

duo (☎ 0871 700 0700; www.duo.com)

Eastern Airways (☎ 01652-680600; www.easternairways.com)

easyJet (☎ 0870 600 0000; www.easyjet.com)

Icelandair (☎ 0845 758 1111; www.icelandair.com)

KLM UK (☎ 0870 507 4074; www.klmuk.com)

Lufthansa (☎ 0845 773 7747; www.lufthansa.com)

Ryanair (☎ 0870 156 9569; www.ryanair.com)

ScotAirways (☎ 0870 6060 707; www.scotairways.co.uk)

Airports

Edinburgh Airport (☎ 333 1000; www.baa.co.uk/edinburgh) is 8 miles west of the city. It has a tourist information and accommodation desk, left-luggage facilities, ATMs, currency exchange desks and car hire agencies.

The **Lothian Buses Airlink service No 100** (☎ 555 6363; www.flybybus.com) runs from Waverley Bridge, just outside the train station, to the airport (one way/return £3.30/5, 30 minutes, every 10 to 15 minutes) via the West End and Haymarket. The Airsaver ticket (adult/child £4.20/2.50) can be purchased on the bus and gives a one-way trip on the Airlink bus plus unlimited travel for one day on all Lothian Bus services in the city.

An airport taxi to the city centre costs around £13 and takes about 20 minutes. Both buses and taxis depart from just outside the arrivals hall.

Edinburgh can be reached via **Glasgow Airport** (☎ 0141-887 1111; www.baa.co.uk/glasgow), 56 miles to the west. Scottish Citylink bus 915 runs from the airport directly to Edinburgh (one way £6.30, every 10 or 15 minutes).

Websites

As well as airline websites, there are a number of efficient online resources for buying good-value plane tickets. Some of the best include:

www.cheapflights.co.uk Lists discount flights to Edinburgh from other parts of the UK and Ireland.

www.opodo.co.uk Site owned by consortium of European airlines; often cheaper than no-frills airlines for short-notice flights.

BICYCLE

Despite its many hills and cobbled streets, Edinburgh is a cycle-friendly city. This is largely due to the efforts of the cycle campaign group **Spokes** (Map p221; ☎ 313 2114; www.spokes.org.uk; St Martins Church, 232 Dalry Rd) and a city council that has pledged to reduce car use.

Visiting cyclists should be aware that the increased popularity of cycling in Edinburgh – and, it has to be said, the inconsiderate behaviour of a selfish minority of cyclists – has caused a backlash and an increase in hostility towards bike riders from both pedestrians and motorists. Follow the Good Cycling Code – be courteous and considerate to others, obey the rules of the road and always give way to walkers, remembering that some people may have impaired hearing or sight. Police have the power to issue on-the-spot fines of up to £40 for offences such as cycling on the pavement, jumping a red light, going the wrong way down a one-way street and cycling after dark without proper lights.

Hire

Biketrax (Map pp222–3; ☎ 228 6633; 11 Lochrin Pl; 🕑 9.30am-6pm Mon-Fri, 9.30am-5.30pm Sat, noon-5pm Sun) Rents out a range of cycles and equipment, including kids' bikes, tandems, recumbents, pannier bags, child seats – even unicycles! A mountain bike costs £15 per day, £10 for extra days, and £60 for one week. You'll need a £100 cash or credit-card deposit and some form of ID. Has a repair service.

Edinburgh Cycle Hire & Scottish Cycle Safaris (Map pp224–5; ☎ 556 5560; www.cyclescotland.co.uk; 29 Blackfriars St; hire per day £10-15, per week £50-70; 🕑 10am-6pm Mon-Sat) The friendly and helpful folk here rent out top-quality bikes; rates include helmet, lock and repair kit. You can hire tents and touring equipment too. They also organise cycle tours in Edinburgh and all over Scotland – check their website for details. Has a repair service.

Edinburgh Bicycle Cooperative (Map pp222–3; ☎ 228 1368; 8 Alvanley Tce, Whitehouse Loan) Does repairs and supplies spares and accessories.

City Cycles (Map pp218–20; ☎ 557 2801; 30 Rodney St) Does repairs and supplies spares and accessories.

BUS

The brand new **Edinburgh Bus Station** (Map pp218–20), for regional and long-distance bus services, is at the northeast corner of St Andrew

Cycling Edinburgh

The city and its surrounding countryside are covered by a wide-reaching network of signposted cycle routes. Many of these are traffic-free and shared by cyclists and pedestrians, but some are simply cycle lanes marked on ordinary roads; the latter are often blocked by parked cars. The main cycle paths follow the routes of former railway lines, and are thus delightfully free of any serious hills. The *Edinburgh City Bike Map* (£4.95), published by Spokes and available from bike shops, shows all the cycle routes in and around the city. Spokes also publish cycle maps for Midlothian, East Lothian and West Lothian.

The main off-road routes from the city centre out to the countryside follow the Union Canal towpath and the Water of Leith Walkway from Tollcross southwest to Balerno (7½ miles) on the edge of the Pentland Hills, and the Innocent Railway Cycle Path from the southern side of Arthur's Seat eastwards to Musselburgh (5 miles) and on to Ormiston and Pencaitland. There are several routes through the Pentland Hills that are suitable for mountain bikes – for details ask at any bike shop or contact the **Pentland Hills Ranger Service** (☎ 445 3383). There's even a dedicated downhill mountain-biking trail at the Midlothian Ski Centre at Hillend.

Sq, with pedestrian entrances from the square and from Elder St. There are information desks and left-luggage facilities. For timetable information, call **Traveline** (☎ 0870 608 2608; www.travelinescotland.com).

Public transport within the city is provided entirely by buses; the two main operators are **Lothian Buses** (☎ 555 6363; www.lothianbuses.co.uk), who run most of the city routes, and **First Edinburgh** (☎ 663 9233; www.firstedinburgh.co.uk), whose buses mainly serve the towns and villages around Edinburgh. You can get timetable information and route maps from the offices listed below. Bus timetables, route maps and fare guides are also posted at all main bus stops.

Adult fares range from 60p to £1; children aged under five travel free and those aged five to 15 pay a flat fare of 50p. On Lothian buses you must pay the driver the exact fare, but First Edinburgh buses will give change. Lothian Bus have a **Daysaver ticket** (£2.50, or £1.80 if purchased after 9.30am Mon-Fri or all day Sat & Sun) that gives unlimited travel on Lothian buses for a day. Night-service buses, which run hourly between midnight and 5am, charge a flat fare of £2.

First Edinburgh Bus Shop (Map pp218–20; Edinburgh Bus Station; 🕑 8.30am-6pm Mon-Sat, 9.30am-5pm Sun)

Lothian Bus Travel Shop (Map pp224–5; Waverley Bridge; 🕑 8.30am-6pm Mon-Sat, 9.30am-5pm Sun)

Lothian Bus Travel Shop (Map pp218–20; 27 Hanover St; 🕑 8.30am-6pm Mon-Sat)

Lothian Bus Travel Shop (Map pp218–20; 7-9 Shandwick Pl; 🕑 8.30am-6pm Mon-Sat)

Lothian Buses Lost Property Office (Map pp218–20; ☎ 558 8858; 1-4 Shrub Pl, Leith Walk; 🕑 10am-1.30pm Mon-Fri)

Top Five Useful Bus Services

The following Lothian Bus services are particularly useful for visitors.

- **28** (every 30 min, Mon-Sat) Runs from St Andrew Sq to the Lawnmarket (closest bus stop to Edinburgh Castle) and on towards Lothian Rd.
- **35** (every 30 min, Mon-Sat) Runs from Edinburgh Airport to Ocean Terminal, and goes along most of the Royal Mile between the Palace of Holyroodhouse and George IV Bridge.
- **41** (every 15 min, Mon-Sat; every 30 or 40 min Sun) Runs from Marchmont Rd (Southside) to Cramond via George IV Bridge (for Museum of Scotland and Royal Mile), George St and Charlotte Sq.
- **42** (every 20 min, Mon-Sat; every 30 or 40 min Sun) Links Stockbridge, Frederick St (for Princes St), George IV Bridge (for Museum of Scotland and Royal Mile), Causewayside (Southside), Duddingston and Portobello.
- **64** (every 30 min, Mon-Sat) Links St Andrew Sq, Waverley Bridge (outside the train station), St Mary's St (lower part of Royal Mile), Our Dynamic Earth, and Palace of Holyroodhouse.

CAR & MOTORCYCLE

Arriving in or leaving Edinburgh by car during the morning and evening rush hours (7.30am to 9.30am and 4.30pm to 6.30pm Monday to Friday) is an experience you can live without. Time your journey to avoid these periods. In particular, there can be huge tailbacks on the A90 between Edinburgh and the Forth Road Bridge.

Though useful for day trips beyond the city, a car in central Edinburgh is more of a liability than a convenience. There is restricted access on Princes St, George St and Charlotte Sq, many streets are one-way and finding a parking place in the city centre is like striking gold.

There's no parking on main roads into the city from 7.30am to 6.30pm Monday to Saturday. On-street parking in the city centre is controlled

by self-service ticket machines from 8.30am to 6.30pm Monday to Saturday, and costs £1.20 per hour, with a two-hour maximum. If you break the rules, you'll get a fine, often within minutes of your ticket expiring – Edinburgh's parking wardens are both numerous and notorious. The fine is £60, reduced to £30 if you pay up within 14 days. Cars parked illegally will be towed away. There are large, long-stay car parks at the St James Centre, Greenside Pl, New St, Castle Tce and Morrison St. Motorcycles can be parked free at designated areas in the city centre.

Plans to tackle traffic include congestion-charging (to be introduced in 2006) for vehicles entering Edinburgh. There will be two cordons – an outer one on the city boundary, and an inner one enclosing the city centre. It will cost £2 to cross either cordon (inbound only, and only one payment per day); the charge will apply to the inner cordon all day long (7am to 6pm), but to the outer one during rush hours only.

Rental

All the big, international car rental agencies have offices in Edinburgh. There are many smaller, local agencies that offer better rates.

Arnold Clark Car Hire (Map pp222–3; ☎ 228 4747; 1-13 Lochrin Pl) One of the best, Arnold Clark is located in Tollcross. They charge from £20 a day, or £100 a week for a small car, including VAT and insurance. The daily rate includes 250 miles per day; excess is charged at 4p per mile. For periods of four days and more, mileage is unlimited.

Avis Car Rental (Map p217; ☎ 0870 606 0100; www.avis.co.uk; 5 West Park Pl, Dalry Rd)

Europcar (Map pp218–20; ☎ 0870 607 5000; www.europcar.co.uk; 63 Carlton Rd)

Thrifty Car Rental (Map p217; ☎ 337 1319; www.thrifty.co.uk; 42 Haymarket Tce)

TAXI

Edinburgh's black taxis can be hailed in the street, ordered by phone (extra 60p charge), or picked up at one of the many central ranks. Taxis are fairly expensive – the minimum charge is £1.40 for the first 340 yards, then 22p for every subsequent 240 yards – a typical 2-mile trip across the city centre will cost around £4 to £5. Tipping is up to you – because of the high fares local people rarely tip on short journeys, but occasionally round up to the nearest 50p on longer ones.

The main local companies are:

Capital Taxis (☎ 228 2555)

Central Radio Taxis (☎ 229 2468)

City Cabs (☎ 228 1211)

Radiocabs (☎ 225 9000)

TRAIN

The main terminus in Edinburgh is **Waverley train station** (Map pp218–20; Waverley Bridge), located in the heart of the city. Trains arriving from, and departing to, the west also stop at **Haymarket train station** (Map p217; Haymarket Tce), which is more convenient for the West End. You can buy tickets, make reservations and get travel information at the **Edinburgh Rail Travel Centre** (☯ 4.45-12.30am Mon-Sat, 7-12.30am Sun) in Waverley station. For fare and timetable enquires, phone the **National Rail Enquiry Service** (☎ 0845 748 4950) or check the timetable on the Railtrack website at www.railtrack.co.uk. Buy tickets at www.thetrainline.com.

ScotRail operates a regular shuttle service between Edinburgh and Glasgow (£8.60, 50 minutes, every 15 minutes).

TRAVEL AGENCIES

American Express (Map pp218–20; ☎ 718 2501; www.americanexpress.co.uk; cnr George & Hanover Sts; ☯ 9am-5.30pm Mon-Fri, 9am-4pm Sat)

STA Travel (Map pp224–5; ☎ 226 7747; www.statravel .co.uk; 27 Forrest Rd; ☯ 10am-6pm Mon-Wed & Fri, 10am-7pm Thu, 10am-5pm Sat)

Student Flights (Map pp224–5; ☎ 226 6868; www .studentflight.co.uk; 53 Forrest Rd; ☯ 9.30am-6pm Mon-Fri, 11am-5pm Sat)

TravelEx/Thomas Cook (Map pp218–20; ☎ 226 5500; www.thomascook.co.uk; 52 Hanover St; ☯ 9am-5.30pm Mon, Tue & Thu-Sat, 10am-5.30pm Wed)

PRACTICALITIES

ACCOMMODATION

Accommodation listings in the Sleeping chapter (p157) are broken down first by neighbourhood, then alphabetically within each neighbourhood heading, with 'Cheap Sleeps' (places that cost less than £25 per person per night) at the end. The average cost of a double room with en suite bathroom is in the £60 to £100 range, with seasonal variations – the highest rates are charged during August and the Christmas/New Year period.

Also see the Sleeping chapter for details of accommodation websites, long-term rentals and self-catering.

BUSINESS

Edinburgh is the second most important business centre in the UK after London and one of the largest financial centres in the European Union (EU). It is also high in the world league table of cities hosting business conferences.

The annual *Edinburgh Business Directory*, published jointly by the City of Edinburgh Council and the Edinburgh Chamber of Commerce & Enterprise, has useful information on the city and its economy. Most of Edinburgh's top-end and mid-range hotels provide business facilities including conference rooms, secretarial services, fax and photocopying services, ISDN lines and use of computer and private office space.

Business Hours

Shops open at least 9am to 5pm Monday to Friday, and most are open on Saturday too. An increasing number of shops also open Sunday, typically from 10am to 4pm, or noon to 5pm. Most supermarkets stay open until 8pm or 10pm daily and a few are open 24 hours.

Approximate standard opening hours are:

Banks (☯ 9.30am-4pm Mon-Fri, some 9.30am-12.30pm Sat)

Cafés (☯ 8am-5pm) If licensed they may stay open for dinner.

Post offices (☯ 9am-5.30pm Mon-Fri, 9am-12.30pm Sat)

Pubs (☯ 11am-11pm Mon-Thu, 11am-1am Fri & Sat, 12.30-11pm Sun)

Restaurants (☯ lunch 11am-3pm, dinner 6pm-9pm or 10pm)

Useful Organisations

City of Edinburgh Council Economic Development Department (Map pp224–5; ☎ 529 4625; 1 Cockburn St) Responsible for integrating economic development, transport and town planning.

Edinburgh Chamber of Commerce & Enterprise (Map p217; ☎ 477 7000; www.ecce.org; Conference House, 152 Morrison St) Provides a wide range of business support services including information technology, start-up and development advice and financial help.

Edinburgh International Conference Centre (EICC; Map p217; ☎ 300 3000; www.eicc.co.uk; The Exchange, Morrison St) Can accommodate up to 1200 people.

Scottish Enterprise Edinburgh & Lothian (Map p217; ☎ 313 4000; www.scottish-enterprise.com/edinburghand lothian; Apex House, 99 Haymarket Tce) Promotes economic development in Edinburgh. It provides support to new and existing business and improves access to jobs.

CHILDREN

Edinburgh has a multitude of attractions for children, and most things to see and do are child-friendly. Kids under five travel free on Edinburgh buses, and five- to 15-year-olds pay a flat fare of 50p. However, you should be aware that the majority of pubs – even those that sell bar meals – are forbidden by law to serve children under the age of 16; only pubs with a restaurant licence can do so.

Buying baby supplies is no problem here – disposable nappies and formula are widely available in pharmacies and supermarkets. See p69 for more information.

Babysitting

For full listings of government-approved child-minding services, check out **Childcare Link** (www.childcarelink.gov.uk). Reliable Edinburgh agencies, charging around £4 per hour, include:

Emergency Mums (☎ 535 1106; mail@emergencymums.co.uk; 21 Lansdowne Cres)

Family Circle Recruitment (☎ 447 9162; www.familycircles.org; 37 Comiston Rd)

Panda's Nanny Agency (☎ 663 3967; www.pandasnannyagency.co.uk; 22 Durham Pl, Bonnyrigg)

CLIMATE

Given just how far north it lies (it's on the same latitude as Labrador in Canada) you might expect Edinburgh's climate to be colder than it is, but the Gulf Stream (a warm Atlantic current) keeps the prevailing westerly winds pleasantly mild. May and June are generally the best bet for dry, sunny weather, but you can expect rain at any time. The weather changes quickly too – a rainy morning can often be followed by a sunny afternoon. A distinctive feature of Edinburgh's weather is the 'haar' – a dense, chilly fog that often blows in from the North Sea when the wind is in the east. You can usually escape it by heading just a few miles inland.

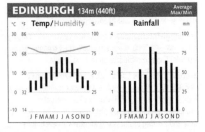

COURSES

Edinburgh university's of **Office of Lifelong Learning** (Map pp222–3; ☎ 650 4400; www.lifelong.ed.ac.uk; 11 Buccleuch Pl) runs summer courses for adults on a wide range of subjects, including Scottish archaeology, Scottish literature, Scottish history and Gaelic language. A one-week course in Scottish Poetry costs £165, while the three-week Elementary Gaelic course costs £275.

Edinburgh is a popular place to learn English as a second language, and is home to many establishments offering a range of intensive courses, summer schools, weekend workshops and specialised English courses (eg for medicine, business or tourism):

Edinburgh School of English (Map pp224–5; ☎ 557 9200; www.edinburghschool.ac.uk; 271 Canongate)

English Language Institute (Map pp222–3; ☎ 447 2398; www.eli.co.uk; 69 Nile Gve, Morningside)

Institute for Applied Language Studies (Map pp224–5; ☎ 650 6200; www.ials.ed.ac.uk; Edinburgh Uni, 21 Hill Pl)

International Language Academy (Map p217; ☎ 220 4278; www.language-academies.com; 11 Great Stuart St)

CUSTOMS

Travellers arriving in the UK from the EU don't have to pay tax or duty on goods for personal use. The maximum amounts of tobacco and alcohol that each person can bring into the country duty free are 3200 cigarettes, 400 cigarillos, 200 cigars, 3kg of smoking tobacco, 10L of spirits, 20L of fortified wine (eg port or sherry), 90L of wine and 110L of beer. People under 17 are not allowed to import any alcohol or tobacco.

Travellers from outside the EU can bring in, duty-free, a maximum of 200 cigarettes or 100 cigarillos or 50 cigars or 250g of tobacco; 2L of still table wine; 1L of spirits or 2L of fortified wine, sparkling wine or liqueurs; 60mL of perfume; and £145 worth of all other goods. Anything over this limit must be declared to customs officers.

For details of restrictions and quarantine regulations, see the HM Customs and Excise website at www.hmce.gov.uk.

DISABLED TRAVELLERS

Edinburgh's Old Town, with its steep hills, narrow closes, flights of stairs and cobbled streets, is something of a challenge for wheelchair users. By law, new buildings must be made accessible to wheelchair users, so large, new hotels and modern tourist attractions are usually fine. However, many B&Bs and guesthouses are in hard-to-adapt older buildings. It's a similar story with public transport. Newer buses sometimes have steps or suspension that lowers for access, but it's always wise to check before setting out. Most black taxis are wheelchair-friendly too.

Many banks are fitted with induction loops to assist the hearing impaired. Some attractions have Braille guides for the visually impaired.

Scottish Tourist Board produces a guide, *Accessible Scotland*, for disabled travellers, and the Edinburgh and Scotland Information Centre has accessibility details for Edinburgh (see p199 for information on both organisations). **Historic Scotland** (☎ 668 8600; www.historic-scotland.gov .uk) and the National Trust for Scotland (☎ 243 9300; www.nts.org.uk) provide details on disabled access and facilities at their properties.

Organisations

Capability Scotland (☎ 313 5510; www.capability -scotland.org.uk; 11 Ellersly Road) Scotland's largest disability organisation, offering advice and info on a range of issues.

Holiday Care Service (☎ 0845 124 9971; www.holidaycare .org.uk; Holiday Care Information Unit, 7th fl Sunley House, 4 Bedford Pk, Croydon, Surrey CR0 2AP) Publishes information guides (£7.50) to Scotland and can offer general advice.

Royal Association for Disability & Rehabilitation (RADAR; ☎ 020-7250 3222; www.radar.org.uk; Information Dept, 12 City Forum, 250 City Rd, London EC1V 8AF) Publishes a guide on travelling in the UK.

Royal National Institute for the Blind (RNIB; ☎ 311 8500, confidential helpline ☎ 0845 766 9999; www.rnib .org.uk; Dunedin House, 25 Ravelston Tce) A good point of initial contact for sight-impaired visitors to Edinburgh.

Royal Nation Institute for the Deaf (RNID; ☎ 0141-554 0053; www.rnid.org.uk; Fl 3, Crowngate Business Centre, Brook St, Glasgow G40 3AP) Publishes a large amount of helpful literature, which they mail out free.

ELECTRICITY

The standard voltage in Scotland, as in the rest of Britain, is 240V, 50Hz AC. Plugs have three square pins, and adapters are necessary for non-British appliances; these are widely available in electrical shops in Edinburgh. North American appliances, which run on 110V, will also need a transformer if they don't have one built in.

EMBASSIES & CONSULATES

Most foreign embassies are in London, but a few countries maintain a consulate in Edinburgh:

Australia (Map pp218–20; ☎ 624 3333; 69 George St) For passport applications and document witnessing only;

for emergencies contact the Australian High Commission in London (☎ 020-7887 5335).

Canada (Map pp218–20; ☎ 220 4333; Standard Life House, 30 Lothian Rd)

Denmark (Map pp214–15; ☎ 337 6352; 215 Balgreen Rd)

France (Map p217; ☎ 225 7954; 11 Randolph Cres)

Germany (Map p217; ☎ 337 2323; 16 Eglinton Cres)

Ireland (Map p217; ☎ 226 7711; 16 Randolph Cres)

Italy (Map p217; ☎ 226 3631; 32 Melville St)

Japan (Map p217; ☎ 225 4777; 2 Melville Cres)

Netherlands (Map pp218–20; ☎ 220 3226; Thistle Court, 1-2 Thistle St)

Spain (Map pp218–20; ☎ 220 1843; 63 North Castle St)

USA (Map pp218–20; ☎ 556 8315; 3 Regent Tce)

EMERGENCY

In an emergency, dial ☎ 999 or 112 (no money needed at public phones) and ask for police, ambulance, fire brigade or coastguard. Other useful phone numbers include:

Edinburgh Rape Crisis Centre (☎ 556 9437; edinirc@aol .com)

Lothian & Borders Police HQ (Map p217; ☎ 311 3131; www.lbp.police.uk; Fettes Ave)

Lothian & Borders Police Info Centre (Map pp224–5; ☎ 226 6966; 188 High St; ☽ 10am-10pm May-Aug, 10am-8pm Mar, Apr, Sep & Oct, 10am-6pm Nov-Feb) You can report a crime or make lost property enquiries here.

GAY & LESBIAN TRAVELLERS

Edinburgh has a small but flourishing gay scene. The city has a fairly tolerant attitude towards homosexuality, but overt displays of affection aren't wise away from gay venues. The age of consent for homosexual sex in the UK is 16.

The website at www.gayscotland.com and the monthly magazine *Scotsgay* (www.scotsgay .com) will keep you informed about gay-scene issues. Also check out *Gay Scotland* magazine (www.outright-scotland.org.uk/gs).

Useful contacts include:

Edinburgh LGB Community Centre (Map pp218–20; ☎ 478 7069; 60 Broughton St)

Lothian Gay & Lesbian Switchboard (☎ 556 4049; www.lgls.co.uk; ☽ 7.30-10pm)

Lothian Lesbian Line (☎ 557 0751; ☽ 7.30-10pm Mon & Thu)

Check out the Entertainment chapter for more information (p131).

HOLIDAYS

On public holidays and bank holidays, banks, post offices and government offices will be closed and public transport may run a reduced service. Many shops stay open, however, except on Christmas and New Year's days.

The following days are public holidays in Scotland:

New Year's Day 1 January

New Year Bank Holiday 2 January

Spring Bank Holiday Second Monday in April

Good Friday The Friday before Easter Sunday

May Day Holiday First Monday in May

Victoria Day Third Monday in May

Autumn Holiday Third Monday in September

Christmas Day 25 December

Boxing Day 26 December

Edinburgh also has its own local holidays on the third Monday in May and the third Monday in September. See also p19.

INTERNET ACCESS

Most hotels that have Internet connection points in their rooms use ordinary RJ-11 sockets; others use a BT phone socket. RJ-11/phone-socket adaptors are widely available in computer and electronics shops, as are UK modem cables with an RJ-11 plug on one end (for your laptop) and a BT phone plug on the other.

There is also an increasing number of WiFi hotspots in the city, which can be used to access the Internet if your laptop has an 80211b wireless card. You can search for wireless hotspots in Edinburgh on websites such as www.wifinder.com and www.hotspothaven.com.

There are many Internet cafés spread around the city, and there are also several Internet-enabled telephone boxes (10p per minute, 50p minimum) scattered around the city centre.

connect@edinburgh (Map pp218–20; ☎ 473 3800; ESIC, Princes Mall, 3 Princes St; per 20 min £1; ☺ as for ESIC – see p199)

easyInternetcafé (Map pp218–20; ☎ 220 3580; www.easy-everything.com; 58 Rose St; per hr £1.60, 50p minimum; ☺ 8am-11pm)

e-corner (Map pp218–20; ☎ 558 7858; www.e-corner.co.uk; Platform 1, Waverley Station; per 20 min £1; ☺ 7.30am-9pm Mon-Fri, 8am-9pm Sat & Sun)

That Internet Café (Map pp222–3; ☎ 0870 770 41 21; www.thatinternetcafe.net; 1a Brougham Pl; per 20 min £1; ☺ 8.30am-10pm)

Internet Café (Map pp224–5; ☎ 226 5400; 98 West Bow, Victoria St; per 30 min £1; ☺ 10am-11pm)

The Web (Map pp218–20; ☎ 229 8883; www.web13.co.uk; 13 Bread St; per 20 min £1; ☺ 9am-10pm)

LEGAL MATTERS

The 1707 Act of Union preserved the Scottish legal system as separate from the law in England and Wales. Although there has been considerable convergence since then, Scots Law remains distinct.

Police have the power to detain anyone suspected of having committed an offence punishable by imprisonment (including any drugs offences) for up to six hours. They can search you, take photographs and fingerprints, and question you. You are legally required to provide your correct name and address – not doing so, or giving false details, is an offence – but you are not obliged to answer any other police questions. After six hours, the police must either formally charge you or let you go. If you are detained and/or arrested, you have the right to inform a solicitor and one other person, though you have no right to actually see the solicitor or to make a telephone call. If you don't know a solicitor, the police will inform the duty solicitor on your behalf.

If you need legal assistance contact **Scottish Legal Aid Board** (Map p217; ☎ 226 7061; www.slab.org.uk; 44 Drumsheugh Gdns).

Possession of a small amount of cannabis is an offence punishable by a fine, but possession of a larger amount of cannabis, or any amount of harder drugs is much more serious, with sentences of up to 14 years in prison. Police have the right to search anyone they suspect of possessing drugs.

You're allowed to have a maximum blood-alcohol level of 35mg/100mL when driving.

Drop litter on Edinburgh's streets and you can be nailed with an on-the-spot fine – a team of red-jacketed litter wardens patrols the city centre on the lookout for offenders.

When You're Legal

In Scotland the following legal ages apply for:

- Drinking alcohol – 18
- Driving – 17
- Heterosexual/homosexual sex – 16
- Smoking – 16
- Marriage – 16
- Voting – 18

MAPS

Lonely Planet's fold-out *Edinburgh City Map* (£3.99) is handy for sightseeing. It is plastic-coated, virtually indestructible and indicates all the major landmarks, museums and shops. There's also a street index.

The Edinburgh and Scotland Information Centre (ESIC; see p199) issues a free pocket map of the city centre. For coverage of the whole city, the most detailed maps are Nicolson's *Edinburgh Citymap* (£3.50) and the Ordnance Survey's (OS) *Edinburgh Street Atlas* (£5.99). You can buy these at the ESIC and at bookshops and newsagents.

The OS's 1:50,000 Landranger map *Edinburgh, Penicuik & North Berwick* (Sheet No 66; £5.99) covers the city and the surrounding region to the south and east at a scale of 1¼ inches to 1 mile (2cm to 1km); it is useful for walking in the Pentland Hills and exploring East Lothian.

MEDICAL SERVICES

Edinburgh Dental Institute (Map pp218–20; ☎ 536 4958; Lauriston Bldg, Lauriston Pl; ☼ 9am-3pm Mon-Fri) For emergency dental treatment, make an appointment here.

Royal Hospital for Sick Children (Map pp222–3; ☎ 536 0000; 9 Sciennes Rd, Marchmont; ☼ open 24 hr) The main casualty department for children aged less than 13 years.

Royal Infirmary of Edinburgh (Map pp214–15; ☎ 536 1000; 51 Little France Cres, Old Dalkeith Rd; ☼ open 24 hr) Edinburgh's main general hospital has a 24-hour accident and emergency department.

Minor Injuries Unit (Map pp214–15; ☎ 537 1330; Western General Hospital, Crewe Rd; ☼ 9am-9pm) For non-life-threatening injuries and ailments, you can attend without having to make an appointment.

METRIC SYSTEM

Like the rest of the UK, Edinburgh has officially moved to the metric system, but road distances are still quoted in miles (1.6km) and beer is still served in pints (568ml). Whisky and other spirits are sold in 25ml or 35ml measures, and petrol is sold by the litre. For conversion tables see the inside front cover.

MONEY

The British currency is the pound sterling (£), with 100 pence (p) to a pound. 'Quid' is the slang term for pound.

Several Scottish banks issue their own bank notes. You shouldn't have trouble changing them in shops etc immediately south of the Scotland–England border, but elsewhere it may be difficult. Although all UK banks will accept them, foreign banks generally do not.

Euros are accepted in Scotland only at some major tourist attractions and a few upmarket hotels – it's always better to have cash in sterling. For more info on money see p16. See also the inside front cover for exchange rates.

ATMs

There are 24-hour ATMs (called cashpoints in Scotland) all over the city, where you can use Visa, MasterCard, American Express (Amex), Cirrus, Plus and Maestro to withdraw cash. Cash withdrawals from some ATMs (especially ones in shops) can be subject to a small charge (about £1), but most are free.

Changing Money

You can change currency and travellers cheques at exchange counters (known by the French term 'bureau de change') scattered throughout the city centre, and in banks, post offices and travel agencies. Banks generally offer the best rates. Be careful using bureaux de change; they may offer good exchange rates but frequently levy outrageous commissions and fees.

American Express charges no commission on cash and Amex travellers cheques, and generally offers a good rate of exchange (slightly better on cash than on cheques). Thomas Cook charges 2% commission, with a minimum charge of £3, on both cash and travellers cheques. Rates of exchange are the same for both cash and cheques.

American Express (Map pp218–20; ☎ 718 2501; cnr George & Hanover Sts; ☼ 9am-5.30pm Mon-Fri, 9am-4pm Sat)

Bank of Scotland (Map pp218–20; ☎ 465 3900; 38 St Andrew Sq; ☼ 9am-5pm Mon-Fri, 10am-2pm Sat)

Fexco (Map pp218–20; ☎ 557 3953; ESIC, Princes Mall, 3 Princes St; ☼ same as ESIC, see p199)

Royal Bank of Scotland (Map pp218–20; ☎ 556 8555; 36 St Andrew Sq; ☼ 9.15am-4.45pm Mon, Tue, Thu & Fri, 10am-4.45pm Wed, 10am-2pm Sat)

Thomas Cook (Map pp218–20; ☎ 226 5500; 52 Hanover St; ☼ 9am-5.30pm Mon, Tue & Thu-Sat, 10am-5.30pm Wed)

Credit Cards

Visa, MasterCard, Amex and Diners Club cards are widely recognised, although some places make a charge for accepting them (generally for small transactions). Charge cards such as Amex and Diners Club may not be accepted in smaller establishments; credit and debit cards like Visa and MasterCard are more widely accepted.

Travellers Cheques

Amex or Thomas Cook cheques are widely accepted in exchange for cash in banks, but (unlike in the US) you can't use them over the counter in shops and restaurants. Bring sterling cheques to avoid changing currencies twice, and take most cheques in large denominations; commission is usually charged per cheque.

NEWSPAPERS & MAGAZINES

Edinburgh's home-grown daily newspapers include the *Scotsman* (www.scotsman.com), a broadsheet covering Scottish and international news, sport and current affairs, and the *Edinburgh Evening News* (www.edinburghnews .com), covering news and entertainment in the city and its environs. *Scotland on Sunday* is the weekend broadsheet from the same publisher.

You can find a wide range of newspapers from around the world at **International Newsagents** (Map pp224–5; ☎ 225 4827; 351 High St, Royal Mile; 🕑 6am-6.30pm Mon-Fri, 7am-6.30pm Sat, 7.30am-6pm Sun Sep-Jul; 6am-midnight Mon-Fri, 6am-1am Sat & Sun Aug).

PHARMACIES

Chemists (pharmacists) can advise you on minor ailments. At least one local chemist remains open round the clock – its location will be displayed in the windows of other chemists. Alternatively, look in the local newspaper or in the *Yellow Pages*. **Boots** (Map p217; ☎ 225 6757; 48 Shandwick Pl; 🕑 8am-9pm Mon-Fri, 8am-6pm Sat, 10.30am-4.30pm Sun) has long opening hours.

POST

Mail sent within the UK can go either 1st or 2nd class. First-class mail is faster (next-day delivery) and more expensive (28p up to 60g, 42p up to 100g) than 2nd-class mail (20/34p). Air-mail postcards/letters (40g to 60g) to European countries cost 38/69p; to South Africa, the USA and Canada 42p/£1.42; and to Australia and New Zealand 42p/£1.56. An air-mail letter generally takes five days to get to the USA or Canada and around a week to Australia or New Zealand.

If you don't have a permanent address, mail can be sent to poste restante c/o Edinburgh's main post office. Amex offices also hold cardholders' mail for no charge.

Main Post Office (Map pp218–20; ☎ 0845 722 3344; St James Centre, Leith St; 🕑 8.30am-5.30pm Mon-Fri, 8.30am-6pm Sat)

Branch Post Office (Map pp218–20; 40 Frederick St; 🕑 9am-5.30pm Mon-Fri, 9am-12.30pm Sat)

Branch Post Office (Map pp224–5; 46 St Mary's St; 🕑 9am-5.30pm Mon-Fri, 9am-12.30pm Sat)

SAFETY

Lothian Rd, Dalry Rd, Rose St and the western end of Princes St, at the junction with Shandwick Pl and Queensberry and Hope Sts, can get a bit rowdy on Friday and Saturday nights after people have been out drinking. Calton Hill offers good views during the day but is probably best avoided at night.

Women should avoid crossing The Meadows (the park that lies between Old Town and Marchmont) alone after dark – several women have been attacked here. And be aware that Coburg St in Leith is a notorious red-light district – lone women here at any time of day might be approached by kerb crawlers.

TELEPHONE

To call Scotland from abroad dial your country's international access code then ☎ 44 (the UK country code), then the area code (dropping the first 0) followed by the telephone number. The area code for Edinburgh is 0131.

You'll mainly see two types of phone booth in Scotland: one takes money (and doesn't give change), while the other uses prepaid phone cards and credit cards. Some phones accept both coins and cards. The minimum charge is 20p.

All phones come with reasonably clear instructions in several languages. British Telecom (BT) offers phonecards for £3, £5, £10 and £20; they're widely available from retailers, including post offices and newsagents.

Mobile Phones

Codes for UK mobile phones usually begin with ☎ 07. The UK uses the GSM 900/1800 network, which is compatible with the rest of Europe, Australia and New Zealand, but not with the North American GSM 1900 or the totally different system in Japan (though some North Americans have GSM 1900/900 phones that will work in the UK). If you have a GSM phone, check with your service provider about using it in the UK, and beware of calls being routed internationally (very expensive for a 'local' call). You can also rent a mobile phone – ask a TIC for details – or buy a 'pay-as-you-go' phone for as little as £40.

Useful codes

Some codes worth knowing are:

International dialling code ☎ 00

International directory enquiries ☎ 153

International operator ☎ 155

Local & national directory enquiries ☎ 118 500

Local & national operator ☎ 100

Local call rate ☎ 0345, ☎ 0845

National call rate ☎ 0870

Premium call rate ☎ 0891, ☎ 09064

Reverse-charge/collect calls ☎ 155

Time ☎ 123

Toll-free call ☎ 0800

TELEVISION

Britain still turns out some of the best quality TV programmes in the world. BBC1 and BBC2 are publicly funded by an annual TV licence and don't carry advertising. ITV and Channels 4 and 5 are commercial stations and do.

There are two Scottish-based commercial TV broadcasters. Scottish Television (STV) covers southern Scotland and some of the western Highlands. Grampian TV transmits to the Highlands, from Perth to the Western Isles, and to Shetland. Both include Gaelic-language programmes. Border TV covers Dumfries & Galloway and the Borders, as well as northwestern England.

These channels are up against stiff competition from Rupert Murdoch's satellite TV company, BSkyB, and assorted cable channels. Cable churns out mostly missable rubbish but BSkyB is monopolising sports coverage with pay-per-view screenings of the most popular events.

TIME

Edinburgh, along with the rest of the UK and Ireland, follows Greenwich Mean Time (GMT) in the winter and British Summer Time (BST) in the summer. BST is GMT plus one hour – the clocks go forward one hour at 2am on the last

Sunday in March, and back again at 2am on the last Sunday in October.

When it's noon in Edinburgh in summer, it's 4am in Los Angeles, 7am in New York, 1pm in Paris (and the rest of Europe), 1pm in Johannesburg, 8pm in Tokyo, 9pm in Sydney and 11pm in Auckland.

Most public transport timetables use the 24-hour clock.

TIPPING

In general, if you eat in an Edinburgh restaurant you should leave a tip of at least 10% unless the service was unsatisfactory. Waiting staff are often paid derisory wages on the assumption that the money will be supplemented by tips. If the bill already includes a service charge (usually 10%), you needn't add a further tip. Tipping in bars is unheard of.

Taxis in Edinburgh are expensive, and drivers rarely expect a tip unless they have gone out of their way to help you.

TOILETS

There are well-maintained public toilets conveniently spaced around the city centre and most have facilities for the disabled. On Princes St there are toilets (open 10am to 10pm) beside St Cuthbert's Church at the western end; on either side of the Royal Scottish Academy (gents to the west, ladies to the east) in the middle; and in Waverley train station at the eastern end. On the Royal Mile, there are toilets at the top of Castle Wynd stairs just outside the castle esplanade (open 10am to 8pm, summer only), and in Hunter Sq (open 10am to 10pm) at the junction with North Bridge. Some busy public toilets, such as the ones at Waverley train station and inside Edinburgh Castle, charge 20p.

Some disabled toilets can only be opened with a special key that can be obtained from the Tourist Information Centre (TIC) or by applying in advance to RADAR (see p195).

TOURIST INFORMATION

Edinburgh and Lothians Tourist Board (www .edinburgh.org) is the city's main provider of tourist information, with an office in the Edinburgh and Scotland Information Centre.

Edinburgh and Scotland Information Centre (ESIC; Map pp218–20; ☎ 0845 225 5121; info@visitscotland.com; Princes Mall, 3 Princes St; ☺ 9am-8pm Mon-Sat & 10am-8pm Sun Jul & Aug, 9am-7pm Mon-Sat & 10am-7pm Sun

May, Jun & Sep, 9am-5pm Mon-Wed, 9am-6pm Thu-Sat & 10am-5pm Sun Oct-Apr) Includes an accommodation booking service, currency exchange, gift and book shop, Internet access, and counters selling tickets for Edinburgh city tours and Citylink bus services.

Scottish Tourist Board (☎ 0845 225 5121; www .visitscotland.com)

Tourist & Airport Information Desk (☎ 0845 225 5121; Edinburgh Airport)

Tourist Information Centre (TIC; ☎ 653 6172; Old Craighall Junction, A1) In a service area on the main A1 road, about 5 miles east of the city centre.

VISAS

Currently, if you're a citizen of Australia, Canada, NZ, South Africa or the USA, you're permitted to stay in Britain for up to six months (no visa required), but are prohibited from working. The Working Holidaymaker scheme, for Commonwealth citizens aged 17 to 27 inclusive, allows visits of up to two years, but arrangements must be made in advance through a British embassy.

EU citizens can live and work in Britain free of immigration control and don't need a visa to enter the country.

All other nationalities should contact their nearest British diplomatic mission to obtain a visa. Standard/one-year multiple-entry visas cost from £36/60.

No extra visas are required for Scotland if you arrive from England or Northern Ireland. For more information, see www.ukvisas.gov .uk or the Lonely Planet website at www.lonely planet.com.

Extensions

To extend your stay in Britain contact the **Home Office, Immigration and Nationality Directorate** (☎ 0870 606 7766; Lunar House, 40 Wellesley Rd, Croydon, London CR9 2BY) *before* your existing permit expires. You'll need to send your passport with your application.

WOMEN TRAVELLERS

Women are unlikely to have any problems, although common-sense caution should be observed, especially late at night (see p198).

For general advice on health issues, contraception and pregnancy, visit a Well Woman clinic – ask at local libraries or doctors' surgeries for the details. In Edinburgh, contact **Well Woman Services** (Map p217; ☎ 332 7941; 18 Dean Tce, Stockbridge).

The Rape and Abuse Line can be contacted toll-free every evening at ☎ 0808 800 0123. Or contact the **Edinburgh Rape Crisis Centre** (☎ 556 9437; edinirc@aol.com).

WORK

EU citizens do not need a work permit to work in the UK. Citizens of Commonwealth countries aged 17 to 27 can apply for a Working Holiday Entry Certificate that allows up to two years in the UK, during which you can take work that is 'incidental' to a holiday. Commonwealth citizens with a UK-born parent may be eligible for a Certificate of Entitlement to the Right of Abode, which allows you to live and work in the UK.

Commonwealth citizens with a UK-born grandparent, or a grandparent born before 31 March 1922 in what's now the Republic of Ireland, may qualify for a UK Ancestry-Employment Certificate, allowing you to work full time for up to four years in the UK.

Visiting full-time US students aged 18 and over can apply for a six-month work permit through the **Council on International Educational Exchange** (☎ 212-822 2600; www.ciee.org; 205 East 42nd St, New York, NY 10017). **British Universities North America Club** (BUNAC; ☎ 203-264 0901; www.bunac.org; PO Box 49, South Britain, CT 06487) can also help organise a work permit.

Seasonal work is available in the tourist industry, in hotels, restaurants and bars. Hostel noticeboards advertise casual work and hostels themselves sometimes employ travellers to staff the reception, clean up and so on. Bars and restaurants also advertise jobs in their windows.

Those with IT skills will be in demand. There are also opportunities for secretaries, receptionists, book-keepers and accountants. Other possibilities include telesales work, nursing and nursery care. A wide range of full- and part-time jobs are advertised in the Recruitment section of Friday's edition of the *Scotsman* newspaper, and online at www.scottishappointments.com.

The minimum wage in the UK is £4.80 per hour, but there is a loophole that allows employers to include tips in this figure; be warned, some restaurants pay as little as £2 per hour plus tips. However, others can pay as much as £5 per hour for bar work, so look around. Telesales work pays around £6 per hour and office work is mostly in the range of £5 to £10 per hour.

Whatever your skills, it's worth registering with a few employment agencies; check the *Edinburgh Guide* website at www.edinburgh guide.com/business/recruitment.htm or the *Yellow Pages* (www.yell.co.uk).

Behind the Scenes

THE LONELY PLANET STORY

The story begins with a classic travel adventure: Tony and Maureen Wheeler's 1972 journey across Europe and Asia to Australia. There was no useful information about the overland trail then, so Tony and Maureen published the first Lonely Planet guidebook to meet a growing need.

From a kitchen table, Lonely Planet has grown to become the largest independent travel publisher in the world, with offices in Melbourne (Australia), Oakland (USA), London (UK) and Paris (France).

Today Lonely Planet guidebooks cover the globe. There is an ever-growing list of books and information in a variety of media. Some things haven't changed. The main aim is still to make it possible for adventurous travellers to get out there – to explore and better understand the world.

At Lonely Planet we believe travellers can make a positive contribution to the countries they visit – if they respect their host communities and spend their money wisely.

THIS BOOK

This 3rd edition of *Edinburgh* was written and updated by Neil Wilson, as was the previous edition. The 1st edition was written by Tom Smallman. This city guide was commissioned in Lonely Planet's London office, and produced by:

Commissioning Editor Amanda Canning
Coordinating Editor Lou McGregor
Assisting Editors Thalia Kalkipsakis & Pete Cruttenden
Coordinating Cartographer Kusnander
Coordinating Layout Designer Laura Jane
Colour Pages Cris Gibcus
Cover Design Maria Vallianos
Artwork Daniel New
Series Designer Nic Lehman
Series Design Concept Nic Lehman & Andrew Weatherill
Managing Editors Jane Thompson & Darren O'Connell
Managing Cartographer Mark Griffiths
Mapping Development Paul Piaia
Project Manager Huw Fowles
Regional Publishing Manager Katrina Browning
Series Publishing Manager Gabrielle Green

Cover photographs by Lonely Planet Images: Stained-glass window, Edinburgh Castle, Bethune Carmichael (top); Memorial to Dugald Stewart, Pat Yale (bottom); House on Calton Hill, Jonathan Smith (back).

Internal Photographs by Lonely Planet Images and Jonathan Smith except for the following: p90 (#1) Glenn Beanland; p90 (#4) Grant Dixon; p90 (#2), p185 Martin Moos; p177 Neil Setchfield. All images are the copyright of the photographers unless otherwise indicated. Many of the images in this guide are available for licensing from Lonely Planet Images: www.lonelyplanetimages.com.

THANKS
NEIL WILSON

Many thanks to the helpful and enthusiastic staff at the Edinburgh & Scotland Information Centre, to the travellers who chipped in with recommendations, and to the various people I pestered for their opinions. Thanks also to Carol Downie for help and advice on restaurants and shopping.

OUR READERS

Many thanks to the travellers who used the last edition and wrote to us with helpful hints, useful advice and interesting anecdotes. Your names follow:

Andrea Bender, Louise Blair, Rebecca Brown, Christopher Calvert, Kate Cogill, Nick Cole, Rhian Croke, Carole M Cusack, Erik Einbeck, Morgan Fallon, Andrea Foxworthy, Trevor Graham, Wolfgang Guenther, Virginia Horscroft, Vlasta Jamnicky, Ingrid Johansson, Kerry Shaz King, Jennifer Levinson, Emma Locock, Barbie Markey, Pam & Lidi McGregor, Pinky McKay, Jane Munns, Keith Murray, Edward Nicol, Ian Oliver, Roger Pedersen, Marie Petrelis, Tracey Phillips, Gillian Rogers, Mark Scheffer, Andrew Schmid, Eugene Sheyn, Lesley Simpson, John Stern, Derek Stewart, Katie Stuart, Claire Swain, Kara Szifris, Cara Smith, Rowland Thomson, Maryanne Twomey, WH Turner, Bernie White, Marc Van Opstal, Katie Young, Graham Yuill.

SEND US YOUR FEEDBACK

We love to hear from travellers – your comments keep us on our toes and help make our books better. Our well-travelled team reads every word on what you loved or loathed about this book. Although we cannot reply individually to postal submissions, we always guarantee that your feedback goes straight to the appropriate authors, in time for the next edition. Each person who sends us information is thanked in the next edition – and the most useful submissions are rewarded with a free book.

To send us your updates – and find out about LP events, newsletters and travel news – visit our award-winning website: www.lonelyplanet.com.

Note: We may edit, reproduce and incorporate your comments in Lonely Planet products such as guidebooks, websites and digital products, so let us know if you don't want your comments reproduced or your name acknowledged. For a copy of our privacy policy visit www.lonelyplanet.com/privacy.

Notes

Notes

Index

See also separate indexes for Eating (p210), Drinking (p211), Shopping (p211) and Sleeping (p212).

Index

SLEEPING

000 map pages
000 photographs

MAP LEGEND

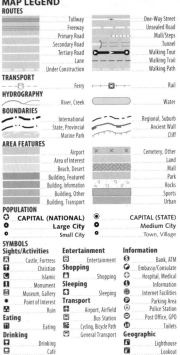

ROUTES

.... Tollway
.... Freeway
.... Primary Road
.... Secondary Road
.... Tertiary Road
.... Lane
.... Under Construction

.... One-Way Street
.... Unsealed Road
.... Mall/Steps
.... Tunnel
.... Walking Tour
.... Walking Trail
.... Walking Path

TRANSPORT

.... Ferry

.... Rail

HYDROGRAPHY

.... River, Creek

.... Water

BOUNDARIES

.... International
.... State, Provincial
.... Marine Park

.... Regional, Suburb
.... Ancient Wall
.... Cliff

AREA FEATURES

.... Airport
.... Area of Interest
.... Beach, Desert
.... Building, Featured
.... Building, Information
.... Building, Other
.... Building, Transport

.... Cemetery, Other
.... Land
.... Mall
.... Park
.... Rocks
.... Sports
.... Urban

POPULATION

⊙ **CAPITAL (NATIONAL)**
● **Large City**
● Small City

◉ CAPITAL (STATE)
● Medium City
● Town, Village

SYMBOLS

Sights/Activities
🏰 Castle, Fortress
🛕 Christian
☪ Islamic
🗿 Monument
🏛 Museum, Gallery
● Point of Interest
🏯 Ruin

Eating
🍴 Eating

Drinking
🍺 Drinking
☕ Café

Entertainment
🎭 Entertainment

Shopping
🛍 Shopping

Sleeping
🛏 Sleeping

Transport
✈ Airport, Airfield
🚌 Bus Station
🚲 Cycling, Bicycle Path
🚐 General Transport

Information
💲 Bank, ATM
✉ Embassy/Consulate
✚ Hospital, Medical
ℹ Information
@ Internet Facilities
🅿 Parking Area
👮 Police Station
✉ Post Office, GPO
🚻 Toilets

Geographic
🗼 Lighthouse
🔭 Lookout
▲ Mountain, Volcano
→ River Flow

Map Section

GREATER EDINBURGH

A **B** **C** **D**

1

Firth of Forth

Granton Harbour

● 10

21
9
16
13
Newhaven

Granton

West Granton Rd
Lower Granton Rd
A901

Starbank Rd
Trinity Cres

Wardie
Starbank Park

Boswall Parkway

Pilton
Crewe Rd North

Pilton Dr
Granton Rd

Trinity

Ferry Rd

Silverknowes

6

2

Muirhouse

To Cramond (0.5mi);
Dalmeny House; The Maltings (0.5mi)

Ferry Rd
B9085

Crewe Rd South

East Fettes Ave

Edinburgh Academy New Field

Edinburgh Academy

Inverleith Pl

Inverleith Row

George Heriot's Sports Ground

Powderhall Stadium

Drylaw

Inverleith

● 12

Warriston Playing Fields

Canonmills
14

Davidson's Mains Park

Davidson's Mains

A90
Hillhouse Rd

To Forth Bridges; South Queensferry;
Port Edgar Marina & Sailing
School (4mi); Inchcolm
Island Ferry (4mi); Queensferry
Museum (4mi); Dundas Castle
(8mi); Hopetoun House (8mi)

See West End & Stockbridge Map (p217)

24

Inverleith Park

Eyre Pl
Dundas St
Albany St
York Pl

Broughton

East Claremont St

3

Corstorphine Hill

Blackhall

Ravelston Golf Course

Craigcrook Rd

Ravelston Dykes Rd

Ravelston

A90

Comely Bank Rd

Craigleith Rd

Queensferry Rd

Dean Village

A90

Queen St

See Old Town Map (pp224-5)

Corstorphine

Murrayfield Rd

Belford Rd

Princes St

See Edinburgh Castle Map (p226)

Edinburgh Zoo

5

Edinburgh University

Coates

Palmerston Pl
Shandwick Pl
A702
Lothian Rd

Lauriston

4

Corstorphine Rd

Balgreen Rd
Saughtonhall Dr

Roseburn Tce

Roseburn St

West Coates
A8

Haymarket Train Station

Murrayfield (S.R.U. Ground)

8

A8

See Dalry & Morningside Map (p221)

Dairy Rd

Dundee St
Union Canal

Fountainbridge

Bruntsfield Pl

The Meadows

Melville Dr

Tollcross

Marchmont Rd

To Queen Margaret College (0.5mi);
Edinburgh Airport (4mi);
Inglison Market (5mi);
Glasgow (42mi)

Carrick Knowe

Whitson Rd

Stenhouse Dr

Stevenson Rd

Westfield Rd

Gorgie Rd

Dairy

Merchiston

Greenhill

Marchmont

5

Saughton Park

Ford's Rd

22

Stenhouse Rd

A71

Saughton Prison

Chesser Ave

Stevenson Dr

A70

Shandon

Morningside

Morningside Rd

Grange

Stenhouse Dr

Calder Rd

Saughton Rd

17

Stedeford Rd

Education Committee Athletic Ground

Charterhall Rd

Blackford Hill

6

To Heriot-Watt
University Campus (2mi);
Ratho (6mi); Adventure Centre (6mi)

Longstone

Inglis Green Rd

Lanark Rd

Murray Burn

25

Craiglockhart Ave Rd

Colinton Rd
Glenlockhart Rd

Craiglockhart Park

Napier University

Craiglockhart

To Hillend; Roslin; Rosslyn Chapel;
Fairmile Inn (0.5mi); Lothianburn
Golf Course (0.5mi); Midlothian
Ski Centre (0.5mi); Swanston (1mi);
Pentland Hill (4mi); Penicuik (6mi)

A702

Comiston Rd

Hermitage of Braid

Braid Hills Dr

Braid Hills Golf Course

Kingsknowe

Union Canal

SIGHTS & ACTIVITIES   (pp47-82)
Alien Rock...................................1 D1
Bawsinch Nature Reserve............2 F4
Craigmillar Castle.........................3 G5
Duddingston Parish Church..........4 F4
Edinburgh Zoo.............................5 A4
Lauriston Castle...........................6 A2
Meadowbank Sports Centre..........7 F3
Murrayfield Stadium.....................8 B4
Newhaven Heritage Museum.........9 D1
Next Generation.........................10 D1
Portobello Turkish Baths.............11 H3
Royal Botanic Garden.................12 D2
Seafari................................(see 21)

EATING   🍴 (pp99-118)
Old Chain Pier...........................13 D1
Rhubarb.............................(see 19)

DRINKING   🍸 (pp119-30)
Bedford House Hotel.............(see 18)
Claremont Bar............................14 D2
Old Chain Pier.....................(see 13)
Sheep Heid.................................15 F4
Starbank Inn..............................16 D1

ENTERTAINMENT   🎭 (pp131-44)
Edinburgh Corn Exchange............17 B5

SLEEPING   🛏 (pp157-70)
Bedford House Hotel....................18 H4
Prestonfield House Hotel..............19 F5
Robert Burns Guest House............20 H4
Travel Inn Edinburgh Leith...........21 D1

INFORMATION
Danish Consulate.......................22 B5
Edinburgh Royal Infirmary...........23 G6
Minor Injuries Unit.....................24 C3
Water of Leith Visitor Centre.......25 B6

LEITH & PILRIG (0131) 332 6780,

| 0 | | 200 m |
| 0 | | 0.1 mile |

A   **B**   **C**   **D**

Western Harbour

Firth of Forth

Leith Docks

Imperial Dock

Leith Dock

Albert Dock

To Newheaven (0.75mi)

Ocean Dr

Victoria Dock

Edinbur Dock

Lindsay Rd

Britannia Way

Victoria Quay

North Leith

Lindsay St

Argyle St

Portland St

Madeira Prince Regent St

Madeira Pl

North Junction St

North Fort St

Commercial St

The Shore

Tower St

Citadel

Dock St

Dock Pl

Timber Bush

Baltic St

Cadiz St

Salamander St

Coburg St

Sandport Pl

Broad St

Bernard St

Burgess Water St

Assembly St

Bath Rd

Ferry Rd

Keddie Gardens

Water of Leith

Mill La

Sheriff Brae

Shore Pl

Maritime St

Mitchell St

Elbe St

Pattison La

Salamander Pl

Portobe (2m

South Fort St

Bangor Rd

Swanfield

Cables Wynd

Henderson St

Giles St

Tolbooth Wynd

Great Junction St

Yardheads

Kirkgate

Constitution St

Queen Charlotte St

John's La

John's Pl

Links Pl

Poplar La

West Bowling Green St

Pirrie St

Kirk St

South Leith

Duncan Pl

Leith Links

Links Gdns

Ashley

Bonnington Rd

Pilrig Park

Pilrig

Rosebank Cemetery

Pilrig Gdns

Pilrig St

Cambridge Gdns

Cambridge Ave

Arthur St

Leith Walk

Dryden St

See Central Edinburgh Map (pp218-20)

SIGHTS & ACTIVITIES	(pp47-82)
Ocean Terminal	1 B2
Royal Yacht Britannia	2 B2
Scotch Malt Whisky Society	3 C4
Scottish Executive	4 C3
Trinity House	5 C4

EATING	(pp99-118)
Brasserie de Malmaison	(see 30)
Britannia Spice	6 B3
Daniel's Bistro	7 B3
Fishers	8 C3
Khublai Khan	9 D4
Raj	10 C4
Restaurant Martin Wishart	11 C4
Waterfront	12 C3

DRINKING	(pp119-30)
Cameo Bar	13 C3
Carriers Quarters	14 C3
King's Wark	15 C3

Old Dock Bar	16 C3
Port o'Leith	17 C4

ENTERTAINMENT	(pp131-44)
Commplex	18 B3
Shore	19 C3

SHOPPING	(pp145-56)
Edinburgh Architectural Salvage Yard	20 A4
Flux	21 C3
Georgian Antiques	22 D4
Kinloch Anderson	23 B3
Tiso Outdoor Experience	24 B3

SLEEPING	(pp157-70)
Ardmor House	25 A6
Balmoral Guest House	26 B6
Balquhidder Guest House	27 A6
Express by Holiday Inn	28 B3
Hotel Bar Java	29 C4
Malmaison Hotel	30 C3

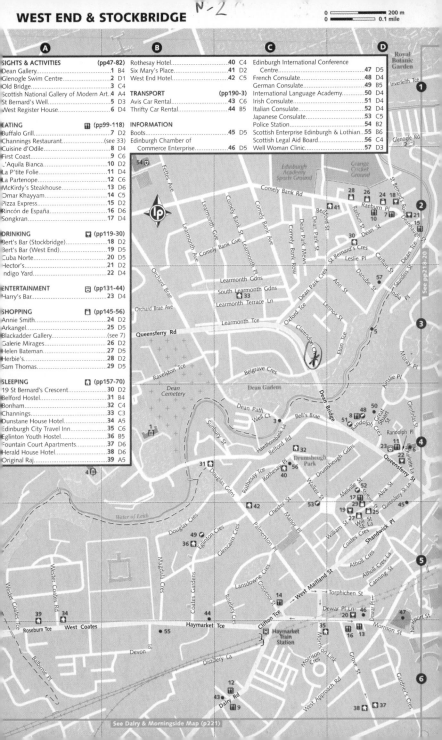

WEST END & STOCKBRIDGE

N-2

| | | 0 | 200 m |
| 0 | | 0.1 mile |

SIGHTS & ACTIVITIES (pp47-82)
Dean Gallery..................................1 B4
Glenogle Swim Centre.....................2 D1
Old Bridge....................................3 C4
Scottish National Gallery of Modern Art.4 A4
St Bernard's Well...........................5 D3
West Register House........................6 D4

EATING 🍴 (pp99-118)
Buffalo Grill..................................7 D2
Channings Restaurant..................(see 33)
Cuisine d'Odile..............................8 D4
First Coast...................................9 C6
L'Aquila Bianca.............................10 D4
La P'tite Folie..............................11 D4
La Partenope...............................12 C6
McKirdy's Steakhouse....................13 D6
Omar Khayyam..............................14 C5
Pizza Express..............................15 D2
Rincón de España..........................16 D6
Songkran...................................17 D4

DRINKING 🍸 (pp119-30)
Bert's Bar (Stockbridge).................18 D2
Bert's Bar (West End)....................19 D5
Cuba Norte.................................20 D5
Hector's....................................21 D2
Indigo Yard................................22 D4

ENTERTAINMENT 🎭 (pp131-44)
Harry's Bar.................................23 D4

SHOPPING 🛍 (pp145-56)
Annie Smith................................24 D2
Arkangel....................................25 D5
Blackadder Gallery.....................(see 7)
Galerie Mirages...........................26 D2
Helen Bateman............................27 D5
Herbie's....................................28 D2
Sam Thomas...............................29 D5

SLEEPING 🛏 (pp157-70)
19 St Bernard's Crescent................30 D2
Belford Hostel.............................31 B4
Bonham.....................................32 C4
Channings..................................33 C3
Dunstane House Hotel....................34 A5
Edinburgh City Travel Inn................35 C6
Eglinton Youth Hostel....................36 B5
Fountain Court Apartments..............37 D6
Herald House Hotel.......................38 D6
Original Raj................................39 A5

Rothesay Hotel............................40 C4
Six Mary's Place...........................41 D2
West End Hotel............................42 C5

TRANSPORT (pp190-3)
Avis Car Rental............................43 C6
Thrifty Car Rental.........................44 B5

INFORMATION
Boots.......................................45 D5
Edinburgh Chamber of
  Commerce Enterprise...................46 D5
Edinburgh International Conference
  Centre....................................47 D5
French Consulate..........................48 D4
German Consulate.........................49 B5
International Language Academy.........50 D4
Irish Consulate............................51 D4
Italian Consulate..........................52 D4
Japanese Consulate.......................53 C5
Police Station..............................54 B2
Scottish Enterprise Edinburgh & Lothian.55 B6
Scottish Legal Aid Board..................56 C4
Well Woman Clinic.........................57 D3

See Dalry & Morningside Map (p221)

A B C D

1 2 3 4 5 6

Inverleith Tce
Water of Leith
Inverleith Terrace La
Howard St
Standard Life HQ
142
Canonmills
Brandon Tce
Canon La
Canon St
Eyre Cre
Eyre Pl
West Annandale St
Broughton Rd
Glenogle Rd
35
Rodney St
181
34
East Claremont St
Bellevue St
Bellevue Rd
Hopetoun St
B901
179
Annandale St
161
180
Perth St
Eyre Tce
King George V Park
Bellevue
Bellevue Cres
182
Gayfield St
Edinburgh Academy
Henderson Row
127 51
Fettes Row
Royal Cres
Scotland St
Scotland La East
East London St
Saxe Coburg
117
West Silvermills La
157
14
75
Broughton St
123
Union St
10
B900
Clarence St
Saint Vincent St
76
Dundas St
Cumberland St
78
London St
54
Broughton Pl
39
42
Hart St
Forth St
107
Hamilton Pl
49
129
St Stephen St
71
Circus La
72
Great King St
169
Drummond Pl
Barony St
Albany La
Kerr St
9 NW
63
44
Circus Pl
Royal Circus
Howe St
Northumberland St
141
Abercromby Pl
83
65
Albany St
York La
82
89
99
97
159
Doune Tce
India St
80
Jamaica La N
Heriot Row
26
Queen St Gdns East
Dublin St
Dublin St La South
York Pl
38
165
104
Omni Centre
Cloucester La
Jamaica St La S
Queen St Gardens
Queen St Gdns West
176
145
110
York La
Elder East
St James Centre
A900
Monument to Dugald Stewa
Moray Pl
Wemyss Pl
Heriot Row
Queen St
Hanover St
29
North St Andrew St
St Andrew Square
195
Elder St
112
Leith St
Calton Hill
172
87
Old Calton Burial Ground
115
Forres St
North Charlotte St
52
174
46
140
48
190
7
15
188
20
43
160
25
149
Waterloo Pl
198
132
197
196
57
138
92
84
199
George St
62
47
70
93
Charlotte Sq
2
12
100
158
186
18
131
148
118
55
79
167
125
Rose St
171
28
134
183
Meuse La
Princes Mall
155
191
Waverley Train Station
North Bridge
73
175
59
94
151
144
139
133
81
55
192
27
East Princes St Gardens
Waverley Bridge
193
Hope St
Charlotte Sq
18
146
66
197
Hope St La
147
90
Princes St
Floral Clock
Ross Bandstand
See Edinburgh Castle Map (p226)
Market St
Cockburn St
Jeffrey St
184
33
137
156
32
Watch Tower
West Princes St Gardens
Edinburgh Castle
Esplanade
North Bank St
The Mound
Ramsay La
Castlehill
Lawnmarket
High St
Old Fishmarket Cl
Blair St
Niddry St
Blackfriars St
A702
A8
189
Castle Tce
124
113
Lothian Rd
114
53
108
135
King's Stables Rd
103
King's Stables La
Johnston Tce
Victoria St
Cowgate
Chambers St
South Bridge
Infirmary St
Candlemaker Row
Chalmers St
Grassmarket
178
143
152
102
37
60
64
Spittal St
West Port
121
Greyfriars Kirk
Forrest Rd
Bristo Place
Lothian St
Charles St
Potterrow
Nicolson St
Morrison St
201
106
74
150
101
119
116
Holy Lawson St
Lauriston St
Lauriston Pl
George Heriot's School
See Old Town Map (pp224-5)
Bread St
173
170
Laurison Pl
Bristo Square
Edinburgh Mosque
40
153
Semple St
East Fountainbridge
High Riggs
166
163
Glen St
Lauriston Gardens
Lauriston Park
194
Charles St La
Crichton St
67
86
50
191
Fountainbridge
Earl Grey St
Ponton St
Dunbar St
Brougham St
105
162
77
Home St
Thornybauk
See Southside Map (pp222-3)
West Chapel St

p217
p218

See p216

E · F · G · H · 1

LP

Leith Walk

Shrub Pl La ● 185

etoun Cres

 36

Haddington Pl

69

Windsor St

Brunswick St

Hillside Cres · Hillside St

Leopold Pl

Royal Tce

58

177 154

alton Hill

17

19

200

Regent Gardens

Regent Tce

Regent Rd

Royal High School

1

Calton Rd

Old Tolbooth Wynd

111

3 · 4

126

Canongate

16

Reid's C

95

Holyrood Rd

168

Saint John St

96

Viewcraig St

Viewcraig Gdns

Dumbledykes Rd

Pleasance Sports Centre

The Pleasance

Brown St

l Pl Richmond La

Saint Leonard's St

120

t Crosscauseway

Buchanan St · Iona St · Dickson St

Albert St

Allanfield

Brunswick Rd

South Elgin St · Elgin Tce

Montgomery St · Brunton Tce · Easter Rd

London Rd

Royal Terrace Gardens

Carlton Tce

Montrose Tce

91

A1

Regent Road Park

Abbeymount · Abbeyhill

Abbeyhill Cres

Croft-an-Righ

Calton New Burial Ground

23

122

Hope Wynd · 24

13

22

30

21

Queen's Dr

● St Margaret's Well

Radical Rd

Salisbury Crags

Holyrood Park

Whinte Trails

Queen's Dr

Hutton's Section ●

Saint Clair St

Eastern Cemetery

Hawkhill Ave

Albion Pl · **Easter Road Stadium (Hibernian F.C.)** ● 8

Albion Rd

Bothwell St

Rossie Pl

East Norton Pl

London Rd

Spring Gardens

Royal Park Tce

Moray Park Tce

Dalgety Ave · Dalgety Rd

Marionville Rd

Wishaw Tce

Lochend Loch

Lochend Park

Duke's Walk

St Margaret's Loch

St Anthony's Chapel 🏛

Arthur's Seat (251m)

See Southside Map (pp222-3)

1 · 2 · 3 · 4 · 5 · 6

DALRY & MORNINGSIDE

0 — 200 m
0 — 0.1 mile

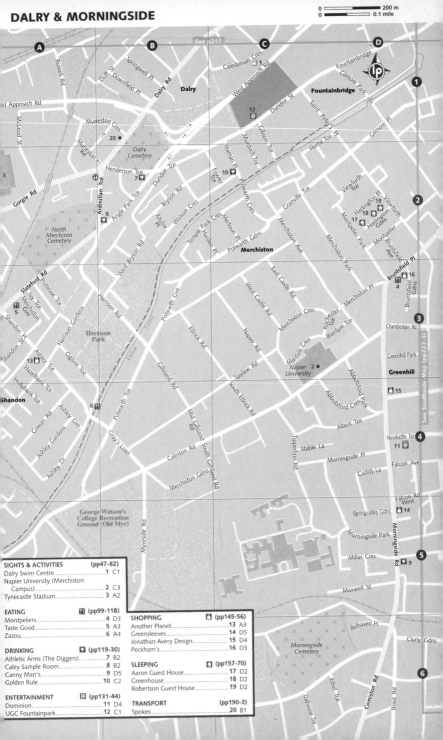

See p217

Dalry

Fountainbridge

Merchiston

Napier University

Greenhill

Brunstfield Gdns

Shandon

Harrison Park

North Merchiston Cemetery

Dalry Cemetery

George Watson's College Recreation Ground (Old Myr)

Morningside Cemetery

See Southside Map (pp222-3)

SIGHTS & ACTIVITIES	(pp47-82)
Dalry Swim Centre	1 C1
Napier University (Merchiston Campus)	2 C3
Tynecastle Stadium	3 A2

EATING	(pp99-118)
Montpeliers	4 D3
Taste Good	5 A3
Zazou	6 A4

DRINKING	(pp119-30)
Athletic Arms (The Diggers)	7 B2
Caley Sample Room	8 B2
Canny Man's	9 D5
Golden Rule	10 C2

ENTERTAINMENT	(pp131-44)
Dominion	11 D4
UGC Fountainpark	12 C1

SHOPPING	(pp145-56)
Another Planet	13 A3
Greensleeves	14 D5
Jonathan Avery Design	15 D4
Peckham's	16 D3

SLEEPING	(pp157-70)
Aaron Guest House	17 D2
Greenhouse	18 D2
Robertson Guest House	19 D2

TRANSPORT	(pp190-3)
Spokes	20 B1

SOUTHSIDE

See p221

A B C D

1 2 3 4 5 6

Thornybauk
Brougham St
Panmure Pl
St Patrick
17
Home St
12
13
46
Lochrin Pl
41
42
Union Canal
27
21
Brougham Pl
Lonsdale Tce
Buccleuch
Edinburgh
University
2
Gilmore Pl
Hailes St
18
Tarvit St
Meadow La
40
Valleyfield St
Levelfield St
Leven St
Leven Tce
9
Upper Gilmore Pl
24
15
The Meadows
Glengyle Tce
Gillespie Cres
16
35
Barclay Pl
Wright's Houses
Bruntsfield Links
Melville Dr
Melville Tce
29
14
6
Whitehouse Loan
Warrender Park Tce
Roseneath Pl
Sylvan Pl
Livingstone Pl
Gladstone Tce
Leamington Tce
Warrender Park Cres
Marchmont Tce
Warrender Park Rd
Roseneath Tce
25
45
Sciennes Rd
43
Marchmont Rd
Marchmont Cres
Chalmers Cres
Hatton Pl
Bruntsfield Pl
Bruntsfield Tce
Bruntsfield
Lauderdale St
Spottiswoode St
Arden St
Argyle Pl
Mansionhouse Rd
Tantallon Pl
Scien
Grange R
Bruntsfield Cres
30 36
Spottiswoode Rd
Marchmont
Cumin Pl
Greenhill Gardens
Greenhill Tce
Thirlestane Rd
Beaufort Rd
Lauder Rd
Greenhill Pk
Saint Margaret's Pl
5
Thirlestane La
Grange
Cemetery
Saint Margaret's Rd
Strathearn Rd
Kilgraston Rd
Greenhill Pl
Strathearn Pl
Hope Tce
Church Hill
Clinton Rd
Blackford Rd
Pitsligo Rd
Carlton Cricket Ground
Newbattle Tce
Grange Loan
Saint Thomas Rd
George Tce
Saint Alban's
Oswald Rd
South Oswald Stt
Blackford Ave
West Relugas Rd
Canaan La
Woodburn Ave
Mortonhall Rd
Neil Gve
44
Charterhall Gve
Charterhall Rd
Cluny Grdns
Midmar Ave
Blackford Pond
Blackford Hill Gve
Ladysmith
Cluny Dr
Midmar Dr
Blackford Hill
Blackford Hill View

4

See pp218-20

SIGHTS & ACTIVITIES	(pp47-82)
Historic Scotland	1 E2
Office of Lifelong Learning	2 D1
Royal Commonwealth Pool	3 F2
Royal Observatory of Edinburgh	4 D6
Warrender Swim Centre	5 B3

EATING	(pp99-118)
Apartment	6 A2
Blonde	7 E1
Chinese Home Cooking	8 E2
Favorit	9 A1
Kalpna	10 E1
Namaste	11 E2
Ndebele	12 A1
Sukhothai	13 B1
Thai Lemongrass	14 A2

DRINKING	(pp119-30)
Bennet's Bar	15 A1
Borough	(see 28)
Golf Tavern	16 A1

ENTERTAINMENT	(pp131-44)
Cameo	17 A1
King's Theatre	18 A1
Queen's Hall	19 E1

SHOPPING	(pp145-56)
Courtyard Antiques	20 A1
Kilberry Bagpipes	21 A1
Meadows Pottery	22 E2

SLEEPING	(pp157-70)
32 Granby Road	23 F5
Amaryllis Guest House	24 A1
Argyle Backpackers	25 C2
Avondale Guest House	26 E3
Ballarat Guest House	27 A1
Borough Hotel	28 E2
Bruntsfield Hotel	29 A2
Bruntsfield Youth Hostel	30 A3
Fairholme Guest House	31 F4
Hopetoun	32 E4
Kenvie Guest House	33 G3
Linden Guest House	34 E4
Menzies Guest House	35 A2
Nova Hotel	36 A3
Salisbury Guest House	37 F2
Sherwood Guest House	38 E3
Southside Guest House	39 E2
Town House	40 A1

TRANSPORT	(pp190-3)
Arnold Clark Car Hire	41 A1
Biketrax	42 A1
Edinburgh Bicycle Cooperative	43 A2

INFORMATION	
English Language Institute	44 A5
Royal Hospital for Sick Children	45 D2
That Internet Café	46 B1

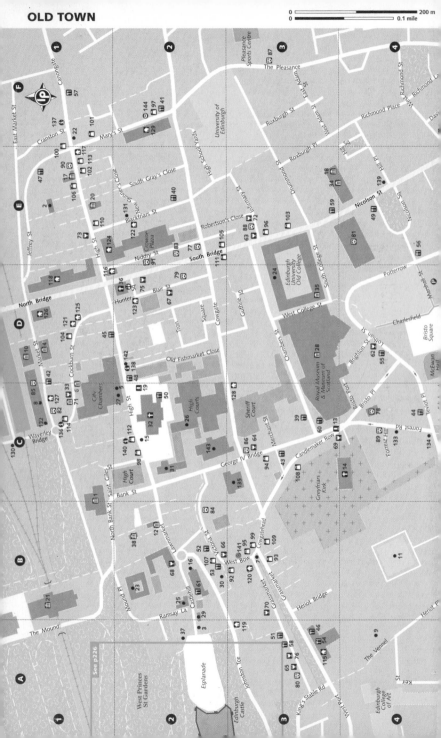

OLD TOWN

0 ————————————— 200 m
0 ————————————— 0.1 mile

EDINBURGH CASTLE

To The Mount, National Gallery of Scotland

Ramsay Ln

Castlehill

Johnston Tce

0.1 mile

To Ross Bandstand

Castle Bank

See Old Town Map (pp224-5)

Statue of Field Marshall Earl Haig

Esplanade

Ticket Office

Sentry

Sentry

Ditch

Ditch

Entrance Gateway

Castle Gift Shop

Audiotape Pick-up Point

Half Moon Battery

Royal Palace

Portcullis Gate & Argyle Tower

Farewell Battery

Lang Stairs

Mons Meg

St Margaret's Chapel

Scottish National War Memorial

Crown Square

Great Hall

Argyle Battery

Pet Cemetery

Castle Bookshop

Queen Anne Building

Mills Mount Battery

Foog's Gate

Military Prison

Entrance to Castle Vaults

One O'Clock Gun

Cart Shed & Cafe

Governor's House

Royal Scots Military Museum

New Barracks

Western Ramparts

Hospital Buildings (National War Museum of Scotland)

Ross Fountain

King's Stables Rd

Castle Tce

Cornwall St

King's Bridge

Grassmarket

DR1